SPORT
Analytics

An Applied Introduction to How Numbers are Changing Sport

J.T. Wolohan

John T. Wolohan

Kendall Hunt

publishing company

Cover image © Shutterstock, Inc.

www.kendallhunt.com
Send all inquiries to:
4050 Westmark Drive
Dubuque, IA 52004-1840

ISBN 978-1-7924-5397-7

Published in the United States of America

To Nicole, the greatest influence in our lives and our biggest fan.

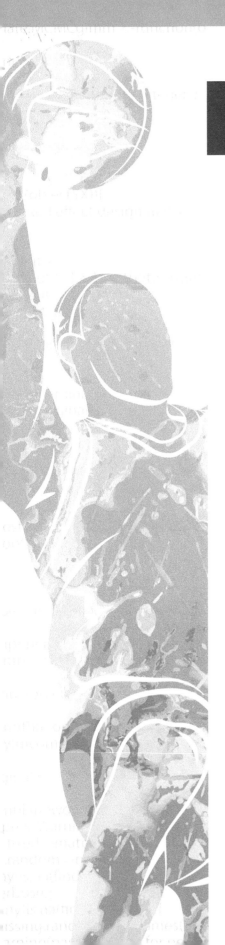

CONTENTS

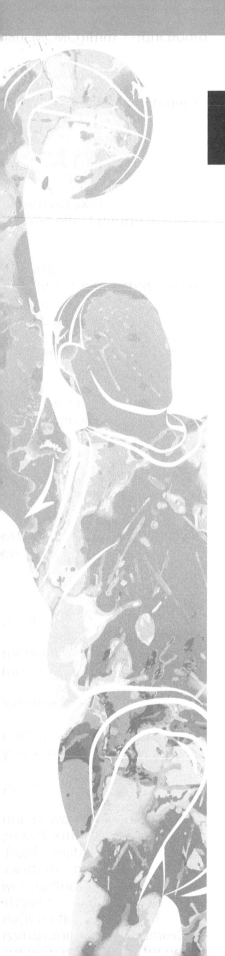

ACKNOWLEDGMENTS

Thank you to Rodney Paul, Shane Sanders, and Christopher Boudreaux for their contributions to the sport business and gambling chapters; their expertise and knowledge were essential in making this book a success. Thank you also to Joshua Mosher for his research help in the esports chapter. Thank you to Chad DeLuca, Director, Twitch Properties at Twitch and Chris Henderson, Associate Manager, Marketing Partnerships at 2K League National Basketball Association for their time and patience answering all of our questions concerning the business of esports.

Special thanks also to Dave Meluni and the faculty of the Syracuse University Sport Analytics program: Justin Ehrlich, Jeremy Losak, and Francesco Riverso. Their help, insight into the world of sports, and patience in responding to numerous questions during the writing process, shaped the final text.

Thanks to the broad community of statistics, mathematics, and sport researchers, analysts and thinkers for their hard work developing the ideas that we present in these pages. Thanks to the developers and maintainers of the R programming language, whose collective contributions make sport analytics broadly accessible and a joy to teach.

Lastly, a special thank you to Kendall-Hunt's Brenda Rolwes, who is a pleasure to work with, and to the many unheralded professionals at Kendall-Hunt for their work on this edition.

J.T. & John

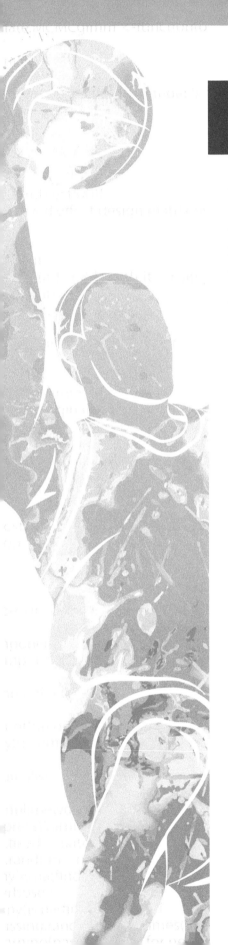

PREFACE

To say that sport analytics is an emerging field would not give sufficient credit to the field's forebearers; to say that sport analytics is an established field would imply too much cohesion among those same forebearers. The progenitors of sport analytics developed the critical body of literature, methods, findings, and concepts over time through a series of hobby-efforts. As an example, consider Mark Glickman, an esteemed statistician with Harvard University, who has done important work applying Bayesian methods to health—and theorizes about new rating systems for games and sport on the side.

The disorderly production of the body of work that now comprises sport analytics is in our view a boon to the field. Sport analytics draws on lively areas of research in mathematics, statistics, economics, computer science, and management. Each of these areas will continue to have much to offer the next generation of thinkers in sport analytics. Undoubtedly, thinkers from additional fields of research will bring their thoughts to bear as well. The speed at which leagues adopted personalized medical technology as preventative measure against COVID-19 foreshadows the impact that the impending era of big biological data will have on the way we understand sport. Ultimately, so long as sport remains a joyous personal respite, sport analytics will always need to make room for innovative hobbyists.

While this book is in many ways a celebration of the diversity of the field of sport analytics, we intend it first and foremost as a practical primer to the aspiring analyst. The diversity of the field does the novice no favors. Entering from any specific sport, one is prone to miss ways of reasoning about sport analytics that emerge from other sports; entering from any specific discipline, one is prone to miss methods of analysis that emerge from other disciplines.

We modestly offer this book as an incomplete canon of methods and findings in sport analytics. We endeavor in these pages to collect and concisely convey critical concepts to facilitate the education of the next generation of sport analysts. To those ends, we lay out foundational observations about sport analytics from the four major American sports, as well as foundational methods for analyzing sport writ large. Ultimately, we hope two things: first, that this text can start the process of demarcating the domain of sport analytics as a sophisticated field in its own right; and second, that this this text can play a catalyzing role in the training of future sport analytics professionals.

We hope you enjoy.

ABOUT THE AUTHORS

J.T. Wolohan is the author of *Mastering Large Datasets with Python*, a top book on practical approaches for processing big data. His writing is endowed by over a decade of experience in software development, artificial intelligence, big data and analytics. J.T. currently works as a data scientist and artificial intelligence researcher. An alumnus of both Syracuse University and Indiana University – Bloomington, in his free time, J.T. likes to run, cook, and spend time with his family. On the best days, he does all three. J.T.'s favorite sports team is the New York Yankees; he is also an avid boxing fan. Originally from Ithaca, N.Y., he currently resides in Washington, D.C.

John T. Wolohan is a sports lawyer, academic, consultant, and author. He joined the Syracuse University Sport Management program in 2011 and the Syracuse University College of Law in 2014. In addition to publishing numerous articles and being one of the lead editors of the book "Law for Recreation and Sport Managers" by Cotten and Wolohan, Professor Wolohan has been teaching and working in the fields of sport management, sports law, and sports media for over 30 years. Professor Wolohan has taught as a visiting professor and served as scholar-in-residence at the China University of Political Science and Law (China), University of Lleida (Spain), Sheffield Hallam University (England), University of Pretoria (South Africa) and as a research fellow for Beijing Sport University (China).

In addition, Professor Wolohan is a highly sought-after expert for the *New York Times, Washington Post, USA Today, The Athletic, Forbes,* NPR, CCTV, and many other news organizations. Professor Wolohan, who is a frequent speaker, panelist, and moderator at professional organizations, law schools, and sport business conferences, received his J.D. from Western New England University, School of Law, M.A. from Syracuse University, and B.A. from the University of Massachusetts - Amherst.

CHAPTER 1

Introduction to Sport Analytics

John Wolohan

LEARNING OBJECTIVES

After reading this chapter, students should be able to:

- Understand and be able to explain the meaning of analytics.
- Explain the meaning of the term sabermetrics.
- Describe descriptive statistics and when they are used.
- Describe inferential or predictive statistics and when they are used.
- Describe how analytics were first introduced into the sports world and for what purpose.
- Identify how analytics are used in the sports world today.

Introduction

In today's digital world, the use of data analytics can be found in virtually every aspect of modern life and business. In fact, consumer data is one of the most valuable commodities a company can own. As a result, every time you go online and visit a website, purchase something using your credit card, send a snap or tweet, or post personal information to your social media page, someone is collecting that information "data" about you. Companies and organizations hope that if they can collect enough data on their current and potential consumers, they can use it to discover some significance in the data or hidden key to predict your future spending and product preferences or help improve their decision-making (Davenport and Kim 2013).

The following are just some of the ways companies are using your data to predict your future behavior and increase revenue. NIKE, through my online purchase history, knows that I traditionally buy a new pair of running shoes every six months. As the time to purchase a new pair gets closer, NIKE will start emailing me suggestions on the latest running shoes I might be interested in based on price, style, and function. Netflix, based on my viewing history, knows that I generally like action and adventure movies or real-life police dramas. However, my history (my data) also shows that on Friday nights between 7 and 9 pm, I tend to watch Disney movies. Based on this data, on Fridays Netflix will suggest other "kid-friendly" movies and shows I might be interested in watching with my family. Video game developers, after collecting data on weapon usage and my general playing style, can use that data to suggest various equipment and weapons upgrades that I might purchase through micro-transactions to increase my enjoyment and keep me engaged in the game. Finally, Amazon, knowing that you purchased the *Sports Analytics* book by Wolohan and Wolohan, will use that data to suggest that you purchase *Mastering Large Datasets with Python* by John T. Wolohan, and other books published by the two authors.

By using the data that they collect on customers and potential customers, companies and sports organizations are seeking to gain a competitive edge over their competitors. Collecting consumer data, however, is not enough. Companies and sports teams need to be able to analyze and understand what the data means and how to incorporate those findings into action. The rest of this book, therefore, explores how organizations and teams are using the data they collect to not only build a winning team on the field, but also off the field to improve customer service, create new products and to help guide with their future marketing and general business decisions (Davenport and Kim 2013).

Who is This Book For?

Most sports analytics books suffer from one major flaw, they are one dimensional. In particular, many sports analytics texts are either grounded in data sciences or sport science. The benefit of this book is that the authors have backgrounds and expertise in both fields. It is this combination, we hope, that will provide readers with a more well-rounded foundation in data science and analytics as well as how those theories apply to the business of sports.

While this book would be appropriate for anyone with a basic understanding of statistics and regression models, it was intended for upper-level undergraduates or as introductory graduate text. In particular, the book is intended as an introduction to the field of sport analytics and the programming language R. As such, there are two major goals to the text. The first goal is to provide the statistical and analytical foundation required for students to do sport analytics. To achieve this, the text introduces the foundational theories of sport analytics while also presenting the practical and theoretical considerations for these methods. While not intended to be a statistics book, the text does use case studies and programming exercises to allow students to work with and apply some of the statistical foundations presented in the text. Therefore, while some understanding of statistics and regression models may be helpful, it is not necessary that students be fluent in quantitative statistics to use the text.

The second goal is to provide an overview of how analytics is being used by various sports businesses both on and off the field. The text uses various examples of how professional and college sports teams and leagues, as well as individual athletes, esports, retailers, and casinos are using analytics in their player evaluation, training, game preparation, and overall business. Although the text uses R to run all the statistical analysis, STATA, SPSS, Excel, or any other statistical package would also work. The text uses R, however because R is the preferred language of economists, statisticians, and front offices throughout sport. Therefore, once you learn R you will be able to take your R skillset with you for as long as you advance in sport analytics.

Additionally, it is hoped that the text will serve as a sport-specific supplement to the education of economics, data science, computer science, mathematics, or engineering students. Although there are several statistical software packages students and professionals can use when analyzing data, this text uses the software program R. Although the text uses R throughout this book, other statistical tools such as Excel and Python will also be used.

What Will This Book Cover?

The book is divided into four sections. The first part of the text examines how analytics looks at discrete events (such as a season in sport) as well as introduces the fundamental idea in statistical regression that performance or behavior can be predicted. The first part also introduces some of the modern analytics tools currently available and used in data analysis. In particular, the section provides a basic introduction to the fundamentals to using R, which is used in the various programming exercises throughout the text.

The second part of the text examines how basic methods and theories in analytics are applied in the world of sports. Instead of focusing on a single sport, the text uses examples from all the major (and some not so major) sports. In particular, the text gives examples on the data teams use to evaluate individual player performance and how they use that information to predict a player's future performance. For example, besides just looking at the box score and traditional player statistics such as batting average, points per game or yards per rushing attempt, the text introduces readers to some of the advanced sabermetric tools used to calculate a player's total contributions to their team in comparison to a replacement-level player. In hockey, the text examines *plus minus,* which measures a player's impact on the game, by examining the difference between their team's total scoring versus their opponent's when the player is in the game and what it does and does not measure. The text compares plus minus to the *Corsi* statistic, which looks at shots on goal. In basketball, the text looks at plus minus and player efficiency rating as well as how to choose effective basketball lineups and how a new player will fit into line projections. In football, the text introduces how to calculate the data for *defense-adjusted value over average (DOVA)* and *defense-adjusted yards above replacement (DYAR)* and other calculations like *RUG*, that examines wide-receivers and other appropriate way of analyzing a football game.

The third part of the looks at more advanced modeling. In particular, the text introduces Monte Carlo Methods, Game Theory, and Optimization Methods and other advanced data methods. In addition, this section explores what is deep learning, how it applies in sport, and what type of data lends itself toward deep learning applications. This section of the text also examines player projections, rankings, and rating systems.

The fourth part of the text examines how analytics is used off the field in the sport industry. In particular, the section examines how analytics is used in everything from ticketing and custom relationship management to marketing. In addition to the use of analytics in the sport industries, this section of the text also looks at the role of analytics in esports, fantasy sports, and sports betting markets. For example, the section examines how the use of analytics in fantasy sports and sport betting haven taken these industries to new levels. The text concludes by looking at the legal and ethical considerations associated with using an athlete's data, especially medical and other personal data.

What is Analytics?

In its most basic form: analytics is the collection and use of data to help make better informed, fact-based decisions. Another useful definition of analytics is that analytics is simply the collection of information "data" and the use of mathematical, statistical, or even qualitative methods to find meanings and patterns in the data to make better, more informed decisions (Severini 2015).

As mentioned above, the use of analytics is practiced by companies everywhere. In the world of sports, analytics is being used in everything from player profiles, player development and training, game preparation and strategy to ticket sales, marketing, and a hundred other ways.

So, how do you start to use analytics to make fact-based decisions? The analytics process can be broken down into four steps:

1. Asking the question
2. Collecting data
3. Analyzing the data
4. Reporting and acting on the results

The first step in any data analysis is to figure out what it is you want to measure or discover. In statistical language, what is your hypothesis? For example, if the owner of a minor league baseball team were to ask you how to make the team more profitable, there are several suggestions you could probably give her. One, she could lay off some of the full-time employees and take on college interns to reduce staff salaries. Two, she could find cheaper ways to travel and less expensive hotels, so reducing costs. Three, she could sell more tickets and increase attendance, thus increasing revenue. All three of the actions above will probably result in short-term higher profits. However, before you can analyze the owner's question and the impact such a decision would have on the overall profitability of the team, you need to know which of the three questions she is really asking.

Once you know the question or issue you want answered, increase attendance through higher ticket sales (the dependent variable), you can move on to the second step: data collection. In order to answer the question or dependent variable, we need to collect data on those variables (independent variables) that effect attendance. Independent variables are variables that influence, directly or indirectly, the dependent variable. So, what variables impact attendance? As you can see in Table 1.2 below, some of the variables include: weather, day of the week, month of the year, game promotion, team performance. (This is just a small list—I am sure you could think of others.) Once you have identified the variables, you start collecting the data. Since attendance numbers are reported, it is easy to collect data on the number of people who attended the game on each day of the week, month of the year, and on what promotional night. If you want to know more about who is attending the game on which day, you will need to develop your own survey or method of collecting the data.

Once you have collected all the data, you can move on to step three: analyzing the data. As collected, the data is simply a bunch of numbers and, depending on the variables you wanted to measure, there could be a large data set of numbers. Analytics, therefore, requires that you find a systemic way to organize all the data collected and analyze it so that you understand what all those numbers mean. While there are a various analytical methods organizations and teams can use, here are three of the most common.

1. Statistical
   a. Descriptive
   b. Predictive
2. Data and Text mining
3. Experimental design

STATISTICAL. There are two major categories of statistics: **descriptive statistics and inferential or predictive statistics** (Frankfort-Nachmias and Leon-Guerrero 2011). Both descriptive statistics and inferential statistics are employed in the analysis of data and both are equally important. ***Descriptive statistics*** or analytics involves procedures that help organize, tabulate, and describe the characteristics of the data collected (Frankfort-Nachmias and Leon-Guerrero 2011). This type of analytics has historically been called reporting data because the statistics are generally only helpful in providing the reader with a current snapshot of what you are analyzing. However, it fails to tell anything about why the result happened or predict what might happen in the future (Davenport and Kim 2013). Descriptive statistics are commonly used by marketers to help create a consumer profile and track product usage. For example, in looking at attendance data for the Florida State League (see Table 1.1), the data shows that there were a total of 816 games played during the 2009 season. The average number of home games played by each team was 68, with a range of 64 to 72. The mean attendance for each home game was 1,457.59. However, as shown in Table 1.1, the range in attendance (9,715 fans) was large. For example, the Lakeland Flying Tigers, an affiliate of the Detroit Tigers, averaged the smallest crowds at 547 fans per game. The Flying Tigers also had the smallest single game crowd of the season with only 129 fans attending one game. The Charlotte Stone Crabs, an affiliate of the Tampa Bay Rays, averaged the largest crowds in the league with 2,731 fans per game. The team with the largest single game attendance was the Fort Myers Miracle which had a total of 9,844 fan attended a game.

TABLE 1.1. Florida state league teams (Paul, Paul, and Yelencsics 2008)

TEAM	Mean Attendance	SD	Games	Range	Min	Max
Brevard County Manatees	834.34	907.35	64	4,894	354	5,248
Clearwater Threshers	1,721.59	1,460.83	71	7,790	520	8,310
Daytona Tortugas	2,395.65	934.17	63	4,327	737	5,064
Dunedin Blue Jays	581.36	266.89	64	1,252	368	1,620
Lakeland Flying Tigers	547.07	623.24	68	2,319	129	2,448
Tampa Yankees	1,528.43	1,039.28	72	3,987	773	4,760
Bradenton Marauders	1,175.07	916.08	66	4,043	490	4,533
Charlotte Stone Crabs	2,731.32	1,452.70	67	6,197	1,143	7,340
Fort Myers Miracle	2,466.80	1,599.77	70	8,777	1,067	9,844
Jupiter Hammerheads	990.76	1,064.19	71	7,490	320	7,810
Palm Beach Cardinals	1,044.55	795.06	70	4,589	337	4,926
St. Lucie Mets	1,452.67	1,007.25	70	4,055	380	4,435
Total	1,457.59	1,277.24	816	9,715	129	9,844

There are four main categories of descriptive statistics: ***measures of frequency***, which are used to show how often something occurs or how often a response is given; ***measures of centrality***, used when you want to identify an average or most common event or response (mean, medium and mode); ***measures of variation***, used to identify the spread of scores by stating intervals (the range) or the difference between an observed score and the mean (standard deviation); and ***measures of position***, used to describe how scores fall in relation to one another (percentile ranks and quartile ranks).

Inferential or predictive statistics moves away from simple counts and describing the characteristics of the data and attempts to make predictions or inferences from the data (Frankfort-Nachmias and Leon-Guerrero 2011). For example, in Table 1.2, the study attempts to determine which variables or factors have a greater influence on per game attendance. The factors examined include winning percentage, city population, day of the week, month of the year, and game promotion. Inferential statistics, generally regression models, are used to identify associations among the variables. By looking at the data, analytics attempts to predict which variables will have the greatest effect on future attendance.

TABLE 1.2. Level of attendance at Florida State League games.

Variables	Model 1	Model 2	Model 3	Model 4	Model 5
Intercept	1711.62***	1307.75***	1640.95***	1574.14***	1237.74***
Winning percentage	1337.10**	1289.03**	1373.06**	1281.57**	1274.70**
City population	.001*	.001*	.001*	.001*	.001*
Per Capita Income	−.04***	−.03*	−.04***	−.04***	−.03***
Food		−161.55†			18.88
Beer		180.75†			−75.41
Merchandise		183.74			48.19
Free Tickets		−407.88**			−153.52
Fireworks		2005.48***			1670.77***
Concerts		1138.63†			966.28
Group Nights		118.93			92.35
Family Nights		173.95†			333.27**
Athlete Appearance		1146.04			1004.89
Theme Night		36.64			−292.62
College Night		−241.58			−427.65
Religious Theme		−280.64			72.58
Doubleheader Game 1		−81.55			−102.65
Doubleheader Game 2		−221.11			−259.75

	Model 1	Model 2	Model 3	Model 4	Model 5
Opening Night		1202.91***			1162.33***
Scout Sleepover		−129.50			−305.58
Dogs to Park		204.60			−194.99
Clear			243.02†		53.24
Cloudy			211.19†		249.83*
Overcast			118.17		33.20
Rain			11.73		−44.49
Sunny			14.36		226.68
Drizzle			−187.70		−289.06
Sunday				−261.23†	−413.09**
Monday				−411.96**	−276.77†
Tuesday				−266.57†	−142.76
Thursday				292.71†	400.47*
Friday				901.08***	570.13***
Saturday				981.46***	501.30**
R squared	0.06	0.33	0.06	0.23	0.38

Notes: N = 816
Model 1 looks at winning percentage and city population and income per capita.
Model 2 adds the effect of game day promotions.
Model 3 adds the effect of game-time weather.
Model 4 adds the effect of days of the week.
Model 5 examines the combined effect all variables.
***$p<0.001$; **$p<0.01$; *$p<0.05$; †$p<0.10$

Using an Ordinary Least Square (OLS) regression model, winning percentage and quality of team play have a positive relationship on fan attendance. However, since minor league teams have very little control over the players they put out on the field, player personnel decisions are all made by the major league affiliate, and so on-field success is not always possible. Fortunately, while the study shows that on-field performance has a significant positive effect of fan attendance, it also supports the findings of others that promotions and game day events, weather, and days of the weeks can also play major roles in determining whether fans attended a game or not.

Not all promotions increased fan attendance, however. Minor league baseball is considered a family-friendly sports product, and promotions such as fireworks, that are geared toward the family, seem to have the largest positive impact on fan attendance. Promotions designed to attract certain groups of fans, such as college, religious groups, or scouts, seem to have the opposite effect and keep fans not affiliated with the groups away from the ballpark.

Also, not surprisingly, the day the game was played was a statistically significant factor, both positively and negatively, in the number of fans who attended games. As expected, weekend days, Thursday, Friday, and Saturday drew larger crowds, compared to the dummy variable Wednesday. Sunday, Monday, and Tuesday were shown to have a negative effect on attendance.

In addition to various statistical methods used, sports teams and organizations also use analytics in data mining and text mining. ***Data mining*** is the process of finding anomalies, patterns, and correlations within large datasets through the automatic or semi-automatic extraction of data using computational algorithmic and statistical methods (Davenport and Kim 2013). Data mining is used by sports businesses and teams to help learn more about their customers and fans, to help with their marketing, and to help increase revenue and improve customer service. Data mining is also being used in esports to help gamers improve and to help game developers track game usage and discover programming issues that make the games difficult or easy and fail to keep the players interested (More information on how esports are using analytics can be found in Chapter 14).

Text mining is like data mining, except that instead of finding anomalies, patterns, and correlations within large datasets, the computers analyze text instead. While probably best known by its use by companies like Twitter, which mines all the tweets being sent, to identify which stories or topics are tending now (Wolohan 2019), text mining is also used by sports business and teams to track customer reaction to new products or developments within the teams. In addition to mining social media and news sites, sports businesses and teams also can mine data from call centers, ticket sales departments, online team forums, and customer surveys. Using text mining, analytics can discover a lot of information about how customers and fans perceive the products and team, and hopefully help with future decisions.

Another important type of analytics used in sports is experimental design. ***Experimental design*** is used to test the reaction of two randomly selected groups, the experimental group, and the control group, by introducing a change to the experimental group and not the control group (Davenport and Kim 2013). For example, the marketing department at the Boston Celtics is interested to know whether their new direct sales campaign is effective in increasing sales. To discover the effect of the new campaign on sales, the marketing department randomly selects a groups of past ticket buyers that it will send the new campaign to (the experimental group), and another randomly selected groups of past ticket buyers to send the existing sales campaign to (the control group). Based on the number of sales from each group, this experiment should allow the marketing department to determine the effectiveness of the new campaign in driving new sales.

The final step in the process, and perhaps the most important, is reporting and implementing the results. Nothing is going to help the owner of our minor league baseball team increase attendance and profits if she and her staff are not willing to act upon the finding. So, what does Table 1.2 above tell us, and how can we increase attendance? First on-field performance has a significant effect of fan attendance. However, as a minor league team, the owner has very little control over which players are on the team from day to day. Therefore, you need to focus less of your marketing on the core product and more on the product extensions, such as game promotions and other special game day events. In addition, since weather and days of the weeks can also play a role in attendance, the team should also take that into consideration. For example, hosting a fireworks night should generate large crowds. Also, since the largest crowds attend games during the weekend, you might want to hold any promotions designed to attract certain groups of fans, such as college, religious groups, or scouts, for mid-week games, since those promotions seem to have a depressing effect on overall attendance.

Qualitative Analytics vs. Quantitative Analytics

There are two general methods of research or analytical methods: quantitative and qualitative. The type of research methods you use will vary depending on the type of data you wish to collect and what you wish to discover from the data.

When most people think of data analytics, they instinctive think of quantitative analytics.

Quantitative analytics looks at all the data collected by an organization or team and transforms it via statistical, mathematical, or computational techniques into useable information that will help explain or predict future events. Organizations and teams typically collect quantitative data on their customers and fans when they purchase products; however, it can also be collected from in-stadium or online surveys, website interceptors, online polls, or telephone sales (Davenport and Kim 2013). In addition, because of the power of the statistical software used today, quantitative analytics allows companies to work with extremely large datasets (Wolohan 2019). This allows teams to track the purchasing behavior of fans from season to season.

The larger our sample size compared to the population we are hoping to analyze, the more likely the results of the analysis can be inferred on to the entire population. For example, if you wish to predict how the current 20,000 season ticket holders will react to an increase in season ticket prices or renewal versus non-renewal, you cannot be very confident in your findings if you only sample 100 season ticket holders. To feel 100% confident in knowing how all 20,000 season ticket holders are going to react, you would need to survey all of them. Since the probability of all 20,000 returning a survey are slim, we can calculate the confidence interval we feel comfortable with based on the number of surveys returned. Therefore, if we wanted a confidence level of 95% on the real value of people who would renew their tickets at the higher price was within ±5% of the results of the survey, statistically you only need 377 season ticket holders to return their surveys. In other words, if out of the 377 surveys returned, 90% of the season ticket holders said they would renew their tickets at the higher price, you should feel 95% confident that out of the 20,000 season ticket holders, between 85%–95%, will renew their season tickets are the higher price. The higher the number of returned surveys, the greater our level of confidence. If I had 645 season ticket holders to return their surveys, the confidence level would be 99% that the real value is within ±1% of the measured/surveyed value.

In other words, if 90% of the 645 season ticket holders who returned surveys said they would renew their tickets at the higher price, you should feel 99% confident that out of the 20,000 season ticket holders, between 89%–91%, will renew their season tickets at the higher price.

While it may be true that most analytics are quantitative, there are cases when qualitative research or analytics is more appropriate to analyze issues facing teams and organizations. **Qualitative research or analytics** is used in discovering broad themes for marketers or as a tool in the early stages of research to help discover areas that may need more in-depth statistical or quantitative analytics (Davenport and Harris 2007). For example, in interviews, focus groups or observations qualitative researchers seek to capture information that might explain certain patterns, opinions, motivations, or other information that might be more difficult to collected in a more structured format like surveys or is difficult to collect and tabulate in a statistical model.

What is Sport Analytics?

With analytics seemingly infiltrating every aspect of our lives, it was not surprising that it would find its way into sports. Professional and college teams, with the help of video and advanced computer statistical software, can track every play and every movement of every player and break down those movements into quantifiable statistics. Analytics are also impacting high school and little league sports. For example, little league baseball players can go online after each game and post data of their at-bats to compare their season statistics with other players on the teams and in the league. In fact, it would be hard to find any professional or major college organization that does not have at least one analytical expert on staff, let alone an entire department dedicated to analytics.

In many ways, sports has always used analytics in one format or another. However, the person widely credited as the first modern sports executive to use advanced statistical analytics to help identify player value is Billy Beane, the General Manager of the Oakland Athletics. Faced with an ever-widening revenue gap between his small-market, low-payroll Oakland Athletics and the large-market, high-payroll teams of the New York Yankees and Boston Red Sox, Beane and his assistant Paul DePodesta sought a new approach. Not wanting to do what the Yankees did, because they would "lose every time, because they are doing it with three times more money than we are" (Lewis 2003, 119), Beane and DePodesta decided that in order to compete with the Yankees, they needed to ignore the traditional baseball statistics, such as batting average (BA) and runs batted in (RBIs), and focus more on newer sabermetrics numbers like slugging percentage (SLG), which measures the total number of bases reached per at bat; on base percentage (OBP), which measures the percentage of times a player reaches base on either a hit, walk, or hit by pitch; and on-base plus slugging percentage (OPS), which looks at a player's OBP and slugging percentage. As detailed in Michael Lewis' 2003 book "*Money Ball*," DePodesta argued that statistically the only two offensive numbers that had any relationship to winning were slugging percentage and on base percentage. Everything else, he concluded, was less important. Therefore, the A's sought out players with a high on base percentage and pitchers that the market had undervalued, often getting them for a fraction of the price (Lewis 2003). While money may have forced the A's to think outside the box of normal baseball thinking, Beane also believed "that the market for baseball players was so fundamentally inefficient, and the general grasp of sound baseball strategy so weak, that superior management could still run circles around taller piles of cash" (Lewis 2003, 122).

While Beane and the A's may not have beaten the Yankees in the playoffs, because of the general on-field success of the low-budget Athletics, major league team owners began to adopt Beane's use of sabermetrics and introduce a whole new breed of General Managers into the game. In 2004, Paul DePodesta would be hired to run the Los Angeles Dodgers. However, the most successful of the new breed of sabermetrics General Managers was Theo Epstein, who was able to use sabermetrics to win World Series with the long-suffering Boston Red Sox in 2004 and Chicago Cubs in 2016.

While Beane may get credit for introducing analytics to baseball, the truth is, sports administrators and executives have always used statistics in one way or other. In fact, professional sports have kept statistical records on player performance since the box score was first developed in 1845 and transformed into our more modern version by Henry Chadwick in 1859 (Lewis 2003). It is because of these statistics, such as batting average and ERA, that we can compare players from one decade with those from another.

While Chadwick may have invented the modern box score, the modern-day Godfather of sport analytics is Bill James. James was one of the first, if not the first, statistician to look at the statistical data collected differently. Beginning in 1977, with the self-publication of "*The Bill James Baseball Abstract: Featuring 18 categories of statistical information that you just can't find anywhere else*," James began to look at more than just a player's batting averages (BA) or earn run averages (ERA). While the first edition may have only sold 75 copies, James' approach to viewing the history of baseball through statistics, which he termed sabermetrics in reference to the Society for American Baseball Research (SABR) influenced a whole new generation of baseball executives and owners (Lewis 2003). SABR was created in Cooperstown, New York, in 1971, as a group of baseball researchers associated with the National Baseball Hall of Fame. The original purpose of SABR was to bring together different professional interested in baseball research. To honor baseball's great researchers, SABR awards the Henry Chadwick Award for their invaluable contributions to making baseball the game that links America's present with its past (Thompson and Hufford 2021).

While baseball may be the sport most associated with analytics, the fact is analytics is used in every sport. In looking at sports analytics, therefore, this text separates its use of analytics into on-field and off-field. On-field analytics, like those used by Billy Beane and Theo Epstein, deal with improving the on-field performance of teams and players. Depending on the sport, on-field analytics examine every pitch, field goal attempt, shot on goal, or pass to discover tendencies or patterns. Sports executives believe that the deeper into the data you dig, the better the chances of discovering the other team's weakness and thereby increasing the chance of winning on the field.

Off-field analytics deal with the business side of sports. Off-field analytics focuses on helping teams increase revenue by improving customer satisfaction and affiliation with the team. Using customer and fan data that is collected by the team when fans purchase a ticket or team merchandise or concessions, teams hope that they can mine the data to help make off-field decisions that hopefully improve the game experience for fans, while also improving the team's overall budget.

The success Billy Beane and Theo Epstein had in baseball also did not go unnoticed by executives in other professional sports leagues. For example, in the NFL, New England Patriots Coach and General Manager Bill Belichick is famous for using data and in-depth analytics to help the team find quality starters cast off by other teams that fit certain positions and can help the team win. Unlike Beane and Epstein, Belichick also had the extra burden of staying under the NFL's salary cap. In 2016, attempting to apply the *Moneyball* principles he learned in baseball, the Cleveland Browns hired Paul DePodesta as their Chief Strategy Officer. In 2021, the Browns would break a 25-year streak of not winning a play-off game. Besides player personal decisions, NFL teams also use analytics to make on field strategic decisions, such as which plays to run or defense to use.

While NBA teams have historically been less quantitatively oriented than baseball and football, there has been an increased use of analytics in the league over the last 15 years so that almost every team has an analytics department (Oliver 2003). The person most credited with introducing analytics to the NBA is Daryl Morey. Morey, who was the General Manager of the Houston Rockets from 2007 to 2020, implemented a style of analytics known as "Moreyball" which favored three-point shots over mid-range jumpers (Keddie 2020).

Today, NBA teams not only record every movement of every player on the court but also have all players wear monitors or wearables, not during games but during practice to measure performance and fatigue. Teams are using all this information to determine which players to draft, based on data collected on the players in college, or sign as free agents, and when to rest players. On the court, analytics have changed the way the game is played (Winston 2009). For example, the analytics show that the reward of taking a three-point shoot outweighs the risk of missing or taking ten-foot jumper when. As a result, during the 2000/01 season, NBA teams averaged 13.7 three-point attempts per game. During the 2019/20 season, that number had jumped to 33 attempts per game.

Like other professional sports, the NHL has also moved beyond the basic statistics historically used: goals, assists, plus/minus, goals-against average, and is now using more advanced analytics. For example, like the three-point attempt in the basketball, advanced analytics has determined the best way to win in hockey is to score more goals than your opponent. As a result, teams now measure puck possession and shot attempts. The two main analytic models used are: Corsi, which measures all shots on goal, and Fenwick, which measures all shots on goal and all shots that miss the net, excluding shots that are blocked.

It should be noted that not everyone believes that the use of analytics has improved sports. When baseball managers feel the need to consult binders using statistics to track every pitch showing the hitters and pitchers tendencies and games that stretch over four hour games, or when football coaches consult their computer tablets and switch up personnel after each play, it is easy to say that analytics have gone too far. However, "while detractors of sports analytics might image a dystopian future of data and analytics driven sports, most people in the know see higher levels of competition resulting from the intelligent use of analytics and … informed choices about player positioning, competitive strategy and in game tactics" (Miller 2016, 194). Those in favor of the use of analytics argue that improved measures on performance data can help teams with player selection and game day strategies (Miller 2016).

Sports Analytics as a Field of Study

While economists have been using statistics to explain or predict future events in other industries for decades, the use of statistical modeling in the sports industry was slow to catch on. One of the reasons for this hesitation was that very few academically trained economists were interested in the field of sports economics. In addition, those economists that were interested in studying sports faced two barriers. The first barrier was that in the field of sport management, most college programs were too small to hire such specialized faculty, so there were limited jobs outside traditional economics departments. The second barrier was that those who stayed in traditional economic departments found their research in sport was undervalued, so publishing research on sports threatened their academic careers.

These barriers started to come down in the last couple of decades with the migration of sport management programs from physical education departments into more traditional business schools. In addition, with the success of analytics, more employers started to look for graduates with specific analytic skills. This move, along with the increased interest in the number of students wishing to study in the area, allowed more academic departments to hire more economics professors interested in sport.

With the increased number of faculty coming into the academic discipline, the next step was a dedicated publication for the field. In 2000, the *Journal of Sport Economics* was introduced. That was followed in 2006 with the beginning of the annual MIT Sloan Sports Analytics Conference, which was co-founded by Daryl Morey and other students at MIT. With a dedicated journal and conference, research into the field of sports economics and sports analytics began to gain legitimacy. This led to the final stage of the evolution. Recognizing the widespread and increasing role of analytics in the sports industry and the need for employees with analytic skills in this rapidly growing field, Syracuse University became the first university to offer a sports analytics bachelor's degree. The program, which began in August 2017, was designed to offer students a degree to match their interests in math, statistics, and computer programming with their love of sport (Reimer 2016).

Summary

Over the last 20 years, the use of analytics has seemingly entered every aspect of modern life and business. As a result, every time you go online and visit a website, purchase something using your credit card, send a snapchat or tweet, or post personal information to your social media page, companies are tracking, capturing, and analyzing your data. With analytics infiltrating so much of daily life, it is not surprising that the use of analytics has gravitated into the sports world. As we will see in the rest of the book, executives in every aspects of the sports industry are using statistical modeling and analytics to determine the best way to perform tasks ranging from coaches evaluating on-field performance, general managers evaluating off-field personnel, and doctors evaluating player injuries to sports bettors evaluating odds and trends, ticket managers evaluating how best to sell tickets, and marketing managers evaluating consumer profiles and how best to market the product to consumers.

Key Terms

Analytics

Sports Analytics

Descriptive Statistics

Inferential or Predictive Statistics

Quantitative Methods

Qualitative Methods

Measures of Frequency

Measures of Centrality

Measures of Variation

Measures of Position

Sabermetrics

Critical Thinking Exercises

- List some examples of how analytics can be used to evaluate on-field performance.
- Discuss some of the methods teams use to collect data on players.
- Discuss how analytics have slowed down the games of the field and may have a negative impact of the way games are played.
- Think about all the methods teams and organizations use to collect data on fans and how that data is used.
- Discuss the difference between qualitative and quantitative analytics and give examples of when you would use each research method.

References

Davenport, Thomas H., and Jeanne G. Harris. 2007. *Competing on Analytics*. Boston: Harvard Business School Publishing.

Davenport, Thomas H., and Jinho Kim. 2013. *Keeping Up with the Quants: Your Guide to Understanding + Using Analytics*. Boston: Harvard Business School Publishing.

Frankfort-Nachmias, Chava, and Anna Leon-Guerrero. 2011 *Social Statistics for a Diverse Society* (6th edition). Los Angeles: SAGE.

Keddie, Paul. 2020. The Return of Moreyball. Double Clutch. https://www.doubleclutch.uk/nba/the-return-of-moreyball/.

Lewis, Michael. 2003. *Moneyball: The Art of Winning an Unfair Game*. New York: W.W. Norton & Company.

Miller, Thomas W. 2016. *Sport Analytics and Data Science: Winning the Game with Methods and Models*. Old Tappan: Pearson Education.

Oliver, Dean. 2003. *Basketball on Paper: Rules and Tools for Performance Analysis*. Washington D.C.: Brassey's Inc.

Paul, Rodney J., and Andrew P. Weinbach. 2013. Firework Saturation and Attendance in Minor League Baseball. *International Journal of Sport Finance* 8, 123–138.

Paul, Rodney J., Kristin K. Paul, and Kyle Yelencsics. 2008. Good Day, Sunshine: Attendance for the Florida State Baseball League. *Southern Business and Economic Journal* 31(4), 218–229.

Reimer, Alex. 2016, May. Syracuse University Will Launch First Sports Analytics Degree in The U.S. *Forbes*.

Severini, Thomas A. 2015. *Analytic Methods in Sports*. Boca Raton: CRC Press.

Thompson, Dick, and Tom Hufford. 2021. *A History of SABR*. Society for American Baseball Research (2021). https://sabr.org/history.

Winston, Wayne L. 2009. *Mathletics: How Gamblers, Managers, and Sports Enthusiasts Use Mathletics in Baseball, Basketball and Football*. Princeton: Princeton University Press.

Wolohan, John T. 2019. *Mastering Large Datasets with Python*. Shelter Island: Manning Publications.

CHAPTER 2

Statistical Programming and Sport Analytics

J.T. Wolohan

> **LEARNING OBJECTIVES**
> After reading this chapter, students should be able to:
> - Install R on your computer.
> - Perform basic arithmetic analytics with R.
> - Calculate "box score" statistics.
> - Create functions in R.

Introduction

Contemporary sport analytics is as much about computers as it is about mathematics, decision theory, and, indeed, sport. In order to be successful in sport analytics, one certainly needs to understand—if not master—the computational aspects of sport analytics. Throughout this book, we will teach computational techniques essential to effective sport analytics. In this chapter, we will begin that process by introducing R.

First, we will talk about what R is and go over some of R's background, as well as where the language is used. Next, we will walk through the steps of installing R on our computers and explore some elementary features of R. To introduce R, the text looks at the Syracuse Orange's 2003 NCAA tournament run. In addition, you will learn how to calculate box-score statistics using R. Next, the text examines univariate analysis. Finally, the text will examine Cam Newton's 2015 MVP season and show how to perform analysis on univariate count and rate statistics in R.

The R Programming Language

R is a statistical programming language in widespread—and growing—use across both academia and industry. It is the preferred language of economists, statisticians, and sport analysts. The rise in big data along with the increasing emphasis that industry is placing on mathematical analysis has made R one of the 15 most popular programming languages in the world. This is despite R being primarily a single purpose language. Apart from SQL—the ubiquitous relational database query language—all of the other languages in the top 15 are general purpose programming languages. R is the foremost statistical computing tool.

In this book, we have chosen to use R because it provides an extensive library of advanced statistical functions. You will be able to use this library to perform complex statistical analysis with convenient programing tools. Additionally, because R is a fully fledged programming language, you will be able to take your R skillset with you for as long as you advance in sport analytics. The R language is used in front offices throughout sport, as well as by data-oriented sport journalists, sport analytics companies, sport marketing companies, apparel companies, and elsewhere across the business of sport.

Getting to Know R

When we think about R, there are two things we want to keep in mind:

1. R is a high-level **scripting language**.
2. R is an **array-oriented programming** language.

These two traits will shape how we interact with R.

R AS A HIGH-LEVEL SCRIPTING LANGUAGE. Scripting languages are designed to be fast and easy to learn. As you'll see later in this chapter, R tries pretty hard to get out of your way and the syntax—compared to other programming languages—is easy to pick up. We'll also often have the option of using scripting languages, like R, in a **read-evaluate-print-loop** (REPL). This is a process whereby we the computer reads our command, evaluates it, prints the output to the screen, and then waits for our next command. We can use the REPL to program interactively—checking in on our work as we progress.

R AS AN ARRAY-ORIENTED LANGUAGE. The next thing that we want to keep in mind as we use R is that R is array-oriented. This means that R expects that we are working with one or more arrays. If you remember your linear algebra, an **array** is a collection of numbers. Many of Rs functions are geared toward working on collections numbers. For example, R has built-in support for array mathematics. Almost any R function that you can use on two numbers will also work on two arrays of numbers. As we will see, this comes in quite handy.

Installing R

To install R, we are going to want to install two pieces of software: R itself, and RStudio. R is the statistical language itself and RStudio is an integrated development environment used to run R. RStudio provides an easy way of keeping track of our R environment, viewing plots we create, installing and loading third-party packages, looking up help, and more.

INSTALLING R FROM CRAN.ORG. To install R, we will go to the R project's homepage and find the appropriate download. The R project's homepage is https://cran.r-project.org/. The first text on the page has three download links: one for Mac, one for Windows, and one for Linux. For both Mac and Windows, clicking on your operating system's link will take you to another page where you can download "base" or "base-R." This is the essential software needed to run R.

INSTALLING RSTUDIO. In addition to R, we are going to want to install RStudio. RStudio is available for free from the RStudio website: https://rstudio.com/products/rstudio/download/. On this page, you will again find links to download RStudio for your operating system of choice. Both the Mac and Windows downloads should be executables that install RStudio.

Both R and RStudio are free software, distributed under free and open-source licenses. R is distributed under the GPL and RStudio is distributed on the AGPL. This means that they will always be free and are available for you to use.

Other Statistical Tools

While we have chosen to use R in this book for the reasons laid out above, there are other tools that one could use to follow along with this book. Tools one might choose for statistical analysis include:

- Microsoft Excel
- Python
- MATLAB, SPSS, or SAS

For the sake of fairness, we'll briefly cover these three options.

USING EXCEL FOR SPORT ANALYTICS. Excel is a common data analysis tool, and the spreadsheet is a self-explanatory and comfortable way to do analysis. Additionally, Microsoft has developed a scripting language for Excel that we could use to achieve any analysis we would want to do in R. Unfortunately, because Excel forces you to look at your data at all times, when we're working with larger datasets, Excel quickly becomes clunky and wieldy.

SPORT ANALYTICS WITH PYTHON. Another tool one might want to use for sport analytics is the Python programming language. Python is very popular among data scientists for its strong support of machine learning. It is also popular with traditional software developers. Python's versatility and ease of use have made it one of the top five most popular programming languages in the world. Python could become the top language in the world within the decade. While Python is an excellent choice for many tasks, we have chosen not to use it because the barrier to entry-level analysis in Python is high, the language's flexibility encourages bad practices, and because most of the features that we would want to use in Python actually work better in R.

MATLAB, SPSS, AND SAS FOR ANALYTICS. MATLAB, SPSS, and SAS are all proprietary numerical computing languages. They are all very similar to R; however, they come with hefty price tags. Additionally, much of their power comes from their optimized, but unique, functions. Because of this, teaching any one is of limited usefulness. You would not be able to learn what you know about SAS to perform a similar task in SPSS. We decided against teaching any of these tools to ensure that you would always be able to take your skills with you.

Box Score Statistics

With R and RStudio installed, we are ready to begin learning analytics methods and we will begin our study of analytic methods with what we call **box score** statistics. Box score statistics are the statistics found in traditional box scores. They are stats that are intended to describe and summarize a game after it has been played. Dating back to the 1800s, the box score is an efficient way of communicating what happened in a game, or many games, to an interested audience. The box score is most commonly associated with baseball, though all of the major American sports have box scores in some format. In this section, we will review common box score statistics, and we will cover their purpose and role in analytics.

The box score was created for baseball and dates back to the mid-1800s. It was a useful way for newspapers, the dominant news medium at the time, to communicate with their audiences what happened in a large number of games. A newspaper may have only enough room in its pages to track the local team. The box score made it possible for a paper to communicate the outcomes of all the games, including the players performances, to a wide audience.

The purpose behind the box score is to summarize what happened in a game. In this way, we can think about box score statistics as the simplest **unit of measurement** in sport analytics. For example, in baseball, a box score will contain measurements of a batters' as-bats, hits, walks, runs, strikeouts, runs-batted-in, and so forth. These are all measurements of a player's performance. We can use these measurements to better understand a player. We might consider a batter who hits a lot of home runs a power hitter, or a player who gets a lot of walks and singles to be an on-base specialist. These traits are evident only because we measure them.

If baseball is the sport where the box score is the most famous, American football is the sport where the box score is the least heralded and most heavily criticized. This is especially true for defensive players, whose performance is typically only measured in terms of tackles, sacks, and interceptions. These statistics in football play much less of a role in the way we think about defensive players. Consider what offenses sometimes do when competing against a lockdown cornerback: they avoid the good cornerback and target his lesser teammates. This has the effect of reducing the corner's tackles and interceptions, despite the fact that he is a good player. In football, box score statistics may be a description of what happened—but with 22 players engaged on every play, simple counts designed to summarize the game can hardly reflect the true nuance of the sport.

Units of Measurement: What We Count

The box score is the starting place to understanding sport analytics because it is an introduction to counting things in sports, and counting is the simplest form of measurement and analysis. Talking about what we count and measure in sport is also important because it illustrates what we do not measure in sport. To be a good sport analyst, it is important to understand what you are measuring and what that measurement is describing.

Remember back to the last section when we suggested that a baseball player who hits a lot of home runs might be considered a power hitter. When we make that assessment based on the number of home runs, we are making a decision. We are deciding that hitting home runs is an important measure. We know, however, that there are lots of factors that influence how many home runs a player might hit in a season. For **example**, players who play in Colorado, where the air is thin, hit home runs more often than those who play elsewhere. Additionally, players who hit especially well to one side of the field or another will hit more home runs in ballparks where that side of the field is shorter.

To drive this point home, let's look at a few more statistics from across sports, what they measure, and what they do not.

TABLE 2.1. Statistics and measurements across sport

Sport	Statistic	Measures	Does not measure
Baseball	Wins	How many games a pitcher wins.	How many runs the pitcher gave up in those wins and how much run support they had.
Basketball	Blocks	How many times a player tipped an opponent's shot.	How many times a player prevented a shot attempt.
Football	Receptions	How many passes did a receiver catch.	How many times did a receiver get open.
Hockey	Points	How many times a player was involved in a goal.	How many times a player disrupted an opponent's possession.
Soccer	Tackles	How many times a player slid and took the ball from an opposing player.	How many times a player intercepted a pass or prevented a player from taking a shot on goal.

Table 2.1 shows that statistics across all of sport reflect these decisions about measurement. When we decide to use a statistic in our analysis, it is important that we think about what that statistic is or is not measuring. This is especially true because there is often a discrepancy between what we are measuring and what we would like to measure. We will come back to this point throughout the book. For now, let's turn our attention to calculating some box score statistics in R.

Calculating Box Score Statistics in R

We started this book with box score statistics because they are commonplace and because they are easy to calculate. This makes them a great way to introduce the power of the R programming language for analytics. In this section, we will look at how we can use R to create and analyze box score statistics.

In this section, we will introduce some new notation specific to using the R programming language. For example, you will often see words in `monospace font`. This notation tells you that we are talking about a specific piece of your code. Additionally, you might see sections of code, like this:

```
> print("I'm a code listing")
[1] "I'm a code listing"
```

These are code listings. Commands preceded by a > indicate code that you should type into an interactive console. Text preceded by a [#] indicates the expected output of that command. Text in code font that is neither preceded by a > or [#] indicates code that should be written in a script.

With that notation in mind, let's take a tour of some of R's capabilities. First of all, R has all the capabilities of a calculator. For example, if we want to find out how many times a baseball player reached base and we know they recorded 2 hits and a walk, we could add those numbers together in R.

```
> 2+1
[1] 3
```

To keep track of our work, we can also assign those numbers to variables. For example, it is easier to understand what we are doing if we assign the number of hits to a variable hits and the number of walks to a variable walks.

```
> hits <- 2
> walks <- 1
> hits + walks
[1] 3
```

We will use the word variable in two contexts throughout this book: in a programming context and in a statistical context. In a programming context, variables are shorthand ways of referring to other parts of code. For example, in the scenario above, hits has become a way of referring to a 2 and walks refers to a 1. Importantly, the values for these variables can change if we assign new values to them.

```
> times.on.base <- 0
> hits <- 2
> walks <- 1
> times.on.base <- hits + walks
> times.on.base
[1] 3
```

LISTING 2.1 Calculating times on base

For a more sophisticated example, let's imagine a scenario from American football. We want to figure out the number of yards per touch a running back had. We know he had 44 receiving yards on 3 catches and 70 rushing yards on 15 attempts. To calculate yards per touch, we simply add together his receiving yards and his rushing yards and divide that number by the number of catches plus rushes.

```
receiving.yards <- 44
catches <- 3
rush.yards <- 70
rush.attempts <- 15

tot.yards <- receiving.yards + rush.yards
touches <- catches + rush.attempts
yards.per.touch <- tot.yards / touches
yards.per.touch
```

LISTING 2.2 Calculating yards per touch

Performing this analysis reveals that the running back had 6.3 yards per touch during the game, with 114 total yards over 18 touches.

Importantly, we can use this same approach to analyze many observations at once. For example, imagine we are trying to total up the number of points scored by a basketball team's starting five, given the number of two point and three point, and free throw shots they each made. We can calculate each of their points all at once using R's array-based logic.

```
> twos <- c(3,2,14,8, 4)
> threes <- c(1,3,0,3,1)
> fts <- c(1,2,4,3,1)
> totals <- twos*2+threes*3+fts*1

> totals
[1] 10 15 32 28 12

> sum(totals)
[1] 97
```

LISTING 2.3 Using array-based to calculate many player statistics at once

There are a couple of things we want to pay attention to here. First, we use the c function to create an array of data. The numbers inside the c, separated by commas, are treated as elements of an array. Second, we can use arithmetic operations on those arrays as if they were normal values. R will default to performing element-wise operations on the arrays. Third, R knows the mathematical order of operations. When we use multiplication and division together, we do not need to specify the order unless we want to make the order explicit or we want to override the order of operations. Lastly, this is the first time we have seen an R **function** in action.

In this code block, we see the sum function. The sum function does what you imagine it would do: it adds together and gets the total of several numbers. In this case, we use it to count the points scored by the five starting players. The sum function is one of many helpful functions in R. Learning these functions is part of learning the R language.

That said, you will have plenty of help along the way. When you want to know more about how a function works, you can type help(<function>) to learn more about that function. This command will bring up the R documentation. R's documentation is the definitive place to look to learn about how a bit of code works. The documentation is often complete with usage examples as well, so you can see the code in action.

Case Study: Syracuse's 2003 NCAA Run

To learn more about R, let's look into Syracuse basketball's 2003 NCAA tournament run. To start, let's look at Syracuse's first game in the tournament against Manhattan. A number three ranked Syracuse, off a disappointing Big East tournament loss to rival UConn, kicks off the tournament against the Manhattan College Jasper's in the Boston Garden. Syracuse's team is led by freshmen forward and future NBA All-Star Carmelo Anthony.

ANALYZING A SINGLE GAME

Let's look at how Syracuse played in that first game. To do that, we will need to load in some data. R has support for a variety of data formats. In this book, we will most commonly be using data in the CSV format. CSV, short for comma separated values, is a common storage format for tabular data, such as the data found in box scores. The way we will load CSV data in R is with the read.csv command.

```
> box.score <- read.csv("./manhattan.csv")
> box.score
...
```

Once you have run these two commands, you should see the box score for the game printed to the screen. You might note that at this point, you have saved the box.score to a variable box.score. This variable is a special type of variable called a data frame. We will be using data frames a lot throughout this book. Data frames are columnar-based representations of tabular data. This means that we can access all of the columns by their names and perform operations on them.

Consider, for example, that we want to know how many points each of the Syracuse Orange scored during that first game against Manhattan. Well, we saw previously how it would be done. We'll add up the number of two point shots each player made times two, plus the number of three point shots times three, plus the number of free throws. Except instead of assigning all of the variables to vectors like we did last time, we can use the column selection notation included in the data frame:

```
> box.score$PTS <- box.score$X2P*2 + box.score$X3P*3 + box.score$FT
> box.score
```

You will notice the use of the dollar sign before the column name. This is the selection symbol in R. It will work for both data frames and lists. Additionally, you will notice that we assigned our result to a column in our data frame called PTS. This column did not exist before, so R will create it for us and append it to the end of the data frame as the final column. When we print the data frame, we can see the points for all of the players.

If we wanted to see only the players' names and their scores, we could use the R data frame subset notation to select just the first and last columns of our data frame. In R, the notation to subset a data frame is two vectors inside of square brackets. The vector in the first position indicates which rows to keep and the vector in second position indicates which columns to keep. An empty vector says to keep all of the rows or columns. For example, box.score[,c(1,19)] can be used to select just the first column of our data frame—the players' names—and the 19th column of our data frame—the players' scores. If we wanted just the first five players' scores, we could do something like this: box.score[1:5, c(1,19)]. This command uses the same explicit vector notation in the second position, but it uses R's built-in sequence notation in the first position to generate a vector containing the numbers 1, 2, 3, 4, and 5.

Let's use this notation to create a bar plot of the first five players' scores. To do that, we will take advantage of a function built-in to R, intuitively called barplot. We can use the barplot function to generate a bar plot, given a variable to plot for the height and a variable by which to separate the data. In this instance, we'll use box.score$Points as our height and box.score$Player as our separation variable.

```
> starting.five <- box.score[1:5,]
> barplot(starting.five$PTS~starting.five$Player)
```

LISTING 2.4 Creating a barplot with R

You will notice that when this chart plots, the plot is limited to showing the scores of the starting five players; however, the four bench players names are still plotted. This is because R interpreted the Player column as a factor. A factor is a variable type in R for categorical variables, categorical variables being those that have a limited number of options. For example, if we were to represent the outcome of a series of games in an array, we would want those to be represented as a factor because there are only a handful of outcomes (typically: win, loss, or draw.) Further, we can order those variables so that good outcomes—such as a win—are better than mediocre outcomes—such as a tie—are better than bad outcomes—such as a loss. To confirm this, we can check the type of the starting.five$Player variable using the class function: class(starting.five$Player). This should print the word factor to your screen.

Sports Analytics

Factors, are a high-performance data structure in R. Internally, to R, they are actually treated as numbers. We can also check to see how the variable is being handled internally by using the typeof function. We use the typeof function when we want to know how the low-level operations that R implements will treat out data. For factors, R handles them as integers. That means that even if we store our variables in R as "wins," "ties," and "losses," R will treat them as 1, 2, and 3. If we store player names as a factor, R optimizes that storage under the hood by storing only a number instead.

In order to make R display only the players represented in the first five rows, we can explicitly convert the data from a factor to another data type: character. We will use the character data type when we want to store text data. Primarily, we will reserve using this data type for when we want to analyze textual data, but it can also be a convenient way to coerce factors to display better in plots and charts. We can coerce factors into character data with the as.character function.

```
> barplot(starting.five$PTS~as.character(starting.five$Player))
```

Analyzing multiple games

Of course, to understand the run Syracuse went on in the 2003 NCAA tournament, we will need more than one game of data. We could load in all of the games one by one by repeating the steps above, but one of the benefits of using computers for analytics is that we can get them to do the repetitive tasks for us. In this subsection, we will learn to load several box scores into a large data frame.

In order to load and analyze multiple box scores at the same time, we will need to do five things:

1. Generate a list of file paths that we would like to open
2. Create an empty data frame to put our data in
3. Loop over the lists of file paths
4. Open the files in the list
5. Add those opened files to the empty data frame

To start analyzing multiple box scores, we need to generate a list of the file paths that we want to open. Conveniently—yet again—R has a built-in function that we can just for this purpose. Fittingly, that function is called list.files. We can pass the list.files function a path pattern and the function will give us back all the files on our system that match that pattern. For example, if we have a folder with data files from 3 months in it, June.csv, July.csv, and August.csv, we can write a pattern to get all the files that start with J and be given back June.csv and July.csv. If we wanted every file in the folder, we could write a pattern that matched everything.

For our specific example, we have six data files that we want to analyze:

1. 01_manhattan.csv
2. 02_oklahoma_state.csv

3. 03_auburn.csv
4. 04_oklahoma.csv
5. 05_texas.csv
6. 06_kansas.csv

Each file is the box score of a single game. In order to select just these files and not any of the other data in that may be in the same folder, we can clue in on some patterns about the files. First, they all start with a zero. Second, they have an underscore in them. And third, they all end in .csv. Using these rules, we can come up with a pattern to load the files.

```
file.paths <- list.files(pattern="0*_*.csv")
```

LISTING 2.5 Listing data files in R

In Listing 2.5, we call the list.files function and we pass it a pattern 0*_*.csv. First, you will notice the pattern we specify starts with a 0, just like all of the data files we want to open. Next, you will notice two star or asterisk characters. In the regular expression pattern matching syntax, these asterisks are called wildcards. Asterisks stand in for any number of anything, including. That means they can match whole words or phrases, as well as nothing at all. Last, you will notice that we conclude the pattern with the .csv ending all our files have. Specifying the ending further limits the results gathered by our pattern.

Next, we need to create an empty data.frame. Earlier in this chapter, we saw how to create a data.frame from a file path using the read.csv function. We can also create a data.frame without putting any data in it. To do so, we call the function data.frame. So that we can access the data.frame latter on, we will assign data.frame to a variable: all.games.

```
file.paths <- list.files(pattern="0*_*.csv")

all.games <- data.frame()
```

The one thing to note here is that we call our variable all.games. even though we do not have any data in it yet. Using a variable in this way is called a **placeholder variable**. We use placeholder variables to create a place to put data later on. In our case, we will be using it to store the data we load in from the files.

In order to load the data from the files and put them into the all.games data frame, we need to **loop** over them. Loops are a programming term that refers to a type of instructions where we tell the computer to do something repeatedly. The most basic of these loops is called the **for loop**. We use the for loop when we want to do something for every item in a sequence. For example, a simple for loop might look like Listing 2.6.

```
for(number in 1:100){
  print(number)
}
```

LISTING 2.6 Looping over numbers and printing them

The loop in Listing 2.6 goes through the numbers between 1 and 100 and prints them to the screen. You will notice a few things about this code. First, you will notice that we use the sequence generation syntax we saw earlier in this chapter to concisely generate the numbers between 1 and 100. Next, you will notice we create a new variable: number. We use the variable number to represent the current place between 1 and 100. As we move from 1 toward 100, the value of number changes to the new value. Lastly, you will notice two curly brackets around the print function. These brackets declare where the logic we want to execute on each loop begins and ends. Everything inside these brackets will be executed each time we loop through the numbers. Code outside will be executed once the loop ends.

In our instance, we will loop over the file.paths variable we created with list.files. With every file that we loop over, we will open that file as we have before, and add it to the all.games data frame we created. To do this, we will use a new function called rbind that combines data frames together row wise. We can see this code illustrated in Listing 2.7.

```
for(path in file.paths){
  all.games <- rbind(all.games, read.csv(path))
}
```

LISTING 2.7 Looping over file paths to box scores and accumulating them

In Listing 2.7, we see a lot of the same conventions that we saw in our first example. Again, we loop over some variable—path—in a sequence—file.paths. This time, however, the logic inside the loop is a little more sophisticated. As promised, we're using the rbind function to modify—indeed over-write—the all.games variable we established before. Every time we go through the loop, we assign the path of a new file to the path variable. We then pass this variable into the read.csv function we use previously to load a .csv file into a data.frame. Except this time, instead of assigning the data.frame we've loaded into a variable, we pass it directly into the rbind function, along with the current all.games variable. The rbind function combines whatever data is in the all.games data.frame with the data being loaded from the current .csv file, we then assign that resulting data frame to the all.games variable. We use the loop to repeat this process until we have no files left to add.

Once we've run this code, the all.games data frame will have all the data we need to analyze Syracuse's 2003 NCAA tournament run. With that data, we can do a few things to look at how the team performed.

1. We'll see how the team performed overall by looking at their totals
2. We'll calculate how many minutes each player was on the court
3. We'll see how many points each player scored during the run
4. We'll find out who score the most, given their time on the floor

CALCULATING OVERALL TEAM TOTALS. To calculate overall team totals from our long data frame, what we will need to do is find the sum of the values in every column. R has a built-in function called apply—one of many similarly named functions that we will learn in this book—that we can use to perform an operation on many database columns all at once. To use the apply function, we pass it three parameters: the data.frame we want to operate on, the direction in which we want to operate, and the function we'd like to use. Because we want to use the sum function—which takes only numerical arguments—we will need to select all the numerical columns of all.games before we pass it in.

```
apply(all.games[,2:ncol(all.games)], 2, sum)
```

LISTING 2.8 Using apply to sum team totals

We can see what this will look like for our data in code snippet in Listing 2.8. We provide the apply function with three parameters. The first is the selection of our data we want to take the sum of, the second is the direction we would like to combine the data, and the third is the function we will be using. In first position, we subset the all.games data frame to only the 2 column and beyond. We do this because these values are all numerical and will work nicely with our sum function. Next, in second position, we pass 2. In R, whenever we have the option of providing a direction, 1 will indicate row-wise and 2 will indicate column-wise. Lastly, we will pass the function we would like to use. In this case, we are looking to find totals, so we will need the sum function.

Once we have run the command, we should see all the box score labels printed to the screen with a number under each label. This number is the team's total for that given statistic. If you are doing things right up to this point, you should see the team with a total of 1200 MP for minutes played. We can verify that this is the right number with some simple arithmetic: 5 players times 6 games times 40 minutes per game. Now that we know we have the right totals for the team—let's find the totals for each of the players.

CALCULATING PLAYER TOTALS. Turning our attention to player totals, let's start by calculating the number of minutes each player played during Syracuse's six-game run through the NCAA tournament. To do this, we are going to use a variation on the apply function: tapply. The tapply function takes a vector, factors to group that vector by, and a function to apply over those groupings.

```
tapply(all.games$MP, all.games$Player, sum)
```

In our specific case, we put the minutes played variable in the first position as the data we would like to operate on, the player variable in second position to split the data, and the sum function in third position to add up all the minutes. This should result in the 2003 Syracuse Orange players' names being printed to the screen with the number of minutes they played underneath. From this, we can see that Carmelo Anthony and Gerry McNamara played the most minutes—218 and 210 minutes respectively—with Hakim Warrick playing the third most minutes: 178. These three are followed up by the rest, who played between 94 and 144 minutes.

Of course, it would be better to calculate the sums of all their statistics all at once, instead of having to sum up each statistic individually. To do that, we can use R's built in aggregate function. When we use the aggregate function, we use a special R syntax for working with data—called a formula—as well as the data structure we would like to work on and the function we would like to use. Like apply and tapply, we use aggregate when we want to do one thing on several data objects at once.

```
aggregate(.~Player, all.games, FUN=sum)
```

To find each players' totals using the aggregate function, we will use the formula: .~Player. This formula says to take all of the data—indicated by the dot—and aggregate it by the Player column of data. We then pass in the all.games data.frame so the aggregate function knows what data we are talking about, and then we specify the sum function so aggregate knows how to roll up our data. If we wanted to find each player's game-by-game averages instead of totals, we could use the mean function in place of the sum function. Let's assign each of these to variables: player.total and player. avgs and take a look at the results.

```
player.totals <- aggregate(.~Player, all.games, FUN=sum)
player.avgs <- aggregate(.~Player, all.games, FUN=mean)
```

CALCULATING POINTS SCORED. While minutes played gives us a sense of how much the coach thought each player mattered, the most basic level at which to assess basketball players is typically the number of points they score. Let's use R and the two new data frames we just created to find how many points each player scored and how many points they scored in an average game.

First, let's take a look at finding the total number of points each player scored. In basketball, shots are worth a different number of points based on where and when they are taken. There are two-point shots, worth two points, three-point shots, worth three points, and free throws, worth one point. To find a player's total points scored, we will take the total number of two-point shots they have made and multiple that by 2, add that to the number of three-point shots they have made multiplied by three, and add that to the number of free throws they made.

Because we are going to want to use this logic twice in our code—once on the player totals and again on the player averages—a good practice is to encapsulate this behavior in a function. Functions are reusable blocks of code that have been assigned to a variable. We have seen and used many built-in functions already, including mean, sum, aggregate, and apply. To create our own, we will wrap our code in a function call.

```
count.points <- function(x){
  x[5]*2 + x[7]*3 + x[9]
}
```

LISTING 2.9 Creating a function for counting points

We can see what this will look like for our points calculating function in Listing 2.9. The code inside the moustache brackets is the code that describes what our function does. In this case, it takes the 5th, 7th, and 9th variables, multiplies them by their point values, and sums them together. The made two-point shots get multiplied by two points and so on. The function wrapper itself describes what variables our function will require. In this case, we are accepting a single array. Lastly, we will notice the variable assignment. This is how we name our function. In this case, I have named our function to calculate players point totals count.points. It is convention to use verb phrases as function names, as we do here.

Once we have this function created, we can use it by calling the variable we have assigned it to. In this case, we want to call our count.points function on our player.totals data.frame and save that output to a variable. Then, once we have that variable, we can add it to our player.totals data.frame to see it in the context of the rest of the players' stats. It's also possible to assign the function output to a column in the data.frame directly. We will use that approach for our player.avgs. Both are shown in Listing 2.10.

```
pts = points.scored(player.totals)
player.totals <- data.frame(player.totals, PTS=pts[,1])

player.avgs <- data.frame(player.avgs,
                    PTS=points.scored(player.avgs)[,1])
```

LISTING 2.10 Using a custom function to augment a data frame.

Listing 2.10 shows two approaches to using our custom function and adding those results to an existing data.frame. In the first, we assign the output of our function to a variable, pts, which we then add to the player.totals data.frame. In the second, we assign the output directly to a column in the player.avgs data.frame. Both methods achieve the same result.

If you inspect the player.totals data.frame, you should now see an additional column, PTS, that contains the total points scored during the NCAA tournament by each player on the 2003 Syracuse Orange. You will notice that Carmelo Anthony scored by far the most points on the team—121—followed by McNamara and Warrick, who scored 80 and 73 points respectively. You might remember that these three players—Anthony, McNamara, and Warrick—also logged the first, second, and third most minutes played.

Let's also take a look at how many points the Syracuse Orange players averaged per game during the 2003 NCAA tournament. For convenient viewing, let's using the square-bracket slice notation to select just the first column, which contains the players' names, and the last column, which contains the points each player averaged. In this view, the picture about who was the second best player on the 2003 Syracuse Orange becomes less clear. McNamara, 13.3 points per game, and Warrick, 12.2 points per game, averaged within a point per game of one another, and Edelin was close behind them both with 11 points per game.

```
> player.avgs[,c(1,19)]
    Player       PTS
1  Anthony 20.166667
2    Duany  7.333333
3   Edelin 11.000000
4    Forth  1.666667
5 McNamara 13.333333
6   McNeil  3.333333
7     Pace  8.000000
8  Warrick 12.166667
```

CALCULATING POINTS PER 30 MINUTES PLAYED. Another way we might want to assess how good each Syracuse Orange player was during the 2003 run was by looking at their **Points per 30 minutes**. Points per 30 minutes is a calculated statistic that tries to get at how many points a player would score in 30 minutes of playing time. This statistic is a useful way to normalize player performances across different teams or playing circumstances. We will touch on some problems with this statistic later on in the book, but for now think of it as a measure of how productive a player was when they were on the court.

Points per 30 minutes is calculated by taking the number of points a player scored, dividing that number by the number of minutes they played, and multiplying the result by 30. We will calculate that value based on each players tournament totals and assign that back to the player.totals data. frame so we can take a look at it.

```
> PP30 <- 30*(player.totals$PTS / player.totals$MP)
> player.totals$PP30 <- round(PP30, 1)
> player.totals[,c(1,19,20)]
    Player PTS PP30
1  Anthony 121 16.7
2    Duany  44 11.8
3   Edelin  66 13.8
4    Forth  10  3.2
5 McNamara  80 11.4
6   McNeil  20  4.4
7     Pace  48 13.3
8  Warrick  73 12.3
```

LISTING 2.11 Calculating points per 30 minutes

In Listing 2.11 we can see how this is done. We define the arithmetic in R, then assign that value to a variable. In order to keep our numbers reasonable, we round the results off to the first decimal place with the round function and then assign the results to a PP30 column of our player.totals data. frame. Then, we can call the 1st, 19th, and 20th columns of our player.totals data.frame to see how many points each player scored and how many points they would have scored over a normalized amount of time.

From this, it becomes even more unclear who the second most important player on the 2003 Syracuse Orange team was. Carmelo Anthony's nearly 17 points per 30 minutes jump off the page, but nobody really stands out among the remaining seven Orange. Five of the players—Edelin, Pace, Warrick, Duany, and McNarama—are between 11 and 14 points per 30 minutes. That is just a single basket per 30 minutes. And indeed, there was quite a lot of talent on this Syracuse Orange team. Anthony, McNarama, Duany, and Edelin were all considered top 100 prospects coming out of high-school. Both Anthony and Hakim Warrick would go on to play in the NBA as well.

Summary

In this chapter, we started learning about the R programming language, a computational tool for sport analytics and data analytics more broadly. We learned about box score statistics—raw measurements of in-game events that are typically recorded for communication, rather than analysis—and we learned how to work with those statistics using the R programming language. Among the R tools that we learned were the sum and mean functions; the apply, tapply, and aggregate functions; and how to create our own functions. Further, we learned how to load in data from files using read.csv.

Additionally, we looked at measurement itself and introduced measurement theory: the study of how people assign numbers to phenomena. Specifically, we looked at this with respect to the popular American sports and how each measurement in a given sport either overlooks or hides information that is relevant to making judgements.

Lastly, we looked at a case study of the 2003 Syracuse Orange men's basketball team during the NCAA championship run. We saw how we could use R to take game-by-game boxes scores to calculate the team's statistics across the entire NCAA tournament. Then we used these statistics to count up how many points each player scored and averaged, as well as how many points they scored on a per-30 minute basis.

Key Terms

Unit of measurement

Box score

Scripting language

Array

Function

for loop

placeholder variable

Critical Thinking Exercises

1. Pick two different sports. For each sport, name one way that players or teams are measured and describe what that measurement successfully measures and what it leaves out. See Table 2.1 for an example.

2. Earned run average is a baseball statistic that is calculated by runs given up, times innings pitched, divided by nine. Write a function in R to calculate ERA given runs and innings.

3. In football, a series of plays by the offense is called a drive. Write a function to calculate the number of yards gained in the following drive using a for loop. Write another function to calculate the number of yards gained using the sum function.

Play	Yards
1	3
2	1
3	65
4	0
5	−3
6	4

CHAPTER 3

Pythagorean Wins and Probability in Sport Analytics

J.T. Wolohan

LEARNING OBJECTIVES
After reading this chapter, students should be able to:
- Define probability and what it means to think about a problem probabilistically
- Identify scenarios in sport in which we can think about the situation probabilistically
- Define the axioms of probability and the properties of random variables
- Identify properties of the binomial and normal distributions
- Generate random variables from the binomial and normal distributions in R
- Define Pythagorean Wins and explain why we want to treat wins as random variables
- Implement Pythagorean Wins in R for a variety of sports

Introduction

In this chapter, we examine probability theory as applied to sport. We look at what probability theory is, cover some axioms of probability theory and some of its core ideas, and apply those ideas to sport. Additionally, we look at two common probability distributions: the normal distribution and the binomial distribution. We apply those distributions to sport and we talk about ways to discuss those distributions, including how we can measure the centrality of a distribution. Lastly, we will examine Pythagorean Wins and consider what it means to think about winning and losing games as a random process. We examine Pythagorean Wins across several sports and consider the adjustments we must make to the approach for different sports and different rulesets across sport.

Probability Theory

Sport analytics is the process of describing sports through numerical models. In many cases, this process is very similar to the objective of probabilistic modeling, where one wishes to find a mathematical representation of the likelihood of some event. For example, we know that Steve Kerr made 86% of his free throws throughout his career. How then, do we model the chance of him making any given free throw? How do we model the chance of him making a series of free throws? How do we model the chance of him making more than some number of free throws if he gets to the free-throw line some other number of times in a game? Probability theory is the pursuit of answers to all of these questions.

WHAT IS PROBABILITY THEORY?

Probability theory is a branch of mathematics that has its roots adjacent to sport in gambling. It is no accident that many **probability** examples involve the use of dice. Early treatises of probability theory were devised to provide advantage at old games of chance. The fundamental concept of probability is that events—such as rolling a specific number, say a 3, on a die—have probabilities or **likelihoods** of occurring. These likelihoods can be expressed as a fraction. For example, with a die, we might represent the likelihood as the number of rolls that will show a 3 over the number of rolls that will not show a 3: ⅙. We would say then, that ⅙ is the probability of rolling a 3 on a standard die.

If we think back to our example above with Steve Kerr, we were performing roughly the same process. We knew that Kerr made ~86/100 free throws during his career, so we assumed that the likelihood of him making any one free throw was equal to 86/100. This is the same process as rolling a die. We represent the number of successes Kerr will have over the number of total attempts.

From these basic facts, we can come up with the axioms of probability. The first of these is that all probabilities are between 0 and 1. This is because we will always think about the likelihood of an event as being the number of times that event will occur out of some total sample space. Returning to the Steve Kerr example, Kerr made 627 out of 727 free throws he attempted during his career. Therefore, the probability of him making any one free throw is approximately 6/7. But the number of free throws he can make will always be less than or equal to the number attempt. Therefore, the probability has to be less than 1. Likewise, the number of free throws made is a count. It can never be less than zero. Therefore, the probability has to be greater than 0. All probabilities follow this pattern.

$$0 \le P(x) \le 1$$

Another axiom of probability is that the probability of an event occurring and an event not occurring add up to 1. Continuing our example, if Kerr makes 6 of 7 free throws, that necessarily means that he will miss 1 of 7 free throws. In probability terms, we will say that these events are **mutually exclusive**. That means that they cannot happen together. For instance, Kerr cannot both make and miss a free throw.

$$P(make) = 1 - P(miss)$$

An extension of the axiom above is that the sum of the probability of all mutually exclusive events is equal to 1. For instance, if we think about a baseball pitcher who knows four pitches—a fastball, a changeup, a curveball, and a slider—the probability that they will throw one of these four pitches is 1. That is, they will only throw pitches they know how to throw. We know that these events are mutually exclusive because one cannot simultaneously throw a pitch that is at once two pitches. For instance, it is impossible to throw a fastball that is also a changeup.

Beyond these axioms, there are also some important rules of probability worth noting. The first of these rules is called the additional rule. This rule states that the probability of either one of two events happening is equal to the probability of both of the events happening added together, minus the probability that they happen at the same time. For mutually exclusive events, such as the pitching example above, this is easy. The probability that a pitcher throws either a fastball or a curveball is equal to the probability that they throw a fastball plus the probability that they throw a curveball.

$$P(curve \cup fastball) = P(curve) + P(fastball)$$

In a more complex example, we might consider the probability of a football defense either playing zone defense or blitzing. For our example, let's assume that the probability of the team playing zone is 1 in 4 and the probability of the team blitzing is 1 in 8. We might, then, be tempted to say that the probability of the team playing zone or blitzing is 3 in 8. However, this would be wrong because a team can both play zone and blitz at the same time: a zone blitz. For example, if a team runs all their blitzes from zone, then the likelihood of the team playing zone or blitzing is 1 in 4 or 2 in 8, because we have to subtract the 1 in 8 chance of a zone blitz from the total 3 in 8 chance.

$$P(zone \cup blitz) = P(zone) + P(blitz) - P(zone \cap blitz)$$

Of course, this begs the question, how do we know the likelihood that two events will happen together? For this, we will say that the probability of two events happening together is equal to the likelihood of an event happening given the second event happens, times the likelihood of the second event happening. For instance, the probability of a zone blitz is equal to the probability of the defense playing zone, times the probability of the defense blitzing when they are in zone; the probability of a player hitting a home run off a curveball is equal to the probability of them hitting a home run when a curveball is thrown, times the probability the pitcher throws a curveball.

$$P(zone \cap blitz) = P(blitz \mid zone) \times P(zone)$$

A related formulation is the conditional probability formulation. **Conditional probability** is when we seek to find the probability of one event given another event has or is occurring. For instance, a pitcher may be interested in finding the probability of the opposing batter getting a hit on given any pitch in their arsenal. A basketball player may be interested in whether their opponent is more likely to score if they drive left or drive right. A tennis player may be interested in knowing whether their opponent is more likely to serve a slice serve or a kick serve on their first service attempt. This value is equal to the probability of the two events happening together, divided by the probability of the conditioning event.

$$P(blitz \mid zone) = \frac{P(zone \cap blitz)}{P(zone)}$$

These rules establish the foundation of probability theory, and their rigorous application provides the foundation for solving any number of probability-related problems, answering any number of probability-related questions. That said, perhaps the most important thing that we can take away from these axioms is that events in sport are uncertain. We do not know what will happen in advance of a season, a game, or even a play. "That's why we play the game."

Observations as Random Variables

When we assign a probability to something, we are admitting that we do not have full information about the event in question. In other words, we are expressing some uncertainty about the outcome of an event. In sport, this is easy. We almost never know exactly what will happen and, when we think we do, we are often surprised. These events—upsets—are some of the most memorable moments in sport. Upsets remind us how little we know about the events that produce outcomes in sport.

This lack of knowledge is referred to as **uncertainty**. We are uncertain in any situation where we have a limited amount of information about how a situation will unfold. For instance, in a heavyweight boxing match. We may believe that one fighter is favored over another—even late in the fight when most of the points are accounted for—but a single knockout punch can change everything and there is no way for us to know if it will come or not. When we have uncertainty about events, it often makes sense to model them as random variables.

Random variables are variables that can take a number of states with some probability. In their simplest form, random variables can be lists of states and probabilities. For instance, we might model Steve Kerr's free throws with a random variable that is a "make" 6 times in 7 and a "miss" 1 time in 7. Likewise, we might model a pitcher's pitches with a random variable that includes each pitch the pitcher knows how to throw and a rate associated with the pitcher throwing that pitch.

Variables that can take an enumerable set of values at enumerable probabilities, such as those named above, are considered discrete random variables. Many random variables we will want to use in sport analytics are discrete. For instance, both examples above are discrete. We can list all the possible states of Steve Kerr's free throws (make, miss) and all the pitches our pitcher knows (fastball, curveball, slider, changeup).

Discrete random variables are typically described using step functions known as probability mass functions. These functions describe the probability of one of the possible states. The **probability mass function** must meet the requirements expressed in our axioms of probability. For instance, its value across its entire range must sum to exactly 1, and each individual point along the range must be between 0 and 1. We might consider the probability mass function for a scenario in which a 75% free-throw shooter is taking two shots. We know that the shooter can make either 0, 1, or 2 free throws. The probability of the shooter missing all of the free throws is .0625; the probability of the shooter making all the free throws is .5625; and the probability of the shooter making exactly 1 of 2 free throws is .375. This list of states is the PMF.

For cases in which we have continuous data, where the outcome can take any number within a range and is not limited to enumerable states, we have **continuous random variables**. Examples of this in sport are metrics like batting average, quarterback rating, or goals against average. There are, in theory, an unlimited number of possibility batting averages, quarterback ratings, and goals against averages that a player can have. Continuous probability distributions give us a way of describing the likelihood of a continuous variable taking any of its possible states. For instance, the likelihood that Derek Jeter hit .300 in a season or that Martin Brodeur had a goals against average of 2.15. In the next several sections of this chapter, we will look at ways of describing the shape of continuous probability distributions.

In sport analytics, we take the stance that these probability functions—probability mass functions for discrete variables and **probability density functions** for continuous variables—are the best way to understand events and outcomes in sport. For instance, when looking at the outcome of a game, we want to think not about whether a game happened exactly as we expected or not (they almost certainly will not). Instead, we prefer to think about how likely the outcome was relative to our expectations and how much, if at all, we need to adjust our expectations to better account for this outcome in the future.

Consider the 2015 NBA finals between Cleveland and Golden State. Cleveland was down a crucial player in Kevin Love and ended up losing the series 4 games to 2. The question of whether this outcome was expected or not is interesting; however, a savvy management would be focused on the question of whether or not the presence of Kevin Love would have changed the shape of the distribution in such a way that the probability of Cleveland winning the series was greater than 50%. And indeed, Cleveland did not overreact to their loss and returned to the finals in 2016, beating the Warriors in a dramatic 7-game series. From this outcome, it would appear that the addition of Kevin Love back into the lineup was enough to bring Cleveland at or near a 50-50 chance of winning a 7-game series against Golden State, though it would be impossible to know.

Probability Distributions

If it is important to think about events as possibly taking a number of different states (e.g., win or lose) with different probabilities, the next important step is to learn how to think about those probabilities. The best way to gain an intuitive understanding of probabilities is to understand a little bit about **probability distributions.** In this section, we will review two probability distributions: **binomial distribution** and the **normal distribution**. The binomial distribution is a common discrete probability distribution that we will use for sequences of events that can take one of two outcomes (e.g., win–lose, make–miss). The normal distribution is a probability distribution that we will use for continuous data that is "bell-curve" shaped.

As just noted, the binomial probability distribution is a function that explains the behavior of sequential, independent, Boolean phenomenon. That is, we can use the binomial probability distribution to model any event with exactly two outcomes: win or lose, make or miss, strike or ball, etc. The binomial distribution is defined by two parameters: the probability of an event occurring and the number of sequential events. To gain some intuition about the binomial probability distribution, let's consider the following example where we will use the binomial probability model to reason about how many games we might expect an NBA team to win.

Going into the season, we won't make any assumptions about how good the team is, so we will say they have a 50/50 chance of winning a random game. We can use the binomial probability distribution to see the likelihood of our .500 team winning some number of games, given that they play some other number of games. The figure below shows probability distribution functions for the .500 team over 5-, 10-, 20-, 41-, and 82-game spans.

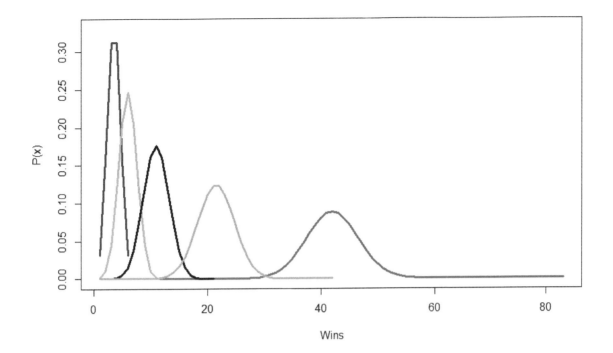

You will note first, that as the number of games goes up, the likelihood of any specific outcome goes down. This should not come as a surprise. In a 5-game stretch, there are only 6 possible outcomes: 0 wins, 1 win, 2 wins, 3 wins, 4 wins, or 5 wins. In an 82-game stretch, there are 83 possible outcomes, so even the most popular outcomes are going to be more rare. Second, you will note that each of the distributions is symmetrical. In the binomial distribution, exceptional events are equally likely in each direction. That is, if the most common outcome for our .500 team is to win 41 of their 82 games, they are equally likely to win 31 and 51 games. We can say that the number of events in the binomial probability distribution stretches or compresses the distribution. In terms of mathematical functions, increasing the number of events increases the **domain** and decreases the **range**.

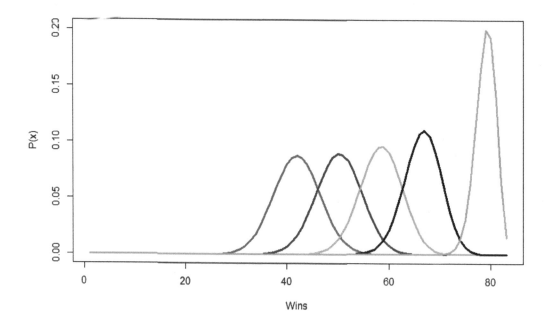

In the next case, we will consider the effect of modifying the probability of winning a random game. The graphic above illustrates the team's probability of winning some number of games out of 82 with true winning percentages of .500, .600, .700, .800, and .950. The first thing you will likely notice about this chart is that the curves shift to the right as the probability of winning increases. This makes intuitive sense: teams that are likely to win more games have a higher probability of winning more games.

What you might find surprising is that as the probability of winning increases, the likelihood of the modal outcome increases. In other words, there is less variation in the outcomes. We are more certain that an especially good team will win a lot of games than we are that an especially average team will win an average number of games. If we think about the effect at play here, this too makes sense though. Imagine a case at the extreme: the United States 1992 Olympic Men's Basketball Team, dubbed the "Dream Team." This team might have a 100% chance of winning against any opponent. We could say with certainty then that they would win all of their games. If we make this team a bit worse, by removing one if its many All Stars and replacing them with a generic player, we get slightly less certain. As the likelihood of outcomes approaches 50%, we decrease in certainty about the event. As the likelihood of the outcome approaches either 0% or 100%, we increase in certainty about the outcome.

Relatedly, you may note that in the case of the team with the 95% winning percentage, the binomial distribution is not symmetric. This is because there is a cap at the number of wins the team can have. The team cannot win more than 82 of 82 games. The number of successes is limited necessarily by the number of events. This causes situations in which probability that would otherwise get distributed out across a range that does not exist gets rolled into the existing range near the side of the limiting factor. In this case, because the team is an exceptionally successful team, this happens on the top end of the range. For an exceptionally bad team, this effect would happen at the bottom end of the range.

R provides convenience functions for working with the binomial distribution. Notably, there are two functions dbinom and rbinom, that you may wish to use. The dbinom function finds the probability of one or more outcomes given a described binomial probability distribution. The rbinom function generates random variates from a described binomial probability distribution. The use of each function is demonstrated below.

```
> dbinom(55, size=82, prob=.6)
[1] 0.03893154
> rbinom(1, size=82, prob=.6)
[1] 47
```

In the first case above, we find the likelihood of a 55 success across 82 events with a probability of success of 60% for each event. In context, we find the likelihood that a .600 team would win exactly 55 games in a 82-game season. The resulting probability, approximately 4%, is the answer to this question. In the second, we use rbinom to generate a random variate representing a single draw from a binomial probability distribution of 82 events with probability .600. In context, this represents a possible outcome of one 82-game season for a team with a .600 winning percentage.

Another common distribution worth knowing is the normal distribution. The normal distribution is the classic "bell curve" distribution. We can use the normal distribution to model most phenomena which we can plausibly expect to take this shape. In comparison to the binomial distribution, the normal distribution is both similar—it is defined by two parameters—and different—it is a continuous distribution and random variates sampled from it can take an infinite number of values. Similar to how we explored the binomial distribution, we will also seek to gain an intuition about the normal distribution through exploring a scenario. In this case, let's imagine a normal distribution that represents the passer rating of NFL quarterbacks.

Normal distributions are defined by two properties: the mean of the distribution and the standard deviation of the distribution. In the chart below, we see four different normal distributions, each with different means. The curve farthest to the left, for instance, has a mean of 80 and the curve farthest to the right has a mean of 95. You will note rather quickly that, besides the curves location along the line, they all look the same. And indeed, because they all have the same standard deviation, all the curves are the same. Changing the mean of a normal distribution results in a shift of that distribution along the X-axis. For instance, consider what might happen if passer rating across the league goes up, as has been happening since the invention of the metric, we would expect that all quarterbacks would post better passer ratings. This is not to say that all contemporary quarterbacks have better passer ratings than all historical quarterbacks, just that the improvement benefits quarterbacks across the league evenly.

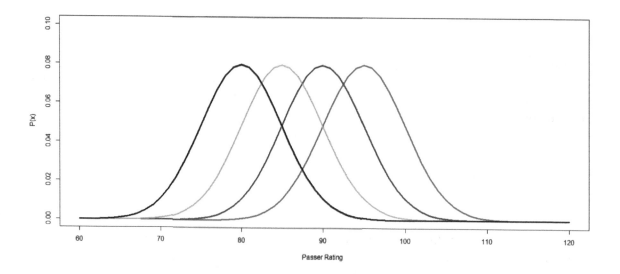

The other way of altering the shape of a normal distribution is by modifying the standard deviation. Standard deviation is a measure of the variation in the distribution. For instance, the league as a whole may have a large variation we need to account for, but if we are attempting to model one specific player, there may be less (or more) variation. Consider the chart below where we compare two distributions, each representing a different quarterback. One is remarkably consistent while the other has great highs and great lows.

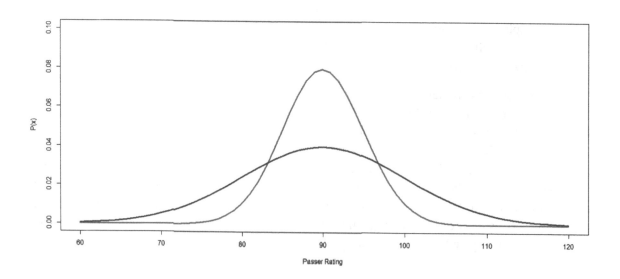

You will note that these two distributions look very different. One distribution is much taller, with an obvious mode and a quick drop off around that point. The other is more diffuse, with a wide domain having probabilities that are well above 0. We can expect the one quarterback to produce performances with a quarterback rating between 80 and 100, while the other we might expect performances between 65 and 115. We expect that they both produce 90 passer-rating performances most often; however, the rate at which they do that is quite different as well. The more stable quarterback in this case produces 90 passer-rating performances twice as often as the quarterback with greater variation in their performances.

More generally, we can note that the effect of increasing the standard deviation of a normally distributed random variable is to increase the rate at which that variable takes values far away from the mean. In contrast, reducing the standard deviation of a normally distributed random variable increases the rate at which it takes values near the mean.

MEASURES OF CENTRALITY

When looking at both the normal distribution and the binomial distribution, we saw that one of the core things we were interested in measuring was the center point of the distribution. Centrality of a distribution is important because it tells us a lot of information about what to expect from random variables sampled from the distribution. Centrality, however, can be measured several different ways. We will usually measure centrality in three ways: mean, median, and mode. In this section, we will review mode, mean, and median of centrality and discuss distributions with different relations between mode, mean, median.

First, **mode** is a measure of centrality that tells us what the most common outcome of a distribution is. In the probability functions we saw above, the mode is represented by the highest point on the curve. This is the point that has the greatest likelihood of occurring and therefore will occur most often if we are drawing variables randomly from the distribution. For a simple example, if we model Mariano Rivera's pitch selection as the following discrete probability function:

```
Cutter: .9
Sinker: .05
Four-seam: .025
Two-seam: .02
Slider: .005
```

Rivera, whose cutter is famous as perhaps baseball's best-ever pitch, throws the cutter in 90% of all pitches. This pitch is clearly the modal outcome—the most common outcome—of the pitch distribution. We can say that the mode of this distribution is the cutter or cut fastball.

Understanding the mode of a probability distribution is helpful because we can use it to reason about what will happen in the most likely case. For instance, if a batter is facing Mariano Rivera, we can say that they will most likely face a cut fastball on the first pitch. Because Rivera's pitch distribution function is so skewed toward the cut fastball, it even makes sense when batting against him to only consider the cut fastball as a pitch. Indeed, one of the reasons that Rivera was so lauded is because batters knew that the pitches incoming were going to be cutters and were unable to effectively bat against him. From 2007 to 2013, Mariano Rivera threw more than 4,500 cut fastballs out of approximately 5,000 total pitches; batters hit only .198 against his cut fastball during that stretch.

Importantly, we cannot really understand mode if we do not understand the degree of the mode. For instance, a more traditional pitcher like Clayton Kershaw may have the following pitch distribution:

```
Fastball: .41
Slider: .38
Curve: .19
Changeup: .02
```

Kershaw throws a mix of fastballs, sliders, and curveballs across a wide range of speeds. His fastball is in the low-90s; his slider is in the mid-80s; and his curveball is in the low 70s. This discrepancy of speeds and the evenness of his distribution makes Kershaw a much different pitcher than Rivera, whose pitches all came in around 93 miles-per-hour. Importantly, when facing Kershaw, we might know that the modal outcome is to face a fastball (41% chance); however, we still should not expect to face a fastball. Indeed, this most common outcome is going to occur less than half of the time. In a short at-bat, it is likely that a batter might not face a single fastball despite the fastball being the single most likely event.

Think back to the normal distributions representing the two quarterbacks earlier in this chapter. The consistent quarterback would have a relatively high frequency of modal outcomes. That is, what would happen most often is going to happen reasonably often. The hot-and-cold quarterback is going to have a relatively less-common frequency of modal outcomes. The most common outcome is going to happen less often, and other outcomes (the hot and the cold) are going to happen instead. Understanding the mode can help us identify what the most common outcome is by definition; understanding the frequency of the mode can help us understand how likely any "average" event is to occur.

The next measure of centrality we want to discuss is the **mean**. The mean is the common average; however, in probability, we prefer to think of the mean as the expected value of a distribution. The expected value of a distribution is the sum of all possible outcomes times the likelihood of those outcomes. If we have an empirical distribution, this value is going to be the exact same as the average.

$$\sum_{x}^{X} P_x \times V_x$$

The mean or expected value of a distribution is an important measure of centrality because it gives us an idea of how to think about value average outcomes. For instance, our marketing team might devise a campaign that encourages 1% of all potential customers exposed to the campaign to attend a game that season. If we want 10,000 different fans attending our games in a season, we can use the expected value of the campaign to determine we will need to get about 1-million exposures.

Expected value is a valuable metric because we can use it in cases like the above, where we want to know the effect of doing something a large number of times. For instance, if we are wondering about which of two players to play, over the course of the season it is probably the right decision to play the player with the greater mean in their distribution of performances. If we are a coach trying to decide whether to kick a field goal or go for it on fourth down, it is probably the right thing to do to select the option with the greater expected value. However, there is also a lot of information hidden by expected value. Notably, the mean of a distribution tells us very little about what is likely to happen at the margins.

Consider again the two quarterbacks, the one with inconsistent performance and the one with consistent performance. Each might have the same mean performance; however, knowing the mean performance for the inconsistent quarterback is of questionable value. This might be a useful measure for a team when deciding if they want to go with a quarterback for a season, but for any given game what use is it? Because the player's performance is so inconsistent, in any given game we may be better off playing a quarterback with lower expected value from their performance. In contrast, we may be better off playing the inconsistent quarterback than another quarterback with an excellent mean performance.

Worse, we may convince ourselves that the expected value of a distribution is all that we need to care about. This is especially common among those with some statistics exposure, but limited understanding of probability. For an obvious example, consider the Hail Mary pass. All observers of football know that the Hail Mary pass is unlikely to succeed; however, when it does, it will often win the passing team the game. There may be plays with higher expected value, but the Hail Mary's upside potential outweighs other considerations. Conversely, we might consider the choice to play or rest a player toward the end of the season. The expected value of a player playing may be for them to have a good performance and exit the game healthy; however, there is always some downside risk of the player being injured. For important players, even this small amount of risk might be too great at the end of the season before the playoffs. We might want to withhold these players from games to avoid this unnecessary risk, even if the expected value of their performance is positive.

The last measure of centrality we will want to look at is the **median** of a distribution. The median of a distribution is its 50th-percentile outcome. That is to say, the point at which 50% of outcomes are higher and 50% of the outcomes are lower. The median is a useful measure of centrality because it helps us reason about distributions that are irregular. Where mode is most useful in helping us understand the most common outcomes of the distribution and the mean is most useful in helping us understand the average outcome, median is useful for helping us think about the middle outcome.

We can benefit from understanding the middle of a distribution when distributions are irregular. For instance, if we modeled the expected score of a soccer or hockey team, we would expect that these scores would be highly skew to the right. That is to say, these distributions have a long right tail where the teams score lots of points, but are mostly clustered around the left side of the distribution. The mode and mean are likely to be uninformative in these situations. The mode is likely to be shared by many teams; the mean is likely to be influenced by a few high-scoring but infrequent events; the median will be more stable.

We might also imagine any number of player metrics, for instance, points per game in basketball. This metric, like most metrics, has a floor. In this case, the floor is zero because points are a counting statistic. Other metrics, for instance, batting average, have an artificial floor because players who bat too poorly typically get cut and replaced with better batters. Most players will score some small number of points per game. However, exceptional players will score a large number of points per game. Using the median can give us a good sense of how effective a player must be to be better than 50% of their peers.

PYTHAGOREAN WINS

In the previous section, we looked at some critical tenants of probability theory and applied it to sport. In this section, we look at a practical example and apply probability theory to the winning and losing of games. In this section, we will explore a phenomenon credited to Bill James, the godfather of Sport Analytics, called **Pythagorean Wins**. We will review James' central observation—that wins are random variables—and look at how we can model wins across sports in terms of points for and against.

Winning and losing is an important part of sport. Some might consider it the only important part of sport. And the emphasis on outcomes, such as winning and losing games, has long been a detraction from those who champion sport analytics. For instance, much has been made of Daryl Morrey's winless exit from Houston after leading the Rockets to adopt an awkward style of basketball that most NBA fans decry. Sport analytics proponents are equally as interested in winning and losing games; however, they recognize that wins are best thought of as random variables. Sport analytics proponents understand that seasons can be made or broken by luck. For example, David Tyree's Helmet Catch that prevented the undefeated New England Patriots from completing a historic 19-0 season. The catch was recognized as remarkably lucky by even, if not especially, those involved in the play. And yet it decided the outcome of the most important game of the 2007–2008 NFL season.

To account for this, sport analytics practitioners consider wins as random variables that need to be estimated and described through a probability distribution. One method of estimating the expected value of wins for a team is to use Bill James' Pythagorean Wins formula. James' formula takes a team's runs scored and raises it to some exponent, and then divides this value by the team's runs scored and runs conceded to some exponent. In the original, the exponent was two. Now, more precise exponents are used to estimate a team's expected wins.

$$Wins = \frac{RunsFor^2}{RunsFor^2 + RunsAgainst^2}$$

This formula makes the simple, but not uncontroversial, statement that teams have an inherent quality that is best represented not by how many games they win or lose but by how many points they score and give up. It also says that some teams are going to underperform relative to their true effectiveness and that some teams are going to overperform. We can consider this luck, though in practice it goes by many explanations. Let's take a look at the 2001 MLB season and look at some of the behavior of both wins and Pythagorean Wins.

To begin our investigation into Pythagorean wins and wins in general, we will first implement the Pythagorean wins formula shown above as a function in R. This function will take the number of runs scored, the number of runs against, and return an estimated win rate. Additionally, we will pass in two optional parameters: the exponent value (known as k) and the number of games across which we want to estimate wins. These later two parameters will help us in adapting the Pythagorean Wins formulation for different sports.

```
pythagorean.wins <- function(r, ra, k=2, n=1){
  r^k / (r^k + ra^k) * n
}
```

The code above shows how we implement this function. As in the original algorithm, this function is mostly elementary arithmetic. The runs a team scored are raised to the power of k, which defaults to two for baseball, and then we divide by the sum of runs and runs against each raised to the power of k. Optionally, we will multiply this value by n to scale the win rate to some number of games. In the base case, we will get the estimated winning percentage. If n was, for example, 162, we would get the number of games a team was expected to win over the course of a season.

Next, we will apply this function to the 2001 MLB season. To do this, we will read in the results of the 2001 season and pass the data from this season into our function. We will use R's automatic vectorization and pass arrays of data into our function and know that we will get an array back out. We will do this for both n = 1 to get the winning percentage and for n = 162 to get the expected number of wins across the season.

```
MLB.2001 <- read.csv("2001-MLB.csv")
MLB.2001$py.rat <-pythagorean.wins(MLB.2001$R, MLB.2001$RA)
MLB.2001$py.exp <- pythagorean.wins(MLB.2001$R, MLB.2001$RA, n=162)
```

Having done this, we have now added two columns to our data frame for Pythagorean Win rate and expected Pythagorean Wins. We will also want to take a look at luck—the degree to which a team deviated from their expected Pythagorean Wins. Teams who deviate from their expected Pythagorean Wins a lot are either going to be very lucky or very unlucky teams. As we will see in a minute, this can impact both successful and unsuccessful teams. To calculate luck, we will simply subtract the expected wins from the actual wins, so that a team with a positive luck won more games than they were expected too and a team with negative luck lost more games than they were expected too.

```
MLB.2001$luck <- MLB.2001$W - MLB.2001$py.exp
```

With this luck calculation in hand, let's take a look at the top five luckiest and unluckiest teams in the league in 2001. We can do this by sorting the data frame and invoking the head command in R. The head command returns the first n elements of an object.

```
> head(MLB.2001[order(MLB.2001$luck),], n=5)
#      Tm   W   L  W.L.   R  RA Lg    py.rat    py.exp      luck
# 12  COL  73  89 0.451 5.7 5.6 NL 0.5088489  82.43352 -9.433516
# 13  MIL  68  94 0.420 4.6 5.0 NL 0.4584055  74.26170 -6.261698
# 11  FLA  76  86 0.469 4.6 4.6 NL 0.5000000  81.00000 -5.000000
# 18  OAK 102  60 0.630 5.5 4.0 AL 0.6540541 105.95676 -3.956757
# 15  CIN  66  96 0.407 4.5 5.2 NL 0.4282089  69.36985 -3.369846

> head(MLB.2001[order(-MLB.2001$luck),], n=5)
#      Tm   W    L  W.L.   R  RA Lg    py.rat    py.exp     luck
# 9   NYM  82   80 0.506 4.0 4.4 NL 0.4524887  73.30317 8.696833
# 17  SEA 116   46 0.716 5.7 3.9 AL 0.6811321 110.34340 5.656604
# 30  TBD  62  100 0.383 4.1 5.5 AL 0.3572036  57.86698 4.133022
# 20  CLE  91   71 0.562 5.5 5.1 AL 0.5376822  87.10451 3.895485
# 4   SFG  90   72 0.556 4.9 4.6 NL 0.5315475  86.11069 3.889307
```

LISTING 3.1. Most and least luckiest MLB teams in 2001

The first statement shows us the five unluckiest teams in Major League Baseball in 2001. We can see that this includes several teams that were expected to be bad, such as the Milwaukee Brewers and the Cincinnati Reds, who were each expected to win less than half their games. And these teams did even worse than that, with the Brewers winning only 42% of their games and the Reds winning barely 40%. However, we also see that bad luck afflicted the very good Oakland As. The A's won 102 games but were actually expected to win nearly 106 games!

The second statement shows us the five luckiest teams in Major League Baseball in 2001. Here, we see a similar story. On one hand, we have the Seattle Mariners. The 2001 Mariners are baseball's all-time winningest team; however, they were quite lucky in achieving this feat. They won 6 games more than the 110 they were expected to win. On the other hand, Tampa Bay posted an abysmal 62-100 record; however, this record was buoyed by luck. Tampa was expected to win only 52 games in 2001. Despite being awful, they should have been worse. Tampa won four more games than expected.

This is an important property of luck in sports: it impacts both the best and worst teams evenly. Good teams can be both lucky and unlucky; bad teams can be both lucky and unlucky. That is not to say that all ways of playing encourage luck to the same degree. For instance, in basketball, we know that three-point shot has more luck in it than the free throw, which is more skill-based. Therefore, teams that focus on the three—an increasingly large portion of the league—are more prone to fits of luck or unluckiness.

Next, let us take a look at how luck is distributed across the league by comparison teams actual wins against their expected Pythagorean Wins. To do this, we will use the ggplot library in R and produce a graph that compares the two. We will also plot a regression line with a 95% confidence band around it. This will help us identify which teams are especially lucky and which teams are about right.

```
library("ggplot2")
ggplot(MLB.2001, aes(x=py.exp, y=W, label=Tm)) +
  geom_smooth(method="lm", level=.95, alpha=.25) +
  geom_point(aes(color=Lg),size=2) +
  geom_text(alpha=1, nudge_y = 2.5) +
  xlab("Pythagorean Expected Wins") +
  ylab("Observed 2001 Wins") +
  theme_bw()
```

LISTING 3.2. Creating a regression plot of actual and Pythagorean wins

This code uses several ggplot charting capabilities. First, we use geom_smooth to produce a regression line indicating the relationship between actual wins and expected wins. Then we use geom_point to place points around the line. And lastly, we plot the team names around the points, nudged ever so slightly upwards so the names and the points don't overlap. The figure resulting from the code can be seen below.

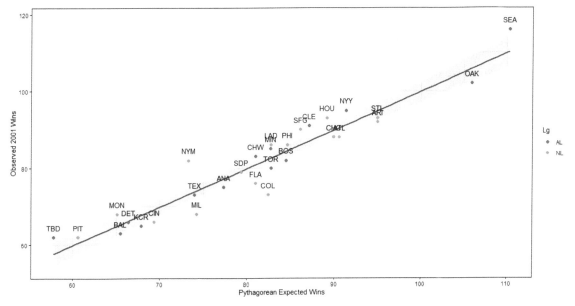

In the picture, we can clearly see the lucky Tampa Bay and Seattle teams hovering above the regression line in the direction of being luckier while on either end of the spectrum in terms of performance, the Mariners being the winningest team and Tampa being the losingest. Through the middle, we see a mixed story. Some teams, like the New York Mets, were very lucky while other teams like Colorado Rockies were very unlucky. Interestingly, we can see that the entire difference between these two teams was luck. The Mets were supposed to win fewer than 75 games but ended up winning more than 80; while the Rockies were supposed to win more than 80 but ended up winning just under 75. Between the two teams, there was more than a 15-game swing in outcome.

This is one of the reasons Pythagorean Wins is an important metric. If the standings can err to such a large degree, how are general managers supposed to use wins and losses to assess their performance? On one hand, they must, because the fans will not be satisfied with the abstract knowledge that their team was unlucky and should have done better in some alternate universe scenario; on the other hand, they cannot, because chasing luck will inevitably lead to bad decision-making. Pythagorean Wins gives general managers a reliable target against which to assess their team performance.

MODELING WINS ACROSS SPORTS

Baseball, of course, is not the only sport in which the Pythagorean Wins concept can be applied, nor is it in the only sport where luck is a factor. Indeed, in many ways, baseball is less lucky than other sports. In this section, we will apply the concept of Pythagorean Wins to other popular team sports—basketball, football, hockey, and soccer—and examine how luck factors across the sports.

We will start by looking at how Pythagorean Wins can be applied to football. In football, we will use a slightly higher exponent than in baseball, indicating a tighter relationship between the point differential of a team and the degree of wins and losses. In football, the exponent we will use is 2.37. Besides this change, to find the expected Pythagorean Wins for NFL teams, we can mostly repurpose the code from above, except we will use data from the 2001 NFL season instead of the 2001 MLB season.

```
NFL.2001 <- read.csv("2001-NFL.csv")

NFL.2001$py.rat <- pythagorean.wins(NFL.2001$PF, NFL.2001$PA, k=2.37)
NFL.2001$py.exp <- pythagorean.wins(NFL.2001$PF, NFL.2001$PA, k=2.37, n=16)

NFL.2001$luck <- NFL.2001$W - NFL.2001$py.exp

head(NFL.2001[order(NFL.2001$luck),],5)
                   Tm W  L  W.L.  PF  PA    py.rat   py.exp      luck
16    San Diego Chargers 5 11 0.313 332 321 0.5199530 8.319248 -3.319248
31      Carolina Panthers 1 15 0.063 253 410 0.2415575 3.864920 -2.864920
10 Jacksonville Jaguars 6 10 0.375 294 286 0.5163400 8.261441 -2.261441
26           Detroit Lions 2 14 0.125 270 424 0.2554776 4.087641 -2.087641
15    Kansas City Chiefs 6 10 0.375 320 344 0.4572546 7.316074 -1.316074

head(NFL.2001[order(-NFL.2001$luck),],5)
                   Tm  W  L  W.L.  PF  PA    py.rat   py.exp      luck
13     Seattle Seahawks  9 7 0.563 301 324 0.4564827 7.303723 1.696277
3        New York Jets 10 6 0.625 308 295 0.5255290 8.408464 1.591536
18          Washington  8 8 0.500 256 303 0.4014382 6.423011 1.576989
```

```
2          Miami Dolphins 11 5 0.688 344 290 0.5998171 9.597073 1.402927
30       Atlanta Falcons  7 9 0.438 291 377 0.3512282 5.619651 1.380349
```

LISTING 3.3. Top and bottom NFL teams by luck

Examining the luckiest and least lucky teams, we find that in football, the lucky teams all tend to be winning teams and the unlucky teams all tend to be losing teams. That is in part a product of the game of football. The NFL is a very balanced league, with a salary cap and a large number of players, which makes it difficult for teams to stay successful over long periods of time. For that reason, the teams tend to be relatively evenly matched. Couple that with the fact that the NFL plays a small number of games, about 1/10th the number MLB does, and you have a league that is much more luck dependent. The small number of games means that NFL teams will be separated by smaller margins, so a swing of a handful of games can be quite impactful. Especially when the difference between making the playoffs and being a .500 team, as with the 2001 New York Jets, can be almost entirely attributed to luck.

In contrast, we can apply the Pythagorean Wins approach to basketball and find a story similar to the one in baseball: both winning and losing teams face swings of luck and there is a long season across which teams have an opportunity to combat their luck. As with the NFL case, we can largely repurpose our code for applying the Pythagorean Wins to the NBA. With basketball, we will use a much larger exponent: 13.91.

```
NBA.2001 <- read.csv("NBA-2001.csv")

NBA.2001$py.rat <- apply(as.matrix(NBA.2001[,c(4,5)]), 1, function(x)
{pythagorean.wins(x[1],x[2],k=13.91)})
NBA.2001$py.exp <- apply(as.matrix(NBA.2001[,c(4,5)]), 1, function(x)
{pythagorean.wins(x[1],x[2], n=82, k=13.91)})

NBA.2001$luck <- NBA.2001$W - NBA.2001$py.exp

head(NBA.2001[order(NBA.2001$luck),],5)
                        Team  W  L    PF    PA py.rat py.exp  luck
24          San Antonio Spurs 58 24 106.6  98.0   0.76  62.57 -4.57
8             Detroit Pistons 32 50 100.0 101.8   0.43  35.93 -3.93
2 9       Washington Wizards 19 63 100.6 107.8   0.27  22.67 -3.67
22   Portland Trail Blazers 50 32 106.5 101.8   0.65  53.46 -3.46
10            Houston Rockets 45 37 106.7 104.2   0.58  47.70 -2.70

head(NBA.2001[order(-NBA.2001$luck),],5)
                     Team  W  L    PF    PA py.rat py.exp  luck
7           Denver Nuggets 40 42 103.7 106.3   0.41  34.00  5.99
13      Los Angeles Lakers 56 26 108.4 104.8   0.61  50.45  5.54
21            Phoenix Suns 51 31 100.3  98.0   0.57  47.55  3.44
```

```
25 Seattle SuperSonics 44 38 105.6 105.6   0.50  41.00  3.00
20  Philadelphia 76ers 56 26 103.6  98.9   0.65  53.79  2.20
```

LISTING 3.4. Top and bottom NBA teams by luck

In basketball, the higher exponent indicates a tighter relationship between the point differential and the expected winning percentage. In basketball, it is common for teams to have higher and lower winning percentages than in baseball. In baseball, where most teams are between .400 and .600, in basketball it is not uncommon for a team to win more than 70% of their games. On the contrary, we almost expect that the best teams in the league will win more than 70% of their games.

Looking at the most and least lucky teams in the NBA in 2001, we see that the San Antonio Spurs, who were the winningest team in the league that year, were plagued by misfortune and won 5 less games than they were expected. This could be, in part, due to their coach Greg Poppavich's then-controversial strategy of resting players mid-season. On the other hand, the Los Angeles Lakers, who would eventually go on to win the title, were the luckiest team in the league, winning 6 games more than they would be expected to based on Pythagorean Wins.

You will also note that in this approach, we are using the apply function in conjunction with our Pythagorean Wins function to produce the expected win rate and expected win totals. This is an alternative way of working with data frames and matrices in R. The apply family of functions is helpful for taking functions that are intended to work on individual numbers and instead working on data in tabular, matrix, or array format.

Next, we will take a look at professional hockey and examine the Pythagorean Expectation across the 2001 NHL season. As before, we will recycle our code changing only the exponent and the length of the season. In hockey, we will use a slightly smaller than 2 exponent: k = 1.93. We also use 82 games, the length of the NHL season.

```
NHL.2001 <- read.csv("NHL-2001.csv")

NHL.2001$py.rat <- pythagorean.wins(NHL.2001$GF, NHL.2001$GA, k=1.93)
NHL.2001$py.exp <-  pythagorean.wins(NHL.2001$GF, NHL.2001$GA,
k=1.93, n=82)
NHL.2001$luck <- NHL.2001$W - NHL.2001$py.exp

head(NHL.2001[order(NHL.2001$luck),],5)

                     Tm  W  L  T OL PTS  GF  GA py.rat py.exp   luck
26      Florida Panthers 22 38 13  9  66 200 246   0.40  32.92 -10.92
2      New Jersey Devils 48 19 12  3 111 295 195   0.69  56.56  -8.56
14 Toronto Maple Leafs 37 29 11  5  90 232 207   0.55  45.49  -8.49
24   Montreal Canadiens 28 40  8  6  70 206 232   0.44  36.32  -8.32
6        St. Louis Blues 43 22 12  5 103 249 195   0.62  50.50  -7.50
```

```
head(NHL.2001[order(-NHL.2001$luck),],5)
```

```
                       Tm   W   L   T  OL PTS  GF  GA py.rat py.exp  luck
17  Carolina Hurricanes  38  32   9   3  88 212 225   0.47  38.65 -0.65
3     Detroit Red Wings  49  20   9   4 111 253 202   0.61  49.77 -0.77
18         Boston Bruins  36  30   8   8  88 227 249   0.46  37.35 -1.35
8         Buffalo Sabres  46  30   5   1  98 218 184   0.58  47.65 -1.65
1     Colorado Avalanche  52  16  10   4 118 270 192   0.66  54.02 -2.02
```

LISTING 3.5. Top and bottom NHL teams by luck

Like basketball and baseball, we can see that misfortune can impact winning teams, like the Devils, who posted a .700 record in a season in which they would come just a game shy of a Stanley Cup victory. On the other hand, we can clearly see that there is a discrepancy between the Pythagorean Wins approach and the way hockey handled close games. In 2001, the NHL allowed for ties. This significantly alters the way we would need to evaluate luck. It also gives you a sense for how precarious any of these metrics are.

For example, the Devils won 9 less games than they were expected to, but they tied in 12 and lost 3 in overtime. Is the Pythagorean Wins expectation that they would have won about 69% of these games? That seems reasonable given their overall performance in 2001 was around this number. However, it is not clear that they should actually be given that higher rating in those matchups, considering their opponents necessarily persisted through a full contest without losing.

We see the same phenomenon in soccer, which we will look at next. In soccer leagues, it is typical for games to end in one of three outcomes: a win, a loss, or a draw. Wins are worth 3 points and draws are worth 1, and at the end of the season teams are evaluated on points instead of winning percentage. Like in hockey, this throws somewhat of a wrench into our Pythagorean Wins process; however, we can of course use the code from before to calculate Pythagorean Wins. We will use 1.7 as the preferred exponent for soccer and because we are using English Premier League data, we will assess performance over a 38-game season.

```
EPL.2001 <- read.csv("EPL-2001.csv")
EPL.2001

EPL.2001$py.rat <- round(pythagorean.wins(EPL.2001$GF, EPL.2001$GA,
k=1.7),2)
EPL.2001$py.exp <-  round(pythagorean.wins(EPL.2001$GF, EPL.2001$GA,
k=1.7, n=38),2)

EPL.2001$luck <- EPL.2001$W - EPL.2001$py.exp

a <- head(EPL.2001[order(EPL.2001$luck),],5)
```

```
b <- head(EPL.2001[order(-EPL.2001$luck),],5)
rbind(b,a)
               Squad  W  D  L GF GA Pts py.rat py.exp   luck
13  Leicester City 14  6 18 39 51  48   0.39  14.74  -0.74
17    Derby County 10 12 16 37 59  42   0.31  11.84  -1.84
10      Southampton 14 10 14 40 48  52   0.42  16.08  -2.08
20    Bradford City  5 11 22 30 70  26   0.19   7.28  -2.28
19   Coventry City  8 10 20 36 63  34   0.28  10.59  -2.59

14   Middlesbrough  9 15 14 44 44  42   0.50  19.00 -10.00
6            Chelsea 17 10 11 68 45  61   0.67  25.41  -8.41
3          Liverpool 20  9  9 71 39  69   0.73  27.92  -7.92
1     Manchester Utd 24  8  6 79 31  80   0.83  31.56  -7.56
15         West Ham 10 12 16 45 50  42   0.46  17.30  -7.30
```

LISTING 3.6. Top and bottom EPL teams by luck

Again, we can see the impact that ties or draws have on the utility of the Pythagorean Wins approach. Many of the top teams are expected to win many more games than they do. For instance, Manchester United and Liverpool, two teams toward the top of the table in 2001, both register as terribly unlucky. However, poor performers like Middlesbrough and West Ham suffer from bad luck as well. On the flip side, almost all of the luckiest teams were quite bad in 2001, with Bradford City and Coventry City both getting relegated following the 2001 season.

For sports like soccer, where draws are a part of the game, they become part of the strategy. A draw against a top team can be a boon to a bad team, while a draw against a bottom feeder is a failure for a good team. In play, teams will even adopt strategies to encourage draws. Ultimately, we must understand the wins and win expectation numbers in their sport-specific context. We would not want to compare luck numbers across sports any more than we would want to compare points for in soccer to points for in football.

Ultimately, Pythagorean Wins are a useful way of thinking about the outcome of a season. They are a good reminder that wins and losses are observations, but there is a significant aspect of randomness to them as well. Winning teams can be lucky or unlucky, and just because a team is having a good (or bad) season does not necessarily mean that the team is fundamentally sound. Teams can have bad fundamentals and be good (good luck) or have good fundamentals and be bad (bad luck). Thinking about wins and losses as a random variable helps us understand this.

Summary

In this chapter, we looked at probability in sport. In particular, we looked at the axioms of probability as applied to sport, the importance of thinking probabilistically about the outcomes of events in sport, and the utility of probability distributions in reasoning about sporting events. Additionally, we looked at the idea of Pythagorean Wins. We saw how Pythagorean Wins can be used to demonstrate the degree to which luck or misfortune impacts a team's performance over the course of a season and how we can come to a better understanding of wins if we think about them as being generated by a random process, instead of as the gold standard of truth about a team's success.

Key Terms

Probability theory	Probability density function
Probability	Probability distribution
Likelihood	Binomial distribution
Mutually exclusive	Normal distribution
Conditional probability	Domain
Uncertainty	Range
Random variables	Mode
Discrete random variable	Mean
Continuous random variable	Median
Probability mass function	Pythagorean Wins

Critical Thinking Exercises

1. In this chapter, we discuss the problems with exclusively reasoning based on outcomes and encourage thinking about sport in terms of probabilities. We discuss how thinking about wins in terms of probabilities offers advantages to general managers. What other aspects of sport would benefit from probabilistic thinking; who would this change in thinking benefit, and why?
2. In the following scenarios, identify whether the scenario represents a discrete probability distribution or a continuous probability distribution:
   a. Baseball pitcher pitch selection
   b. Winning time of Olympic 400m event
   c. Direction of shot by a soccer penalty kick taker
   d. Speed of a slapshot in hockey

3. In the following scenarios, identify whether the binomial distribution or the normal distribution is better to model the scenario and why:
   a. Number of free throws made by a basketball player in 15 shots
   b. Player's free throw percentages across the NBA during a season
   c. Number of hits a baseball player will record in 30 at-bats
   d. Batting average for a player over the season
   e. Completed passes by a quarterback in 35 pass attempts
   f. Quarterback rating over four seasons
4. Find the Pythagorean Win rate and estimated Pythagorean Wins for the following run, goal, or point totals and sports:
   a. A baseball team with 53 runs for, 35 runs against, over 24 games
   b. A baseball team with 35 runs for, 27 runs against, over 11 games
   c. A basketball team with 918 points for, 916 points against, over 9 games
   d. A soccer team with 12 goals for, 4 goals against, over 5 games
   e. A football team with 105 points for, 109 points against over 4 games

CHAPTER 4

Baseball and Sport Analytics

J.T. Wolohan

LEARNING OBJECTIVES

After reading this chapter, students should be able to:

- Describe the importance of on-base and value-based metrics in baseball
- Identify and define on-base metrics such as OBP, OPS, and wOBA
- Calculate value-based metrics like OBP, OPS, and wOBA in R
- Identify and define value-based metrics like VORP and WAR
- Calculate value-based metrics like VORP and WAR in R

Introduction

In Chapter 3, we looked at teams and an approach that general managers could use to assess how much luck was involved in a team's performance over a given period. The idea being that a manager is charged with delivering a winning team, and understanding if the team is under- or overperforming can help the manager correct when they need to correct and avoid changing up the team if they are expected to do better. But when it is time to change the team, how does the manager know what to change and how to change it? That is the question at the root of most **player-evaluation analytics**: which players provide a team the best chance of winning?

In this chapter, we will look at four different player evaluation analytics in baseball: on-base percentage, on-base plus slugging, value over replacement player, and wins above replacement. We will begin by looking at the question of measuring player skill, its similarities and differences with the measurements that we have seen so far in this book, such as runs scored, and free throw percentage. Then we will move on to a discussion of on-base metrics—discussing on-base percentage and on-base plus slugging. We will discuss the motivation for those measures and look at how to apply them using R. Next, we will do the same for player value metrics. We will introduce the notion of a **replacement player** and discuss some of the decision theory that drives player evaluation metrics, look at theory and arithmetic behind value over replacement player and wins over replacement player, and apply those metrics over real Major League Baseball data using R.

Measuring Players

Professional sport is a business, and players are a huge part of that business. Generally, players will make teams money in three ways: (1) increasing the quality of the team, resulting in a better on-field or on-court product; (2) increasing the quality of players around them, resulting in a better on-field or on-court product; and (3) by bringing fans to the game through their personal appeal (Hausman and Leonard 1997). While the third facet of player value—personal appeal—mostly belongs in a discussion about superstar players, the first two qualities, which both relate to the on-field performance of a team, apply to non-star players as well. That is, owners and managers who are interested in raising the most revenue from their team have an interest in winning games.

In the NBA, best estimates suggest that a win was worth approximately $827,000 in the seasons between 2002 and 2010 (Berri, Leeds, and von Allmen 2015). Across the other major American sport leagues—baseball, hockey and football—these values range from just over $300,000 per win in the NHL to $650,000 for MLB. For the 2001 Seattle Mariners who won 112 games, that means that $71+ million in revenue is a direct result of their on-field performance (Table 4.1). In the NBA and MLB, the importance of fielding a winning is especially important to the bottom line. Winning teams in these sports stand to make $20 million more than their losing counterparts.

TABLE 4.1. The value of wins across major American sports

	Poor	Average	Good
NBA	$16M	$33M	$41M
MLB	$39M	$48M	$61M
NFL	$3M	$5M	$7M
NHL	$11M	$12M	$14M

Poor performances are considered to be 20, 60, 5 and 35 wins in the NBA, MLB, NFL NHL; average performances are considered 40, 75, 8, and 40 wins; and good performances are considered 50, 95, 12, and 45 wins.

So far though, we have not looked at any ways to measure how players contribute to wins. We have looked at traditional box score statistics for players; however, many of these measures can be deceptive for reasons we addressed in Chapter 2. Consider a baseball player's home run total. If a player hits a lot of home runs, but every time they do not they strike out, it is entirely possible they are harming the team by leaving runners on base when they could otherwise be advanced or brought in to score. Or consider a basketball player's points per game numbers. If a player is taking a lot of shots and scoring a lot of points, we generally think of that as a good thing. But if that player is taking shots away from players who could score even more points, they are harming the team. That is, it is as important that we understand what box score statistics do not measure as what they do measure.

On-Base Metrics

The first two metrics that we will look at can be considered on-base metrics. That is, on-base percentage and on-base plus slugging. These two measures are commonly abbreviated OBP and OPS. In many ways, these metrics are the beginnings of modern sport analytics. These measures are at the heart of Michael Lewis's *Moneyball* (2003), which chronicled Billy Beane and the Oakland Athletics' analytics-driven approach to baseball.

In this section, we will first look at OBP. We will look at why OBP matters, how it differs from other statistics, and we will use R to calculate it. Then, we will turn to a derivative metric: OPS. We will discuss slugging percentage, the importance of OPS, and how to calculate it using R.

On-Base Percentage

In baseball, OBP is a metric that measures the frequency with which a player gets on base by any means. This includes hitting the ball, getting walked or hit by a pitch. This metric is often contrasted with the much more popular metric: batting average. Batting average measures the number of times a player gets a hit instead of making an out. Batting average is the traditional metric. And though old in and of itself, OBP can be considered an advanced metric.

Contrasting Batting Average and OBP

A baseball tradition that dates back to before the existence of Major League Baseball is to award the player with the greatest batting average at the end of each season a **batting title.** In the modern MLB, two batting titles are awarded: one for the American League—the Rod Carew American League Batting Champion—and one for the National League—the Tony Gwynn National League Batting Champion. The first ever batting title was awarded in 1876 to Ross Barnes, who recorded a batting average of .429 during the National League's inaugural season. Many of the greats of the sport claim batting titles among their accomplishments, including legendary players such as Honus Wagner and Ty Cobb; mid-century heroes such as Roberto Clemente, Stan Musial, and Ted Williams; and modern greats such as Miguel Cabrera, Wade Boggs, and Tony Gwynn.

And while the metric is prestigious, it is also simple. Calculating batting average requires only two other measures. The number of **hits** that a batter has recorded over a given time period—typically a season. And the number of **at bats** that a batter had during that time period. In baseball scoring, a player records a hit when they hit the ball and reach base safely, without the fielding team making an error or a **fielder's choice**—when the fielding team could just as easily get out one of a number of baserunners. At bats are a baseball metric that attempts to measure how many of a player's plate appearances were agentive. That is, during how many **plate appearances** was the batter supposed to do something? At bats are calculated by taking a player's plate appearances—the number of times the stepped up to home plate—and subtracting the following: the number of times they were walked, the number of times they were hit by a pitch, the number of times they recorded a sacrifice hit, and the number of times they were awarded a base due to interference.

In practice, both of these metrics are counting statistics. Both hits and at bats are recorded by a scorekeeper during the game and totaled up over the course of the season. Batting average, being a simple ratio of the two, can therefore be calculated rapidly by plugging the two new updated numbers into a calculator or through division by other means. The formula for batting average is shown below.

$$AVG = \frac{H}{AB}$$

Of course, as we were describing the metric, it becomes obvious that using batting average to measure hitters comes with implicit opinions about the things that are important for a hitter to do. For example, if you are not rewarding hitters for sacrifice hits—by not tallying these numbers in either hits or at bats—you are not encouraging **small ball**, a style of baseball that emphasizes stealing bases, sacrifices, and placing runners in the best position to score on single-base hits. Likewise, you are not rewarding players who have good eyes for the strike zone or otherwise reach base regularly on walks. This might be desired if you want your team to swing for the fences, but a walked batter is still a baserunner. It was for these reasons that Billy Beane emphasized OBP over batting average. Beane saw value in many of the aspects of the game that other front offices did not.

OBP has a few more inputs that batting average; however, as the name implies, the metric is still a simple ratio. OBP is calculated as the number of hits, walks, times a player is hit by a pitch, over the number of at bats, walks, times hit by a pitch, and sacrifice hits. It is perhaps easiest to think about OBP as batting average that also rewards players for walks and getting hit by pitches, while punishing them for sacrifice hits.

$$OBP = \frac{H + BB + HBP}{AB + BB + HBP + SF}$$

OBP has no history of glory as batting average does, though all the career leaders in OBP are universally recognized as among greatest players ever to play baseball, including Ted Williams, Babe Ruth, Lou Gehrig, Barry Bonds, Ty Cobb. And while for these players, on base percentage is perhaps unnecessary—their greatness can be illustrated through the use of more traditional statistics—for journeymen, OBP can often identify meaningful differences between players. Consider the statistical excerpt from the 1992 to 1993 MLB season shown in Table 4.2.

TABLE 4.2. AVG and OBP of select players from 1992 to 1993 MLB season

Name	Tm	AVG	OBP	OB/500
Tony Phillips	DET	0.276	0.387	194
Rene Gonzales	CAL	0.277	0.363	182
Scott Cooper	BOS	0.276	0.346	173
Glenn Davis	BAL	0.276	0.338	169
Bob Zupcic	BOS	0.276	0.322	161
Mike Devereaux	BAL	0.276	0.321	161
Thomas Howard	CLE	0.277	0.308	154
League Average	**-**	**0.259**	**0.328**	**164**

In Table 4.2 we see seven players who all had roughly the same season with respect to batting average; however, there are some meaningful differences we can identify if we use OBP. For the most obvious example, let's consider the year of Detroit Tiger's utility man Tony Phillips and Cleveland Reds outfielder Thomas Howard. Both batters had similar batting averages—with Howard actually recording a slightly higher average: .277 versus .276. When it came to reaching base safely, however, Phillips did much better, recording an OBP of .387 versus Howard's OBP of .308. Compared to the league average, both were better hitters than the average batter when we consider the traditional metric: batting average. When we consider OBP; however, we find that Phillips was actually much better than average and Howard was much worse than average.

If we use these rate statistics and extend them over 500 attempts—a number everyday players can easily hit in a season—we find that Phillips would have reached base nearly 200 times, while the league average player would have reached base only 164 times, and Howard 10 times less than that. This means that when it comes to reaching base safely, Phillips was better than Howard by about 30 percent. And indeed, this is reflected throughout both their careers. Phillips played for 18 years and Howard only 11.

This type of analysis, where we are distinguishing between journeymen players is not common in sports bar talk, sports radio, or talking-head sports TV shows such as First Take; however, it is at the core of the sport analytics value proposition. If a front office can receive 30 percent more value by replacing Howard with Phillips, they would stand to win a considerable number of additional games. Indeed, there is a strong relationship between OBP and runs scored, while the same relationship is not as powerful for batting average (Beneventano, Berger, and Weinberg 2012).

On-Base Plus Slugging AND Weighted On-Base Average

In baseball, of course, players are not limited to a single base per plate appearance. Players can hit doubles, triples, or even home runs—gaining multiple bases in a single attempt. To measure this, a variety of metrics has been devised. In the simplest form, each of these activities is counted separately as a single, double, triple, or home run. In more sophisticated approaches, these events are given weights based on their importance and divided by some number—often a neighbor of plate appearances. These metrics propose to measure how powerful a hitter is in addition to their aptitude for reaching base.

There are three of these metrics worth knowing: slugging percentage, OPS, and weighted on base average. In this subsection, we will look at each of these metrics and compare them to one another and to OBP, with respect to what they do and do not measure.

Slugging Percentage

First among the metrics that attempt to measure power is slugging percentage. A misnomer, slugging percentage is not a percentage at all; however, like batting average, it is a simple ratio of two other statistics: **total bases** and at-bats. Total bases, in baseball, is the number of bases a player reached on any hit.

$$TB = 1 \times 1B + 2 \times 2B + 3 \times 3B + 4 \times HR$$

$$SLG = TB/AB$$

From these definitions, we can make some implicit assumptions. First, we see the same problem we saw with batting average: walks are not considered. That is, a player who reaches base often by holding their bat instead of swinging it will not be rewarded or valued by slugging percentage. Second, slugging percentage considers each base to be worth the same amount. That is, a double is worth twice as much as a single while a triple is worth three times as much. Numerically, this is convenient, but intuitively, it does not make much sense. We know that players on second and third can score on most base hits—so the difference between a triple and double does not seem right at 50 percent.

That being said, slugging percentage does one thing right that batting average does not: it attempts to reward players for hitting for power. And players who can hit for power are more valuable than players who cannot. Home runs, obviously, put points on the board automatically, and doubles and triples have greater power to bring in runners than singles, and also place the batter in better position to score as a runner.

On-Base Plus Slugging

To resolve the problems with slugging percentage, Thorn and Palmer (1985) concocted a new metric: OPS. As it sounds, OPS is a simple calculation: calculate OBP and slugging percentage and add them together. OPS has two major advantages: its simplicity and its intuitive correctness.

On the matter of simplicity, one of the biggest advantages of OPS is that almost anyone can calculate it, given that OBP and slugging percentage were—at the time of OPS' onset—commonplace and adding three-digit numbers is simple by hand and on the computer. OPS is also simple to understand. Indeed, Bill James (2008), used a school-grade-like heuristic for evaluating players by OPS. James assigned As to players whose OPS was above .9, Bs to those above .83, Cs to those above .76, and Ds to those above .7. Players below .7 were considered below average, poor, or very poor hitters.

For intuitive correctness, we can look at the record books. The greatest hitters in the game, Babe Ruth and Barry Bonds, hold 8 of the ten single season records for OPS—and all five of the top five highest single season OPS totals. The remaining two seasons are marks set by Ted Williams, a triple crown winner and the most recent player to record a batting average above .400 in a single season.

The shortcomings of OPS are the shortcomings of the two metrics from which OPS is composed: namely, it does not make a concerted attempt to move beyond that which is easily calculated. The problem that we see with slugging percentage—the arbitrary linear weighting of extra base hits equal to the number of bases reached—cascades into OPS. Additionally, because OBP considers walks, and slugging percentage does not—OPS also implicitly weights a walk as half as valuable as a hit. It is not clear that this is the right approach either. More recently, Kim (2012) suggested that a weighted OPS, using a ratio of 1.3:1, favoring OBP over slugging percentage, is a better predictor of run scoring.

WEIGHTED ON BASE AVERAGE

OBP and slugging percentage both attempt to correct for important parts of the game that batting average overlooks. OBP attempts to correct for batting average overlooking walks, while slugging percentage attempts to correct for batting average overlooking extra-base hits. Combining these measures into OPS is an attempt to correct for both—incorporating the value of getting walked and the value of recording extra-base hits—but the analytically inclined will recognize OPS as a useful heuristic, but an overly simple approach. To correct this, Tango et al. in their book "*The Book: Playing the Percentages in Baseball*" (2007) introduced weighted on-base average (wOBA).

wOBA is an approach that attempts to assign linear weights to the positive outcomes that a batter can create while at bat: walking, getting hit, recording a single, double, triple, or home run, and divide these by the number of opportunities a batter has to create these positive outcomes. That is, wOBA is an attempt to measure how much good a batter will do in any given opportunity to hit. Importantly, wOBA cannot be calculated using a player's stat line alone. It is typically calculated specific to a given season and the value of walks, singles, doubles, triples, and home runs for a given season.

In order to find the value of each of these events, we use what is called a run-expectancy matrix. This matrix records every possible state combination—in terms of outs and base runners—and the number of runs that we would expect that batting team to record in that situation. For example, consider the run-expectancy matrix in Table 4.3.

TABLE 4.3. Example run-expectancy matrix

Runners	No outs	1 out	2 outs
---	0.50	0.25	0.10
1--	0.85	0.50	0.25
-2-	1.10	0.65	0.35
12-	1.40	0.90	0.45
--3	1.30	0.95	0.35
1-3	1.70	1.10	0.50
-23	1.90	1.40	0.60
123	2.30	1.60	0.75

In Table 4.3, we can see that at the start of each half inning, the batting team is expected to score approximately half a run. That is, over the course of a nine-inning game, we expect each team to score approximately 4.5 runs. As an inning progresses, our expectations about how a team will perform in that inning will change. For example, at the start of the half inning, we might expect the team to record half a run; however, after the lead-off hitter records a single, we now have 1 runner on and no out—so we expect the team to score .85 runs. This single is said to be worth .6 runs because when we compare the expected runs to the game state after the single (1 runner on, no out: .85 expected runs scored) to the expected runs scored for the game state where the batter got out (no men out, 1 out: .25 expected runs scored), we find a difference of .6.

Game logs are used to calculate run-expectancy matrices and then again to find the impact of each type of batting outcome. In order to build a run-expectancy matrix, one would read a large number of game situations and, for each, count up the occurrences of the situation and the runs scored in the half inning following that situation. For example, consider Table 4.4, describing a half inning of baseball, from a 1996 ALCS between the Baltimore Orioles and the New York Yankees. In this inning, the first of an eventual 5-3 Orioles win, the Yankees first three hitters record singles, before Cecil Fielder grounds into a rally ending double play.

TABLE 4.4. Play log from bottom of the 1st inning 1996 ALCS

Orioles	Yankees	Outs	Runners	Batter	Pitcher	Outcome
0	0	0	---	Derek Jeter	David Wells	Single
0	0	0	1--	Tim Raines	David Wells	Single
0	0	0	12-	Bernie Williams	David Wells	Single
0	1	0	1-3	Cecil Fielder	David Wells	Double play
0	2	2	---	Tino Martinez	David Wells	Flyout

If we were to update a run expectancy matrix using this log, we would read each line and then indicate the number of runs scored following that situation and that we saw the situation. For example, we would read the first line and record that we saw a situation with no runners on and 0 outs and later observed two runs being scored. Then we would record the second situation: no outs, a runner on first, and two runs eventually scored. Next, we'd record the third situation: runners on first and second, no outs, two runs scored. We would do this until we had recorded all the game logs that were both available and germane to the period we are interested in—usually a season or several seasons.

Once we had done that, to calculate weights for wOBA, we would go over the logs again and this time credit each outcome for the expected run change they created. For instance, working from Table 4.3, we would credit Derek Jeter's lead-off single with 0.6 runs expectancy—the difference between a runner on first and no outs and no runners on and one out. Tim Raines' single would be worth more: .9 expected runs. Subsequently, Bernie Williams' third single would be worth even more: 1.8 expected runs. Williams' single would get one full run for the run he drove in and .8 expected runs from the difference between runners on first and third with no outs (1.7 expected runs) and runners on first and second with one out (.8 expected runs).

A common formula for wOBA may be considered as follows. Its exact implementation may vary based on the years used to calculate expected run value.

$$wOBA = \frac{.72 \times BB + .75 \times HBP + .9 \times 1B + 1.24 \times 2B + 1.56 \times 3B + 1.95 \times HR}{PA}$$

On-Base Metrics in R

From a practical perspective, we can implement functions in R to calculate all of these metrics from the counting statistics of which they are composed. These calculations are shown in Listing 4.1.

```
make.OBP <- function(h,bb,hbp,ab,sf){
  (h+bb+hbp) / (ab+bb+hbp+sf)
}


make.singles <- function(h,b2,b3,hr){
  h-b2-b3-hr
}


make.SLG <- function(h,b2,b3,hr,ab){
  b1 <- make.singles(h,b2,b3,hr)
  (b1+2*b2+3*b3+4*hr)/ab
}


make.wOBA <- function(h,b2,b3,hr,pa,bb,hbp){
  b1 <- make.singles(h,b2,b3,hr)
  (.72*bb+.75*hbp+.9*b1+1.24*b2+1.56*b3+1.95*hr)/pa
}
```

LISTING 4.1 On-base metrics in R.

The functions for calculating the on-base metrics all serve as convenient ways of repeatedly doing the necessary arithmetic for these metrics. There is no magic going on in any of the code in Listing 4.1. The only point of real interest that you will want to note is the use of a function we create—make.singles—that takes metrics that are commonly available to derive the number of singles a batter has hit for. Singles are not typically counted on their own, perhaps because of their mundane nature, but we need them for both slugging percentage and weighted on base average.

With these functions in hand, we can perform the calculations on any number of batters' stat lines by reading in that data and then using the apply function across the data. In the example shown in Listing 4.2, we will read in data from the 1992 season and calculate these statistics for all players.

```
al.1992 <- read.csv("AL.1992.batting.csv")
make.singles <- function(h,b2,b3,hr){
  h-b2-b3-hr
}

al.1992$OBP <- apply(
  al.1992[,3:13],
  1,
  function(x){make.OBP(x[4],x[8],x[10],x[2],x[11])}
)

al.1992$SLG <- apply(
  al.1992[,3:13],
  1,
  function(x){make.SLG(x[4],x[5],x[6],x[7],x[2])}
)

al.1992$OPS <- with(al.1992, OBP+SLG)

al.1992$wOBA <- apply(
  al.1992[,3:13],
  1,
  function(x){make.wOBA(x[4],x[5],x[6],x[7],x[1],x[8],x[10])}
```

LISTING 4.2 Calculating OBP, SLG, OPS, and wOBA with apply

In Listing 4.2, we first read in the data using the read.csv function which we have seen in previous chapters. Then, we use the apply function to map each of our metric functions row-wise across the data by specifying 1 as the "direction" for apply. We specify only the numeric columns of the data.frame that we read in—columns 3 through 13—so that R can implicitly convert this data. frame to a matrix. We also need to pair the correct column numbers with functions. We do that with an anonymous function taking an array of values and then pass in only the values we need to satisfy the function's parameters. For example, we need to pass in walks—x[8]—to OBP because the function requires it, but we do not need it for SLG.

At this point, you should be able to investigate the data.frame and find the value of these advanced metrics for each of the 50 players in the data.frame. Table 4.5 shows the top 10 American League batters, by wOBA. You can reproduce these results with a single line of code:

```
top.wOBA <- al.1992[order(-al.1992$wOBA),][1:10,c(1,14,15,16,17)]
```

TABLE 4.5. Top 10 AL players in 1992 by wOBA

Name	OBP	SLG	OPS	wOBA
Frank Thomas	**0.439**	0.536	**0.975**	**0.422**
Edgar Martinez	0.404	0.544	0.948	0.408
Mark McGwire	0.385	**0.585**	0.970	0.407
Danny Tartabull	0.409	0.489	0.898	0.395
Ken Griffey Jr.	0.361	0.535	0.896	0.383
Dave Winfield	0.377	0.491	0.867	0.377
Kirby Puckett	0.374	0.490	0.864	0.375
Shane Mack	0.394	0.467	0.860	0.374
Mickey Tettleton	0.379	0.469	0.848	0.372
Paul Molitor	0.389	0.461	0.851	0.371

In Table 4.5, we can see that many of the metrics track one another very closely. Indeed, it appears that Frank Thomas was far and away the best AL hitter in 1992, leading the league in OBP, OPS, and wOBA. Though he did trail slugger Mark McGwire, who would later go on to set the single season home-run record and be embroiled in a steroid scandal.

We can assess empirically the degree to which all of these metrics move together by looking at their correlation. Correlation is the statistical measure of covariance between two variables. That is, when one variable changes, how much can we expect the corresponding variable to change. Correlation metrics can range from −1 to 1, with numbers toward either extreme representing greater correlation and numbers closer to zero representing no correlation. We can calculate correlation for our metrics in R using the cor built-in.

```
cor(al.1992[,c(11,14:17)])
```

Performing that command should result in a matrix. We present the lower triangular version of that matrix in Table 4.6.

TABLE 4.6. Correlation between on-base metrics

	AVG	OBP	SLG	OPS
OBP	0.539	-	-	-
SLG	0.232	0.253	-	-
OPS	0.439	0.679	0.882	-
wOBA	0.469	0.814	0.763	0.976

From Table 4.6, we can see that there are some very strong correlations between our metrics. OBP has strong correlations with wOBA and AVG, while SLG has strong correlations with wOBA as well. That OPS is strongly correlated with both OBP and SLG should not be surprising—given that it is comprised of the two metrics in even parts; however, we do see that SLG is more influential in determining OPS than OBP. The reverse seems to be true for wOBA, which correlates more strongly with OBP than with SLG. The most surprising correlation of all, however, is between OPS and wOBA. The correlation of .976 is so close to 1 that they are almost perfect predictors of one another. This is true despite all of the statistical and methodological problems of OPS that the sophisticated expected runs approach of wOBA was designed to correct.

Lastly, let us look at a histogram of these four measures to see how they are distributed across the league. These histograms are shown in Figure 4.1.

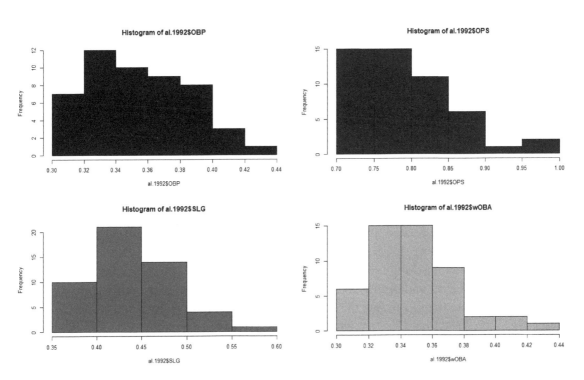

FIGURE 4.1. Histograms of OBP, OPS, SLG, and wOBA for 1992 AL batters

Across these four histograms, what we see is that all four metrics are skewed to the right or positively skewed. At first glance, this might be surprising. We might expect there to be a traditional bell-curve shape to the skill of batters in the American league, with equal numbers of batters performing below average as above average. However, if we think about the processes at play in professional sports, it becomes obvious that this cannot be the case.

Professional sports leagues are not random samples of the general public. Instead, they are made up of the upper echelons of talented individuals. If we consider a bell curve for the batting skill of the entire population, the selection of this curve that makes it to play professional baseball is only the 800 or so best hitters in any given year. Of those 800, most are just good enough; however, a few are truly exceptional.

Value Metrics

The observation that most players in professional baseball are clustered toward the bottom end of performance poses a challenge for general managers: which selection of many players of medium skill will help us win? As shown earlier in this chapter, it is sometimes possible to differentiate between journeymen by identifying undervalued aspects of the game—this is the *Moneyball* approach. If the entire league is valuing batting average and underpaying players with good relative OBP or slugging percentage, then we can succeed by investing in those players. Unfortunately, those days are mostly gone. Now, there are two major metrics used to assess relative player value: *Value Over Replacement Player (VORP)* and *Wins Above Replacement (WAR)*. In this section, we will look at both those metrics and calculate them in R.

VALUE OVER REPLACEMENT PLAYER (VORP)

The metric VORP attempts to calculate the marginal value of a player based on the difference between the runs they have created, the outs they have made, and the expected performance of a replacement-level player over that same period. Marginal value is an economics term that refers to the amount one favors something over something else. For instance, if you go to a hockey game and they have cola soda for $1 and orange soda for $2, your marginal value for orange soda over cola soda needs to be more than $1 to buy the orange soda. Similarly, if it is 2016 and we are selecting between two outfielders: Brett Gardner, who we will need to pay $13.5 million, or Kevin Pillar, who we will need to pay $500,000, we would need Gardner to be worth more than $13 million to us in order to sign Gardner over Pillar.

VORP FOR BATTERS

So far, we have primarily been looking at metrics for batters. VORP is can be used for both batters and pitchers. We will use different formulas for each metric; however, we will retain the same underlying concepts. In this subsection, we will look at calculating VORP for batters as well as some necessary sub-calculations that are themselves useful metrics. As noted in this section's introduction, VORP looks at marginal value by assessing runs created over outs. For batters, the formula for VORP is below:

$$VORP = OutsMade \times \frac{RunsCreated}{OutsMade} - \frac{ReplacementRunsCreated}{ReplacementOutsMade}$$

To calculate the players value over how a replacement player would have performed in the same span, we multiply the number of outs they have made by the difference between their ratio of runs created to outs made and the ratio of runs created to outs made for a replacement-level player. It follows that the only things we need to calculate VORP are ways of calculating runs created, outs made, and a method of assessing a replacement-level player. It turns out, this first piece is slightly contested.

There are two effective ways of assessing runs created, one of which we have already seen. One way of assessing runs created, as we have seen above, is to use linear weights for batting events. The other method is to use Bill James' runs created metric. Starting with the linear weights approach, because we have seen it already—one way to calculate runs created is to calculate the change in expected runs scored for each batting outcome and then multiply the number of times a player achieves that outcome by its expected value.

$$wOBA = \frac{.72 \times BB + .75 \times HBP + .9 \times 1B + 1.24 \times 2B + 1.56 \times 3B + 1.95 \times HR}{PA}$$

We performed this calculation for wOBA and then went on to divide by the number of plate appearances to get a sense of how much value a player created per appearance. If we skip the division, we have an estimate of runs created.

Second, we could use James' runs created (RC) metric. This metric has many forms, each increasing in complexity; however, it is sufficient to know the simplest of them:

$$RC = OBP \times SLG \times AB$$

This simple metric roughly estimates the runs created by a given player using readily available box score metrics. That said, we know that it falls apart for truly exceptional players because their OBP and SLG numbers will be much, much higher than a normal player. Consider Barry Bonds in 2004, who had OBP and SLG numbers double the league average.

Choosing one of these approaches, we will then calculate outs. The calculation for outs is straightforward: we take plate appearances and subtract hits, walks, and hit by pitches. That is, we find all the times a player went up to bat and subtract all the times they did not make an out.

With these two sub-components of VORP in place, all that remains is to find the same values for a replacement player. This will be the baseline against which we compare to arrive at the marginal utility or value of the player we are investigating. A common heuristic approach to doing this is to take league total runs created and league total outs made and multiply those values by some discount rate constant, depending on how productive we believe readily available replacement players to be.

$$\frac{ReplacementRunsCreated}{ReplacementOutsMade} = \frac{LeagueTotalRunsCreated}{LeagueTotalOutsMade} \times DiscountRate$$

In practice, this discount variable can range from .7 to .9, with .8 being the default rate. The most common reason for varying this rate is the differing defensive responsibility of players in baseball. For example, catchers tend to be more defensive minded. It is fair then to use a lower discount rate when assessing their value. It is important to note here that although we can—and many do—vary the discount rate based on defensive importance, the VORP metric does not make any attempt at measuring defensive value. That is, VORP should not be interpreted as a measure of a player's overall value: rather, it only encapsulates their offensive value.

Offensive VORP in R

There is little magic to calculating VORP in R. Much like the calculations for on-base metrics we performed earlier in the chapter, the VORP calculations are straight arithmetic. For ease of reuse and clarity, we place these calculations into R functions. The functions for calculating the necessary components for VORP—both the linear weights version and the runs created or "simple" version—are shown in Listing 4.3.

With these functions in hand, we will then need to apply the functions to our data frame. To do that, we will use the same row-wise apply approach that we took earlier in this chapter. We will use a throwaway anonymous function to select the requisite variables from each row and place them in the right spots as determined by our functions. This will add the necessary columns to our data frame to use R's vectorized arithmetic for the remainder of our calculations. These final calculations are shown in Listing 4.4.

```
make.linearRC <- function(h,b2,b3,hr,bb,hbp){
  b1 <- make.singles(h,b2,b3,hr)
  (.72*bb+.75*hbp+.9*b1+1.24*b2+1.56*b3+1.95*hr)
}
make.simpleRC <- function(OBP, SLG, AB){
  OBP*SLG*AB
}
make.outs <- function(PA, H, BB, HBP){
  PA-H-BB-HBP
}
```

LISTING 4.3 Functions for calculating Offensive VORP

In Listing 4.3, you will note that we use the with function so that we do not need to keep using the dollar-sign syntax for column selection. This is a convenient approach when we need to select many named columns from a data frame. You will also note that this final step mirrors the mathematical formula introduced earlier in this section.

Having loaded the data into a data frame, it is worth looking at some aspects of VORP. Here, we'll examine three: the relationship between the two different types of VORP; the relationship between OPS and VORP; and the overall distribution of VORP. These aspects are all shown in Figure 4.2. First, it is worth validating that even though we can measure runs created in two different ways, both approaches achieve roughly the same outcome when it comes to VORP. The correlation between these two variables for our 1992 dataset is greater than .97. The two versions of VORP are almost perfect predictors of one another.

```
# AL LEAGUE TOTALS FOR 1992
# Linear runs created: 27333
# Simple runs created: 9742
# Outs: 58592
al.1992$RpO.L <- with(al.1992, RC.L/outs)
al.1992$RpO.S <- with(al.1992, RC.S/outs)
al.1992$VORP.L <- with(al.1992, (RpO.L-(27333/58592)*.8)*outs)
al.1992$VORP.S <- with(al.1992, (RpO.S-(9742/58592)*.8)*outs)
```

LISTING 4.4 Functions for calculating Offensive VORP

Second, it is worth comparing VORP to OPS. After all, the distribution of OPS was one of the reasons we were interested in VORP in the first place. In Figure 4.2, we can see that OPS and VOPR are strongly correlated, but there are distinct groups of players who offer better than expected or worse than expected value based on their OPS. Indeed, it would be wise for a general manager to use a chart like this to assess a player. Comparing VORP and OPS helps answer the question: compared to other players with similar box score statistics, is a given player a good deal or a raw deal?

Third, we see that the distribution of value, as determined by VORP, is unevenly distributed, with most players clustered toward the left and a few stretching out to the right. In our dataset, we only have data for the top 50 players in the American League. It appears that in 1992, you could count on a player of this caliber to get you between 20 and 50 runs more than a replacement-level player. The ten best players in the league would get you 60. And only the very best player was worth more than 100 runs.

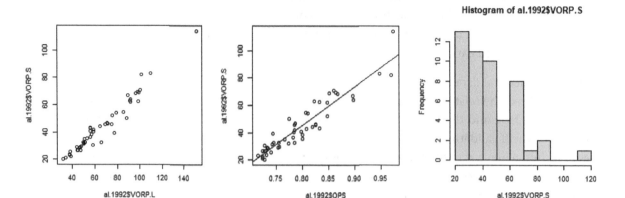

FIGURE 4.2. Examining three facts about VORP

Over a more complete set of data—for example, all the players of 1992 instead of just the 50 best—we would see a wider range of VORP values and, indeed, even some negative VORP values. The bottom tier of players in Major League Baseball who may play only a few games are occasionally worse than the replacement-level ones. Players who are worse than replacement level will quickly find themselves sent down to the minor leagues because their marginal value to the team is negative.

VORP for Pitchers

We can apply the notion of VORP to pitchers as well. For pitchers, the notion of value is the opposite of the notion of value for batters. Where we judge batters by how many runs they create per out, we judge pitchers by the number of runs they prevent per out. Otherwise, the two metrics—VORP for batters and VORP for pitchers—are very similar. Both metrics assess the run creation rate as attributed to a specific player and extended over a number of outs.

For pitchers, VORP is the number of innings a pitcher has pitched, times the replacement rate of giving up runs—their Run Average (RA)—minus the pitcher's specific RA over 9. In this case, 9 is used because Run Average is a metric that attempts to look at how many runs a pitcher would give up in a standard 9 inning game. Dividing the difference between the replacement level pitcher and the specific pitcher by 9 normalizes this value to an inning.

$$VORP = IP \times \frac{ReplacementRA - RA}{9}$$

To calculate this metric, we can see we need two values: the run average for the pitcher and the replacement run average. Run average, for its part, is a straightforward metric equal to 9—the number of innings in a game—times the number of runs a pitcher has given up divided by the number of innings that pitcher has pitched. We use this same formula for our replacement payer calculations; however, like with batters, we use a discount rate factor to go from league average to replacement average. For pitchers, discount rates are greater than 1 because giving up more runs is worse than giving up fewer. We will also use two different replacement rates—one for starters and one for relievers—because being a starter is more difficult than being a reliever. As the game has evolved and continues to evolve, these rates may need to be adjusted—for instance, to account for new pitching roles like the closer, who pitches only at the end of games in tight situations, or setup pitcher, who pitches primarily in situations where a close is coming soon.

$$ReplacementStarter = 1.35 \times LeagueRA - 0.66$$

$$ReplacementReliver = 1.70 \times LeagueRA - 2.25$$

Pitching VORP in R

Calculating VORP for pitchers is much the same as calculating VORP for batters. We'll need to create functions for the requisite sub-metrics and we will need to calculate the replacement level. For this example, we will treat every pitcher as if they were a starter. The code for this can be seen in Listing 4.4.

```
make.RA <- function(R, IP){
  9*(R/IP)
}

make.VORP.p <- function(IP, RA, Repl){
  IP * (Repl-RA)/9
}

AL.Repl <- make.RA(R=9802, IP=20329) * 1.35 - 0.66
```

LISTING 4.5: Functions for calculating pitchers' VORP

In Listing 4.5., we create two functions: one to make Run Average and one to make VORP itself. The Run Average function takes the runs a pitcher has let up and the innings they have pitched and performs the necessary arithmetic to calculate Run Average: nine times runs over innings pitched. The VORP function similarly takes the innings pitched by a pitcher, their Run Average, and the replacement level Run Average, and calculates VORP according to the formula from earlier in the chapter. We will again use these functions on our entire data frame by way of the apply function. That can be seen in Listing 4.6, along with two sorts of the data that allow us to inspect the top 15 and bottom 15 pitchers from the 1992 American League, according to VORP.

```
pitchers$RA <- apply(pitchers[,3:14],
            MARGIN=1,
            FUN=function(x){make.RA(x[8],x[6])})


pitchers$VORP <- apply(pitchers[,3:15],
            MARGIN=1,
            FUN=function(x){make.VORP.p(x[6],x[13],AL.Repl)})

head(pitchers[order(-pitchers$VORP),c(1:5,8,16)],15)

head(pitchers[order(pitchers$VORP),c(1:5,8,16)],15)
```

LISTING 4.6: Applying VORP to pitcher data

That can be seen in Listing 4.6, along with two sorts of the data that allow us to inspect the top 15 and bottom 15 pitchers from the 1992 American League, according to VORP. The code in this section uses the same patterns as that from Listing 4.2. Table 4.7 shows the top and bottom five pitchers from our dataset.

TABLE 4.7. Top 5 and bottom 5 pitchers from 1992 by VORP

Name	Tm	W	L	ERA	IP	VORP
Mike Mussina	BAL	18	5	2.54	241	69.2
Roger Clemens	BOS	18	11	2.41	246.2	62.2
Kevin Appier	KCR	15	8	2.46	208.1	61.2
Jack McDowell	CHW	20	10	3.18	260.2	55.29
Charles Nagy	CLE	17	10	2.96	252	54.55
Mike Flanagan	BAL	0	0	8.05	34.2	-14.25
David Wells	TOR	7	9	5.4	120	-14.69
Les Lancaster	DET	3	4	6.33	86.2	-16.21
Scott Scudder	CLE	6	10	5.28	109	-17.04
Dave Otto	CLE	5	9	7.06	80.1	-17.73

Sports Analytics

Table 4.7 features Hall of Famer Mike Mussina and 7-time Cy Young Award winner Roger Clemens as the best pitchers in the league, according to VORP. You will also note that of the top five pitchers by VORP, all of them are starters: pitching more than 200 innings. This highlights the value of a pitcher's endurance. 1992 Cy Young Award winner Dennis Eckersley, a reliever for the Oakland Athletics, pitched only 80 innings—only enough to accumulate a VORP of 29.

The bottom five pitchers of 1992 feature a mix of relievers and starters; however, Dave Otto, Scott Scudder, and David Wells—all back-of-the-rotation starters—performed the worst according to VORP. This highlights the damage that an unreliable starting pitcher can do to a team. Even though as in Wells' case he has a nearly .500 record, his VORP demonstrates that Toronto would have been better with another pitcher.

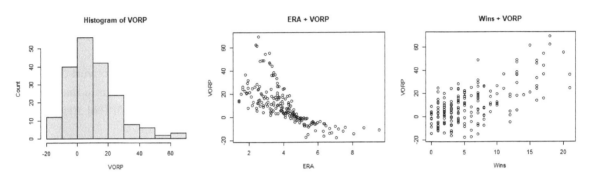

WAR—Wins above replacement

FIGURE 4.3. Patterns of VORP for pitchers

Before leaving replacement value, we will examine the three charts in Figure 4.3 to better understand VORP for pitchers. First, from our histogram of VORP scores, we see a strong right skew in the data. This is as expected: remember, most players are at or slightly above replacement level; a few players will be below replacement level: either on their way into or out of the league; some players are greatly above replacement level.

We can also see that VORP is correlated with, but by no means perfectly associated with, the common pitching metrics of ERA and Wins. With ERA especially, we see a strong correlation on the upper end of ERA. Pitchers with high ERAs will have low VORP scores; in fact, it is almost impossible for a pitcher with an ERA above league average to have a positive VORP score. On the lower end of the ERA spectrum, we see the correlation between VORP and ERA loosen up. For these pitchers, it becomes more about endurance: how many innings can a pitcher contribute giving up fewer runs than a potential replacement.

With wins, the correlation is much weaker, especially as pitchers accumulate more wins. This points to winning games being a matter of luck to some degree—a pitcher cannot rely on only their performance, but they also need help from the offense. And indeed, we can see that some pitchers with VORPs near zero can win quite a few games.

Estimating Player Contributions to Wins

As discussed in the first section of this chapter, a win in baseball may be worth upwards of $650,000 to a team. Therefore, it is worth attempting to assess how much each player—both position players and pitchers—contributes to a team's wins and losses. Winning games is also an easy way for the lay or non-analytic oriented sporting audience to understand or interpret a statistic. To that end, baseball has begun to rely on a metric called Wins Above Replacement (WAR).

Unlike the most metrics we have viewed so far, WAR does not have a standard implementation. Rather, various baseball analytics groups publish their own versions of WAR, often with proprietary and undisclosed logic behind them. The logic, however, is much the same as VORP: Calculate the difference between the player in question and a replacement-level player, and then convert this value into wins. A simple version of WAR can be estimated using VORP and a rule of thumb that says 10 runs contributed is equivalent to 1 win. That is, a VORP of 10 is a WAR of 1, a VORP of 30 is a WAR of 3, a VORP of 60 is a WAR of 6, and so on.

```
al.1992$WAR <- al.1992$VORP.S/10
pitchers$WAR <- pitchers$VORP/10

# Print the top 10 hitters and pitchers
head(al.1992[order(-al.1992$VORP.S),c(1,2,24)],10)
head(pitchers[order(-pitchers$VORP),c(1:2,17)],10)
```

LISTING 4.7 A simple version of WAR

In Listing 4.7, we can see how we would go about calculating WAR in R. The rule-of-thumb based approach is purely arithmetic, once we have VORP calculated. We can use R's vector arithmetic logic to calculate WAR for our entire data set without the use of apply. The last two calls print the top 10 hitters and pitchers to the screen. From this, we can see that Frank Thomas was worth about 3 wins more than the second best hitter in 1992, and 4 wins more than the best pitcher—Mike Mussina.

More sophisticated WAR calculations may try to take into Thomas' defensive contributions. Note that here we did not grade Thomas' against the first-baseman replacement level, which is quite high because the defensive standards for the position are low. Indeed, all of the top hitters from 1992 are First Basemen and should have their scores decremented.

Summary

In this chapter, we reviewed advanced metrics for player evaluation in baseball, looking at on-base metrics and replacement-adjusted metrics. In doing so, we emphasized the importance of having metrics that reflect the value of actions in a game. In particular, we saw that in approaches like wOBA we can calculate the impact of each at bat to the win probability of a game. Further, we discussed the importance of understanding player value not in a vacuum, but as their marginal value. The marginal value of a player is the value they provide over their replacement. In metrics such as VORP, this replacement player is represented by some fraction of the league average contribution. Lastly, we explored how player value can be translated into wins through WAR. Throughout this chapter, we saw practical examples of how these metrics can be implemented in R.

Key Terms

On-base percentage
Slugging percentage
On-base plus slugging
Weighted on-base average
Run expectancy

Replacement level player
Marginal value
Value Over Replacement Player
Wins Above Replacement

Critical Thinking Exercises

1. The on-base plus slugging metric, OPS, has a high correlation with weighted on-base average.
    a. If given the choice between the two metrics, which would you rather use to justify player personnel decisions?
    b. Why might you prefer OPS?
    c. Why might you prefer wOBA?
2. In this chapter, we saw that the top-50 players in MLB in 1992 were worth between 20 and 100 runs over the course of a season; however, that this distribution was highly skewed to the right. That is to say, the majority of the good players are only marginally better than average, while a few elite players are much better.
    a. As a general manager, how would you use this information to inform salary negotiations?
    b. What stance would you take toward elite players?
    c. What stance would you take toward average or good players?
    d. How might this change in a salary cap sport?

3. For pitchers, VORP is highly correlated with ERA; however, many of the pitchers with the lowest ERAs will not have the highest values. This is because many of the pitchers with the lowest ERAs will be elite relief pitchers (e.g., closers and set-up pitchers).
   a. Why would relief pitchers have a lower VORP than a starting pitcher?
   b. Why might we be willing to pay a higher-ERA starting pitcher more than a lower-ERA reliever?
4. We saw in this chapter that VORP and WAR are highly correlated with OPS (for hitters) and ERA (for pitchers.)
   a. Why is it still useful to think about VORP and WAR instead of OPS or wOBA?
   b. What are the advantages of VORP and WAR for comparing players across positions?
6. Using the 2002 MLB pitching data provided, calculate VORP and WAR for each of the top 199 pitchers by innings pitched. Who are the five best pitchers by VORP? How do they compare to the top five pitchers from 1992? Plot a histogram of the pitchers by VORP. How does this histogram compare to the histogram from 1992?

References

Beneventano, Philip, Paul D. Berger, and Bruce D. Weinberg. 2012. Predicting run production and run prevention in baseball: the impact of Sabermetrics. *International Journal of Business, Humanities and Technology* 2(4), 67–75.

Berri, David J., Michael A. Leeds, and Peter von Allmen. 2015. Salary determination in the presence of fixed revenues. *International Journal of Sport Finance* 10(1), 5.

Hausman, Jerry A., and Gregory K. Leonard. 1997. Superstars in the National Basketball Association: Economic value and policy. *Journal of Labor Economics* 15(4), 586–624.

James, Bill. 2008. *The Bill James Gold Mine 2008.* Chicago: ACTA Publications.

Kim, Hyuk Joo. 2012. Effects of on-base and slugging ability on run productivity in Korean professional baseball. *Journal of the Korean Data and Information Science Society* 23(6), 1065–1074.

Lewis, Michael. 2003. *Moneyball: The Art of Winning an Unfair Game.* New York: W.W. Norton & Company.

Lopez, Javier, Daniel J. Mundfrom, and Jay R. Schaffer. 2011. What makes a winning baseball team and what makes a playoff team. *Multiple Linear Regression Viewpoints* 37(2), 23–28.

Thorn, John, and Pete Palmer. 1985. *The hidden game of baseball.* Boston: Doubleday.

Tango, Tom M., Michael G. Lichtman, and Andrew E. Dolphin. 2007. *The book: Playing the percentages in baseball.* Lincoln: Potomac Books, Inc.

CHAPTER 5

Hockey, Basketball, and Sport Analytics

J.T. Wolohan

LEARNING OBJECTIVES
After reading this chapter, students should be able to:
- Identify advanced metrics used in hockey, such as the Corsi statistic
- Identify advanced metrics used in basketball, such as PER and TS%
- Explain why Usage Rate is important to understand in basketball
- Explain why basketball is thought of in terms of efficiency
- Analyze hockey data using advanced metrics in R
- Analyze basketball data using advanced metrics in R

Introduction

In the previous chapter, we examined player valuation in baseball using on-base metrics and player value metrics. Baseball was an excellent place to begin our discussion of player evaluation analytics for two reasons: first, baseball has a long history of analytics; second, baseball has a large volume of readily available statistics. We do not get those same luxuries with every sport. Some sports have been culturally impervious to analytics and some sports produce little useful data. In this chapter, we will look at two other sports—ice hockey and basketball—and examine the player evaluation metrics available in those two sports.

First, we will look at hockey. In hockey, we will examine the ubiquitous plus/minus statistic, as well as more advanced metrics that attempt to measure the latent contributions of a player while they are on the ice. Namely, we will look at the Corsi statistic and adjusted plus-minus. We will also implement these metrics in R. Then, we will move on to analyzing basketball. We will start with basketball's traditional box score metrics, noting some of their drawbacks. Then we will move on to some of the shooting efficiency metrics. Lastly, we will discuss PER and Usage Rate. We will implement several of these methods in R.

Player Value In Hockey

We will begin our discussion of player evaluation of analytics in sports that are not baseball with hockey. Hockey has, like baseball, several convenient box score measurements that have long been used to assess players. For example: goals and assists. In fact, hockey might be most well-known for the *hockey assist,* a term that refers to how hockey credits an assist to the player who passed the puck to the player who passed the puck to the player who scored. In other sports, it is traditional to limit assists to only the player who immediately preceded the goal scorer.

In this section, we will specifically look at two hockey metrics: **plus-minus**, and the **Corsi** statistic—intended to be an improvement over plus-minus. Additionally, we will implement both metrics in R. Lastly, we will look at some of the drawbacks with "lineup" metrics such as plus-minus and the Corsi statistic, as well as ways we can normalize the data to address that issue.

PLUS-MINUS IN HOCKEY

Plus-minus, which is also written as +/− or ±, is metric that attempts to measure a players joint offensive and defensive contributions to his team. It has a simple implementation: one takes the number of points scored while a given skater was on the ice and subtracts the points scored by the opponent while that skater was on the ice.

$$\pm = Goals - GoalsAgainst$$

Beyond that simple implementation, there are two additional implementations of plus-minus worth knowing: full-strength plus-minus and situational or weighted plus-minus. For full-strength plus-minus, only goals that are scored while both teams are at full strength are counted toward a player's plus-minus. This eliminates power play, penalty shot, and shootout goals. Situational plus-minus considers the numbers of players on ice at the time of a given goal and credits the player with a value equal to the number of players on the player's team over the number of players on the opposing team. Teams that are short-handed when they score, then, will be credited with values greater than one, while teams that score while on the powerplay will receive credit equal to less than a regular goal. In practice, the full-strength plus minus is often used as the "standard" plus minus. The situational plus-minus is considered a better metric by the analytically inclined.

CALCULATING PLUS-MINUS IN R

To calculate plus-minus in R, we need access to game log data. The NHL currently makes game logs available on their website. We can parse these logs to identify which players were on the ice when a goal was scored and calculate plus minus. These reports contain events, as well as the players who were in the ice at the time of a given event. For the purposes of calculating plus-minus, we will look only at goal-type events.

A common way to store this event data is in a format called JSON—JavaScript Object Notation. JavaScript Object Notation is a convenient human and machine readable way of storing data and metadata together. We will avoid diving too deep into JSON in this text; however, because it's often a convenient form for storing complex data, we do need to give a brief introduction to it.

One of the reasons we will often prefer JSON to other data storage formats is because we can store metadata along with our data. In its most simple form, this metadata can simply be labels for the data values. An example of a hockey goal might be as shown in Listing 5.1.

```
{
    "scoring_team": "Anaheim",
    "Anaheim": [15,10,19,4,6,31],
    "Detroit": [93,8,40,2,55,35]
}
```

LISTING 5.1 JSON data for a hockey goal

In Listing 5.1 our example goal event contains three pieces of information: the scoring team, the players on ice for the Anaheim team, and the players on ice for the Detroit team. The players are, in this instance identified by their jersey number. In this listing we have an example of several different data types. We have the string or character type—which is used to represent the name of the scoring team. We also have two array types, which we use to hold the numbers representing the players who were on ice. Importantly, this information is all relatively well organized, given that each data element—scoring team, and the two team's lineups—have labels.

Of course, we might be able to do a better job labeling the data. We might prefer to label "Anaheim" as "On_Ice_Anaheim" or "Anaheim_skaters"; however, labeling data is often a trade-off between clarity, concision, and utility. Oftentimes, when we receive a dataset, we'll be lucky if it has any labels or metadata at all. JSON data, at the very least, will tend to come with some labels.

To work with JSON data in R we will use an R library aptly named "rjson." This library has only two functions worth knowing: fromJSON and toJSON. The fromJSON function can take either a file-path or a character object containing a valid JSON string and convert it into a complex R object. The toJSON function goes the other way: it converts an R object into a valid JSON string, which could then be written to a file as text if we were so inclined.

For this example, we'll first load data into R by bringing in the rjson library—you may need to install this library if it's not already installed—and then by using the fromJSON function to load a file containing JSON into an R object. This is shown in Listing 5.2.

```
#install.packages("rjson")
library("rjson")
pme <- fromJSON(file="plus-minus-events.json")
```

LISTING 5.2 Loading in JSON data using R

From here, we'll need a way of going over the events in this object. We will use a familiar strategy: we will define a function and then use R's apply capabilities to use that function on each event. The function we design will convert each event into a format suitable for calculating plus minus. A convenient format for this is a matrix—a two-dimensional array. We can use a 2×99 matrix to store the impact of each event on every possible player for each team, with every player taking a spot in the matrix corresponding to their jersey number.

Looking back at Listing 5.1, we would want to increment the 4th, 6th, 10th, 15th, 19th, and 31st columns of the row corresponding to Anaheim's players and decrement the 2nd, 8th, 35th, 40th, 55th, and 93rd columns of the row corresponding to Detroit's players. If we do this for every event, we will end up with a number of 2×99 matrices that we can then add together to find the plus-minus total for each player for a given game. Or, if we have properly laid out data, for any period of time in which we have events.

```
event_to_matrix <- function(event){
  event.matrix <- matrix(data=0, nrow=2, ncol=99)
  e <- event[[1]]
  ifelse(e$scoring_team=="Anaheim",
         {Anaheim_value=1; Detroit_value=-1},
         {Anaheim_value=-1; Detroit_value=1})
      for (player in e$Anaheim){
        event.matrix[1, player] <- Anaheim_value;
      }
      for (player in e$Detroit){
        event.matrix[2, player] <- -Detroit_value;
      }
      return(event.matrix)
    }eturn(event.matrix)})}
```

LISTING 5.3 Converting a goal event to a matrix in R

Listing 5.3 shows what an R function to perform this calculation looks like. In this function, we take in an event and use it to populate a matrix representing that event. We start this by generating an empty matrix which we will later populate with the adjustments for each player. Next, we figure out which team scored. In this example, we are looking at data between Anaheim and Detroit—so we will check the scoring_team variable to see if it contains the string Anaheim or Detroit. If Anaheim scored, we will set the value to assign to each Anaheim player as 1 and the value to assign to each Detroit player as -1. If Detroit scored, we will reverse the values so that the Anaheim players are receiving a -1 and the Detroit players receive a 1. Once we have done this, we loop through all of the players on each team and replace the value in the matrix (a zero, because we created an empty matrix) with their corresponding team's value: 1 if they were on the scoring team and -1 if they were getting scored on. Remember, each player is represented as an element in the matrix. In this case, matrix element 1, 10 represents Anaheim forward Corey Perry.

Last, we will apply this function to all the data we loaded into R from the JSON. We will need to use R's dollar-sign selection notation to select the events and then convert those events to an array-first; apply only works on array objects. From there, we will use apply again—this time with the built-in sum function—to add these matrices together. This will give us the totals for each player over the course of all the events.

```
events.by.player <- apply(FUN=event_to_matrix,
                          X=as.array(pme$events),
                          MARGIN=1)

matrix(apply(X=events.by.player,
             MARGIN=1,
             FUN=sum),
       nrow=2)
```

LISTING 5.4 Creating a player-events matrix in R

When you have run the code from Listings 5.1, 5.2, 5.3, and 5.4, the output will be a 2 × 99 matrix that contains the plus-minus value for each player in the game.

Before moving on from plus-minus, it makes sense to spend a second talking about what it feels like to do the type of analysis we just performed on hockey data, as compared to the early analysis we performed on baseball data. With the baseball data, we mostly used arithmetic approaches from observed metrics. The simple observations—hits, runs, walks, strikeouts, etc.—were useful, even for calculating nuanced advanced metrics. In hockey, we are avoiding this approach from the start. The information contained in the counting metrics—in hockey: goals and assists—is less useful than the nuanced play-by-play level data, the line data, the who did what and who was where. With hockey data, we need to comb over the details more specifically. This is in part because hockey—like basketball, football, and soccer—is a highly relational sport.

CONTINUUM OF TEAMWORK SPORT

In order to understand how nuanced our analytics need to be, it can help to think of sports along a continuum from less teamwork to more teamwork. The more teamwork is involved in a sport, the less we can rely on individual measures to capture the richness of the sport. The less teamwork is involved in a sport, the more we can rely on individual measures. To illustrate this point, let's first consider this spectrum at both ends: sports with little teamwork and sports with the most teamwork.

Starting with sports with little teamwork, it makes sense to think about individual sports such as tennis, athletics, boxing, and most other Olympic sports. We can assess the performance of a singles tennis player, for example, almost exclusively by looking at statistics about their own play—there simply are no teammates to bring into the analysis. We can look at serve accuracy, serve speed, forehand and backhand accuracy, forehand and backhand speed, time spent in various parts of the court—and all of these will result in a meaningful summary of the match and a meaningful assessment of a player's performance. In low-teamwork sports, individual statistics are highly representative of their performance.

On the opposite end of the spectrum is a sport like football. At any given time, a football team has 11 players in play for each side; however, these players switch quite regularly and top-level metrics often hide nuances. For example, consider a team that has a large number of passing yards for a game. This situation could occur either because (1) the team ran up the score on their opponent and vastly outscored them or (2) the team was behind for most of the game and had to pass a lot in order to try and close the gap. In high-teamwork sports, individual's statistics are not very representative of their performance; they rely heavily on their team to perform well.

TABLE 5.1. Popular American sports along a teamwork continuum

Less teamwork				More teamwork
Athletics	NASCAR	Baseball	Basketball	Football
Boxing		Softball	Hockey	Soccer
Golf		Tennis (doubles)	Lacrosse	
Swimming		Volleyball		
Tennis (singles)				
Wrestling				

Table 5.1 shows popular sports placed along the continuum, from involving less teamwork to involving more teamwork. You will note that hockey, the sport that we are talking about in the first half of this chapter, and basketball, the sport we are talking about in the latter half of this chapter, are in the same grouping. A lot of the methods we use to analyze one sport can (and are) used in the other. A distinction here, however, is that in basketball, scoring opportunities are more prevalent. This volume makes individual statistics more reliable. The counterpoint would be soccer, which has so few scoring opportunities, that individual statistics are only a crude representation—and often provide little to no insight into the value of midfielders or defensive players.

Corsi Statistic

In addition to plus-minus, another metric that is popular in hockey is the Corsi statistic. We can think of this metric as plus-minus for shots, whereas plus-minus is a measure of goals. By definition, the Corsi statistic for a player is the ratio of shots, blocks, and missed shots taken by their team, over the same quantity for the other team.

$$Corsi = \frac{Shots_{For} + Blocks_{For} + MissedShots_{For}}{Shots_{Against} + Blocks_{Against} + MissedShots_{Against}}$$

Like plus-minus, there are also variations of the simple Corsi. The Corsi Rate or Corsi Percent are the two components of Corsi expressed as a percentage. This metric is useful because it can help differentiate between a player who has a low Corsi score because their team both took a few shots and their opponent took few shots and a player whose Corsi score is low because their team and their opponents take about an equal number of shots.

$$Corsi = \frac{Corsi_{For}}{Corsi_{Against}}$$

$$Corsi_{Rate} = \frac{Corsi_{For}}{(Corsi_{For} + Corsi_{Against})}$$

Additionally, there is an ice-time adjusted Corsi. This metric attempts to normalize Corsi for over the length of the game, or over the length for which a player is typically on ice, in order to facilitate comparisons between players who play different numbers of minutes. A good number of minutes to use to normalize the Corsi statistic by is 20—a number of minutes that most starters for a given game will surpass, but few second stringers will. This would seem to make Corsi an indicator of a player's impact on a game should they be in a starter role.

$$Corsi_{20} = \frac{(Corsi_{For} - Corsi_{Against})}{Minutes} \times 20$$

Calculating Corsi Metrics in R

Because Corsi is a modification of plus-minus, we can use a slight modification of our plus-minus code to calculate the various Corsi metrics. The major change we will need to make is to calculate is to include shots, blocks, and missed shots into our event list and discard goals—which the Corsi metric does not use. Another change we will make is that we will calculate the two parts of the Corsi metric—$Coris_{For}$ and $Corsi_{Against}$—separately as positive values, instead of calculating the offensive and defensive contributions together.

We start the process of calculating the Coris metric by reading in the events. For this example, the data is in a common informal format called JSON lines. In this format, each event is saved as its own event as a JSON object to a line in a plain text file. This is especially common for data where the information comes in an unpredictable and uneven sequence—such as the plays in a game. We can read the file into R line by line using R's readLines function, and then when we apply over that function to calculate the Corsi metrics, we will parse each line from JSON into an R object.

The data for this game comes from two simulated hockey matches between the AHL's Albany Devils and the Syracuse Crunch. We will need to read through each event, decide which team to credit for the offensive or defensive event, and then credit all the players on that team. Like with plus-minus, we will loop over the relevant players and increment a matrix where each player is represented by a single value. Because this is synthetic data, we only have 10 players—so we will update a 2 × 10 matrix—representing 2 teams of 10 players each.

```
corsi.events <- readLines("corsi.events.jsonl")

corsi.addition <- function(event, offensive=T){
  event.data <- fromJSON(event)
  if (offensive) {t = "Syracuse"} else {t = "Albany"};
  corsi.array <- matrix(array(20, data=0),nrow=2)
  if (event.data$event_team == t)
      {for (player in event.data$on.ice.syr){
        corsi.array[1, player] <- 1;}
  } else {
      for (player in event.data$on.ice.alb){
        corsi.array[2, player] <- 1;
      }
  }
  return(corsi.array)}

offensive.events <- lapply(FUN=corsi.addition, X=corsi.events)
defensive.events <- lapply(FUN=corsi.addition,
                           X=corsi.events,
                           offensive=F)

offensive.corsi <- Reduce(x = offensive.events, f= `+`)
defensive.corsi <- Reduce(x = defensive.events, f= `+`)

offensive.corsi/(offensive.corsi+defensive.corsi)
```

LISTING 5.5 Calculating Corsi scores in R

Listing 5.5 shows how we can calculate the Coris rating of all the players for the game. You will note that we create one function—corsi.addition—which is responsible for converting a game event into a matrix of values, indicating which players should be credited with either an offensive shot or a defensive shot-against. This function works by converting the event from JSON to R with the fromJSON function, determining which team the event corresponds to, and then incrementing the values for that team. The corsi.addition function also has a defensive variation which we can set by specifying offensive=F. This credits the opposing team with giving up a shot against in the same manner.

Once we do this for each event, we are left with two lists of event matrices. We can use R's Reduce function to sum all of the values of these matrices. Somewhat counterintuitively, we do not actually use the sum function for this. In R, the sum function returns a single value—the sum of all the values—while the addition operator, which we can turn into a function by surrounding it with ticks, provides us with a range of addition options for single values, arrays, matrices, and so forth.

Once we have reduced the events, we have calculated the offensive and defensive Corsi rankings for each player for these simulated games. Using the raw numbers, we can see which players were on ice the most when their team was taking shots—offensive Corsi—or when the opposing team was getting shots off on them—defensive Corsi. Listing 5.5 shows both of these metrics for each of the 20 players who played in the two games. From this, we can see that player four for Syracuse was on ice for the most offensive players—represented by the highest offensive Corsi—while player 6 from Albany was on ice for the fewest shots against—represented by the lowest defensive Corsi.

We can also see each player's Corsi rating in Listing 5.6. Remember, Corsi rating is a player's offensive Corsi metric—the number of shots taken while they are on the ice—over that same value plus their defensive Corsi—the number of shots taken by the other team while they are on the ice. The players who have the highest rating—again player 4 from Syracuse and 6 from Albany—are the players for which, when they were on the ice, their team out shot their opponent the most.

```
> offensive.corsi

      [,1] [,2] [,3] [,4] [,5] [,6] [,7] [,8] [,9] [,10]
[1,]    25   26   30   36   25   23   28   31   29    17
[2,]    27   23   25   23   27   19   22   22   19    23

> defensive.corsi

      [,1] [,2] [,3] [,4] [,5] [,6] [,7] [,8] [,9] [,10]
[1,]    20   27   26   24   21   21   23   26   21    21
[2,]    30   28   27   26   19   17   33   31   32    27

> round(offensive.corsi/(offensive.corsi+defensive.corsi),2)

      [,1] [,2] [,3] [,4] [,5] [,6] [,7] [,8] [,9] [,10]
[1,] 0.56 0.49 0.54 0.60 0.54 0.52 0.55 0.54 0.58  0.45
[2,] 0.47 0.45 0.48 0.47 0.59 0.53 0.40 0.42 0.37  0.46
```

LISTING 5.6 Offensive and defensive Corsi scores

Team and Line Adjustments for Plus-Minus

With both Plus-Minus and the Corsi metrics, there is a shared problem: bad players can be elevated by playing on otherwise good teams. Consider a hypothetical example where 4 NHL players and a 10-year old are playing against a pick-up team at the local rink. The four NHL players will, trounce the amateurs, regardless of the contributions of the 10-year old. We might imagine that the professionals would score 15, perhaps more, goals over their less-talented opponents. Would it be right then to use plus-minus and suggest the 10-year old is better than every player on the opposing team? Of course not.

To solve this problem, we need a way to get at the contribution each player is making to their team's overall chance of scoring. Likewise, it would be nice to have a measure of players' impact on their team's overall chance of being scored on. The common approach to this problem is known as Adjusted Plus Minus—though in implementation, it bears little resemblance to plus-minus. In hockey, this approach was popularized by Macdonald (2011); however, it was prevalent in basketball circles before that (see Ilardi and Barzilai 2008).

This approach is the first non-arithmetic approach to sport analytics we see in this book. This means that the calculations for Adjusted Plus Minus cannot be made using simple addition, subtraction, multiplication, and division. That said, we will still describe the formula for Adjusted Plus Minus here and calculate Adjusted Plus Minus using R later in this section.

Adjusted Plus Minus poses the question "will the team score during this shift" and considers (1) the offensive skill of each player to be the probability that they contribute to their team scoring on shifts in which they play and (2) the defensive skill of each player as the probability that their opponent does not score on shifts in which they play. We can think of Adjusted Plus Minus attempting to get at two values for each line: $P(Goal_{for})$ and $P(Goal_{against})$. When we calculate Adjusted Plus Minus, we solve for the values that each player contributes to these probabilities. These values become the players ratings.

To solve for these weights, we need the following: the outcome of every shift; the players who played on offense that shift; the players who played on defense that shift; the goalie who played that shift; and the length of the shift (if we want to later adjust by time-on-ice.)

$$Outcome = OffensivePlayers + DefensivePlayers + Goalie$$

In practice, we will use a vector of variable weights to represent each aspect in the equation above and solve for these weights using an ordinary least squares or similar approach. This process is known as regression analysis. Regression analysis is a technique where we solve for the values of a number of unknown variables by fitting them to our known data, according to a formula. There are a variety of forms of regression, each covered in depth elsewhere. To learn more about practical application of regression approaches in R, we strongly recommend Frank Harrell's book on *Regression Modeling Strategies: with Applications to Linear Models, Logistic and Ordinal Regression, and Survival Analysis* (2015).

Because we are solving for the probability of a goal on any given shift—a variable that will either be a 0 or a 1—we use a variation of the general regression approach called logistic regression. This approach represents the output of our equation as a probability between 1 and 0 and is otherwise used for classification problems. For our purposes (and as is often the case in regressions) we are less interested in the output of our model than the weights it optimizes towards.

TABLE 5.2. Example design matrix for APM

Outcome	O1	O2	O3	O4	O5	O6	O7	O8	O9	O10	D1	D2	D3	D4	D5	D6	D7	D8	D9	D10	G1	G2
0	1	1	1	1	1	0	0	0	0	0	0	0	0	0	0	-1	-1	-1	-1	-1	0	-1
0	0	0	0	0	0	1	1	1	1	1	-1	-1	-1	-1	-1	0	0	0	0	0	-1	0
1	1	1	1	1	1	0	0	0	0	0	0	0	0	0	0	-1	-1	-1	-1	-1	0	-1
0	0	0	0	0	0	1	1	1	1	1	-1	-1	-1	-1	-1	0	0	0	0	0	-1	0
0	1	1	1	1	1	0	0	0	0	0	0	0	0	0	0	-1	-1	-1	-1	-1	0	-1
0	0	0	0	0	0	1	1	1	1	1	-1	-1	-1	-1	-1	0	0	0	0	0	-1	0
0	1	1	1	1	1	0	0	0	0	0	0	0	0	0	0	-1	-1	-1	-1	-1	0	-1
1	0	0	0	0	0	1	1	1	1	1	-1	-1	-1	-1	-1	0	0	0	0	0	-1	0

Table 5.1 shows an example of what a design matrix might look like to calculate the adjusted plus-minus for 12 players—10 skaters and two goals—over four shifts. In statistics, a design matrix is a matrix of variable observations that we use to represent our data—typically for the purposes of multivariate regression, as is our case here, or other techniques such as analysis of variance or analysis of covariance. In our case, you will note that we have twenty columns representing our 10 players. These columns contain Boolean variables indicating whether or not a player was on the ice during a given shift. From the design matrix, we can identify that players O_1 through O_5 play for one team and players O_6 through O_{10} player for the opposing team. We can notice this because those players are either always (or never) on the ice at overlapping times. You will also note that when players are on offense, we represent their presence with a 1; however, when they are on defense, we represent their presence with a −1. This is because good defense performance reduces the likelihood of a goal being scored—so to obtain a positive value for a player's defensive skill, we use a negative weight. Goalies, for this reason, are always represented as −1. Lastly, you may note that despite this example being for four shifts, we have eight rows in our matrix. This is because each row represents one team's perspective. In hockey—unlike in baseball or football—there is no distinction between offense and defense. All players are playing both at the same time.

In our example, you will note that the five players for each team are always on the ice at the same time. This is often—but not always the case in hockey. That is what makes this approach powerful. We can use it to capitalize on the situations where players play on lines they do not typically play on—either because of injury, exhaustion, penalty, or otherwise—and use that information to arrive at an assessment of players' skill. For a practical example, let's look at how to calculate these values in R.

To calculate adjusted plus-minus, we will typically need to parse through play-by-play data. In this example, we are going to start with some play-by-play data and, indeed, the entire design matrix already constructed. We will read the matrix into R and then perform a ridge regression on the matrix (Macdonald 2012). Ridge regression is the regression technique favored for adjusted plus-minus because its regularization reduces the error in APM ratings. The code for this process can be seen in Listing 5.7.

```
apm.design.matrix <- read.csv(file = "adjusted.plus.minus.data.csv")
players <- MASS::lm.ridge(Outcome ~ . + 0, data=apm.design.matrix)
data.frame(players$coef)

                players.coef
Katie.A.         0.13120573
Sammie.B.        0.10203791
Patricia.C.      0.08616041
Annie.D.         0.09679994
Tiffany.E.       0.12621475
Yasmin.G.        0.04659703
Michelle.H.      0.08649984
Daisy.I.         0.03182531
Eva.J.          -0.01449360
Rachel.K.        0.06824096
Nancy.L.         0.06948204
Hazel.M.         0.07374977
Melissa.N.       0.08030919
Isobel.O.        0.07522068
Eliza.P.         0.05635817
Alish.Q.         0.09079109
Maryam.R.        0.05826557
Isla.S.          0.10771628
Elizabeth.T.     0.10182299
Sofia.U.        -0.29250000
```

LISTING 5.7 Ridge regression for calculating APM

We can see from Listing 5.7 that, though the process of setting up the design matrix may be involved, calculating the APM from that matrix is rather simple. In our data, we can see that most of the players are about average. Some players are notably bad: Sofia U., for example. And some are a little above average, such as Katie A. and Tiffany E.

In practice, excellent players will have APM as high as .5 or .6, while the worst players will have APM as low as -.4 or -.5. We can also use this same process to calculate adjusted Corsi statistics. This attempts to more accurately indicate how many shots a player is worth. A good player may be worth up to 10 shots per game using this adjusted Corsi process while bad players are typically worth a loss of 6 to 8 shots per game.

Player Evaluation in Basketball

Having looked at hockey already, we can now turn our attention to basketball. In many ways, basketball is the same game as hockey. Each sport (usually) has five players who are responsible for both offense and defense. Offensive possessions and defensive possessions alternate as teams either score or commit turnovers. And each sport fundamentally comes down to putting the ball through the net, or the puck in the back of the net, more times than your opponent.

The chief difference between the two sports is pacing. Hockey is a small sample-size sport compared to basketball. Whereas in professional hockey each team may take about 30 shots in the average game, in modern professional basketball each team will take between 80 and 100 shots in the average game. This means we might have 60 events to analyze in a hockey match, but 200 to analyze in a basketball game. Of course, this also means we can count smaller events in basketball. And we do.

In basketball, we keep track of a handful of metrics in addition to the points and assists that make up the vast majority of hockey analysis. Further, basketball is complicated by the fact that not all basketball shots are worth the same number of points. Free throws are worth a single point, standard field goals are worth two points, and three point field goals are worth three points. In recent years, the discrepancy in point values across shots has been emphasized by analytics-oriented teams who are increasingly moving to three-point centric game plans.

In this section, we first review the traditional metrics associated with basketball. Then we discuss some of the advanced metrics associated with basketball, namely effective field goal percentage, true shooting percentage, and player efficiency rating. Lastly, we discuss Usage Rating, a statistic that is helpful for understanding the degree to which a player can be relied on by their team.

Traditional Metrics

Because of basketball's higher volume when compared to hockey, more nuanced events are tracked in the typical basketball box score. In this section, we will review those events as well as what they do and do not measure. We will first look at the offensive metrics and then we will turn our attention to the defensive metrics.

The classic offensive basketball metrics are the same as those we find in hockey: points and assists. In addition, we will also typically find the number of makes and misses, split up by the three shot types: two-point field goals, three-point field goals, and free throws. Points and assists are obvious in their importance—one wins basketball games by scoring more points than their opponents—but they are also deceptive. A large number of points does not necessarily mean a player was helping their team the most, merely that they were shooting the ball a lot. Players like Russell Westbrook and Kobe Bryant are notorious for their ball-dominant style of play that does not necessarily translate into winning performances. Likewise, players can fall into the trap of over-assisting, passing up good open shots in order to get an assist. The shot-type count metrics are helpful for understanding how a player comes by their points. We can identify categories of players: physical players (lots of 2-point attempts and free throws), balanced players (mix of 2-point attempts and 3-point attempts), three-point specialists (more 3-point attempts than we might expect), etc. The trick here is that not all shot attempts of the same kind are created equal. An open corner three, for example, is easier to make than a contested half-court heave; a slam dunk is a better shot than an off-balance long-range 2-pointer.

On the defensive side, the common metrics you will hear about are going to be rebounds, steals, and blocks. Rebounds can be both an offensive and a defensive metric, but 75% to 80% of rebounds one gets will come from the defensive side of the ball. Rebounding is an important aspect of basketball because it gains or keeps possession of the ball; however, there are many flaws with simply counting the number of rebounds. Most obviously, there are often defensive rebounding situations where the rebound is—for all intents and purposes—uncontested. That is, there are many defensive players who may get the rebound, but no offensive players with a legitimate chance at recovering the ball. In these situations, a player will be credited with a rebound that was worth no marginal value to the team. Steals and blocks, on the other hand, are almost always valuable—though they are rare. Steals are when a defensive player strips the ball from an offensive player or intercepts a pass. Blocks are when a defensive player puts their hand between a shot ball and the net. Both of these have the very obvious impact of taking a scoring chance away from the offense. Steals are slightly more valuable because, definitionally, they result in a change in possession. Blocks do not always result in a change in possession, and it is possible for a block to occur and the offensive team to still score on that same possession—though this is rare in practice.

ADVANCED BASKETBALL METRICS

In order to expand on these baseline metrics—especially the offensive metrics—basketball analysts have devised a handful of advanced metrics that can be derived from the box score. In this section, we will review three of those metrics. We will first review effective field goal percentage and true shooting percentage. Both of these metrics attempt to assess how valuable a player is as a scorer, by taking into account the number and type of shots they take. Lastly, we will review Player Efficiency Rating (PER), a heuristic-based metric devised by John Hollinger to assess comprehensive player value. Now largely replaced by the more rigorous Box Plus Minus—which we treat on its own in a subsequent section—PER is still a useful indicator of a player's overall impact on a game.

EFFECTIVE FIELD GOAL PERCENTAGE

Effective Field Goal Percentage is the first of two advanced metrics that we will discuss that attempts to correct for the advantage players who are good at making three-point shots convey to their team. Since three-point shots are worth an extra point than two-point shots, they are 50% more valuable. This leads directly to the following formula for Effective Field Goal Percentage:

$$eFG\% = \frac{FG + (.5 \times 3P)}{FGA}$$

Effective Field Goal Percentage is the number of total field goals made (two pointers and three pointers), plus one half the number of 3-point field goals made, divided by the total number of field goal attempts. So, a player who made 3 of 8 shots, including 2 of 3 three-point shots, would have an Effective Field goal percentage of 50%. Effective Field Goal percentage is a useful means of comparing similar types of players; however, shot volume is still going to factor heavily into the utility of Effective Field Goal percentage. Low-volume shooters who take high-percentage shots—think centers and power forwards—will still have a higher rating in this metric when compared to shooters who are taking higher volume or lower-likelihood shots. The exception to the rule is Steph Curry, who in 2019 had an Effective Field Goal percentage of .604, despite taking nearly 500-shots more than any other player with a rating above .600.

Similar, and indeed related to, Effective Field Goal percentage is True Shooting Percentage. True Shooting Percentage is a metric that attempts to measure a player's shooting skill, to include their performance on free throws, which Effective Field Goal percentage omits. To do this, True Shooting Percentage normalizes the number of points a player scores by the number of field goal attempts they take, plus an average rate of foul-shots awarded. The formula for this is as follows:

$$TS\% = \frac{PTS}{2\,(FGA + .44 \times FTA)}$$

This metric has the effect of both crediting players who make more three-point shots as well as players who can get to and score from the line. Conversely, players who are unable to get to and score from the foul line at an average rate will be punished by this metric.

Given the similarity between Effective Field Goal Percentage and True Shooting Percentage, it makes sense to compare the two and look at correlations. We can readily implement both of these metrics in R and perform this correlation analysis. To do this, we will design two functions—one each to calculate Effective Field Goal Percentage and True Shooting Percentage—and then apply those functions to a data frame of 2019 NBA data. We can then plot the two metrics against one another and find the correlation between them.

```
calculate.efp <- function(fg,x3p,fga){
  efp <- (fg+x3p/2)/fga
  return(efp)
}

calculate.tsp <- function(pts,fga,fta){
    tsp <- pts / (2*(fga+.44*fta))
    return(tsp)
}

nba.2019$EFP <- calculate.efp(nba.2019$FG,
                              nba.2019$X3P,
                              nba.2019$FGA)
nba.2019$TSP <- calculate.tsp(nba.2019$PTS,
                              nba.2019$FGA,
                              nba.2019$FTA)

ggplot(nba.2019, aes(x=EFP, y=TSP)) +
  geom_point() +
  geom_smooth(method="lm") +
  facet_wrap(nrow = 1, vars(Pos))

cor(nba.2019$EFP, nba.2019$TSP)
# 0.9088409
```

LISTING 5.8 Comparing eFG% and TS% on 2019 NBA data

The code in Listing 5.8 is a translation of the mathematical formula presented above into R code. We then apply these two functions on the corresponding values from our 2019 data to calculate the metrics for each of the players in that dataset. The plot function at the end produces a chart, which is presented below in Figure 5.1. The correlation function at the end produces a correlation score. A score of .9 indicates that the two metrics are very strongly correlated. We would probably only want to use one for our analysis.

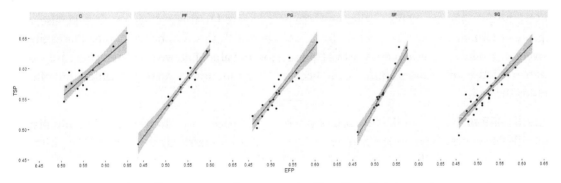

FIGURE 5.1. True shooting percentage and effective field goal percentage

Figure 5.1 shows how well correlated the two metrics are for the top 100 shot takers in the league. It also gives us a sense of how we can expect different players to perform across positions—again, this is largely due to the number and type of shots they are taking. We can see that each of the point guard and shoot guard graphs have notable outliers: Steph Curry (PG) and Joe Harris (SG). In 2019, Joe Harris finished second in the league in both eFG% and TS%, behind center Clint Capella. This is exceptional for a shoot guard, though Harris takes fewer shots than one would expect from a bona fide star, with only about 10 per game. In contrast, Curry carried a heavy load for his team in 2019, taking 20 shots per game—twice as many as Harris—with eFG% and TS% ratings still top-5 in the league.

Ultimately, the choice between the two metrics is one of personal preference. Both are better than strict field goal percentage and simpler to understand than PER which we have yet to discuss. However, each must be put in the context of a player's performance with respect to both position and their usage.

Player Efficiency Rating

Next among the advanced metrics we will review is PER. The PER metric, originally devised by early basketball analytics pioneer John Hollinger, has largely fallen out of favor now, so we will not give it the full treatment we have other metrics; however, it is worth discussing the ideas behind the metric. Hollinger's PER is designed to calculate how much a player contributes to their team's performance by assigning point values to all of the things they do and then weighting those actions by how frequently they occur based on minutes played and pace of play. For example, in the part of Hollinger's PER formula that deals with blocks and steals, he assigns a full average value of a possession to a steal and a fractional average value of a possession to a block. This is because, as we noted above, not all blocks are recovered by the defensive team.

We can also see here the idea of an "average value of a possession." Average value of a possession is the idea that every time a team has the ball, they are expected to score some number of points. They can score more than this number (a good possession) or fewer than this number (a bad possession); however, the outcome of any possession needs to be compared to this average result. Likewise, acts that gain, sustain, or a giveaway a possession should be worth this number of points. For example, turnovers in Hollinger's system are worth -1 possession in value. Likewise, missed shots are worth a negative fraction of a possession in value because they function as turnovers unless the offense rebounds the ball.

Hollinger's PER is also one of the first places where we see pace normalization coming into play in basketball. Pace normalization is when we weight a counting metric by the pace of play, with the logic that in basketball, all possessions end with the other team getting the ball back. Therefore, if you play fast and score a lot of points, the other team will also have a chance to score a lot of points. Value comes not from scoring more points by taking more shots, but by having the most efficient possessions possible knowing that your opponent will get the same number of possessions.

Critics of PER dismiss the metric as crude and biased, in part because some believe that Hollinger crafted the metric with Michael Jordan's preeminence in mind. A more balanced critique of the metric is that it attempts to approximate team-effects, while not accounting for them as directly as a more sophisticated statistic like Box Plus Minus. In many ways, PER is best thought of as a correlate to the NFL's Passer Rating: a good metric that is useful and has a simple-enough calculation; however, being a single-metric rating, it masks a lot of nuance.

TABLE 5.3. Top players of 2019 by PER

Player	Pos	Tm	PER	USG%
Giannis Antetokounmpo	PF	MIL	30.9	32.3
James Harden	PG	HOU	30.6	40.5
Anthony Davis	C	NOP	30.3	29.5
Nikola Jokić	C	DEN	26.3	27.4
Karl-Anthony Towns	C	MIN	26.3	28.9
Joel Embiid	C	PHI	26.1	33.3
Kawhi Leonard	SF	TOR	25.8	30.3
LeBron James	SF	LAL	25.6	31.6
Nikola Vučević	C	ORL	25.5	28
Rudy Gobert	C	UTA	24.6	17.8

The top 10 players of the 2019 season by PER are presented in Table 5.3. In this table, we can see some of the same bias we saw before, where high-efficiency centers perform the best. And this is at the height of the three-ball era when the center position is supposedly dead. However, we also get the sense that PER is roughly measuring the right things when it comes to identifying the most valuable players. Antetokounmpo, Harden, Davis, Leonard, and James would all have been in discussion for the MVP. Antetokounmpo did end up winning the award; Leonard led the Toronto Raptors to the NBA title and won the Finals MVP award. Just outside the top 10 are also a handful of excellent players, including 2019 All-NBA players Steph Curry, Kevin Durrant, Damien Lillard, and Kyrie Irving.

Ultimately, PER is a good approximation of a player's value that can be derived almost entirely from common box score stats. It has some gaps and it suffers the same "over-valuing the big" problem that many NBA stats do; however, it can be relied on as a good indicator of player value. PER is effective as a starting point for a more nuanced conversation about player value.

Usage Rate

The last metric we will examine attempts to measure a concept we have been bringing up time and again when discussing basketball: Usage Rate. Usage Rate is a metric that attempts to measure how integral a player is to their team's offense. Players with high Usage Rates are expected to do a lot of work to make the offense function; players with low Usage Rates are more of a cog in the system and come by their metrics a little more serendipitously. Generally speaking, higher Usage Rate players will be better and lower Usage Rate players will be worse. This, however, is almost entirely because coaches prefer to organize their teams around their best players. Additionally, most players' performances will be middling at low usage rates, increase at some rate as their usage rate increases up to some threshold, and then decrease as they are forced to do more and more on their own. Only the best basketball players are able to sustain high performance at high Usage Rates.

Before diving into the math behind Usage Rate, turn back to Table 5.3 where we can see Usage Rate next to PER. From the table, we can see that Harden has a much higher Usage Rate than Antetokounmpo, indicating he plays a bigger role on his team. And indeed, whereas Antetokounmpo took 17 shots per game, Harden took nearly 25, nearly 50% more. In some sense, PER accounts for this already—it performs possession weighting—however, Usage Rate suggests that Harden has a heavier burden on each of his possessions than Antetokounmpo has on his. Thus, even though their performances are comparable, Antetokounmpo is doing so under better circumstances. Would Antetokounmpo be able to sustain his highly efficient play if asked to take a step up in importance to his team? In many ways, that line of thinking is an explanation for why Milwaukee has, to date, had lackluster postseason performances: Antetokounmpo performs well in the more casual regular season, but is unable to truly take over a game in the playoffs.

To calculate Usage Rate—an approximation of the percentage of a team's plays "used" by a player when they are on the floor—we take the number of field goals, free throws, and turnovers a player accumulates, multiplied by one-fifth the team's minutes played, and divide that by the player's minutes played times the same quantity for the team. The formula for this is shown below.

$$Usg\% = \frac{(FGA + .44 \times FTA + TOV) \times MP_{TM}/5}{MP \times (FGA_{TM} + .44 \times FTA_{TM} + TOV_{TM})}$$

You will notice similarities between the calculations here and the formula for True Shooting Percentage. The key addition here is turnovers. We are not concerned with turnovers for True Shooting Percentage because we can easily imagine a great shooter who just happens to be clumsy with the ball. Usage Rate, however, measures the number of possessions that end with the ball coming out of a player's hands—turnovers matter.

To take a look at Usage Rate in action, let's examine Kobe Bryant's Usage Rate across his 2008 MVP season. We will look at his game by game usage rate and true shooting percentage. This will give us an idea of how Kobe's shooting performances changed as his shot volume increased. In order to do this, we will transcribe the algorithm above into R and apply it to a data frame containing Kobe's statistics as well as Laker team statistics.

```
calculate.usg <- function(mp,fga,fta,tov,mp.t,fga.t,fta.t,tov.t){
  num <- (fga+.44*fta+tov)*(mp.t/5)
  denom <- (fga.t+.44*fta.t+tov.t) * mp
  return(num/denom)
}


kobe.2008$usg <- with(kobe.2008,
  calculate.usg(MP,FGA,FTA,TOV,
             MP.TM,FGA.TM,FTA.TM,TOV.TM)
)


kobe.2008$tsp <- calculate.tsp(kobe.2008$PTS,
                          kobe.2008$FGA,
                          kobe.2008$FTA)


plot(kobe.2008$usg, kobe.2008$tsp)
cor(kobe.2008$usg, kobe.2008$tsp)
# -0.1353705
```

LISTING 5.9 2008 Kobe Bryant by game TS% and Usage Rate

You will note from this analysis that the correlation between Kobe's Usage Rate and True Shooting Percentage is negative, suggesting that the more he shoots, the worse he shoots (Listing 5.9). This is, largely, to be expected. And when we examine the graph of Kobe's performances, in Figure 5.2, we see that his very best performances are all (relatively) low Usage Rate performances. That said, what made Kobe special is that even with a Usage Rate above 30% he was still able to achieve a TS% over 60% regularly, turning in great shooting performances despite being the center of his team's offense.

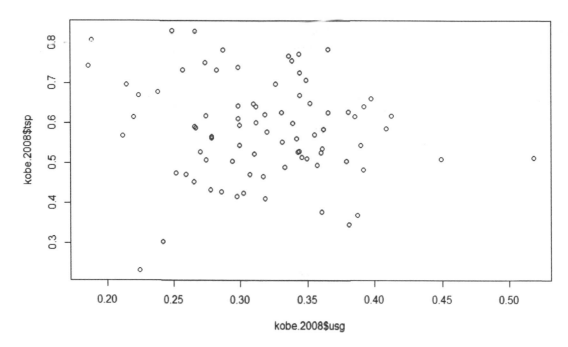

FIGURE 5.2. Kobe Bryant 2008 usage rate and TS%

You will note from this analysis that the correlation between Kobe's Usage Rate and True Shooting Percentage is negative, suggesting that the more he shoots, the worse he shoots. This is, largely, to be expected. And when we examine the graph of Kobe's performances, in Figure 5.2, we see that his very best performances are all (relatively) low Usage Rate performances. That said, what made Kobe special is that even with a Usage Rate above 30% he was still able to achieve a TS% over 60% regularly, turning in great shooting performances despite being the center of his team's offense.

Summary

In this chapter, we reviewed metrics for analyzing hockey and basketball: two similar games that share many of the same principles. Indeed, many of the metrics that we discussed in the hockey sections, such as plus-minus and adjusted plus-minus, can be used in basketball as well. Specific to hockey there are statistics like the Corsi metric, which give players credit for the shot ratio while they are on the ice. Specific to basketball, there are enhanced shooting metrics, like eFG% and TS%, comprehensive metrics like Player Efficiency Rating, and player centrality metrics like Usage Rate. Additionally, we looked at how many of these metrics can be calculated in R and saw examples of the metrics used in analysis.

Key Terms

Plus-minus

Corsi statistic

Hockey assist

JSON

Design matrix

Teamwork

Corsi Rate

Corsi Percent

Adjusted plus-minus

Ridge regression

True Shooting Percentage

Effective FIeld Goal Percentage

Player Efficiency Rating

Efficiency

Usage Rate

Critical Thinking Exercises

1. Hockey and basketball are different sports, but a lot of the methods to analyze them can be shared across sports, in particular, plus/minus and adjusted plus-minus are useful in both. What is it about the two sports that make them amenable to the same analysis?

2. In hockey, we focus on shots and shot differential, while in basketball we focus on point differential. Why do we want to focus on shot differential in hockey? Why do we focus on point differential in basketball?

3. In hockey, we find ourselves facing unusual situations with some regularity. Possessions can start in different places on the court and teams can field different numbers of skaters due to power plays or pulled goalies. How might a player being on an offensive power play specialty unit affect their statistics? How might a player being on a defensive power play specialty unit affect their statistics? How might we adjust for these differences?

4. In basketball, increased three-point shot accuracy has revolutionized the game, however, even the best three-point shooters such as Steph Curry still have lower TS% than the top centers. Why then has three-point shooting been so influential? How may the relationship between TS% and Usage Rate contribute to this effect?
5. Advanced plus-minus is preferred over even the most advanced box score metrics. Why do we need a metric like advanced plus-minus for basketball and hockey, when we can readily rely on box score metrics in baseball?

References

Harrell Jr, Frank E. 2015. *Regression modeling strategies: With applications to linear models, logistic and ordinal regression, and survival analysis.* Switzerland: Springer.

Ilardi, Steve, and Aaron Barzilai. 2008. *Adjusted plus-minus ratings: New and improved for 2007-2008. 82 Games.* http://82games.com/ilardi2.htm

Macdonald, Brian. 2011. A regression-based adjusted plus-minus statistic for NHL players. *Journal of Quantitative Analysis in Sports* 7(3). doi:10.2202/1559-0410.1284

Macdonald, Brian. 2012. Adjusted plus-minus for NHL players using ridge regression with goals, shots, fenwick, and corsi. *Journal of Quantitative Analysis in Sports* 8(3), 1–24.

CHAPTER 6

Football and Sport Analytics

J.T. Wolohan

LEARNING OBJECTIVES

After reading this chapter, students should be able to:

- Define and describe the traditional metrics for measuring football performances.
- Identify the problems and gaps with football's box score metrics.
- Identify how advanced metrics such as WPA and EPA address these problems.
- Define and describe how WPA and EPA measure player performance.
- Compare and contrast the DVOA, WPA, and EPA metrics.
- Gather and analyze NFL play-by-play data with R.

Introduction

Football is America's favorite sport and, more than that, American's favorite thing to watch on TV. The Super Bowl can dependably be expected to record the greatest number of viewers of any TV program in any given year. The College Football Championship can, likewise, be counted on to place in the top 10, alongside a host of NFL playoff matchups and Sunday night football games. Perhaps relatedly, football is also America's most heavily bet sport. More than 25-million Americans place bets on the Super Bowl alone, totaling over $5 billion. This is to say nothing of the money that is bet during the season or the money bet illegally—according to the American Gaming Association, 38-million Americans bet on the NFL throughout the year—or money wagered on fantasy sport leagues. Fantasy Football is estimated to have a market size of around $19 billion, a number that is actually greater than the $15 billion in revenue generated in 2019 by the NFL.

Naturally, this interest in football has brought analytics into the game of football. Unlike other sports, however, football has been surprisingly resilient to the impact of advanced metrics. This has been for a variety of reasons, but chief among them is the trouble of measuring the wide variety of things that can account for the success or failure of any play. Unlike baseball—which is broken up into isolated, repeated duels between pitcher and batter—or hockey and basketball—which are back-and-forth small team efforts—football is a series of repeated plays drawn up by coaches who are engaged in a highly violent form of chess and executed by 22 of the world's most physically gifted athletes each play. For any given football game, each team's coach might have up to 200 offensive plays to select from; fewer than a third will see use in a game, which consists of between 60 and 80 offensive snaps for each team on average.

That said, there have been many attempts at measuring performance in football, and those attempts have evolved over the years. In this chapter, we will examine some of those attempts. We will begin with some of the traditional measures for assessing the performance of football players and teams; many of these metrics are still widely used in fantasy sports. Then, we will look at some of the advanced metrics. You will recognize many of the ideas behind these metrics from the ideas present in the previous chapters: assess performance not by what happens, but by comparing what happens to what is expected to happen and its impact on the game. Lastly, we will review some of the metrics used in football betting—as it is an increasingly important part of the business of football.

Box Score Metrics for Football

Much like the other sports we have looked at so far, football has a variety of traditional counting or box score metrics. These are the simple metrics one can come by from watching the game and tallying what happens. Unfortunately for football, these metrics matter much less than in other sports. In baseball, the nature of the game makes it such that we can count what matters. In basketball and hockey, the collaborative nature of the sports make the connection between player performance and winning less strict; however, we can still generally trust that players who are scoring lots of points or netting lots of goals are advantageous to have on the team—even if we are not quite certain how good they are relative to other high-performers. In football, even this goes out the window.

Consider, for example, a quarterback whose team is always behind. The team's coach is going to call more passing plays, leading to the quarterback throwing the ball more often, leading to the quarterback recording more completions, yards, and—in all likelihood—touchdowns. This fact is compounded by the fact that teams that are losing by multiple touchdowns at the end of the game face what is known as a "prevent defense." These defenses are designed to allow lots of small plays and force the offense to use up a lot of time. The result is that a lazy offense can compile a lot of yards, and even points, without coming anywhere close to winning the game. The yards acquired in this way will also typically be passing yards. And therein lies the problem of football statistics: how do we differentiate between a good quarterback—one who makes plays for his team and can uniquely lead them to victory—versus a quarterback who's box score metrics are simply bolstered by a bad defense or aggressive play calling?

Setting that question aside for the moment, it is important to discuss the traditional box score metrics of football if for no other reason than that they are widely used in evaluating fantasy football matchups. As noted earlier, fantasy football is a multi-billion-dollar industry with a market size greater than the revenue of the NFL itself. Whatever problems we have with the metrics as player and team evaluation tools, we should understand them. In football, box score metrics are broken down along four categories: passing metrics, rushing metrics, receiving metrics, and defensive metrics.

The passing metrics are the metrics most strongly associated with quarterbacks. Given that the quarterback is the most important player on the field, these metrics are often the most highly scrutinized. But as noted earlier in this section, applying strict scrutiny to the quarterback metrics may not be wise—there is too much that can be hidden between game conditions and play calling. That all said, the prime box score metrics that one will look at when evaluating passing are: number of touchdown passes, passing yards, and completion percentage. In fantasy sports, touchdown passes and passing yards are going to be the most important metrics. Completion percentage is an acceptable proxy for passing accuracy, which is what it attempts to measure; however, we should be aware that pass play design, receiver skill, and pass selection will play heavily into completion percentage. The high completion percentage plays, such as bubble screens and even variations of the jet sweep—traditionally understood as a running play, involving a wide receiver taking a handoff following a pre-snap motion—can artificially inflate a quarterback's completion percentage.

Because of the importance of passing the football, the attention paid to quarterbacks, and the difficulty of measuring their impact, there are also two additional box score metrics used to rate quarterbacks: passer rating, the statistic used by the National Football League; and passer efficiency, the statistic used in college football. Both measures attempt to do the same thing: count what a quarterback does and boil it down to a single number. In general, these metrics behave in the ways you would expect. Long completions that result in touchdowns will increase the ratings, incompletions and interceptions decrease the ratings, but whether they accurately reflect quarterback performance as implemented is certainly debatable. Both metrics—passer rating and passer efficiency—rely on five measures: passing yards, passing touchdowns, passing completions, interceptions, and pass attempts. College football's passer efficiency system is a simple linear weighting of the first four measures—passing yards, passing touchdowns, passing completions, and interceptions—divided by the number of pass attempts. The NFL's passer rating attempts to establish baseline levels of performance before doing the same thing.

To discuss the two metrics, it is helpful to look at the code in R, shown below. We will discuss passer efficiency first because it is simpler and then discuss passer rating. Passer efficiency is, as noted, a set of linear weights applied to the metrics yards, touchdowns, completions, and interceptions all over the number of attempts. Yards, touchdowns, and completions have positive weights of 8.4, 330, and 100, respectively. Interceptions have a negative weight of 200. A drawback of the passer efficiency rating is that it has somewhat nonsensical bounds, with a lower bound in the negative 700s and an upper bound in the thousands. In practice, college quarterback ratings will be capped somewhere in the 200s.

```
# NCAA Passer Efficiency
passer.efficiency <- function(yards, tds, cmp, ints, att){
  efficiency.rating <- (8.4*yards+330*tds+100*cmp-200*ints)/att
  return(efficiency.rating)
}
```

The NFL passer rating remedies these drawbacks of the college passer efficiency score by bounding the components of their rating, creating a stable score that can range from a worst-case 0 to best-possible 158.3. Each component of the rating—which assess yards per attempt, touchdowns per attempt, and completions per attempt—versus a "league average" value—can vary between 0 and 2.375. The sum of those four ratings is then divided by 6 and multiplied by 100.

```
# NFL Passer Rating
bound.term <- function(x){
  if(x>2.375){return(2.375)}
  if(x<0){return(0)}
  return(x)
}

passer.rating <- function(yards, tds, cmp, ints, att){
  y.rtg <- bound.term((yards/att-3)*0.25)
  t.rtg <- bound.term((td/att)*20)
  c.rtg <- bound.term((cmp/att-0.3)*5)
  ints  <- bound.term(2.375 - (ints/att)*25)
  rating <- ((y.rtg + t.rtg + c.rtg + i.rtg)/6)*100
  return(rating)
}
```

LISTING 6.1 Calculating Passer Rating in R

Both passer ratings face much the same argument that all the box score metrics in football face: they are too simple of a measure. An analytical reader might notice some similarities between these approaches and the idea behind weighted on base average in baseball. The key distinction, of course, being that weighted on base average's linear weights were arrived at through empirical means directly associated with a critical game outcome: runs scored. Passer rating is based in empirical data from the 1960s; however, because the metrics designers—Don Smith of the Pro Football Hall of Fame and Seymour Siwoff of Elias Sports Bureau—were using the box score statistics as their starting point, the flaws in these metrics inevitably permeate the passer rating and passer efficiency metrics.

Moving on to rushing metrics, the statistics most commonly used to assess running backs, the numerical picture becomes much simpler. For running backs, we are primarily concerned with how often they run the ball (carries), how many yards they get when they run the ball (yards), how many yards they get per run (yards per carry), and any touchdowns or fumbles they make while running. To a degree, these metrics can reflect the skill of a runner; however, they are heavily influenced by play calling, the strength of the blockers, and strength of other aspects of the offense, and situation. For example, Mike Shanahan, Super Bowl winning coach of the Denver Broncos, had six running backs run for more than 1,000 yards in his 14-year tenure as head coach of the Broncos. This was due in large part to Shanahan's scheme and his reputable offensive line.

Increasingly, rushing statistics are also becoming a way to capture a quarterback's contribution to the game. For example, in 2019, Lamar Jackson led his team in rushing, recording more than 1,200 yards on the ground while averaging nearly 7 yards per carry. The value of quarterbacks running yards should, however, be understood differently than the value of running back running yards. The rushing yards and carry numbers for running backs are typically reflective of play calling. The head coach needs to call plays—or the quarterback needs to audible into plays—which results in the back being handed the ball. In contrast, quarterback running yards will typically happen on "broken plays," plays that have gone off script, or scrambles. More coaches are scripting designed quarterback running plays as quarterbacks prove themselves capable athletes; however, the volume of these runs for the average running quarterback will be between 5 and 10 a game, or between 1/16th and 1/6th of the total plays. A running back may carry the ball between 15 and 30 times per game—between 1/5th and one-half of the total plays.

The third category of metrics—receiving metrics—is the dominant statistic for wide receivers and tight ends; however, some running backs accumulate a meaningful portion of their total yardage from catching passes as well. Receiving metrics are our way of recording who catches passes and what happens when they catch those passes. There are six standard receiving metrics: yards, receptions, touchdowns, targets, and yards after catch. Yards, receptions, and touchdowns should all be somewhat familiar from their parallels in the rushing world. Yards is the total number of yards gained on plays where the player catches the ball; receptions is the total number of times a receiver catches the ball; touchdowns is the total number of touchdowns a player scores after catching a pass.

The additional two metrics, targets and yards after catch, do not have parallels in the rushing world. Targets is the number of times a pass was intended for the receiver but the receiver did not make the catch. This statistic is strongly related to another metric: drops; however, the definition of a drop—much like an error in baseball—is fuzzier and less likely to be found in most box scores. Targets, unlike drops, also gives us a sense of how the team was hoping to use a player. If a player received 12 targets, that might mean that getting a specific receiver the ball was up to 20% of a team's game plan. Targets can be a good indication for fantasy players which receivers will be consistent performers and which will be inconsistent; a stretch of high-target games likely means a team is comfortable including that player in their game plan.

Yards after the catch, lastly, is a metric that attempts to measure the receiver's post-catch contribution to the offense. While the primary way most receivers contribute to the offense is by running routes and catch passes, they can also contribute by running with the ball and evading defenders. This is an increasingly important metric in the age of spread offenses, bubble screens, and other short-route passing attacks. Because the yards after catch metric favors players who are likely to catch the ball in space, it does slightly favor running backs and tight ends, who are more likely to catch the ball in the flat away from defenders—in the case of running backs—or in the center of the field between the linebackers and safeties—in the case of tight ends.

In addition to offensive metrics, there are also several defensive metrics. The defensive metrics are, among all the crude box score metrics, the crudest of the lot. Defense in the NFL is decidedly a team activity. Even for supposedly individual statistics such as sacks or interceptions, it is not hard to imagine (common) circumstances where one player causes the event that is ultimately recorded for another. Consider a pash rush situation where a defensive tackle forces the quarterback to roll to their right—directly into the arms of a defensive end. The defensive end gets credit with the sack, but it was the defensive tackle who created the initial pressure. Or imagine that the quarterback throws the ball haphazardly down field in an attempt to evade the sack and the ball finds its way into the ready hands of a free safety. We will credit the safety with the interception, but was it not the defensive tackle who precipitated it in the first place? Over careers, defensive statistics such as tackles, sacks, and interceptions can have some meaning—but even then it is not clear. After all, exceptional corners interceptions will drop dramatically after their breakout year because teams wise up to the fact that the corner is a talented ball hawk; they will elect to throw the ball to the other side of the field. Likewise, elite pass rushers will begin to face double teams and stunt blocks, helping their teammates pressure and sack the quarterback, but harming their own numbers.

That said, there are four metrics that will commonly be associated with defensive players: tackles, sacks, forced fumbles, and interceptions. Tackles and sacks are recorded when a defensive player tackles the ball carrier and, in the special case of a sack, when that ball carrier is the quarterback behind the line of scrimmage. Forced fumbles and interceptions are both turnover-related metrics. Forced fumbles are recorded when a defensive player knocks the ball from the hands of an offensive player in a situation where either team may recover the football. The forced fumble occurs regardless of which team recovers the ball. That is, the player will still be credited with a forced fumble if they knock the ball loose from the running back's hands and one of the offensive linemen recovers the fumble. Interceptions occur when a defensive player catches a pass.

As noted, the box score metrics in football remain important largely because of their connection with fantasy football. Fantasy football games are decided based on players' performances, as measured by these traditional box score metrics. In fantasy sports, it is not relevant whether or not a running back's 125 yards helped their team win or if a quarterback's four touchdowns came in garbage time when the defense was resting. In fantasy sports, what matters is the total a player records. This creates a misshapen view of the game for fantasy owners, who can end up over valuing players who do not contribute to their team's success but still record big numbers.

An example of this type of player can be seen in Maurice Jones-Drew. Jones-Drew was a running back for the Jacksonville Jaguars for 7 years and a 3-time Pro Bowler. Over this time, Jones-Drew was consistently a top-10 fantasy running back, but his Jacksonville Jaguars had very little success. Does this make Jones-Drew's performances a success? Certainly, he was successful if your metric is "would he help my fantasy team?"; however, in Jones-Drew's best year—2011, when he led the league in rushing—the Jaguars won only 5 games and fired their coach mid-way through the season. (For more on fantasy sports, see Chapter 15).

Advanced Metrics for Football

In the previous section, we reviewed the box score metrics for football and noted the many drawbacks of them. In this section, we will look at the advanced metrics, the ways that those metrics attempt to resolve the drawbacks of traditional box score metrics, and how those metrics work. We will begin by covering a variety of simpler metrics that we can think of as slightly smarter variations of the traditional box score metrics, i.e., things we would want to include in a box score but might be too complex or nuanced. Then we will move on to a series of value metrics: Expected Points Added, Win Probability Added, and—the current holy grail of football analytics—defense-adjusted value over average.

The first two advanced metrics we will look at are passing metrics: air yards and air yards per attempt. Air yards is defined as the number of yards the ball travels in the air during a receiving play. If you remember the yards after catch statistic from the previous section, air yards can be defined as air yards = total yards - yards after catch. Air yards per attempt is this number divided by the number of attempted throws by a quarterback. This number might seem trivial, but it is actually a strong indicator of quarterback performance for two reasons: player caller trust and quarterback aggression.

The first reason this metric is useful is the same as the reason we should be so skeptical of many of the other passing metrics: situation and play calling matter. Air yards is a metric that can only be improved by quarterbacks making risky, downfield throws. In this way, air yards is an indicator of the trust an offensive staff has in their quarterback's play. And while teams can be mistaken about the amount of talent on their team, most play callers are generally attempting to get the best results; the game—and their jobs—depend on them doing so. For this reason, a quarterback who has a high air yards per attempt should be thought of as, at least, a trusted quarterback. These players are at least a step above the "game manager" type of quarterback who is capable of holding on to a win, but not contributing to one.

Second, air yards are indicative of quarterback aggression and the possibility for chunk plays. One of the key strategies in defensive football is to extend offensive drives. If the defensive can make the offense run a lot of plays, they increase the likelihood of the offense hurting themselves by committing a penalty or their own likelihood of an exceptional play, such as a sack or an interception. These plays can put the offense "behind the chains," in situations where they are unlikely to convert the first down. Passers who are aggressive and can win large chunks of yardage for their team in a single play can bypass this defensive strategy. These chunk plays are especially predictive of scoring drives for that reason.

Further, there is yet another air yards metric—intended air yards—that doubles down on this idea that a quarterback's willingness to throw the ball downfield and a coach's willingness to call such plays matters. Intended air yards is the total number of air yards a quarterback would have from their passes regardless of if those passes were completed or not. This metric measures how aggressive a quarterback is over a season. The average variant of this metric, intended air yards per attempt, measures how aggressive a quarterback's average throw is. An excellent example of how this metric can change under different circumstances is with Tom Brady's movement from the New England Patriots to the Tampa Bay Buccaneers. With the Patriots in 2019 to 2020, Brady had 7.6 intended air yards per attempt; with the Buccaneers the following season, Brady averaged 9.1 intended air yards per attempt. Meanwhile, Brady's average yards per attempt, total yards, and touchdowns also increased. The change in scheme—from a more conservative scheme to a more aggressive scheme—as we can see from the intended air yards, is one reason that football commentators speculated Brady might have left New England.

The air yards metrics are, in many ways, a heuristic for measuring the coaching staff's confidence in their player more than they are measuring the ability of the player themselves. After all, many quarterbacks simply will not be put in positions to throw the ball down the field. That this is useful shows the intricacy of football as a game and the challenges we face with developing analytics in it. In no other sport would we attempt to measure a coach's like for a player. Indeed, in baseball, we tend to think that coaches fundamentally misunderstand how to use their players and that players succeed on their own merits, potentially despite poor situational decision-making by coaches. In football, it is nearly impossible to parse player performance, play calling, and team composition apart.

That said, there are two ways that we can attempt to parse out player performance: Expected Points Added and Win Probability Added. These two metrics are related in their calculation and theory, though slightly different in their application. Expected Points Added attempts to measure the offensive contribution of individual players by taking the difference of the amount of points an offensive player contributed to their team, by comparing observed points accumulated in situations in which that player was involved against the expected points a generic team would have accumulated. Win Probability Added is similar except, instead of points, we use win probability—the likelihood of the team winning the game—and instead of only awarding players who touched the ball as we do in Expected Points Added, we reward every player on the field.

EXPECTED POINTS ADDED

Expected Points Added is football's parallel to baseball's weighted on-base average. The idea is the same: for each situation where an offensive player touches the ball, there exists an expected number of points that the team should earn. For example, on 1st and goal from the 1 yard line, this number might be 6.8 points. For 2nd and 15 with 85 yards to go, this number might be closer to 1. After each play, there will be a new situation and a new expected number of points. For instance, we might imagine the 2nd and 15 becomes a 3rd and 1 with 71 yards to go; that might have an expected value of 2 points. We would credit the players involved in that play—let's say it was a run for simplicity, so just the running back—with a positive 1 point of Expected Points Added. And we would do this for every offensive player and every play, over the course of the season.

Of course, this relies on understanding the expected points from any given situation. And this is calculated much the same way it is for wOBA baseball; the only difference is that there are many more situations. Using historical NFL play-by-play data, we can constitute a table of situations and expected point values for every situation we would like to consider. Different calculations of expected points average will vary in how exactly they do this, just like different formulations of wOBA will use different linear weights. For instance, we may decide to chunk up the field into 10-yard segments instead of considering each yard as its own unique situation. This would create some strange anomalies in our data—for example, having the ball on the 29 would be treated the same as having the ball on the 21, while having the ball on the 19 would be treated differently than having the ball on the 21—however, many of these abstractions are innocent enough to be justifiable to increase the sample size. Traditionally, expected points will include down, yards to go, field position, and may include other variables such as time remaining and score differential.

Expected Points Added is, in many ways, a very straightforward metric. Higher numbers are better and typically we will only want to compare within position groups. For instance, it is probably not fair to compare wide receivers and running backs; the two positions are asked to play different roles. Running backs are expected to provide a foundation of yards and receivers are expected to stretch the field and gain yards in large chunk plays. Receivers should have higher Expected Points Added per play but running backs should have higher cumulative Expected Points Added because they are involved in more plays. Of course, this will not be true for all receivers and all running backs.

Naturally, elite quarterbacks—who touch the ball the most and where there is arguably the largest gap between the best players and the worst players—will have the greatest cumulative EPA numbers. Good quarterbacks may be worth more than 80 points to their team, as measured by EPA, and a great quarterback may be worth more than 100 points. In Patrick Mahomes' 2018 MVP season, he was worth more than 125 points to the Kansas City Chiefs, as determined by EPA. That accounts for almost all of the point differential between the Chiefs and their opponents, who the Chiefs managed to outscore by 144 points.

WIN PROBABILITY ADDED

Win Probability Added is at once a more sophisticated and more crude measure than Expected Points Added. In a sense, it is more sophisticated because Win Probability Added measures something more abstract—a team's probability of winning the game—and almost always includes variables that are optional in EPA—namely time remaining and score. In another sense, it is more crude because whereas expected points average is applied only to players who touch the ball on a given play, Win Probability Added is applied to every player who was on the field during a play. This makes it harder to distinguish between good players and players on good units—though the hope is that over time this smooths out.

To take a look at how Win Probability Added is calculated, let's consider it for a player, say a passing rushing specialist who plays predominantly on passing downs. The player comes in a 2nd and long play, on the first series of the game, when the score is tied at zero. The two teams are evenly matched, so the win probability at the start of the play is 50%. The player beats a double team and sacks the quarterback deep in the backfield setting up a 3rd and 14. Still early in the game and a tie score, the win probability on this next play is 50.1%. The player gets a 0.1% added to their Win Probability Added. Late in the game, that same player comes in when their opponent is driving, a critical 3rd and 4 with a minute remaining on the clock and down by 3 points—winning percentage 70%. This time, the player bursts through the line unblocked, only to be flattened by a pulling guard from the other side of the line. The opponents running back skips into the secondary where they are met head on by a safety, who forces a fumble that the defense recovers! With the turnover, the team's winning percentage is not 99% and the player gets a 29 percentage points added to their Win Probability Added.

At first glance, this might seem like a strange metric for a few reasons. First, it is clear that in the first situation—the sack—the pass rusher was more influential than in the second—the fumble caused by the safety; however, the pass rusher gets far more credit for their contribution on the second play than the first. How can this make sense? Over a season, a defensive starter may play close to 1,000 snaps and a specialist may play 300 to 500 snaps. With sample sizes this large, we do not need our measurements to be perfect—so long as they are accurate and consistent we can use them to make meaningful judgments. Over the course of a season, we expect all players to be in enough plays where their teammates make something good happen without their involvement at all that the resulting Win Probability Added reflects their contribution.

Second, it is entirely possible for players to do good things on plays where the outcome is bad from a win percentage perspective. Imagine a safety that makes a critical open field tackle after a completion deep down field. Would the play have been better if the safety missed the tackle? Certainly not. But they will still be punished because of the deep completion. To get around this, we will sometimes use a metric called Positive Win Probability Added. Positive Win Probability Added is similar to Win Probability Added except, as the name suggests, we only consider the positive changes in Win Probability. So, players are only getting credit for the good that they do, while not (necessarily) being punished for the bad that they do. Of course, because we are either using a cumulative or a per snap version of these metrics, negative results—which are given a 0 Win Probability Added—are still counting against the player, simply not as much as they might otherwise.

As you might have picked up on from the examples, Win Probability Added and positive Win Probability Added are both metrics that we tend to prefer for defensive players—though they certainly make sense for offensive players as well. For offensive players—especially skill position players—we will tend to prefer Expected Points Added because it is simple for us to rationalize only crediting the players who touch the ball with the outcome of the play. In contrast, because defense has far fewer effective individual metrics, we are a lot less picky about the metrics we do have to evaluate defensive players. Because our points of comparison are exceptionally crude measures like sacks or interceptions, Win Probability Added makes an excellent metric for defensive players.

Defense-Adjusted Value Over Average (DVOA)

If we think about Expected Points Added and Win Probability Added as the Weighted On-Base Average for football, then DVOA—**Defense-Adjusted Value Over Average**—is the Wins Above Replacement for football. DVOA takes the core ideas from Win Probability Added—that each player should get credit for their performance on a play based on how much it contributes to their team's likelihood of winning—and combines it with the fundamental observation from WAR—that a baseline player would have done *something* and sometimes that something will even be a good thing. In order to understand how good a player is, we should only be giving them credit for the things they do that an average player would not do.

Consider seven-time Super Bowl winner Tom Brady. Brady has a reputation as a quarterback sneak specialist. When it is feet to go for either a first down or a touchdown, Brady has an excellent conversion rate. But how should we incorporate this into our overall understanding of the value Tom Brady brings to a team? First, and foremost, these situations tend to be low frequency, so while being good at the quarterback sneak is certainly of some benefit, it is not the first trait that one would look for when selecting quarterbacks. Second, the situations in which Brady is sneaking are high-conversion percentage plays. Brady might convert a 75% play at a 95% rate, in which case he should be given credit for the 25% of conversions he is making that a replacement player is not making—but we do not want to reward Brady for the 75% of plays that any competent NFL quarterback could make. In contrast, one of the areas where Brady—and most good quarterbacks—succeed relative to their peers is on third down. Third down conversions are critical because they keep the drive alive and prevent the opponent from having a chance to score. If Brady does only slightly better than his peers on third down—say 2 to 3%—this can have a massive effect on his value over the course of a game (10-15 third downs), a season (150-250 third downs), or a career (several thousands of third downs). What is more is that because these third down plays are highly valuable, every success will have a relatively large impact on the outcome of a game versus a standard play. That said, we would still not want to give Brady credit for *every* third down. Again, even the most average NFL quarterback will complete some percentage (about 40%) of third downs.

To this end, we can use DVOA. DVOA is largely considered the best available metric in advanced analytics of football. Produced authoritatively by Football Outsiders (2021), a sport analytics and media company, DVOA is a metric that we can apply to any number of football entities worth analyzing including units—offense, defense, special teams—and skill-position players. Football Outsider's write that in many ways, DVOA is a counter-metric to the traditional metrics which, while flawed for a number of reasons, are incredibly popular with (and important to) the fantasy-football playing fanbase.

Across all the entities we might want to apply DVOA to, the metric is calculated in more or less the same fashion. Simply, we are finding the expected degree and rate of success for a situation and contrasting that with observed performances. To do this, DVOA includes a number of factors: many of the aspects we were already considering for Expected Points Added and Win Probability Added, such as down, distance, field position, and time, but new measures as well, such as strength of opponent. Further, Football Outsider's DVOA metric uses some semi-statistical heuristics to tailor the metric, such as red-zone and touchdown bonuses. These bonuses allow Football Outsider's to reward teams and players for their performance in the areas of the game that matter most—scoring points—even if there is a dash of art to their construction of this metric.

For practical purposes, we cannot work through a full DVOA example in this chapter—as desirable as that may be—however, we can review some pseudo-code that represents that computations that would be involved in a DVOA calculation. This will allow us to discuss, in specific, the considerations of DVOA. And, if you would like to download and parse the NFL's play-by-play data, you should be able to modify the pseudo-code that follows to derive your own DVOA metrics.

Zoomed out, there are four broad steps to calculating DVOA. First, we need to parse the game logs into the data we want to use for DVOA. Second, we need to find the number of "**success points**" earned on each play (every DVOA calculation will use a proprietary blend of factors here and differ slightly). Third, we will find the expected success points per play based on our data and the average observed results. We can do this either by literal averaging or through regression-based approaches; a combination of the two is most likely to be the best in practice. Fourth, we will find the success points accumulated by the players or units under investigation and compare those with the expected results; we will typically represent the results as a cumulative value—that can be interpreted as "number of successful plays a player created versus a replacement player"—or a percentage value—that can be interpreted as "increase in success likelihood over a replacement player."

To access and parse NFL game logs, we are most likely to want to use the NFL's play-by-play API. The NFL's API provides access to semi-structured play-by-play data in JSON format and much of the information we will want has, very conveniently, already been parsed for us. We can see a subset of the data that the NFL provides us below.

```
{
  "id": "c6d7b2bb-7f2a-42ac-86a8-d4f80612c165",
  "orderSequence": 12,
  "game": {
    "id": "f82cc9dd-e5bc-49c1-8ae4-fd78a7acad51"
  },
  "drive": {
    "id": "1a4a11cd-4295-48a8-a0db-c318faddb91e"
  },
  "quarter": 1,
  "possessionTeam": {
    "id": "d9a98a6a-6955-46c7-a67f-b37c2bf1673f"
  },
  "down": 4,
  "yards": 11,
  "playType": "PLAY",
  "gameClockStartTime": "14:51",
  "gameClockAtSnap": "14:51",
  "gameClockEndTime": "13:59",
  "playClockDuration": 40,
  "playClockStop": 15,
  "isGameClockActiveAfterPlay": true,
  "description": "(:09) (Shotgun) 12-A.Rodgers pass long right to
18-R.Cobb for 53 yards, ...",
  "yardsToGo": 10,
  "isGoalToGo": false,
  "yardLineSideTeam": {
    "id": "d9a98a6a-6955-46c7-a67f-b37c2bf1673f"
  },
  "yardLineNumber": 25,
}
```

LISTING 6.2. JSON representation of an NFL play.

In R, the most convenient way we will have to work with this data is through the nflfastR library. This is a library specifically for working with NFL play-by-play data. We can use it to query the NFL API and manage the results. To see this in action, let us use the library to query a play from the 2017 Ravens at Steelers game. First, we will need to install nflfastR and load it. Then, let's retrieve the full 2017 schedule with the fast_scraper_schedules function. This gets all the games from 2017 and gives us the ID for each. We will need the game IDs to query game play-by-play. You will also note that having the game IDs for a single season would allow us to easily process an entire season's worth of data if we developed a means of converting game IDs into sequences of play condition-success points pairings. Then, for our toy example, we can find all of Baltimore's away games. We will then use the ID for the Baltimore–Pittsburgh matchup and scrape that game's data with the fast_scraper function. This loads each play of the game into a data frame-like structure for us. You can see below that we can query any play of the game by looking up the play number. Below, we look up the 53rd play of the game: a successful completion by Ravens' quarterback Joe Flacco.

```
install.packages("nflfastR")
library('nflfastR')

schedule <- fast_scraper_schedules(2017)
schedule[which(schedule$away_team=="BAL"),]$game_id
game_data <- fast_scraper(game_id="2017_14_BAL_PIT")

game_data[53,]
game_data[53,]$desc
# "(11:04) 5-J.Flacco pass short right to 37-J.Allen pushed ob at PIT
41 for 20 yards (98-V.Williams) [90-T.Watt]."
```

LISTING 6.3. Interacting with NFL play data using nflfastR

Each game data entry also has much of the necessary play-by-play metadata associated with each play description. For instance, yardline_100 shows how far to the goal line the team started and yrdstogo contains the number of yards needed for a first down.

With this data in hand, we would want to come up with a success points equation. As noted previously, this algorithm likely implements heuristics based on historical observations. For example, the folks at Football Outsiders refer to the 40/60/first-down rule proposed in The Hidden Game of Football as one such heuristic. This rule proposes that a first-down play is successful if it gains 40% of the yards needed for a first down; a second-down play is successful if it gains 60% of the yards needed for a first down; and a third-down play is successful if it gains a first down. We could implement this heuristic in R as follows.

```
simple.succes <- function(play){
 if(play$down==1){
   if(play$yards_gained >= .4*play$ydstogo){
     return(1)
   } else return(0)
 }
 else if(play$down==2){
   if(play$yards_gained >= .6*play$ydstogo){
     return(1)
   } else return(0)
 }
 else if(play$down==3){
   if(play$yards_gained >= play$ydstogo){
     return(1)
   } else return(0)
 }
}
```

LISTING 6.4. A simple NFL play-success function in R.

You will note that we take in a play—a line the data-frame-like structure returned by the nflfastR library—and output 1s and 0s depending on whether or not the play was a success, implementing the simple heuristic above. We would want to, of course, come up with a more nuanced version of this approach if we were implementing DVOA in earnest. For example, losses of yards may result in negative success. Touchdowns or large gains in yards may result in successes greater than 1.

With this algorithm in hand, we would then apply it to every play for the season. You already know how to do this because we have used the apply-family of functions throughout this book for largely this same purpose. Because our data is in a data frame, we will want to use the mapply variation of apply. Remember that we will have to either modify our scoring algorithm to use positional calls to data—instead of labeled calls—or parameterized calls. In the case below, we have opted to parameterize the variables we are interested in using for our play-success algorithm.

```
plays <- game_data[which(is.na(game_data$down)==F),]
mapply(simple.succes, plays$down, plays$ydstogo, plays$yards_gained)
```

For a simple analysis, we might look at how successful Baltimore and Pittsburgh were respectively. For instance, we may be interested in finding out how successful Baltimore and Pittsburgh were overall as well as how successful they were when running or passing, specifically. To do that, we can add play-specific metadata to our success data and use R built-ins for analysis. The code below shows how we could find the number of success and rate of success on running plays and passing plays, respectively.

```
success.df <- data.frame(team=plays$posteam,
                         play.type=plays$play_type,
                         success=play.successful)
aggregate(success~team,
          data=success.df,
          FUN=function(x){c(mean(x), sum(x))})
aggregate(success~team+play.type,
          data=success.df,
          FUN=function(x){c(mean(x), sum(x))})

#      team  play.type  success.1   success.2
# 5    BAL        pass  0.4571429  16.0000000
# 6    PIT        pass  0.5671642  38.0000000
# 11   BAL         run  0.6538462  17.0000000
# 12   PIT         run  0.4375000   7.0000000
```

LISTING 6.5. Analyzing successful plays in a football game.

From this analysis, we can see that Baltimore was slightly more successful on average; however, Pittsburgh had more successful plays overall. Further, Pittsburgh achieved much more success passing the football, while Baltimore achieved balanced success with 16 successful passing plays and 17 successful running plays. Because we know that passing is more impactful than running—yards per attempt often being somewhere around 6 or 7 and yards per rush often being somewhere between 3 and 4—all things being equal we would rather be Pittsburgh in this situation. And indeed, Pittsburgh would go on to win this game, albeit narrowly. In this specific game, Baltimore was buoyed by their special team's performance—including a 40 yard punt return—and several long passes from quarterback Joe Flacco. In contrast, Pittsburgh was more consistent throughout and outgained Baltimore by more than 125 yards.

Lastly, from a DVOA perspective, we would take all of these success calculations and use them to come up with estimates of average outcome in any situation we are interested in. For example, using the Baltimore-Pittsburgh game data, we can come up with a simple regression that takes into account down and yards to go and use that to develop an estimated success rate for every given game situation. The regression model will assign weights to down and distance and we can use the expand.grid function to produce a new data frame with every possible combination of down and distance we are interested in—in this case, I've selected 20 yards to go, 15 yards to go, and every integer less than 10. Then we can "predict" the success on that down to get the average success rate in such a scenario.

```
success.lm.df <- data.frame(down=plays$down,
                            to.go=plays$ydstogo,
                            success=play.successful)
success.lm <- lm(success~as.factor(down)+to.go+0, data=success.lm.df)
summary(success.lm)

expected.success <- expand.grid(down=c(1,2,3,4), to.go=c(20,15,10:1))
expected.success$exp <- round(predict.lm(success.lm, expected.suc-
cess),3)
expected.success[order(expected.success$exp,decreasing = T),]

#     down to.go    exp
# 45    1     1   0.742
# 41    1     2   0.717
# 37    1     3   0.693
# 33    1     4   0.669
# 47    3     1   0.664
# 29    1     5   0.645
# 43    3     2   0.639
# 25    1     6   0.620
# 39    3     3   0.615
```

LISTING 6.6. Analyyzing play success-rate by down and distance

Sorting the data by expected success rate, unsurprisingly we find that first and short situations have the highest likelihood of success. For example, a first down and one play is going to be successful 74.2% of the time. Somewhat counterintuitively, third and short situations are also high likelihoods of success—even higher than second and short. We can imagine that teams may take more risks on second and short, resulting in fewer "simple successes" but more big successes—which our 40/60/first-down heuristic does not account for.

With these scores in hand, we can calculate a toy version of DVOA for the Ravens and Steelers. To do so, we would find the expected outcome in each of the situations they faced and the actual outcome. We can then compare those numbers to see how well the respective teams did against their expectation. Because all of this is based on a single game of data, we should anticipate that the expected outcomes are going to very closely match the observed outcomes; with a larger sample of data to base our expectations on, teams performances in any individual game will vary more.

```
success.lm.df$exp <- round(predict.lm(success.lm, success.lm.df),3)
success.lm.df$tm <- plays$posteam
aggregate(success~tm,
          data=success.lm.df[which(success.lm.df$down!=4),],
          FUN=sum)

#     tm success
# 1 BAL      33
# 2 PIT      45

aggregate(exp~tm,
          data=success.lm.df[which(success.lm.df$down!=4),],
          FUN=sum)

#     tm    exp
# 1 BAL 32.636
# 2 PIT 45.384
```

LISTING 6.8. Using a regression to analyze play success.

From this, we can see that Baltimore performed slightly better than expected and Pittsburgh slightly worse. Of course, we can also see that Pittsburgh was expected to have about a dozen more successful plays than Baltimore over the course of the game—and they did do that, likely a big part of their victory. Again, a single game is not the best sample from which to draw expected results—we would be better off doing it for the entire season or several seasons.

Summary

In this chapter, we looked at two kinds of NFL metrics: box score metrics and advanced metrics. The box score metrics, as we noted, suffer from a variety of problems—mostly arising from the number of players involved in any given football play. The advanced metrics attempt to resolve this problem, largely by spreading out the rewards to a number of players or across an entire unit while simultaneously abstracting the good things that players are doing. For instance, with DVOA we saw that an abstract "success points" is used in lieu of yards. With Expected Points Added, we are measuring the number of points an offensive player contributes to their team.

When it comes to traditional box score metrics, there are metrics for most of the ways that offensive players contribute to a game. Quarterbacks even have their own passing meta-metric: passer rating, which aggregates various passing statistics into a single statistic. In contrast, defensive players have relatively few metrics and their performance is much harder to measure. This is especially true because good things defensive players do can often result in statistical bonuses for their teammates. For instance, if a defensive end collapses the pocket and the quarterback gets sacked as they are rolling away from the pressure, all of the credit for the sack goes to the player making the sack, not to the defender who caused the quarterback to roll out.

The advanced metrics attempt to solve this, largely by ignoring the discrete counting metrics and instead using abstract definitions of value. For instance, while calculating Win Percentage Added, we may give a defensive player credit for any good thing that happens while they are on the field and then the Law of Large Numbers is trusted to help differentiate the contributions among players. DVOA, arguably the most important advanced metric in football right now, expands on this concept by giving players or units only credit for the good things they do that also would not have been done by a league average player or unit.

Key Terms

Passer efficiency	DVOA
Passer rating	Drive
Expected points	Air yards
Win probability	Yards after catch
EPA	40/60/first rule
WPA	Success points

Critical Thinking Exercises

1. Pick a traditional football box score metric. What do we purport to capture with the metric and what aspect of that does it fail to capture? Identify how team composition and play design may influence the presentation of this metric.

2. Passer rating has been highly correlated with team success; however, for many reasons, it remains a flawed measurement of quarterback performance. What are some scenarios in which a passer might achieve a high passer rating despite not being a particularly impactful quarterback? What are some scenarios in which a talented quarterback may have a low passer rating?

3. Instead of measuring productivity by counting yards, the advanced metrics in football use abstractions such as expected points, win probability, and "success points." Why is it more important to have these abstractions in football than in other sports? Consider the example of a 6-yard completion on 3rd and goal from the 5-yard line versus that same completion on 3rd and 8.

4. Expected Points Added and Win Probability Added can both be used to measure offensive player performance. Why might we prefer Expected Points Added over Win Probability Added when it comes to evaluating offensive players but Win Probability Added when evaluating defensive players?

5. DVOA uses a concept of success instead of expected points or win probability. Win probability and points both correspond to real on-field outcomes: winning games and scoring points. Why might success points, which are not tied to outcomes, be better than the alternative? Why might success points be a worse idea than win probability or points?

6. At the end of this chapter we presented a simplified version of DVOA. Use the R code provided to gather three games worth of play-by-play data and find the average likelihood of success on run and pass plays on 1st, 2nd, and 3rd downs across all three games. How does this differ from the success rates of the Ravens and Steelers in the game we analyzed?

References

Advanced Football Analytics. 2015. *Glossary.* https://www.advancedfootballanalytics.com/index.php/home/stats/stats-explained/glossary

Carroll, Bob N., Pete Palmer, and John Thorn. 1988. *The hidden Game of Football.* New York: Warner Books.

Football Outsiders. 2021. *Methods to Our Madness.* Football Outsiders.com https://www.football-outsiders.com/info/methods

Pro Football Hall of Fame. 2005. *NFL's Passer Rating.* Pro Football Hall of Fame.com. https://www.profootballhof.com/news/nfl-s-passer-rating/

Sports Reference College Football. n.d. *College football stats glossary.* Sports Reference.com. https://www.sports-reference.com/cfb/about/glossary.html

CHAPTER 7

Monte Carlo Methods in Sport Analytics

J.T. Wolohan

Introduction

Sports pose a serious problem when it comes to the application of traditional statistical methods: namely, the problems we want to study—such as team and player performance—often have many sources of uncertainty and risk, and the results are correlated in unforeseeable ways. To know this, we only have to think about a truism in football: the teams that go into the playoffs the healthiest are the ones that are the most successful. Injuries, which are at least a semi-random event, can cost teams games or even ruin entire seasons. Also, since teams do not play identical schedules, the way those injuries manifest can have a dramatic impact on the results.

Consider a football team with a star quarterback—famously the most impactful player on the field in determining the outcome of a game. The team plays each of their division opponents twice; however, they play one of their opponents once at the beginning and once at the very end of the season, and they play another a few weeks apart during the middle of the season. Now consider what happens if the star quarterback gets a small mid-season injury such as a high-ankle sprain? The first division opponent has to play the star quarterback twice; the second division opponent avoids playing the star quarterback altogether. That potentially serves as a four-game nudge in favor of the team that played the injured quarterback. In a short, 16-game NFL season, even a small effect like that is almost insurmountable.

And that scenario is greatly over simplified. Consider college football, a sport with more than 100 teams, where each team has a hundred players, all of whom are liable to get injured, have problems with their grades, run afoul of NCAA regulations, or otherwise run into personal issues. To properly assess all the potential outcomes in a scenario like that with traditional statistical methods is to admit that you are sweeping a lot of meaningful phenomena under the rug. Luckily, we do not have to do this. We can use a method called **Monte Carlo experimentation**, or **Monte Carlo analysis**. Monte Carlo analysis is a technique that uses repeated sampling from probability distributions to make statistical estimates about a situation.

In this chapter we will look at Monte Carlo analysis and its applications to sport. Specifically, we will learn the basics of Monte Carlo analysis and how to apply it to sport problems increasing in complexity. Additionally, we will look at Markov chain Monte Carlo simulations, an advanced application of the Monte Carlo technique to event sequences—like those found in many sporting scenarios.

An Applied Introduction to Monte Carlo Analysis

"Joltin" Joe Dimaggio Was A New York Yankees Center Fielder, An All-Star In Three Decades (1930s, 1940s, and 1950s), and the holder of what is—perhaps—the most unassailable record in American sports: the 56-game hitting streak. The year was 1941 and DiMaggio, who was the Major League batting champion the two prior years, accomplished a feat so incredible, it largely overshadows his

MVP performance and World Series title in that same season. Many commentators have called the record unbreakable.

During those 56 games, DiMaggio had 91 hits, including 15 home runs, and batted an impressive .408. His record has been challenged credibly only once since, by Pete Rose, who topped 40 consecutive games with a base hit in 1978. Given this, we can say that the event is certainly rare; however, from an analytics perspective, we would like to know how rare. We can solve this problem in two ways, using our knowledge of probability or through Monte Carlo simulations.

First, let's make some assumptions about the scenario. Let's assume that DiMaggio has four plate appearances in every game. And his true batting average—the likelihood of getting a hit during any at bat—is equal to .352, his batting average from the previous season. With these assumptions, we can use probability theory to estimate the likelihood of a player of DiMaggio's caliber recording a 56-game hit streak. We simply find the probability of DiMaggio recording a hit in a single game and then calculate the likelihood of 56 such events. In R, we can find the former using the binomial probability function and the latter using by raising that number to the 56th power.

```
pbinom(0,4,.352, lower.tail = F)**56
# 1.916443e-05
```

We could also calculate this number using Monte Carlo simulations. Monte Carlo simulations operate a bit differently. In a Monte Carlo simulation, we will generate random numbers in a pattern that represents the scenario under examination, and then we can do simple arithmetic—typically averaging—to find an approximate answer. This means that we will need to create a function that represents a streak and then repeat that streak many, many times until we are satisfied that we can estimate the probability.

The first step is to create the streak function. Our streak function will take a number of games and return the length of a consecutive game hit streak over that number of games. We will want to loop through a sequence of games, generate a random number to determine if DiMaggio was able to get a hit in that game or not, and then respond accordingly. If DiMaggio did not get a hit, we will end the streak; if DiMaggio did get a hit, the streak continues. Like before, we will use the binomial probability distribution, except this time we will generate random numbers instead of using properties of the distribution itself.

```
streak <- function(games=56){
  for(game in 1:games){
    if (rbinom(1, size=4, prob=.352) < 1){
      return(game)
    }}
  return(game)
}
```

Once we have our streak function set, we will need to run simulations of it. To aide with this—and other simulations in this chapter—we will create a simulate function and then pass our streak function into that as a parameter. The simulate function needs to run some arbitrary function a number of times and record the results of each. We will do this by applying a function passed in as a parameter over an 0-initialized array. Having the simulate function will allow us to easily compare simulations and change the size of our simulations.

From there, it is a matter of passing our streak into the simulate function we have created. We can then find the number of 56-game streaks and divide that number by the number of simulations to find an estimate of the probability. We will complete this last step using the array filter mechanisms in R and the division operator.

```
simulate <- function(fn, N=1e3){
    sapply(
      array(0,N),
      function(x){fn()}
    )
}

simulations <- simulate(streak, 1e5)
length(simulations[simulations==56])/N
# [1] 1e-05
```

LISTING 7.1. A simple Monte Carlo simulation.

The obvious aspect to notice here is that the result we get will—almost certainly—not match the mathematically derived result from above. This is understood to be the case with Monte Carlo simulations. Monte Carlo simulations are used to approximate solutions—they will rarely arrive at the exact solution. That said, this is often sufficient. Additionally, Monte Carlo simulations can be used in situations where mathematically deriving the solution is impractical.

To examine that, let's make the DiMaggio scenario a little more complex. Instead of assuming DiMaggio has exactly four at-bats in every game, let's introduce a probability distribution to represent the number of at-bats that DiMaggio gets. Let's also change the scope. Instead of searching for the probability of DiMaggio getting a hit in 56 consecutive games, let's find the probability of DiMaggio recording a 56 consecutive-game hitting streak in a 162-game season.

To do this, we will need to define a new streak function. Instead of looping through 56 games, we will loop through a full 162-game season and find the maximum number of consecutive games DiMaggio would have recorded a hit in that simulated season. We will also construct an at-bats function to randomly determine how many chances DiMaggio has in a game to get a hit. For purposes of this scenario, we will assume that DiMaggio gets 3 at-bats in 1-in-10 games, 5 at-bats in 1-in-4 games, and 4 at-bats in the remaining games. We will use random variables drawn from the uniform distribution to determine how many at-bats DiMaggio gets in a given game.

If you compare the code from our second streak function to the code to our first streak function, you will find the two mostly similar. The changes in the second streak function revolve around trying to find the maximum streak over the course of a season. To this end, we need additional variables to capture the streak in progress and the maximum streak. Then, we can loop through a season of games and update the maximum streak every time a streak ends. We calculate the end of a streak in the same way as before, except we are now using a variable number of at-bats.

```
number.of.at.bats <- function(){
  u <- runif(1)
  if(u<.1){return(3)}
  else if(u<.75){return(4)}
  return(5)
}

streak.2 <- function(batting.avg){
  max.streak <- 0
  streak <- 0
  for(game in 1:162){
    hits <- rbinom(1, size=number.of.at.bats(), prob=batting.avg)
    if (hits<1){
      max.streak <- max(c(streak, max.streak))
      streak <- 0
    }
    streak <- streak + 1
  }
  return(max.streak)
}

streak.2.sims <- simulate(streak.2, 1e5)
length(streak.2.sims[streak.2.sims>55])/1e5
# 0.00061
```

LISTING 7.2. Estimating DiMaggio's streak-likelihood with a simple Monte Carlo model

From this analysis, we find that the likelihood of a DiMaggio-caliber player recording a 56-game hitting streak in a season is approximately .06%. That means that if DiMaggio played in 1600 seasons, he might be expected to record one such streak. This adds to the sense of how exceptional DiMaggio's feat was. DiMaggio, one of the greatest-ever baseball players, could play through his 13-year career 100-times and plausible be expected never to match his consecutive game hitting streak.

Of course, even DiMaggio's own greatness clouds how rare this feat was. After all, most players are not nearly as good at hitting as DiMaggio. DiMaggio's .352 batting average would put him in contention for the league batting title every year, and he would win it in many years. No player in baseball recorded a season-long average better than DiMaggio's .352 between the 2010 and 2020 Major League Baseball seasons. Let's update our scenario to look at the likelihood of any player recording a 56-game hitting streak during a 162-game Major League Baseball season.

To do this, we will need yet another function for our Monte Carlo simulation: this time to represent a season. For this example, we will assume that there are 150 players in Major League Baseball who will play in enough games to put together a 56-game hitting streak and that their batting averages are distributed normally, centered around .270, with a standard deviation of .03 points. We will generate players randomly following this formula, and then use the season-long streak function we developed earlier in this section for each player before finding the maximum streak for the season.

```
streak.by.season <- function(players=150){
  synthetic.player.avgs <- rnorm(n=players,mean=.270,sd=.03)
  synthetic.player.streaks <- sapply(synthetic.player.avgs, streak.2)
  return(max(synthetic.player.streaks))
}

N=1e4
season.simulations <- simulate(streak.by.season, N)
length(season.simulations[season.simulations>55])/N
# 0.0002
```

LISTING 7.3 Estimating the likelihood of DiMaggio's streak for all of baseball.

Again, we can use the same simulate function to run our function many times and perform a simple average to find the result. In this example, we perform 10,000 runs and find that in only two seasons a batter achieves a streak of more than 55 games. This puts some serious support behind the widely held idea that DiMaggio's record is the most unassailable in all of sport. If the entire history of Major League Baseball was replayed 35 times, DiMaggio's record would be matched or surpassed perhaps only once.

In the next section of this chapter, we will take a step back from the applied example we just worked through and examine two interacting pieces of Monte Carlo analysis: the deterministic logic of the simulation and the repeated random sampling. First, the use of relatively straightforward, plain-English algorithms is one of the things that makes Monte Carlo simulations so attractive as an analytical tool. We can use Monte Carlo analysis to make statistical statements about problems that we can describe the rules for, but not necessarily denote mathematically. For many without formal math backgrounds, this is extraordinarily powerful because thinking in mathematical operations is not intuitive. And even for those trained in math—such as Stanislaw Ulam, the famed nuclear physicist and mathematician who invented Monte Carlo analysis to analyze solitaire—Monte Carlo methods can save time. It is often more expedient to express a problem through a Monte Carlo formulation than through discrete mathematics.

Second, in all of our analyses we were performing many, many random samples. In our first example, we were generating random numbers for each of the 56 games. We then performed this process several thousand times. If you ran the code as written, you generated 5.6 million random numbers to arrive at your estimation of the likelihood of DiMaggio's 56-game hitting streak. In the final example, we generated 150 random numbers representing each player and then for each player, we generated two random numbers for each of 162 games. Simulating a single season like this sampled 48.00 random numbers; simulating 10,000 seasons like we did, sampled 486 million random numbers. This is the magic of Monte Carlo simulations: instead of working precise mathematical calculations to find an exact answer, we can use random numbers to find an approximate or estimated answer.

Monte Carlo Analysis

Monte Carlo analysis is a practical technique, arriving at answers to important problems through sheer force of will and computing power, instead of mathematical sophistication. As noted in the previous section, Stanislaw Ulam, a nuclear physicist discovered the technique when analyzing probabilities of a card game. An excellent mathematician, Ulam's first instinct was to try and solve the problem using calculus. Then, flustered by his inability to solve the problem—potentially because he was suffering from a fever at the time—Ulam resorted to a brute force estimation of the answer by generating random game states on the computer. Subsequently, Ulam would apply these techniques for computationally approximating differential equations to his main field of study: nuclear physics.

Card games are actually an excellent—and simple—arena to prove out Monte Carlo simulations, if you are yet to be convinced of their efficacy. For instance, we might consider the chance of drawing a spade from a deck. If you know anything about card games, you will already know that a standard deck consists of 52 cards. Those 52 cards in turn consist of 13 cards in each of the four suits: spades, hearts, diamonds, and clubs. Therefore, we know that the true probability of drawing a spade is 1-in-4 or 25%. But we can also derive this fact through Monte Carlo simulation.

To do, let us follow the script we established in the previous section. We will create a function for drawing cards and then find the percentage of spades drawn. However, instead of running this simulation only once with a large number of samples, like before, let's run the simulation several times with an increasing number of samples. In this example, we will run a draw of three cards, of five cards, of 10 cards, of 100 cards, of 1,000 cards, and of 1 million cards.

For this, we create a function that draws a card at random by sampling from the uniform distribution—because we know the cards are evenly distributed across the suits—and we assign a part of the distribution to each suit. Spades, in this case, get the range from [0, 13]. We then use our simulate function to run this function many times. Lastly, we find the percentage of cards we drew that were spades. To perform this several times, we construct an array of values to loop through and use those values as the number of runs.

Observing the results—which will vary from the results of a run you perform yourself, in all likelihood—we can see that for low numbers of simulations, we are nowhere close to accurate. In our 5-card sample, we draw two spades, leading us to believe that there is a 60% chance of drawing a spade. This is more than twice as high than what we know the correct answer to be. However, as the number of cards increases, the percentage guess gets increasingly accurate. Indeed at 100 and 1,000 cards sampled, we are often only by two percentage points. By the time we are at 1 million cards drawn, we have the number down exactly: 25%.

```
draw.a.card <- function(){
  card <- runif(1,min=0,max=52)
  if(card<=13){return("Spade")}
  if(card<=26){return("Club")}
  if(card<=39){return("Heart")}
  return("Diamond")
}

Ns <- c(3,5,10,100,1e3,1e6)
pcts <- array(0, 6)
for (i in 1:6){
  N <- Ns[i]
  draw <- simulate(draw.a.card, N)
  pct <- length(draw[draw=="Spade"])/N
  pcts[i] <- pct
}

data.frame(Ns, pcts)
#     Ns        pcts
# 1 3e+00 0.3333333
# 2 5e+00 0.6000000
# 3 1e+01 0.4000000
# 4 1e+02 0.2300000
# 5 1e+03 0.2210000
# 6 1e+06 0.2499910
```

LISTING 7.4. Analyzing simple card games with Monte Carlo analysis.

Of course, for an example like this we would not want to use a Monte Carlo simulation: it is far easier to just reason about the suits and determine the probability. That said, the line between when we can reason about the probability and when we cannot, is rarely a bright one. It is helpful to have both tools in our toolbelt.

Because Monte Carlo simulations are defined by repeated random sampling, it makes some sense to think about types of random sampling we might be interested in using. R has several probability distributions built in that we can take advantage of—and many more that are available in the same pattern from the software repository CRAN. Before moving on, let's look at some of the most common probability distributions and the sport scenarios in which you might use them.

Normal Distribution

The normal distribution is the class bell curve distribution with which you are probably the most familiar. This distribution is fat in the center and thin on the tails. It is a good choice for data that is both continuous and for which outliers are relatively rare. For instance, earlier in this chapter we used the normal distribution to model batting average. This is probably incorrect. Batting average is likely asymmetrical because players who bat too low will be demoted to the minors, but no manager would ever sit a player for hitting too well. That said, batting average is close enough to normal that the assumption is plausible. Other things we might want to use a normal distribution for are player performance—which we might assume to be normally distributed around some "true value" for that point in their career—or team performance—which again we might assume to be randomly distributed around a "true form" value.

The normal distribution is defined by two parameters: the mean and the standard deviation. The mean is the central point of the distribution. The standard deviation dictates the width of the bell curve. The larger the standard deviation, the wider the curve. The smaller the standard deviation, the more narrow the curve. If the distribution is wide, then values can take a wide range; if the distribution is narrow, then we expect values to take only a narrow range. A good rule of thumb is that values will fall within plus-or-minus 2.5 standard deviations from the mean. So, if we assume batting average to follow a normal distribution with a mean of .270 and a standard deviation of .2, then we would expect to find batting average values between .220 and .320.

In R, we generate values from the normal distribution using rnorm function. The rnorm function takes three parameters—one for each of mean and standard deviation—and another for the number of variables that we want to generate. For instance, we could generate 9 random batting averages with the following snippet:

```
rnorm(9, .270, .02)
# 0.237 0.280 0.275 0.262 0.260 0.233 0.235 0.250 0.251
```

Binomial Distribution

Another common distribution we will use for Monte Carlo simulations is the binomial distribution. The binomial distribution is ideal for counting successes (or failures). For instance, if we expect a college football team to win 75% of their games and they play 11 games in a season, we could use the binomial distribution in a Monte Carlo simulation approximating the answer. We might also use the binomial distribution for the chance of a basketball player making some number of shots or a customer buying something from a concession stand.

Binomial distributions are defined by two parameters: the number of trials and the probability of success. A binomial distribution with a larger number of trials is going to contain larger numbers than one with a smaller number of trials because there is a higher opportunity for success. For instance, it would be trivial for a professional basketball player to make 50 free throws out of 100, but impossible for them to make 50 free throws in only 10 attempts. Likewise, the greater the probability of success, the greater the numbers we will expect from our binomial distribution. Again, in the free throw example, a talented free throw shooter might make 90% of their free throws. We would expect that shooter to make more shots over the same number of three throw attempts than a free throw shooter with a free-throw percentage of only 60%.

In R, the binomial distribution is made available through the rbinom function. The rbinom function has three parameters: one for the number of random variables we would like to generate and two for each of size and probability. We can, for example, generate the number of free throws a 90% free throw shooter and a 60% free throw shooter make if each takes 10 attempts.

```
> rbinom(1,10,.9)
[1] 8
> rbinom(1,10,.6)
[1] 5
```

In this instance, the 90% shooter made 8 of their free throws and the 60% shooter made 6 of theirs. If we run this scenario enough times, there will certainly be times where the 60% shooter outperforms the 90% shooter. If you increase the number of samples generated by each, you can see this play out.

Uniform Distribution

The uniform distribution is perhaps the simplest statistical distribution. Random variates from the uniform distribution will be between 0 and 1 and every number drawn has the same probability. So, the chance of getting .653 is the same as the chance of getting .231 is the same as the chance of getting .917. We can use this property of the distribution to specify—as precisely as we are able—the probability of an event, and then randomly determine whether it happens or not. For instance, if we know a soccer player makes 90% of their passes successfully, we can draw a variable from the uniform distribution and if it is equal to or below 0.9, we would consider the pass a success; if it is not, we would consider the pass a failure. Similarly, we could do this with first-serve accuracy in tennis, a player's chance of hitting a shot in basketball, or play selection by a football team.

Like the previous distributions, the uniform distribution is available to us in R in the convenient runif function. The runif function draws one or more variables from the uniform distribution and it takes 1 parameter, with two optional scaling factors. Like the other distribution functions we have looked at, the first parameter of runif will determine how any random variates are generated. The optional scaling parameters allow us to cast the uniform variate to any range.

This scaling parameter can be used to simplify the math for situations in which we want to make a "random choice." For instance, from our card example in an earlier section, we generated numbers between 0 and 52. Every integer break in this range corresponded to a single card in the deck. For instance, 0 to 1 might have been the 2 of Spades, 1 to 2 might have been the 3 of Spades, 2 to 3 might have been the 4 of Spades, and so on.

```
> runif(1)
[1] 0.456871
> runif(3, max=100)
[1] 51.76177 55.43302 27.70662
```

The code above shows two uses of runif. The first generates a single random variable between 0 and 1. The second shows how we can generate three random variates between 0 and 100. On their own, these random variates are not particularly interesting. Typically, we will want to add deterministic rules to the back end of uniform variate sampling to make them meaningful.

If anyone is still unconvinced in the efficacy of Monte Carlo methods, we can also use the runif function to produce results from conditional probability rules. For instance, consider the probability of two fifty-fifty events occurring. We know that this value should be 25% because 50% times 50% is 25%. We can replicate this using Monte Carlo and demonstrate that over enough simulations the result converges to .25.

```
and.prob <- function(ps){
   for (p in ps){
      u <- runif(1)
      if (u>p){ return(0) }
   }
   return(1)
}

for (n in c(1,3,5, 10, 100, 500, 1000, 1e6)){
   results <- simulate(function(){and.prob(c(.5,.5))}, N=n)
   print(mean(results))
}
```

In the code block above, we create a function that takes in a sequence of probabilities and returns 0 if any of these conditions "fail" and a 1 if they all succeed. We can then pass this function, wrapped up in an anonymous function, to our simulate function to run simulations of it. You will note that the small samples—1,3,5,10, and even 100—can be pretty far from .25. But as we approach a large number of samples, we converge to the true value: .25.

Bootstrapping and Jackknifing

Monte Carlo simulations are excellent for situations in which we want to estimate a value but calculating the value is unfeasible. In these scenarios, we know there to be a true solution and we trust that our probabilistic estimate will be able to approximate it. Sometimes, however, our problem will be more statistical in nature. We may have something that we want to estimate—often the mean or variance of a probability—but we do not know enough about the underlying processes that produce this value. In these scenarios, we can use the **bootstrap technique**. The bootstrap technique is a technique, related to the Monte Carlo we discussed earlier, where we resample from an empirical sample to estimate a true distribution.

Consider, for instance, the question of whether one football player or team "has another's number," that is, performs much better than they are expected to against that specific opponent. For instance, during the New England Patriots' dynastic run from 2001 to 2019 it was widely believed that the Denver Broncos—a solidly mediocre team during that time—had an advantage over the Patriots. We could use the bootstrap to find the extent of the Broncos advantage over the Patriots during this time.

In order to do this, we will take our data and draw random samples from it a large number of times—typically between 50 and 200. A hundred random draws from our observed sample is a good rule of thumb that can be used, unless there is a specific reason to deviate from this number. We will then use this sample to estimate the true values. For instance, we can take the 1st and 99th percentile values to obtain a 98% confidence interval about the advantage the Broncos had during this time.

To achieve this in R, we will use a process similar to what we did with the Monte Carlo simulations, only instead of using a distribution function and drawing from that, we will use the sample function and draw from observed results. Otherwise, the process will remain the same. Code for this example can be seen below.

```
broncos.pats <- c(-9,11,8,-4,8,14,10,-31,3,-18,
                  -35,-10,-3,10,-22,6,2,-13,-25)
results = simulate(fn=function(){
  mean(sample(broncos.pats, 20, replace = T))
  }, N=100
)
hist(results)
#    Min. 1st Qu.  Median    Mean 3rd Qu.    Max.
# -15.550  -7.312  -4.825  -4.654  -2.075   3.900
quantile(results, c(.01,.99))
#      1%      99%
# -14.5105   3.1575
```

LISTING 7.5. Using the bootstrap to anlayze winning likelihood.

You will note that we are taking the average of the results from each sample, that we are sampling 20 times with replacement, and that we are repeating this process 100 times. We use 20 samples here because it's a round number close to the number of observations we actually have: 19. We perform this process 100 times because 100 is our default assumption for bootstrapping, and we take the average because that is the statistic we are most interested in. Lastly, we generate a histogram of the results, produce a five-number summary, and generate our two quantile values for the 1st and 99th percentiles. Results are shown above, but your numbers may vary slightly due to the randomness involved in the bootstrap process.

How are we to interpret these results? First, we can look at the quantiles we generated—the bootstrap version of a confidence interval—and note that zero is safely within this range. From this, we should infer that the Broncos and the Patriots are evenly matched over this period. Or at least that we do not have enough evidence to say otherwise. We can compare these results to a more traditional statistical confidence interval approach, such as the one generated by R's t.test function. We will note that the confidence ranges and point estimates are both close. However, our bootstrap approach, being a numerical solution, is impervious to many of the concerns about the underlying data being normally distributed.

```
t.test(broncos.pats,conf.level = .98)

# 98 percent confidence interval:
#  -14.083785    3.767996

# mean of x
#  -5.157895
```

How are we to interpret these results? First, we can look at the quantiles we generated—the bootstrap version of a confidence interval—and note that zero is safely within this range. From this, we should infer that the Broncos and the Patriots are evenly matched over this period. Or at least that we do not have enough evidence to say otherwise. We can compare these results to a more traditional statistical confidence interval approach, such as the one generated by R's t.test function. We will note that the confidence ranges and point estimates are both close. However, our bootstrap approach, being a numerical solution, is impervious to many of the concerns about the underlying data being normally distributed. In order to confidently use the student's t-distribution approach, we would have needed to justify this assumption of normality. And looking at the distribution of the sample data—which you can inspect using the hist function in R—we would have a difficult time satisfying that assumption.

Indeed, we are going to have a problem satisfying the normality assumption often in sport analytics. Events in sports are often bounded. For instance, the number of points a basketball player can score in a game is 0 bounded at the lower end. No player, bad as they may be, can score fewer than 0 points in a game. The upper limit, however, is infinite in theory and practically bounded somewhere in the 100s. This has the effect of creating right skew distributions: distributions where the right tail of the distribution is long, and there may either be a small left tail or no left tail at all.

Let us take a look at this in practice while considering a special implementation of the bootstrap: the **jackknife**. The jackknife, or jackknife estimation, is a process for estimating parameters of a sample—most often variance or a related attribute—by averaging together unique subsamples of the original sample. In the following example, we will use the jackknife to estimate the variance in scoring for Kobe Bryant during the 2005 to 2006 NBA season. That means that when calculating a jackknife estimation of Bryant's scoring variance, we will sequentially emit one game from the subsample and average together the results.

In 2005 to 2006, Kobe Bryant led the NBA in points, points per game, free-throws attempted, and shots attempted, and shots made. The Laker's performance that year was largely dependent on Kobe's heroism. Thus, there is plenty of reason for the Laker's to be interested in the variance of Kobe's performance. High variance would lead to a fickle Laker's squad—capable of beating any team and losing to any team; a low variance would represent a dependable output that could be counted on game to game.

As previously described, there are reasons we should be suspicious that we can use to satisfy the assumptions of normality when dealing with points scored. A convenient alternative is to use the bootstrap, as we explored earlier in the chapter. In this case, we will instead use the jackknife, a special case of the bootstrap that leaves out observation out of a number of subsamples equal to the number of observations and averages the statistic in question across those subsamples.

The first step to computing Jackknife variance estimate is computing the Jackknife mean. The Jackknife mean is the mean of systematic subsamples wherein each subsample omits a single observation. In R, we will compute these samples ourselves by looping through the number of observations—in this case, 80, one for each game Kobe played in 2005 to 2006—and drop a single observation from each.

```
points <- array(0,80)
for (game.num in 1:80){
    xs <- c(kobe.06[0:(game.num-1)], kobe.06[(game.num+1):81])
    points[game.num] <- mean(xs,na.rm = T)
}

x.bar <- mean(points)
```

Above, we are populating an empty array with the average number of points for each subsample. Then finally, we calculate the Jackknife mean by taking the average of these subsample means. You will note that each sample omits exactly one observation and that no two samples omit the same observation.

With the Jackknife mean in hand, we can then calculate the Jackknife variance. To do this, we will employ a similar approach, except instead of finding the mean of each subsample, we will find the variance for each subsample using the Jackknife mean as our reference point. As a reminder, sample variance is equal to the sum of the squares of the distances between each observation in a sample and the mean of that sample, divided by one less than the number of observations in the sample. For example, the variance of a sample containing 3,4,5 would equal 1: [(3-4)^2+(4-4)^2+(5-4)^2] / 2.

The code below demonstrates what this process looks like in R. You will note that except for the line computing the variance statistic, this process is identical to the process used above to compute the Jackknife mean. You will also note that we take advantage of R's vector arithmetic in the variance calculation. Subtracting a vector from a singleton, in this case, results in a new vector where that subtraction operation is performed on each element.

```
var <- array(0,80)
for (game.num in 1:80){
   xs <- c(kobe.06[0:(game.num-1)], kobe.06[(game.num+1):81])
   var[game.num] <- sum((x.bar-xs)^2,na.rm = T) / 79
}


jack.var <- mean(var)
```

With the Jackknife variance in hand, we may be wondering how this value compares with the standard sample variance, or how the associated standard deviations compare. We can easily compare our Jackknife findings to the traditional findings using R's built-in variance and standard deviation functions. From this, you will note that the Jackknife variance and standard deviation are lower than their traditional correlates. This might be somewhat surprising as the Jackknife is a conservative indicator; however, we know from the sample, a large degree of the variance is coming from a single event: Kobe's 81-point game.

```
> jack.var
# 109.065
> sqrt(jack.var)
# 10.44342
> var(kobe.06)
# 110.4456
> sd(kobe.06)
# 10.50931
```

Kobe's 81-point game is an excellent example of why we would choose to use the Jackknife (or bootstrap) in the first place. Even at Kobe's incredible 35-points per game average, an 81-point game represents a 46-point increase over what we expected. Of course, as we discussed, it would be impossible for Kobe to perform 46-points worse than expected. For that to be the case he would need to score negative 11-points.

Bootstrap Monte Carlo

While the bootstrap and Jackknife approaches are typically used to estimate statistical parameters for the purpose of statistical testing—for example, estimating whether or not two sample means or variances are similar—we can also use the bootstrap approach in a Monte Carlo simulation. Within the context of a Monte Carlo simulation, the bootstrap method replaces random draws from an assumed distribution. That is, instead of generating random numbers, we are drawing randomly from a sample with replacement.

As an example, we might think about the scenario from earlier in this chapter where we were trying to estimate the likelihood of a DiMaggio-length hit streak occurring. In our ultimate Monte Carlo simulation, we made an assumption about the batting average distribution of Major League ballplayers that we knew was incorrect; however, we hand-waived that and deemed it sufficient for our estimate. A better option may have been to use a sample of previous season-long batting averages and draw samples from that using the bootstrap.

We might have, for instance, taken the 150 batters with the most at-bats from each of the past five seasons (or longer, if we wanted), and then randomly drawn 150-observation samples from this pool to create our pool of simulated batters. The benefit of using a bootstrapped distribution in situations like this—where the data is available—is that we do not have to think so hard about the underlying data, nor would we be asked to defend assumptions about the probability distributions chosen. A weakness of the Monte Carlo approach is that assumptions about distributions can seem arbitrary and the bootstrap resolves this. In this way, the bootstrap makes up for the weaknesses of the Monte Carlo, increasing its justifiability.

We can see a comparison of the two approaches in R below. You will note that the two solutions are largely the same. To shift from a standard Monte Carlo simulation to a Monte Carlo simulation that uses the bootstrap, we primarily need a data source. Once we have the data in hand, sampling from that data source with replacement is all that is necessary to complete our bootstrap. You will notice that below we use the sample function, as above, specifying a specific column of the data frame that we have read in.

```
# Standard Monte Carlo
streak.by.season <- function(players=150){
  synthetic.player.avgs <- rnorm(n=players,mean=.270,sd=.03)
  synthetic.player.streaks <- sapply(synthetic.player.avgs, streak.2)
  return(max(synthetic.player.streaks))
}

N=1e3
season.simulations <- simulate(streak.by.season, N)
length(season.simulations[season.simulations>50])/N
# 0.008

# Bootstrapped Monte Carlo
players.150 <- read.csv(file="/path/to/150-batting.csv")
bootstrap.mc.season <- function(players=150){
  bootstrapped.players <- sample(players.150$Avg, players, replace=T)
  synthetic.player.streaks <- sapply(bootstrapped.players, streak.2)
  return(max(synthetic.player.streaks))
}

N=1e3
season.simulations <- simulate(bootstrap.mc.season, N)
length(season.simulations[season.simulations>50])/N
# 0.007
```

LISTING 7.6. Using a bootstrapped Monte Carlo simulation to estimate the likelihood of a baseball streak.

In this toy example, it turns out that the two approaches produce relatively the same result: in a fewer than 1% of seasons will a player have a hitting streak of greater than 50 games. Given the small number of simulations we have run in this case, we would want to be pretty cautious about making any statements about the equivalence or difference of the actual numbers.

Markov Chain Monte Carlo Simulations

So far in this chapter, we have looked at applications of the Monte Carlo simulation to scenarios where the events are statistically independent, i.e., where the outcome of an event—for example whether or not a batter gets a hit—is independent from previous events—for example, the outcome of previous at bats. In sport, we are not always going to be comfortable with this assumption. For instance, we may consider a basketball game. When a player starts to shoot well, it is common for their teammates to pass them the ball more. In basketball there is a widespread "hot hand" idea: players believe that a player who is on a shooting streak—that is, that they are making a lot of shots—will continue to shoot well. Thus, those players will get the player with the "hot hand" the ball, resulting in a greater number of shots per game. This has the effect of early-game hot streaks inflating or deflating the performance of the player over the course of the game. Our previous methods would not be able to handle a situation like this. To model a scenario like this, we can, however, use a technique called **Markov Chain Monte Carlo** simulation.

Markov Chain Monte Carlo simulations are simulations that consist of random draws from multiple probability distributions—Monte Carlo simulations—but where the probability distributions within the simulation are influenced by the outcome of previous events. The **Markov Chain** part of the name indicates that the probability of the scenario will be entirely encapsulated in the most recent event. To understand the Markov Chain, we might consider the 1-and-1 free throw in college and international basketball. In these sports, players who are fouled while not in the act of shooting may be awarded a special type of free throw: they take the first free throw and, if they make it, they then get to take a subsequent free two, the second free throw being conditional on the first. This scenario is perhaps the simplest Markov Chain: the shooter either makes or misses the free throw. If they miss, they are no longer shooting; if they make the shot, they score a point and shoot again.

Markov Chain Monte Carlo simulations can, of course, become much more sophisticated than this. For example, we might consider modeling the 64-team NCAA March Madness tournament. We might know each team's expected performance against each other team. We could use this information to run random simulations about who might win any given game. The outcome of each round would produce probabilities for the next round and the next round, until the tournament was complete. One could then use those simulations to find the probability of each team reaching any given round of the NCAA tournament.

To investigate the Markov Chain Monte Carlo approach in more detail, we will investigate a smaller example: the NCAA Division I College Football Playoff. Each year since 2014, a 13-person committee selects four teams to play off against one another, culminating in a national champion. In the 2018 to 2019 season, the four teams nominated into the playoff were the SEC champion Alabama, the ACC champion Clemson, unaffiliated Notre Dame, and the Big-12 champion Oklahoma. In the first round of the playoff, Alabama and Oklahoma faced off in the top-versus-bottom matchup, while Clemson and Notre Dame faced off in the other game. The winners of those two games— Clemson and Alabama—played one another in the final, which was ultimately won by Clemson.

We might wonder what probability each team had of winning the final. Of course, this is complicated by the fact that Clemson, should they advance to the final as they did, may have a different chance of winning against Alabama than against Oklahoma. Likewise, with all of the other teams. The Markov Chain Monte Carlo can help us resolve this.

To set up our Markov Chain Monte Carlo in this scenario, we will first create a function that represents a game. Our simplification of a football game will treat each as a draw from a binomial distribution. The probability of success for this distribution will be determined by the relative power rankings of each team. The greater a team's power ranking, the greater their chance of winning the game. This is an imperfect representation of a football game but is sufficient for this example—and is often sufficient in sport in general.

```
game <- function(t1, t2){
  outcome <- rbinom(1,1,(t1/(t1+t2)))
  if (outcome) {return(t1)}
  return(t2)
}
```

Our game function will take in the power ratings of the two teams as parameters, use the rbinom function to generate a random number, and then output the power ranking of the winner. In this function, we can see the roots of our Markov Chain forming. We can see that the distribution from which we are sampling—in this case the binomial distribution—is going to be dependent on the two teams that are playing. We also know that each of the four teams will have at least some probability of winning in the first round, thus, we cannot be sure a priori what precise distribution we will be sampling from in the second stage of the playoffs.

Below, we can see the playoff function implement this idea. The first round of playoff games is resolved by the 1-4 and 2-3 matchups. Those teams go on to the final game, wherein they compete in yet another game—which is modeled in the exact same way as the first. The team that emerges from the ultimate game is the winner of the playoffs.

```
playoffs <- function(t1,t2,t3,t4){
  finalist.1 <- game(t1,t4)
  finalist.2 <- game(t2,t3)
  winner <- game(finalist.1, finalist.2)
  return(winner)
}
```

Of course, running this simulation one time is of no interest to us. We will want to run this scenario many times so we can take advantage of the benefits of Monte Carlo and approximate the true probabilities of each team winning. To do this, we will use a familiar pattern: we will construct an empty array and populate it with values from runs of our simulation. We can then perform analysis on the results. In this case, we will perform a simple division operation to find the rate at which each team is winning the final game.

```
N <- 1e5
runs <- array(0,N)

#Power Ratings
AL<-10;CLM<-15;ND<-4;OK<-7

for(n in 1:N){
 runs[n] <- playoffs(AL,CLM,ND,OK)
}

round(table(runs)/N,3)
```

```
#     4      7     10     15
# 0.067 0.157 0.273 0.502
```

In the results here, we find that Clemson is winning about 50% of the time, with Alabama winning a little more than a quarter of the time, Oklahoma winning about 15% of the time, and Notre Dame winning just over 5% of the time. Again, because all of these numbers are an approximation from the Monte Carlo, we would want to take them with a grain of salt. Of course, we could also run the scenario many times or use the bootstrap to estimate the parameters resulting from our Monte Carlo.

The bootstrap provides a convenient way to reason about the results of our Monte Carlo approaches. In this scenario, we will examine bootstrap estimates of four variables: the championship likelihood for each of the four playoff teams. Like before, to do this we will create an array and append to the array the results of our bootstrap samples. In this case, we will perform the bootstrap 100 times, with no reason to believe any more or any fewer is necessary. For each run of the bootstrap, we will sample from our simulation and calculate the probability each team had of winning the playoff during bootstrap of simulation. We will then accumulate these results in our results array. When this process is done, we can use the apply function to find the five-figure summary for each value.

```
N2 <- 100
boot.results <- c()
for (n in 1:N2){
  boot.playoff <- sample(runs, 1000, replace=T)
  win.probs <- round(table(boot.playoff)/1000,3)
  boot.results <- rbind(t(matrix(win.probs)), boot.results)
}

apply(boot.results, MARGIN =2, summary)
#              [,1]    [,2]    [,3]    [,4]
# Min.     0.05200 0.12700 0.23800 0.46900
# 1st Qu.  0.06200 0.14950 0.26100 0.49500
# Median   0.06700 0.15700 0.27200 0.50500
# Mean     0.06729 0.15673 0.27141 0.50457
# 3rd Qu.  0.07200 0.16500 0.27800 0.51400
# Max.     0.08600 0.19200 0.32500 0.54800
```

Doing this gives us a good bit more information than the point estimates we gathered from the simulation. Here, we can see that the probability of Clemson winning is somewhere between 46% and 55%. Likewise, Alabama has a large range of probabilities as well: from 23% up to 33%. Oklahoma and Notre Dame, with smaller overall chances of winning the playoff, have smaller ranges. We can also say with certainty that there is a clear hierarchy. Clemson will always have a better chance than Alabama, who will always have a better chance than Oklahoma, who will always have a better chance than Notre Dame. You may wish to play around with the power rating values in this example and see how changing those values alters these estimates.

Summary

In this chapter, we reviewed Monte Carlo simulations and other methods associated with the use of random sampling to perform statistical calculations, including the Bootstrap, the Jackknife, and Markov Chain Monte Carlo simulations. We demonstrate how these techniques are useful for a variety of tasks that would prove challenging or intractable through traditional methods. The Monte Carlo simulation technique, which draws randomly from probability distributions, can be used for estimating the outcome of probabilistic events when we know the underlying distributions of a phenomenon. The more sophisticated Markov Chain Monte Carlo simulation can be used when the probability of events is intertwined in a non-obvious or non-trivial fashion. Both of these methods produce stochastic outputs. We can then use the bootstrap and jackknife approaches to assess the likelihood of various events resulting from these simulations.

Key Terms

Monte Carlo Simulation

Monte Carlo Experiment

Normal distribution

Binomial distribution

Uniform distribution

Bootstrap technique

Jackknife technique

Markov Chain Monte Carlo

Markov Chain

Critical Thinking Exercises

1. Marshall Jones, a basketball player, is a very sensitive shooter; he shoots much better at home than he does on the road. When Jones' is at home, his points per game can be modeled by the Poisson (rpois) distribution using a lambda of 19. When Jones is on the road, his points per game can be modeled by the Poisson distribution using a lambda of 13. Design a Monte Carlo simulation to estimate Jones' performance of the course of an 82-game season where he plays 41 games at home and 41 games on the road.
   - How many points do we expect Jones to average per game?
   - What is maximum number of points that we expect Jones to record in a single season?
   - What is the minimum number of points that we expect Jones to record in a single season?
2. Wide receivers will typically catch more passes than tight ends. If we model the number of catches a wide receiver is going to make with a Poisson distribution with lambda 7 and the number of catches a tight end is going to make with a Poisson distribution of lambda 5, design a Monte Carlo simulation to find out how often the tight end will out-catch the wide receiver.

3. Of course, when receivers are thrown to, they do not always catch the ball. Drops and tipped passes are very much a part of professional football. Use the Bernoulli or Uniform distributions to add a chance that each player above drops the pass to your Monte Carlo simulation.
   - When the receiver has a catch rate of 85% and the tight end has a catch rate of 80%, how often does the tight end out-catch the receiver?
   - When the receiver has a catch rate of 75% and the tight end has a catch rate of 80%, how often does the tight end out-catch the receiver?
   - When the receiver has a catch rate of 50% and the tight end has a catch rate of 90%, how often does the tight end out catch the receiver?

4. A simple key to the game of golf is keeping the ball on the "fairway"—the well-groomed part of the course from which it is easier to make shots. Design a Markov Chain Monte Carlo simulation to estimate how a golfer will do on a hole, if we assume the following:
   - The golfer's first shot will land on the fairway 80% of the time.
   - Every subsequent shot from the fairway has an 80% chance of staying in the fairway.
   - Each shot from the fairway modifies the number of shots needed to complete the hole, by -2, -1, 0, or +1 shots with uniform probability.
   - Every subsequent shot from the rough (off the fairway) has a 50% chance of making it back to the fairway.
   - Each shot from the rough modifies the number of shots needed to complete the hole, by -1, 0, +1, or +2 shots with uniform probability.

5. In boxing, there is a saying that "styles make fights." A young fighter enters an amateur boxing tournament. They would need to defeat five consecutive other fighters to win. Design a Markov Chain Monte Carlo simulation to estimate the likelihood that the fighter wins the tournament assuming the following:
   - The fighter has a 80% chance of beating puncher style fighters, and any given round has a 50% chance of featuring such a fighter.
   - The fighter has a 75% chance of beating boxer style fighters, and any given round has a 30% chance of featuring such a fighter.
   - The fighter has a 65% chance of beating counter-puncher style fighters, and any given round has a 20% chance of featuring such a fighter.

6. Modify the example above to account for the fact that Southpaw boxers will tend to have an advantage due to their opponents unfamiliarity. Any given opponent has a 10% chance of being left handed and this decreases the fighter's likelihood of beating this opponent by 5% for the puncher, 10% for the boxer, and 15% for the counter puncher. What is the new likelihood that the fighter wins five consecutive fights and wins the tournament?

References

Chawla, Sanjay, Joël Estephan, Joachim Gudmundsson, and Michael Horton. 2017. Classification of passes in football matches using spatiotemporal data. *ACM Transactions on Spatial Algorithms and Systems (TSAS)* 3(2), 1–30.

Fernandez, Javier, and Luke Bornn. 2018. *Wide open spaces: A statistical technique for measuring space creation in professional soccer.* Conference paper at the MIT Sloan Sports Analytics Conference. https://www.researchgate.net/publication/324942294_Wide_Open_Spaces_A_statistical_technique_for_measuring_space_creation_in_professional_soccer

Fernandez, Javier, Luke Bornn, and Dan Cervone. 2019. *Decomposing the immeasurable sport: A deep learning expected possession value framework for soccer.* Conference paper at the MIT Sloan Sports Analytics Conference. https://www.sloansportsconference.com/research-papers/decomposing-the-immeasurable-sport-a-deep-learning-expected-possession-value-framework-for-soccer

Fonseca, Sofia, João Milho, Bruno Travassos, and Duarte Araújo. 2012. Spatial dynamics of team sports exposed by Voronoi diagrams. *Human Movement Science* 31(6), 1652–1659.

Further Readings

Davison, A. C., and D. V. Hinkley. 1997. *Bootstrap methods and their application* (No. 1). New York: Cambridge University Press.

Robert, C. P., G. Casella, and G. Casella. 2010. *Introducing monte carlo methods with R* (Vol. 18). New York: Springer.

Robert, C., and G. Casella. (2013). *Monte Carlo statistical methods.* Springer Science & Business Media.

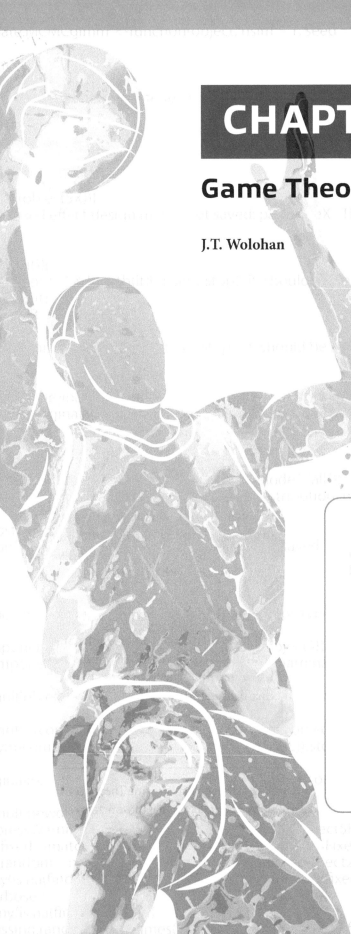

CHAPTER 8

Game Theory in Sport Analytics

J.T. Wolohan

LEARNING OBJECTIVES

After reading this chapter, students should be able to:

- Use a payoff matrix to a model decision-making scenario
- Identify dominating and dominated strategies
- Identify the different considerations for single play and repeated play games
- Identify zero sum and collaborative games
- Perform the calculations necessary to minimize regret

Introduction

In the 1940s, mathematician **John von Neumann** pioneered a new interdisciplinary domain of mathematics that would come to be known as **Game Theory** (Von Neumann and Morgenstern 1947). von Neumann was inspired by the way economic decision-makers—such as businesses, sport franchises, players and coaches—interact with one another and respond to shifting payoffs. Consider the following example:

> *Nike is debating signing a highly regarded college prospect, Javon Wolf, to a shoe contract. Javon is fresh off a 25 point-per-game Freshman season for his University and is considering going pro. Javon's father, however, was a professional NFL player, and several NFL teams are making their interest known to Javon as well. Javon's value to Nike is much higher if Javon plays professional basketball—where his face will be on TV unobstructed by a facemask—as opposed to professional football—where he will be one of 22 masked and helmeted players on the field at any given time. How does Nike decide what to do?*

In the example, there are two economic actors: Nike and Javon Wolf. Nike is making the decision about whether or not to offer Javon millions of dollars in a shoe deal. Javon is deciding whether he wants to play professional football or professional basketball. If Javon goes pro in football, Javon may be happier, but he will be of much less value to Nike. If Javon goes pro in basketball, he will be of much more value to Nike. Game Theory is the study of situations like this, as well as the rules and strategies that decision-making actors can use to ensure they make the best decisions.

The applications of Game Theory to sport are plentiful. Game Theory naturally applies to sport competitions themselves; for helping coaches and players make better decisions on the field of play. We can also apply Game Theory widely in the business of sport. For instance, as we saw earlier, in the domain of sport marketing. Many non-sport applications of Game Theory concern the worlds of business, politics, and public policy—so wherever it is that sport interacts with those fields, there is often an application of Game Theory to be found.

In this chapter, we will review the principles of Game Theory through their application to sport. We will first pursue an introduction to Game Theory. Then we will look at types of games—different rules or circumstances under which decision-makers can be constrained. Next, we will examine various strategies for decision-makers, including von Neumann's own **minimax** decision rule. Lastly, we will look at some differences between Game Theory and other decision theories.

What is Game Theory?

Game Theory is the mathematical study of rational strategic decision-making. That is, Game Theory concerns itself with (1) situations in which actors need to make decisions; (2) strategies that those actors can use to determine the correct decision; (3) mathematical representations of decision-making situations; (4) applications of the above to the real world—or in the theoretical case, an imagined world.

The critical words defining game theory are rational, strategic, and decision-making. Rational ideas suggests that each actor in the situation must have the ability to assess their payouts under various scenarios. Irrational actors cannot do this. Do note that there is a difference between an actor behaving irrationally and an actor not conforming to our misunderstanding of their perception of the payoffs. For example, consider the scenario we introduced with Nike and Javon Wolf in the introductory section of this chapter. If Nike offers Javon a large shoe deal knowing that he is likely to make more money on his first NBA contract than his first NFL contract and therefore reasons that he must rationally choose going in the NBA, Nike is making an assumption about the payoff for Javon. Javon may not value the monetary difference between his first contract in the NBA and the NFL, instead highly valuing continuing his father's legacy as a professional football player. This is not irrational behavior, even if it is unexpected to Nike. Correctly modeling the payoffs of the other decision-maker is a critical component to Game Theory.

Second, Game Theory assumes that decision-makers are strategic. That is, decision-makers are considering their payoffs and have some approach to doing so. For instance, a soccer coach who is very interested in playing an attacking style early in the game to score goals and later switches to a defensive style to preserve the lead is making strategic decisions about the value and risks of goals. The opposite of strategic might be a boxer who only has a single style, for example, a brawler who cannot fight defensively and only knows how to attack cannot behave strategically. A pitcher with only one pitch, for example, Mariano Rivera, cannot behave strategically. Note here that strategic is not the same as successful. Mariano Rivera, with only his devastating cut fastball—baseball's greatest pitch—is a unanimous Hall of Famer. Smokin' Joe Frazier, who was highly dependent on an aggressive, brawler style of boxing beat the highly strategic Muhammed Ali in The Fight of the Century. One exceptional option is better than several less-good options; however, these scenarios are not particularly relevant to game theory.

Third, game theory involves decision-making. For a situation to be evaluated in a game theoretic sense, there must be different options for the various actors involved. The options do not need to be good—in fact, in some of the simpler games we will use to demonstrate the principles of game theory, some of the options will be quite bad—but the options need to exist. Luckily, there are few examples in sport where we run into forced moves. For instance, even in positions where the what is apparent—such as a soccer penalty kick where one must shoot on goal, or a third-and-long in football where one more or less must throw—the how is still up for debate—should the penalty taker kick right or left?; which play should the coach call? Nevertheless, it is important to call out the decision-making aspect because ultimately, decision-making is the subject of Game Theory. Game Theory gives us insight into how we can evaluate decisions and decisions strategies of multiple actors in a mathematical context.

Game Theory Notation and Simple Games

Before looking at some of the classes of games we can evaluate using Game Theory—and principles for reasoning about those games—we first need to cover some notation for representing games. Games in Game Theory are most often represented using a **payoff matrix**. For example, let's consider a soccer penalty kick. The penalty taker can shoot either left or right, and the goalie can defend either left or right. If the two select the same direction, the kick is blocked. If the two select different directions, the kicker scores a goal. This scenario is represented in **Table 8.1.**

TABLE 8.1. Game theory notation for a soccer penalty kick

		Goalie	
		Block Left	Block Right
Kicker	Kick Left	0, 0	1, -1
	Kick Right	1, -1	0, 0

In this set up, you will note that each player in the game—in the case the kicker and the goalie—has been assigned to either the rows (the kicker) or the columns (the goalie.) Each player has also had their options enumerated: left and right for each the kicker and the goalie. At the intersection of these options is the **payoff**. The payoff is the reward or punishment a player gets in a given situation. For instance, if the kicker goes right and the goalie goes left, the kicker benefits (scores a goal) and the goalie loses (concedes a goal.) If the kicker goes left and the goalie goes left, then the kicker does not benefit, but the goalie is not harmed. We can see from this representation that even though the goalie has no opportunity to gain from their performance, they can still have a preference to avoid the harm of giving up a goal.

To consider a more complex example, let's return to the example of Nike and Javon Wolf from the introductory section of this chapter. Remember, Nike is trying to decide how much to invest in Javon, while Javon is trying to decide whether to play basketball or football. We might represent the payoff matrix for the situation as follows.

TABLE 8.2. Shoe sponsorship payoff matrix

		Javon	
		NBA	NFL
Nike	Big contract	10, 25	-5, 15
	Small contract	20, 15	3, 7

You will note instantly that this payoff matrix is much more complex than the one for the soccer penalty kick. For example, there are multiple situations where both parties benefit. In fact, of the four situations, both parties benefit in three of the four situations. The only scenario where a party is harmed is if Nike offers Javon Wolf a big contract and Javon decides to go to the NFL where the cost of sponsoring him will not make back the investment. If Nike offers Javon a big contract and he goes to the NBA, or they offer him a small contract, all parties benefit. Of course, both parties benefit the most financially if Javon goes to the NBA. Laid out like this, we can clearly see the allure for Javon of going to the NBA. Both of his NBA options **dominate** his NFL options. That is, regardless of what Nike does, Javon's payoff is higher by going to the NBA. Similarly, Nike's option of offering a small contract dominates their option of offering a large contract because regardless of what Javon decides, Nike's payoff in the small contract scenario is better. However, it is important to remember that both of these dominations occur as a result of simplifying the scenario. If Nike offers Javon a small contract, there is potential he will not take the contract at all. And for Javon, there are non-financial issues that must be factored into the payoff matrix.

Utility Theory

In the last section we introduced a game to help us think about what Nike might consider when offering a soon-to-graduate collegiate athlete a sponsorship deal. This situation is unusual, but not altogether unheard of—though it is more common with football and baseball than football and basketball. Tom Brady, Russell Wilson, John Elway, and—of course—Deion Sanders all faced the question of whether to play professional football or baseball. Sanders is the only athlete to ever win both a Super Bowl and a World Series.

For athletes, this question comes down to more than finances. It comes down to love of the game, a desire for fame, and even family connection to a sport or the desire to strike out on one's own. These amorphous concepts can be hard to value in analytical models; however, in game theory, we will attempt to do so through what is known as **utility theory**. Utility theory is a theory of preference that attempts to order outcomes, events, possibilities—and where possible assign numerical values to them—in accordance with the preferences that an individual holds for those outcomes. For instance, when John Elway was drafted in 1983 by the Baltimore Colts, he revealed to the Colts that his preference for playing football was greater than his preference for playing baseball, but his preference for playing baseball for the New York Yankees—a team he had played summer ball with the year prior—was greater than his preference for playing football for the Colts. In that case, we might represent Elway's preferences as follows:

Option	Preference
Denver	10
Yankees	3
Colts	1

For Elway, each scenario has some value—after all, he is about to become very, very wealthy no matter what he chooses—however, there is a clear preference. Furthermore, the preference involves more than simple monetary values. His preference for playing for the Yankees is informed by the Yankees history, their success as a franchise, and the likelihood of winning a World Series there—which he very well might have done, as the Yankees won two titles during Elway's football career.

Utility—the unit of analysis in game theory—can often be difficult to measure. One of the tools we have to measure utility is **revealed preference**. Revealed preference is the simple observation that people choose to do what they prefer over the things they do not prefer. Revealed preferences may conflict with outside perceptions of people's interests and even their people's stated interests. This is something we see quite often when free agent players hit the open market. The players will often state that they want to go to a competitive team. This is their stated preference. Then, when the off-season is over, the player will most often find them signed to a large contract with an uncompetitive franchise. This is their revealed preference. The player states that winning gives them greater utility, while in reality the money gives them more utility. Of course, this may not be due to the money itself. Perhaps the athlete is influenced by the opinion of their spouse, in which case satisfying their spouse could give them a high degree of utility. This was rumored to be the case, for instance, in 2014 when Carmelo Anthony was selecting his new basketball home, with interest from the Los Angeles Lakers, the Chicago Bulls, and the New York Knicks. Anthony's wife, La La, who was a successful media figure in her own right, was said to greatly prefer New York to the alternatives. Perhaps co-incidentally, La La Anthony began starring in a New York-based television series the year before Carmelo Anthony signed with the New York Knicks.

One of the problems with revealed utility, of course, is that it somewhat assumes that people make good decisions. And if good decision-making was easy, then game theory would not need to exist. One of the ways around this problem is by thinking in terms of **expected utility.** Expected utility is a risk-weighted form of utility that varies—more so than standard utility—across individuals. For instance, a professional poker player may have a high tolerance for risk while a professional soccer coach may have a low tolerance for risk. These risk tolerances change the expected utility each will get from a situation. A riskier situation is less palatable to the soccer coach, who discounts the situation simply by virtue of its risk. The risky situation, in contrast, may be exciting to the poker player, who prefers a high-upside benefit.

Through the rest of this chapter, we will put most of the problems with measuring utility itself aside—though the problems are real and weigh heavily on decision-making in sport. Before we set aside these points altogether, consider which of the following alternatives you might prefer:

- $5 million/year to play your favorite sport or $25 million/year to play your least favorite sport
- Going undefeated in the regular season or winning the league title
- Beating your rival or beating the league's best team

- Acquiring a star player who will make the team worse but more popular or acquiring an unknown player who will make the team better
- Tanking for one year to get a high-draft pick or spending 3 years as a middle-of-the-pack team
- Building a new state-of-the-art stadium or renovating an old historic stadium

Types of Games

To continue to discuss the games from Tables 8.1 and 8.2, it will help to have language to talk about types of games. In this section, we will introduce the Game Theory terms for talking about games, as well the strategic considerations for those games.

ZERO-SUM GAMES

The first category of games that we will look at are **zero-sum games**. Zero sum games are games like the one expressed in Table 8.1 where the sum of each cell of our payoff matrix totals to zero. That is, every time one player benefits, the other player must suffer. Most sports are like this. If one team scores a goal, their opponents give up a goal. If the batter gets a hit, the pitcher gives up a hit. This winner/loser binary is ubiquitous across the on-the-field aspect sport. Off the field, zero-sum games are less common. For instance, consider Table 8.2. None of these situations were zero-sum. In fact, in most of the situations the players were just deciding how to divide a large pie.

Zero-sum games are intrinsically competitive. The structure is such that whenever one player benefits, the other is harmed an equal, opposite amount. The curiosity of zero-sum games revolves around the degrees of winning and losing and how different strategies can impact those outcomes. For example, consider the following example:

> Bayern Munich and Arsenal are about to face off in the second leg of their UEFA Champions League knockout phase matchup. Arsenal won the first game 2-1 at Bayern, so they have a 1 goal lead overall and 2 away goals in hand. For Bayern to make a comeback and advance to the next round, they would need to beat Arsenal by 2 or more goals; or they would need to score 3 or more goals at Arsenal, while still winning by 1 goal. Arsenal can advance with a win, a draw, or a 1-nil loss.

This is a zero-sum game. Any benefit that is accrued by Arsenal necessarily comes at the expense of Bayern Munich. Any benefit that is accrued by Bayern Munich is at the expense of Arsenal. Unlike the penalty kick example we saw earlier, however, the payoff matrix here exposes an interesting—albeit intuitive—strategy for Arsenal.

TABLE 8.3. Champions League knockout phase payout matrix

		Bayern Munich			
		Attacking	Normal	Counter Attacking	Defensive
Arsenal	Attacking	10, -10	25, -25	5, -5	50, -50
	Normal	-5, 5	15, -15	10, -10	50, -50
	Counter Attacking	25, -25	10, -10	50, -50	50, -50
	Defensive	20, -20	35, -35	50, -50	50, -50

Examine the payoffs in Table 8.3 and you will note that Arsenal has the advantage no matter what they do—resulting from their numerous ways to advance to the next round. Bayern, in contrast, has an uphill climb to advance under each scenario. While this is true, this is obviously an oversimplification of the situation. This oversimplification is one of the flaws of a payoff-matrix oriented approach to making decisions. Often, one number is not sufficient to represent the complexity of a situation. For instance, each cell of this table actually represents the average of many possible outcomes. This average is sufficient for our toy example here, but often insufficient in practice because the distribution of outcomes can be distributed unevenly—the distribution can be skewed. In these cases, more nuanced understanding of the relationship between the benefits of various outcomes and their likelihood is necessary.

All that aside, we can see that there are some strategies that are obviously bad for Bayern—most notably, the defensive strategy. If Bayern plays the defensive strategy, they are guaranteed their worst payout. Arsenal is in a similar boat. Their attacking, and normal strategies are dominated by the defensive strategy. This suggests that they should never use these strategies—even if they have a positive payout expectation—because the expectation of a positive payout is greater with another strategy. In turn, this means that Bayern has no incentive to play its counterattacking strategy because the strategy is only effective against Arsenal's normal and attacking strategies, which—as we just noted—they will never play. The effect is that the 4 × 4 game—where each team has four strategies, is compressed to a 2 × 2 game, with each only having two strategies. This compressed game is shown in Table 8.4.

TABLE 8.4. Compressed Champions League knockout phase payout matrix

		Bayern Munich	
		Attacking	Normal
Arsenal	Counter Attacking	25, -25	10, -10
	Defensive	20, -20	35, -35

Compressing the game, we see strategies that are familiar to anyone who has ever watched the second leg of a Champions League knockout phase, or, more generally, anyone who has ever watched the second half of a blowout. The team with the lead—Arsenal in this case—is highly incentivized to play defensive strategies because a high-scoring game gives their opponent more opportunities to win. The team trailing—Bayern Munich in our example—is highly incentivized to play aggressive strategies because the defensive strategies eliminate all chances of victory.

Table 8.4 also represents an example of a game where there is no **pure strategy**—a strategy that is composed of strictly using one option—that is best for either player. Arsenal's counterattacking strategy can be countered by Bayern using the normal strategy, which in turn can be countered by Arsenal adopting a defensive strategy, which Bayern would counter by adopting an aggressive strategy. Instead, each adopts a **mixed strategy**. Mixed strategies are composed of multiple strategies, chosen randomly at some ratio related to the rate at which we expect the opponent to play their corresponding strategies. In other words, Arsenal will try to play the counterattacking strategy regularly enough that Bayern is disincentivized from using their attacking strategy, but not so often that Bayern can always play their normal strategy to exploit Arsenal in return. The proper mixed strategy for each team—the ideal rate at which each player should select each strategy—is called the **Nash Equilibrium** (Nash 1950). John Nash—the mathematician and economist behind the Nash Equilibrium, as well as the subject of A Beautiful Mind—showed that all games that are played to be won, **finite games**, have such an equilibrium.

SYMMETRIC GAMES

To explore Nash Equilibrium, let us consider a **symmetric game**. Symmetric games are those where the payoff matrix is symmetric. In other words, a game where you can change the position of the players—rows and columns—without changing the game. Symmetric games are pretty rare in sport, but they are common in sport business. For example, consider the case of two teams—Arizona and Montreal—bidding on a free-agent player. If both of the teams bid high, the player will randomly choose a team—but that team will need to overpay. If both teams bid low, again the player will randomly choose a team; however, this time the team that ends up with the player will be happy because they receive a great deal. If one team bids high and one team bids low, then the team that bids high will be satisfied because they get the player for a reasonable amount, while the team that bids low will suffer because they did not get the player.

TABLE 8.5. Symmetric matrix for bidding on a free agent

| | | Arizona | |
		High	Low
Montreal	High	-2.5, -2.5	5, -2
	Low	-2, 5	4, 4

Looking at the payout matrix in Table 8.5, we can see the symmetry. If we swap the labels of the two teams-Arizona and Montreal—the payoffs for the teams does not change. Indeed, nothing about the game does. That is what makes the game symmetric.

We can also see from Table 8.5 that there are no dominant strategies. Each team would prefer to bid low, assuming they could ensure that the other team would also bid low; however, if one team was committed to bidding low, they leave themselves open to exploitation by the other team, which will be more satisfied by bidding high. To resolve this, and prevent any exploitation by the other team, the two teams will converge on behavior that approximates the Nash Equilibrium.

For symmetric and zero-sum games, we can find those strategies—one strategy in the case of a symmetric game—with the following technique: first, we find all the pure strategies that a player may want to play; then, we find the expected value of those strategies; lastly, we find the probabilities that must be assigned to each pure strategy to create a mixed strategy to make the opponent indifferent to their realistic strategies.

For example, in Table 8.5 we can see that each player has an expected value of 1.25 when they bid high and 1 when they bid low.

```
high.ev = (-2.5x + 5y)/2 = 1.25
low.ev = (-2x + 4y)/2 = 1
```

From this payout schedule, each team would be incentivized to bid high, assuming that the other team was picking from either of their strategies evenly. To correct for this, the teams should play the bid-high strategy more. This will punish the other team if they blindly bid high because the value from bidding high is driven by the chance of bidding high when the opposing team bids low. The correct rate for the team to bid high is the rate which makes expected values of the two functions—the high-bid strategy and the low-bid strategy—equal. In our scenario, this rate is approximately bidding high 2/3rds of the time and bidding low 1/3rd of the time.

So far, all of the games that we have looked at have assumed that the game's players are making their decisions simultaneously. These games are, intuitively, called **simultaneous games.** Simultaneous games are those in which the players must make their decisions without information about their interlocutors past behavior or in which there is no time component. In contrast to simultaneous games, **sequential games** are games in which one player goes first and then another goes second. While both simultaneous and sequential games are important for modeling many aspects of sport—neither is typically appropriate for the on-the-field component. The on-the-field aspect of sport is most properly modeled as a **repeated game.** Repeated games are those in which a base game is repeated many times. In this section, we will look at each of these three types of games: simultaneous, sequential, and repeated games.

Simultaneous games are games in which all players must make their decisions at effectively the same time as their opponents. These types of games are common in sport business—where inaction itself must be treated as a strategy with its own distinct set of payoffs—and in some simplified on-field scenarios, for example, a soccer penalty kick or the final play of a football game. In simultaneous games, we have no information about the tendencies or behaviors of interlocutors. Therefore, we will often want to play a Nash Equilibrium strategy to stabilize the game, though this is not always the case. We will discuss other strategies—and their use cases—later in this chapter.

Sequential games are games in which players take turns in one after the other, with information about what their opponents did on previous turns. An example of this is drafts, whether professional or fantasy. During a draft, teams take turns selecting a strategy: selecting a player or trading their pick. The strategy they chose changes the payouts for the teams that will act later by changing the players available to select. These teams must then make a new decision given this updated information, while also understanding that their actions will ripple downstream and influence the strategies other teams will take later in the draft. Popular sequential games include poker and chess. Chess is an example of a sequential game with **perfect information**—that is, the player to act knows all the relevant information about what their opponent chose to do. Poker is an example of a sequential game with **imperfect information**—that is, the player to act knows some information about what their opponent chose to do, but not all the information that is necessary to play perfectly.

Repeated games are games in which a series of simultaneous games constitutes a larger game. This is the best way to think about most on-the-field sports. Perhaps the most obvious example is football. Each down represents a game during which the two teams must select a strategy (a play). Then, they simultaneously run those plays, evaluate the results, and select another strategy for the following down. In soccer or basketball, we might think of a possession as the simultaneous game to be repeated. In sport media, programming can be modeled as a repeated game: the networks make decisions about which sports to bid on and which games or shows to air. This process repeats then weekly, quarterly, and seasonally.

Consider the following games, representative of a sequence of football downs. In the first game, shown in Table 8.6, we see a simplification of what each team may do. The offense has three options: run, pass short, and pass deep; and the defense has three options: man, zone, blitz. The game, considered in total, is a zero-sum game. A quick analysis of the game will reveal that two options—the deep pass for the offense and the blitz are superfluous. The offense will always do better with a run or a short pass, and the defense will always do better playing man or zone defense.

TABLE 8.6. First down payoff table

			Defense		
			Man	Zone	Blitz
Offense	Run		2, -2	1, -1	1, -1
	Pass Short		1, -1	1, -1	3, -3
	Pass Deep		-2, 2	-1, 1	-3, 3

Let us imagine that the offense chooses to run—a strategy that strictly dominates passing short against the man and zone defenses of the defense—and the defense plays a man defense. The result of the play is a 2-yard gain. The game is then repeated with a new payoff Table 8.7 reflecting the new reality of 2nd and 8.

TABLE 8.7. Second down payoff table

			Defense		
			Man	Zone	Blitz
Offense	Run		2, -2	1, -1	1, -1
	Pass Short		2, -2	1, -1	3, -3
	Pass Deep		-1, 1	-1, 1	-3, 3

In the payoff table for second and 8, we can see a few changes. Notably, passing short and deep have both gained in value. Both of these plays are likelier than runs to gain the necessary yardage for a first down, but have the risk of an incomplete pass. You'll note that in this specific payout table, the short pass dominates the other two strategies—running and passing deep—so we can assume that the offense will adopt this strategy. The defense will adopt a zone defense to minimize their loss against this strategy.

Of course, as we remember from earlier in the chapter—and from a lifetime of watching sports—the outcome that is probabilistically most likely is not always the one that occurs. Nor will it in our example. Let us suppose that the second-down play took a negative turn for the offense: their slot receiver dropped a clear first down after finding themselves on the receiving end of a ferocious tackle from a linebacker who had dropped back in the zone defense. The next game will take place at 3rd and 8 and the offense will be without their key slot receiver—who needs a play to catch his breath. The payout table for third down can be seen in Table 8.8.

TABLE 8.8. Third down payoff table

		Defense		
		Man	Zone	Blitz
Offense	Run	-4, 4	-4, 4	-2, 2
	Pass Short	-3, 3	-2, -2	-3, 3
	Pass Deep	-1, 1	-1, 1	-4, 4

Looking at Table 8.8, we instantly notice the changing of the tides. The offense has gone from having positive expected payoffs in most scenarios, to negative expected payoffs in all scenarios. This is a quintessential aspect of repeated games: the previously played games influence the payoffs of the subsequent games. In this case, the defense benefits from the sequence of events and finds themselves in a highly advantageous situation.

In a third and long situation, the offense is out of good options. They need to pass deep in order to attempt to convert the first down—even though doing so is unlikely to succeed—but they cannot exclusively focus on this strategy. If the offense committed to only passing on third and long, the defense would know that it could blitz. Instead, the offense needs to adopt a mixed strategy that balances the defense's payouts and makes them indifferent to the three options. In other words, they need to play their Nash Equilibrium strategy. If you have ever watched a game and wondered why a coach calls a flaccid draw run or screen pass on third and nine, know they are doing so to nullify the defense's natural preferences.

Looking at Table 8.8, the first step we will want to take in finding the Nash Equilibrium for the offense is eliminating the short pass option. Passing short is never the best option for the offense—it is bested by passing deep against man and zone defenses and by running against the blitz. Because it is never the best alternative, we can safely exclude it from the offense's Nash Equilibrium strategy. We also note that when we remove the pass short strategy, the man and zone defenses become the same strategy: they have the same payouts against the run and the pass deep strategies of the offense. This means we can safely collapse them into a single strategy. This consolidated payoff table is shown in Table 8.9.

TABLE 8.9. Third down payoff table

		Defense	
		Don't Blitz	Blitz
Offense	Run	-4, 4	-2, 2
	Pass Deep	-1, 1	-4, 4

The updated table payoff matrix in Table 8.9 shows the small inclination of the defense to blitz on third and long. They are getting 3 points of expected value versus 2.5, assuming the offense was playing strategies at random. Of course, the offense will be playing their Nash Equilibrium instead to nullify any strategic benefit the defense may get. This strategy, somewhat counterintuitively, will involve running more than passing, to encourage the defense away from blitzing. If you do the arithmetic out, it ends up that the offense's Nash Equilibrium strategy is to run ⅗ of the time and pass deep ⅖ of the time.

Importantly you will note that in the toy example we worked through over the last few paragraphs, we did not mention many of the factors that complicate these decisions in a real-life game of football. To name but a few: time, score, weather, the importance of the game, personal player statistics, and the personal motivations of the coaching staff. All of these factors would subtly influence the payoff matrix and, because of our inability to account for most of them, render game theory highly theoretical for actual gameplay.

Types of Strategies

So far, we have talked mostly about types of games, their relevance in sport, and how to stabilize these games through the use of Nash Equilibrium strategies: mixed strategies that play in such a fashion that the opponent is indifferent to all their choices. We briefly discussed dominant strategies and dominated strategies, but because the advice here is so obvious—play the dominant strategy as much as possible and never play the dominated strategy—there is little to say. In this section, we will look at four other types of strategies in game theory. Two of these strategies—minimax and maximin—are applicable toward any game, while two—the tit for tat and grim trigger strategies—are appropriate exclusively for repeated games.

First, let us take a look at the **minimax strategy**. The minimax strategy is a strategy in game theory where a player tries to minimize the maximum loss they could incur. The strategy is highly valuable in situations where the player already has an advantage and will likely benefit in the long run from conservative play. Consider, for instance, the 4th quarter of a regular season basketball game. The game was competitive up until the final 5 minutes, when the home team went on a 15-point run and opened up a big lead. The away team might choose to sit their best players using the minimax strategy. Sure, they are going to lose the game, but they were likely to lose under all circumstances. By sitting their best players, they can avoid the risk that those players get hurt: a far greater negative than the loss of a single game. This strategy is often employed to excess at the end of seasons when a team may sit many or most of their starters once they have clinched a playoff berth.

Additionally, consider the relegation system in Premiere League soccer. If a team finishes at the bottom three of the league, they get demoted to the EFL Championship. Under these circumstances, many bad teams will play conservatively to try and eke out points from a draw—and help them avoid relegation—instead of playing aggressively to win the match. The minimax strategy makes sense in this situation because the downside to being demoted is far greater than the downside to not winning any individual match.

The minimax strategy is often used in situations like the aforementioned where the downside risk is much greater than the upside opportunity; however, it is also rationally adopted in most **infinite games** (Sinek 2019). Infinite games are those in which the primary motivation of the players is not to win, but to keep playing. For example, in Premier League soccer, or—especially—in sport business. Companies play an infinite game in so far as their primary, if unspoken, goal is to stay in business—stay in the game and continue "playing." If we consider the case of basketball shoe companies, Nike is clearly the top dog, while Under Armor, Adidas, Puma and Reebok all play for a piece of second place. For these bottom four companies—Under Armor, Adidas, Puma, and Reebok—beating Nike is not the goal. It is scarcely a dream, if they are being honest with themselves. The goal is to continue selling basketball shoes. To stay profitable enough to stay in the market, with the hopes that they will catch a big break or that Nike's basketball empire will falter. For these companies, the minimax strategy makes a lot of sense. They want to minimize the amount they could lose on any one sponsorship deal, while still ensuring they have a presence in the NBA. Meanwhile, Nike is willing to make riskier—more expensive while potentially more lucrative—deals, such as signing rookie Zion Williamson to a $75-million sponsorship before he had ever played in a professional game.

Under some conditions, this strategy can be known as the **maximin strategy**. The maximin strategy involves maximizing one's minimum gain. For example, thinking back to Table 8.2 where we discussed the college athlete deciding between the NFL and the NBA, it would not make sense to think about the athlete minimizing their loss because they stand to gain a substantial amount under all conditions. In this circumstance, it makes more sense to think about maximizing the minimum gain.

In some more advanced applications of the minimax strategy, we may think not about the pure minimax strategy, but about **minimax regret**. In the minimax regret strategy, one attempts not to minimize their maximum loss, but minimize the maximum amount of regret they will feel. Regret, in game theory, being the payoff you received minus the payoff you expected. For example, in the trivial example of the soccer penalty kick, if the kicker kicks the ball in the same direction the goalie goes to make the same they will have regret that they did not kick the ball the other direction. If they kick the ball in the opposite direction of the goalie, they will score a goal and feel no regret at all.

To see this strategy in action, consider Table 8.10 that illustrates how a shoe company may consider offering a shoe deal to a college basketball player who is on their way to the NBA. The shoe company can either offer the basketball player a big contract or a small contract; the basketball player can either turn out to be bad, good, or great. If the shoe company offers the player a big contract and the player is bad, the shoe company loses a lot of money. If the shoe company offers the player a big contract and they are good, the deal will be neutral—the player will sell enough shoes to make up for the money spent on the sponsorship. If the player is great, the shoe company stands to gain a lot of money and the player will be loyal to the shoe company because they signed a big deal when they were young. In contrast, if the shoe company offers the player a small contract, they lose very little if the player is bad and stand to gain a little if the player is good; however, the ceiling for if the player is great is lower. If the player turns out to be great, they will likely leave to find another company that supports them more.

TABLE 8.10. Payoff table for shoe-deal regret

		College Basketball Player		
		Bad	Good	Great
Shoe Company	Big contract	-5	0	15
	Small contract	-1	2	5

By the pure minimax strategy, the shoe company should offer the player a small contract—that way they only stand to lose a small amount. However, this would be the wrong choice from a regret perspective. If the player turns out to be great, the shoe company will have a lot of regret about not signing the player when they could have. To see this, let's look at the regret matrix in Table 8.11.

TABLE 8.11. Shoe-deal regret matrix

		College Basketball Player		
		Bad	Good	Great
Shoe Company	Big contract	6	2	0
	Small contract	0	0	10

In Table 8.11 we have calculated the regret for each outcome by taking the maximum possible payoff under a given situation (bad, good, great) and subtracting the outcome that would be observed. For example, if the player is bad, the best outcome for the shoe company is to give the player a small contract (-1), so their regret in that case would be zero. Their regret if they gave the player a big contract would be that best possible outcome minus the observed outcome (-5). From this table, we can see that if the player is bad or good, the small contract makes more sense: there is no regret in either situation. However, if the player is great, offering them only a small contract leads to a lot of regret. The company will wish they had invested in the player when they had the opportunity.

If the company is operating under a minimax regret strategy, then they will try to minimize their maximum regret. If they offer the player a big contract, their maximum regret is 6: the player turns out to be bad and they lose a lot of money on the sponsorship. If the company offers the player a small contract, their maximum regret is 10: the player is exceptional and they both miss out on a big branding opportunity. In this scenario, they will play the big contract strategy exclusively.

You will note that the minimax strategy and the minimax regret strategy offer different solutions to the decision problem. The minimax strategy is considered to be more conservative because it attempts to reduce the absolute loss. The minimax regret strategy is considered to be more correct because it attempts to incorporate information about our true preferences.

TIT FOR TAT

While the minimax and minimax regret strategies are both individual-focused strategies, not all game players operate this way. Indeed, in some games, players may have the opportunity to cooperate with one another. Unsurprisingly, these games are called **cooperative games**. Cooperative games are those in which players have the opportunity to forge alliances or otherwise make pro-social acts that can benefit the other players of the game. These scenarios rarely come up in sport—although they do appear occasionally and we will take a look at one—however, they occur frequently in sport business.

To start thinking about cooperative games, we might consider bikers in any given leg of a multi-day race. Biking is a laborious endurance sport where longer races are composed of smaller races that take place over a number of consecutive days. Each smaller race—to the extent that they can be called small—may be hundreds of miles long, requiring four to five hours of biking at a competitive speed. A tactic that the bikers use to make their lives easier is drafting. Drafting is when a biker rides closely behind another—a teammate or other collaborator—in order to avoid the natural wind resistance of leading the pack. In long races, the pack of leaders may all allow one another to draft off of each other for a time, understanding that they will all benefit from faster times in the race and fresher legs the following day if they do not need to face the wind resistance the entire race (Hoenigman et al. 2011). Of course, the bikers are still competing and only one can win the race.

In this situation, a biker may wish to use a **tit-for-tat** strategy. In the tit-for-tat strategy, the player defaults to cooperating with their interlocutor and then subsequently matches their previous move. In the instance of the bikers, this would mean allowing others to draft off of you for a time, and then attempting to draft off of them. If they let you draft off of them, you would in turn let them draft off of you again. If they do not let you draft, you would similarly not allow them to draft until they reciprocated by letting you draft them.

This strategy has several benefits. First, it allows the player to seek the benefits from cooperation, should they exist. The bikers are all better off if they can draft one another, so having a default posture of cooperating is beneficial. Second, it prevents a player from being taken advantage of too much. The biker will only allow others to draft them for so long, before they try to draft off of another. Subsequently, they will only extend the advantage of drafting off them a second time to other bikers who had allowed them to draft. Third, the biker allows themselves to benefit from cooperation—even with those who have previously been uncooperative. This can pay off late in the race, when the bikers are tired. If an opponent, having attempted to separate from the biker through a particularly tough part of the course where they were not allowing the biker to draft them, is open to cooperating later in the race, both bikers still stand to benefit from lower times should they draft off of one another again. The tit-for-tat strategy says that the biker will accept an offer to cooperate, assuming that the competitor makes it first after having violated their original cooperation.

The tit-for-tat strategy is well suited for games where cooperation is of high value and "backstabbing" behavior is of relatively low risk. For instance, the tit-for-tat approach is highly appealing early in a race—when there are many hours of benefit to be gained from cooperation—but loses appeal toward the end of the race, when the risk that your opponent breaks from the cooperative pattern to try and win the race increases. There are lots of situations like this in business where companies can cooperate and avoid the risk of going head-to-head with their competitors. Fortunately, there are typically laws against this type of cooperation—often called collusion.

GRIM TRIGGER

A more primitive version of the tit-for-tat strategy that can be useful in games where the benefits from cooperation and the risks of a defecting opponent are more balanced is the **grim trigger** strategy. A player following the grim trigger strategy will initiate play cooperating with their opponents—similar to the tit-for-tat strategy—and continue to cooperate until an opponent violates this cooperation. Once an opponent violates the cooperation, the player will then attempt to inflict maximum losses upon their opponent, or at least not cooperate with them anymore.

The classic example of a grim trigger application comes from the Cold War's theory of mutually assured destruction, wherein the two nuclear powers—the United States and Russia—would agree not to use their nuclear weapons up until the point that the other used theirs. At such a time, the other would use all of their nuclear weapons, inflicting maximum losses on their opponent, even if it led to their own destruction as well.

In sport, the cooperation between a player and a team can often take the form of a grim trigger strategy. The player and the team may cooperate for some time while they both find it mutually beneficial; however, when the player decides to leave, they may start to degenerate the team's coaching staff, the ownership and management of the team, and even other players on the roster. Depending on the efficacy of these statements, they may be harming the team by making the team less attractive to other players. Similarly, a team may share with other teams information about the player's off field conduct or team-held medical information about the player that could influence the amount or duration of the player's next contract.

Summary

Game theory is a general purpose theory of decision-making that can be effectively applied to the analysis of sport, as well as numerous other areas such as business (including sport business and sport marketing) and even international relations. Game theory's primary innovations emerge from expressing decision-making situations in terms of payoff matrices and deriving techniques for selecting the best strategies. These strategies can take the form of a single approach—in the case of a pure strategy—or of multiple different approaches played randomly at some optimal frequency— mixed strategies. Game theory also offers us insights into how individuals should behave over multiple runs of the same situation and how individuals may cooperate in semi-cooperative situations. In this chapter we saw how game theory may be applied everywhere from sport business to competitive cycling.

Critical Thinking Exercises

1. When we think of sport, we typically think of zero-sum games; however, many sport scenarios are not zero-sum games. Can you identify scenarios in sport where both actors in a game may benefit?

2. Regret is a concept that we can use to help us make decisions. The table below shows the payoff matrix for a football play.
   a. Find the corresponding regret matrix for the following payoff matrix.
   b. Identify the strategy to minimize regret.

		Play outcome	
		Successful play	Unsuccessful play
Play call	Hail Mary	10	-1
	Short pass	3	-1
	Run play	1	-1

3. Below is a payoff matrix for a basketball possession
   a. What strategy should the offense employ? Why?
   b. What strategy should the defense employ? Why?
   c. How might the payoff matrix help us understand the prevalence of zone defense in college basketball but its (near) absence in professional basketball?

		Defense	
		Man	Zone
Offense	Three	1.2, -1.2	1.5, -1.5
	Two	.9, -.9	.8, -.8

4. What type of games would you consider the following sport activities?
   a. Play calling
   b. Contract negotiation
   c. Sport gambling
   d. Trading a player

5. In game theory, we express the value of outcomes in terms of utility, a concept that stands in for the preference of an actor. Consider the following payoff matrix for two owners, one who has a revealed preference for on-field success over profit and one who has a revealed preference for profit over on-field success.
   a. How might their payoff matrix differ?
   b. How would salary caps or floors adjust the values of the payoff matrix?

		Outcome	
		Win	Lose
Expenditure	High		
	Medium		
	Low		

Key Terms

Game theory

John Von Neuman

Minimax

Payoff

payoff matrix

domination

utility theory

revealed preference

expected utility

zero-sum games

pure strategy

mixed strategy

Nash Equilibrium

finite games

symmetric game

simultaneous games

sequential games

repeated games

perfect information

imperfect information

infinite games

maximin strategy

minimax regret

tit-for-tat

grim trigger

References

Hoenigman, R., Elizabeth Bradley, and Allen Lim. 2011. Cooperation in bike racing—when to work together and when to go it alone. *Complexity* 17(2), 39–44.

Houthakker, H. S. 1950. Revealed preference and the utility function. *Economica, 17*(66), 159–174.

Nash, John Forbes. 1950. Equilibrium points in n-person games. *Proceedings of the National Academy of Sciences* 36(1), 48–49.

Savage, L. J. 1951. The theory of statistical decision. *Journal of the American Statistical Association* 46(253), 55–67.

Sinek, Simon. 2019. *The Infinite Game.* New York, NY: Penguin.

Von Neumann, John, and Oskar Morgenstern. 1947. *Theory of Games and Economic Behavior* (2nd rev. ed.). Princeton, NJ: Princeton University Press.

CHAPTER 9

Optimization Methods in Sport Analytics

J.T. Wolohan

> **LEARNING OBJECTIVES**
> After reading this chapter, students should be able to:
> - Describe the process of numerical optimization
> - Identify opportunities to use optimization approaches in sport
> - Translate sport analytics problems into optimization equations
> - Design and run optimization equations using R

Introduction

Most of sport analytics focuses on means of measuring, describing, or estimating what happens on the field of play. The idea being that once those measurements are complete, the resulting decisions become obvious. For instance, if we know which of the two batters has a better on-base percentage against left handed pitchers and we are wondering which of the two should take a key at-bat in the bottom of the 9th, well, the decision is fairly straightforward. Similarly, if in basketball a team is issued a technical foul and their opponent is deciding which of their players to take the free throw, they simply select the player with the best free throw percentage. Some decisions make themselves. Of course, others do not.

For instance, consider a scenario that we will look at in depth later in this chapter: we want to make six daily fantasy sports lineups that give us the greatest chance of winning a large payout. For each lineup we can select any player in the league for each position, but the overall lineup cannot cost us more than $100. From the players available, how do we select lineups that are most likely to win money? Here, even simple—if impractical—heuristics, such as "select the best players," will fail. The best players may do better on average, but what is their likelihood of having exceptional games that week? Furthermore, what is their likelihood of having exceptional games at a low cost such that we can fit them all on the same lineup?

To solve complex problems like this, where we have a combination of targets, in this case fantasy points scored, and constraints, number of players, positions, cost, we will use a technique called optimization. Optimization is a means by which we represent complex scenarios in a series of mathematical functions and then find the points of those functions that best correspond with our desired outcomes. For instance, maximum points in a weekend of fantasy sports.

Perhaps the most common place for optimization approaches to be used is on the business side of sport. Optimization approaches are widely applicable to sport marketing, supply chain, and inventory management. In these instances, we will have objectives such as "acquire the most new customers" or "sell the most tickets," while also having constraints such as "do not spend more than $5,000." Throughout the rest of this chapter, we will look at the techniques to represent these problems mathematically and then solve them using analytics.

An Overview of Optimization

In this section, we will give an overview of the mathematical background of optimization so that we can later apply it to complex scenarios in sport. We will start by looking at function minimums and maximums. Then we will look at how to optimize linear functions. And finally, we will look at combinatorics—which we have had a brief but informal introduction to earlier in the section on probability—and at combinatorial optimization, which are quite useful in the task of lineup selection.

One of the key insights into basketball is that it does not matter how many points a team scores but rather the rate at which they turn possessions into points. This is because teams, roughly speaking, get the same number of possessions per game. So, if the Boston Celtics average 105 points per game on 1.1 points per possession and the Los Angeles Lakers average 115 points per game on .98 points per possession, Boston actually has the better offense, despite Los Angeles having the higher scoring offense. This insight trickles down to the player level as well. For instance, in Kobe Bryant's final game he took 50 shots, scoring on only 22, for a field goal percentage of 44%. The Laker's as a team, that game and often throughout Bryant's career, actually had a higher field goal percentage than Bryant himself. So despite Bryant scoring the most points on the team, he was bringing down the team's rate of scoring and making them worse overall.

Of course, Bryant's percentage was low precisely because he was asked, or was asking himself, to do so much. Players who are asked to carry a team must take more shots. The more shots a player needs to take, the less selective they can be with their shots, the harder each shot becomes, and the lower their field goal percentage gets. This process happens differently for different players. Some players—the stars of the league—can take a high number of shots and still perform at a high level. Others find their productivity drop quite rapidly after being asked to take anything more than a marginal role. It makes sense, then, for us to be interested in finding the maximum number of shots that a player can take before their field goal percentage—or efficiency rating or effective field goal percentage or whichever statistic you prefer—dips below that of a substitutable player on the team.

This type of problem is called a **maximization** problem. We have a function, the player's efficiency by way of the number of shots they are taking, and we try to find the greatest or maximum value it can take. Its opposite is called a **minimization** problem. Minimization problems are those in which we have a function. For instance, the amount of money we need to spend on facilities upgrades while still being able to attract top recruits and we try to find the smallest or **minimum** value it can take.

Maximization and minimization make natural sense for **quadratic** functions. Quadratic functions are functions in which the largest term is of the second degree. Canonically, they take the form of $y = ax^2+bx+c$. Quadratic functions also take the shape of a single curve. We can say that these functions are either **concave** or **convex**, depending on the way that they curve. Concave quadratic functions curve downwards and have a single maximum. Convex quadratic functions curve upwards and have a single minimum.

As an example then, we may model a player's efficiency percentage as a function of the number of shots they take using a concave quadratic function.

```
efficiency = -0.001(shots+5)^2+.05*(shots+6)
```

If we graph this function, which you are encouraged to do using R, we can find that the player's efficiency rating peaks at 20 shots, before tailing off sharply. From this graph, we can start to understand how we might properly deploy this player in a game. We need to find a way to get them at least 10 shots, but want to limit them to no more than 30 shots. This is their sweet spot where they can be an effective contributor to the team.

In R, we can find their optimal number of shots by using the optimize function. We can use the optimize function to find the maximum or minimum of a function. In this case, we are looking for the maximum because we are seeking the number of shots at which the player is the most efficient. To use the optimize function, we need to turn our equation into an R function and then call that function with optimize.

```
eff <- function(shots){
  -.001*((shots+5)^2) + .05*(shots+6)
}

optimize(eff, interval=c(1,40), maximum = T)
```

You will note how similar the efficiency function is to the quadratic we noted above. You will also note the syntax for the optimize function. Optimize takes three parameters: the function we would like to optimize, the interval over which we want to optimize, and whether we are looking for a maximum or a minimum. The function we are looking to optimize over is the mathematical description of the scenario or problem we are trying to solve. The interval over which we want to optimize are the X-axis bounds on our problem. Here, we are not interested in situations where the player takes fewer than 1 shot and more than 40 shots. If they take no shots at all, their efficiency rate is irrelevant to the team's performance; if they take 40 or more shots, the team is likely in dire straits and seeking a heroic performance. Lastly, we use the maximum parameter to tell R whether or not we are seeking a maximum or a minimum. The optimize function—and most optimization problems—are designed as minimums by default. We can change minimization operations into maximization operations by negating the function. You will notice that the code below produces the same effects of the code above.

```
eff <- function(shots){
  -1*(-.001*((shots+5)^2) + .05*(shots+6))
}

optimize(eff, interval=c(1,40))
```

In this code, we have negated our efficiency function and found the minimum, but the outputs are the same—except for the objective, which is now negative.

For more practice with the optimize function, let us consider another case for maximization: pass play selection in football. In football, teams are presented with the option of passing or running on

Sports Analytics

every offensive down. In general, it is best to have some balance between these options. You can refer to the chapter on game theory for a dive into why that is. For this chapter, it is enough to know that the more a team favors the pass, the more their opposition can defend against the pass and limit its effectiveness. We might model the effectiveness of a pass play with a function in R like this:

```
yards.per.pass <- function(passes){
  -3*(passes+.35)^2 + 5*passes + 7
}
```

As the percentage of passes increases, so does the effectiveness of any given pass play—up to a point. After that point, the effectiveness of passing the ball decreases for every additional pass. This is functionally equivalent to the scoring efficiency example we looked at earlier and, indeed, we will solve the problem in the same way.

```
optimize(yards.per.pass, interval = c(0,1), maximum = T)
# $maximum
# [1] 0.4833333
# $objective
# [1] 7.333333
```

You will not in this example, we call the optimize function with the yards.per.pass function as the function to maximize and we do so over the interval 0 to 1. That is because yards per passes expects a percentage of pass plays as an input and percentages must always be between 0 and 1. Again, we specify that we are looking for the maximum value. The results of our one-liner are the passing rate at which we achieve the maximum yards per pass (48%) and the yards per pass we will achieve at that rate (7.3 yards per pass). From this example, we know that we should strive to run the ball slightly more than pass to optimize our passing game.

Unfortunately, unlike the two examples above, we will rarely have well defined quadratic equations to maximize or minimize in practice. Therefore, in order to use the maximization and minimization techniques, it becomes important that we know how to perform an empirical estimation of a quadratic function. We can think of this as the same as fitting a linear regression model to data; however, instead of fitting a linear model, we will fit a polynomial model.

To take a look at this, we will examine the case of predicting the optimal temperature for a minor league baseball game. The minor league team has data from attendance last season and is hoping to use weather forecasts for the upcoming summer to plan their marketing events, such as fireworks and bobblehead giveaways, around days when attendance might normally be down.

To do this, the first thing we will do is to read in the data. We will do this with the same read.csv function we have been using throughout the book. Then, we will try to fit a quadratic model. We assume a quadratic model will be a good fit here because we can imagine that when the temperature is too cold or too warm, people will not want to be at a baseball game. We will use the linear model function you are already familiar with plus a quadratic I term. Then, we will call optimize on the resulting model to find the ideal temperature for a baseball game.

```
data.2017 <- read.csv("path/to/minor.league.att.2017.csv")
quadratic.model <- with(data.2017,  lm(att ~ temp+I(temp^2)))
summary(quadratic.model)
```

You should find most of the code above similar to linear models we have used earlier in this book. The only new aspect will be the inclusion of the quadratic I term. We need to use the function I here in order to freeze the quadratic term, otherwise R will convert it into a non-quadratic linear model. The I function gives objects a special AsIs class that prevents R from modifying them without good reason.

From there, we can summarize the quadratic model to observe the terms. The coefficients here correspond to the coefficients of the dependent variable in our quadratic equation. You may need to take the numbers out of scientific notation in order to place them in the optimize function, depending on the scale of your model.

```
optimize(function(temp){(-4.5*(temp^2))+(716*temp)-23960},
         interval = c(65,110),
         maximum = T)

# $maximum
# [1] 79.55556
# $objective
# [1] 4520.889
```

Finally, we can call the optimize function. Here, we use an anonymous function instead of a named function, because we will only use this function once for the purpose of the optimization. The weights assigned to each term of this function come directly from the summary of our quadratic model. The interval here is bounded—more or less—by the observed temperatures from last season. We could, of course, extend the model to any temperature, but we have no reason to believe that people would want to attend a baseball game more at temperatures below 65 degrees or above 110 degrees than somewhere within that range. And lastly, we select a maximum because we are trying to maximize the number of people who will want to come to the stadium. The results suggest that 80 degrees is the perfect temperature for a baseball game and that 4,500 people can be expected to attend the game at that temperature. Therefore, special attractions, such as fireworks, may be best scheduled for cooler or warmer nights to boost attendance.

While the optimizing of quadratics is intuitive, finding the highest or lowest point on a curved line, the process of coming up with the quadratic equation, is often not. When we have historical data we can sometimes estimate a quadratic function, but often we will not have historical data. In these situations, we can often turn to a technique called **linear function optimization**. Linear function optimization finds the optimal outcome under a series of constraints that we have expressed as a sequence of linear equations.

For example, consider the following scenario:

> *A sport apparel company must decide how to split its production between producing basketball shoes and football cleats. Basketball shoes earn $100 in profit while football cleats earn only $75. Basketball shoes are more sophisticated to produce, requiring 6 units of "Proprietary Shoe Material" (PSM), whereas football cleats require only 3 units of PSM. The factory can use at most 200 units of PSM each day. Basketball shoes also take longer to make--5 shoes per hour, whereas football cleats can be made faster, at a rate of 6 cleats per hour. The factory can only operate for 8 hours each day.*

This situation describes a common scenario in sport business. We know the physical constraints on our apparel, our advertising, or our marketing activities, but we might not know exactly how to allocate our resources given those constraints. In the above instance, for example, it is not clear how much of each item—basketball shoes and football cleats—we should produce. The basketball shoes are more profitable per unit, but we cannot produce as many units or produce them as fast. Some combination of the two is probably the right answer, it is not clear how we ascertain what that correct mixture is. Linear optimization is how we find the right mixture.

In R, we will solve problems of this sort using the lpSolve library. The library gets its name from an alternate name for linear optimization: **linear programming**. These two terms, linear optimization and linear programming, refer to the same thing. It is important that you know both terms. Those coming from applied mathematics or other disciplines where programming does not carry the same connotation of writing computer code will often use the phrase linear programming. We prefer linear optimization in this book because it is more descriptive.

In order to solve a linear optimization problem, we must take the pertinent data from our scenario—the objectives and the constraints—and encode them into a format suitable for the R solver. This involves constructing an objective array, a constraints matrix, an array of constraint limits, and an array of directionality. The objective array encodes the payoffs for our options: the profit on each shoe in the instance above. The constraints matrix indicates the amount each unit of each option contributes to our constraints: the PSM and time consumed by each unit of shoes. The constraint limits indicate the maximum amount of each constrained resource we have: the maximum amount of PSM we can use and the maximum amount of time we have. And the directionality array indicates the direction of our constraint: above or below.

```
library("lpSolve")

objective.arr   <- c(100, 75)
constraint.mat  <- matrix(data=c(6,3,
  (1/5),(1/6)),
                              nrow=2,
                              byrow=T)
constraint.lim  <- c(200, 8)
directional.arr <- c("<=", "<=")

linear.opt <- lp(direction = "max",
                objective.in = objective.arr,
                const.mat = constraint.mat,
                const.rhs = constraint.lim,
                const.dir = directional.arr)
```

LISTING 9.1. Optimizing shoe production in R.

We see above how to encode this information in a format suitable for the lpSolve library. We construct the four data structures we need: the objective array, the constraints matrix, the constraint limits, and the directional array. For the objective array and the constraints matrix, you will note that we keep the order of our options the same: the basketball shoes always come in first position and the football cleats are always in second condition. For the constraint limits, the order of the variables corresponds to the order of the constraints. In this case, the PSM comes first and the manufacturing time comes second. The directional array follows the same pattern and corresponds to the constraint limits.

Once we have done all of this, calling it with the lp function produces an lp.object that contains the solution. We can access that solution, intuitively, by calling the solution attribute.

```
linear.opt$solution
# [1] 23.33333 20.00000
```

In this instance, we see that the factory should produce 23 and ⅓ units of basketball shoes and 20 units of football cleats. Of course, we cannot sell one-third of a pair of shoes. To remedy this, lp has an additional option that we can use to force the solution into integers, preventing fractional results. The option is called all.int.

```
linear.opt <- lp(direction = "max",
                objective.in = objective.mat,
                const.mat = constraint.mat,
                const.rhs = constraint.lim,
                const.dir = directional.arr,
                all.int = T)

linear.opt$solution
#[1] 20 24
```

Using this option, we get a different mix of shoes. Assuming we want to end every day with shoes we can ship and no shoes in progress, we should then produce 20 basketball shoes and 24 football cleats to maximize our profits.

STADIUM IMPROVEMENT DECISION-MAKING WITH LINEAR OPTIMIZATION. In order to get more practice with linear optimization, let's take a look at another scenario, this time from the world of college athletics.

> *Syracuse University is looking to expand their basketball arena: Manley Field House. Manley currently seats 12,000. Syracuse would like to add 7,000 seats to their stadium while maximizing the amount of money they can make off of those seats. When adding seats, Syracuse has the option of selecting from club seats, comfort seats, and standard seats. Club seats earn Syracuse $500 per seat per game, and Syracuse can construct a club seat for $1000 per seat; comfort seats produce $150 per seat per game and can be constructed for $300 per seat; standard seats produce $55 per seat per game and can be constructed for $150. Syracuse would like to spend no more than $3 million on the upgrades and they would like to add at least 1000 standard seats.*

Again, we can decompose this problem into a series of linear functions. The optimization—what we want to maximize in this case—is the amount of revenue, so we will construct our objective matrix using the revenue generated per game per seat. Our primary constraint is the budget: we cannot spend more than $3 million, so the cost of each seat matters. We also, however, have a goal of adding 7,000 seats and at least 1,000 regular seats. Both of these are constraints. Each seat contributes exactly 1 unit of seating toward the overall seating capacity of the stadium, while only the regular seats contribute to the regular seat total. You can see how this is put into practice below.

```
objective.mat    <- c(500, 150, 55)
constraint.mat   <- matrix(data=c(1000, 300, 150,
                                  1, 1, 1,
                                  0, 0, 1),
                        nrow=3,
                        byrow=T)

constraint.lim  <- c(3000000, 7000, 1000)
directional.arr <- c("<=", "=", ">=")

linear.opt <- lp(direction = "max",
              objective.in = objective.mat,
              const.mat = constraint.mat,
              const.rhs = constraint.lim,
              const.dir = directional.arr,
              all.int = T)

linear.opt$solution
# [1] 1500 4500 1000
```

LISTING 9.2. Optimizing stadium renovations using R.

You will note the similarities between the two linear optimization problems. The key change here is that there are three options—club, comfort, and standard—instead of only two. There are also three constraints: overall cost, overall capacity, and standard seating capacity. This results in a 3 × 3 constraint matrix. Again, the columns correspond to each option and the rows correspond to each constraint. You will also notice that the directional array uses the full range of inequality symbols. We want to spend no more than $3 million on renovations, add exactly 7,000 seats, of which at least 1,000 must be standard seats.

Using this process, we find that the optimal way to add seats is to add 1,500 club seats, 4,500 comfort seats, and 1,000 regular seats. As desired, this adds exactly 7,000 seats to the overall seating capacity of Manley Field House, of which 1,000 will be standard seats, satisfying that requirement. In order to find the amount of additional revenue that will be generated per game, we can take the sum of the solution times the objective array. We find that this stadium expansion will bring in nearly $1.5 million in additional revenue each game.

```
sum(linear.opt$solution*objective.mat)
# [1] 1480000
```

MAXIMIZING LINEUPS FOR ICE HOCKEY. Crudely, we can also apply this approach to on-the-field decisions as well. For instance, we might consider the following scenario in which a hockey coach is trying to determine the optimal play-time targets for her players.

> The University of Massachusetts coach is preparing for the upcoming collegiate hockey season. She has to decide how to split the playing time between her 19 college athletes. On average, she will need to field a five-player line—3 attackers and 2 defenders—for three 20-minute periods. Her 19 players each have unique strengths and weaknesses when it comes to playing offense and defense, some excel in the offensive role, others excel in the defensive role, and some are balanced. Additionally, no player is effective on ice when they have played for more than 18 minutes. Overall, she would like to maximize the box plus-minus of her team.

Unlike the previous scenarios, which have had relatively few options and constraints, it is clear from the numbers in the example above, 19 players, for instance, that we will have a large number of options and constraints. We will have:

- one constraint for each player mandating that they cannot play more than 18 minutes.
- one constraint for the play time of offensive players, totaling exactly 180 minutes—3 attackers, playing for three 20-minute periods.
- one constraint for the play time of defensive players, totaling exactly 120 minus—2 attackers playing for three 20-minute periods.

and, like always, we will have an optimization condition: maximize our box plus-minus.

It makes sense to start framing our problem by focusing on the optimization array first. In this scenario, each player has two ways they can contribute: as an offensive player or as a defensive player. Therefore, we will need two entries in the array for each player. Since we have 19 players, that means we will need a 38-element array. To construct this, we will read the data in from the provided and then flatten the data so that all the defensive contributions come after all of the offensive contributions.

```
hockey.players <- read.csv("/path/to/hockey.players.csv")
objective.in <- c(hockey.players$Off, hockey.players$Def)
```

With the optimization objective set, what remains is to encode our constraints in a matrix representation. As discussed above, we have three classes of constraints: an offensive play time constraint, a defensive play time constraint, and a by-player constraint. The offensive play time for the team must total 160 minutes; the defensive play time for the team must total 120 minutes; and the play time for each player can exceed no more than 18 minutes. For clarity, we will assemble these constraints separately and combine them together into a single matrix at the end.

The offensive play time and defensive play time constraints are similar to the constraints we have seen before. Each constraint has one global total we are trying to stay below, so we will need one line in our matrix for each constraint. Because each of the first 19 elements in our objective array corresponds with an offensive contribution—time spent on offense—and the second 19 elements in our objective array corresponds to a defensive contribution—time spent on defense—what we want to construct is two mirrored arrays: one with a 1 in the first 19 elements and 0s in the rest; one with zeros in the first 19 elements in 1s in the rest. To achieve this, we will use the rep function to repeat 1s and 0s the necessary 19 times and the c function to combine the arrays resulting from the rep function. We will do this once for the offensive minutes constraint and then simply reverse this—with the rev function—for the defensive minutes constraint.

With this, we turn to the more complicated player minutes constraint. Each player can play a maximum of 18 minutes, split in any way on an offensive line or a defensive line. Time on offense and time on defense contribute to this evenly. Remembering that the first 19 elements of our objective array correspond to offensive performance and the second 19 elements of our objective array correspond to defensive performance, we know that for the first player the proper constraint array would be a 1 in the 1st and 20th places, with zeros in all other locations of a 38-element array. We would then need to do this for each player, such that player 2 has 1s in the 2nd and 21st places, player 3 has 1s in the 3rd and 22nd places and so on.

As a shortcut to constructing this, we can use what is known as an **identity matrix**. An identity matrix is a **diagonal matrix** in which all the non-zero values are 1. A diagonal matrix is one in which the only non-zero elements in the matrix exist along its diagonal. Diagonal matrices are almost always **square matrices**; matrices with the same number of rows and columns. For our purposes, we need to impose 19 constraints on each of our 38 options. So, we will need to concatenate two 19 × 19 identity matrices. The resulting matrix, 19 × 38, will take the form of the one described loosely above—where each player's time on offensive and defensive is accounted for.

From here, we need to combine these constraints. To do that, we will simply stack the constraint matrices on top of one another: the offensive minutes first, the defensive minutes second, and then the per-player minutes last. We will do that with the rbind function that you have seen throughout the book.

Lastly, we must provide the constraint limits and directionality. Both of these will be 21 element arrays—one for each row of our constraint matrix. The targets will be: 180, the total number of offensive minutes; 120, the total number of defensive minutes; and 18, the maximum number of per player minutes. The caveat here is that the 18 must be repeated 19 times, once for each player. Likewise, the directionality of the constraints will be equivalency twice—once each for the total offensive and defensive ice time—and then the less than constraint 19 times, once for each player.

```
off.min      <- c(rep(1,19), rep(0,19))
def.min      <- rev(off.min)
player.min   <- cbind(diag(nrow=19,ncol=19),
                      diag(nrow=19,ncol=19))
const.mat <- rbind(off.min, def.min, player.min)
const.rhs <- c(180, 120, rep(18, 19))
const.dir <- c("=","=", rep("<",19))
```

LISTING 9.3. Preparing to optimize hockey lineups.

Having constructed both the optimization objective and the constraints, we are ready to perform the linear optimization. We will do so as we have throughout this chapter, using the lp function. We can also do some pretty formatting of the solution so that the results are easier to read. The results for this are shown in the Table 9.1.

```
play.time <- lp(direction="max",
                objective.in = objective.in,
                const.mat = const.mat,
                const.dir = const.dir,
                const.rhs = const.rhs)

players2 <- cbind(hockey.players, matrix(play.time$solution, ncol=2))
names(players2) <- c("Off","Def","Off.Time","Def.Time")
players2$Tot.Time <- with(players2, Off.Time+Def.Time)
players2[order(-players2$Tot.Time),]
```

LISTING 9.4. Optimizing hockey lineups in R.

From the table we can see that most players are best off specializing on the side of the puck where they provide the most value. For instance, despite the fact that the best offensive player would also be the best defensive player, it makes sense for them to play solely on offense because they are more effective on offense than on defense. We also see that the coach should follow the simple strategy of playing her best players and sitting the weaker players.

TABLE 9.1. Collegiate hockey play-time optimization results

Player	Off	Def	Off.Time	Def.Time	Tot.Time
1	2.8	2.07	18	0	18
2	2.29	-0.07	18	0	18
3	1.57	0.5	18	0	18
4	1.09	0.83	18	0	18
5	0.9	0.48	18	0	18
6	0.85	0.33	18	0	18
7	0.63	0.83	0	18	18
8	0.6	-0.53	18	0	18
9	0.58	-0.29	18	0	18
10	0.54	0.7	6	12	18
11	0.53	0.47	10	0	10
12	0.45	-0.51	0	0	0
13	0.4	1.44	0	18	18
14	0.37	-0.42	0	0	0
15	0.29	1.21	0	18	18
16	0.19	1.08	0	18	18
17	-0.19	0.18	0	0	0
18	-0.2	1.01	0	18	18
19	-0.55	1.14	0	18	18

As it turns out, only one player needs to split time between offense and defense. Player 10 will play most of their time on defense, mostly in the weakest defensive rotation; however, they will also play a few minutes on offensive in the weakest offensive rotation as well. You will note that in Table 9.1 that player 10 spends less time on offense than player 11, despite being better on offense. This is because, like player 1 who was more valuable on offense than they were on defense, player 10 is more valuable on defense than they are on offense.

COMBINATORIAL OPTIMIZATION

In the previous section, we looked at optimization problems in which we could reasonably be expected to design constraint matrices and enumerate the constraints. However, some problems do not lend themselves to such solutions so neatly. Consider, for instance, the NFL draft. If you are a general manager heading into the NFL draft, you have, assuming you have not traded away any of your picks, the opportunity to select seven new players. If we assume there are 300 players eligible to be drafted, that means there are two-hundred quadrillion (2e17) ways one could select those seven players.

It is common around the NFL draft for media figures to put out mock drafts, guesses about which team will take which player for each spot in the first round. Assuming no team can trade their first round pick, which of course, they can in reality, and that there are only 45 players who are "good enough" to be first-round picks, there are 19 quattuor-decillion (1.9e46) ways that the first round of the draft could unfold. That is to say nothing about later rounds, where more players are good enough to be drafted.

All that is to say that it becomes intractable very quickly for us to manually construct systems of constraints for problems like **the assignment problem**. The assignment problem is a classic mathematical problem in which we have two sets of things, such as players and open roster spots, and we must optimally match the things in the two sets such that our value is maximized or our cost is minimized. Some version of this problem is what general managers in sport, and more commonly fantasy sport, wrestle with every day. The assignment problem also garners attention from a wide range of other industries. For instance, Uber and Lyft must approximate answers to this problem; however, instead of assigning players to roster spots, they assign available cars to rideshare users. In this section, we will look at approaches for solving the assignment problem by examining two case studies: that of lineup selection in basketball and roster selection for daily fantasy sports.

ROTATION SELECTION IN BASKETBALL

In basketball, a common form of the assignment problem is that of rotation design. Basketball teams can only play 5 players at any given time. Traditionally they will play one center, two forwards, and two guards; however, this is no longer the gospel that it was historically. Teams now experiment with a variety of "small ball" lineups, including three forwards and two guards, or even two forwards and three guards. Different players are better suited for some rotations than others. For instance, some forwards are great small ball forwards, with the ability to run the floor, shoot from distance, and defend smaller, faster guards, whereas other forwards are more traditional forwards: they prefer to play physical in the mid-range or low post and can defend bigger, stronger centers. NBA coaches have the unenviable job of attempting to identify their team's strongest rotations over the course of the season and then deploy these rotations appropriately to exploit their opponents' weaknesses.

On a standard NBA roster with 6 guards, 5 forwards, and 4 centers, there are 2,400 possible 2-guard, 2-forward, and 1 center combinations. Of course, most of these lineups will never be played. Only the best lineups need to be played. In order to find the rotations, it helps to think about the NBA team and rotation in terms of a **graph**.

Graphs are a mathematical structure for a set of objects with some relationship between objects in that set. For instance, we may imagine a graph of professional athletes and the professional teams they have played for. The athletes and teams would constitute the objects. Whether the athlete played for a given team would be the relationship. Graphs are described in terms of **nodes** (or **vertices**) and **edges**. Nodes are the entities in a graph. Edges are the relationship between nodes. In mathematical graphs, no entity may appear on the graph twice; however, there may be multiple edges between a pair of nodes.

To simplify the scenario and introduce the graph concept, let us limit our scenario to the two forward positions. If there are five forwards on the team and two possible forward spots on a rotation, then our graph would have 7 nodes—one for each player and one for each spot—and 10 edges, 1 each connecting each player to each edge. In optimization problems, we will most often concern ourselves with weighted graphs: graphs where the relationships have numbers associated with them. These numbers, weights, will represent the strength of the connection between any two edges.

TABLE 9.2. Matrix representation of weighted bipartite graph of Boston forwards

	Small Forward	Power Forward
Paul Pierce	1/25	1/15
Kevin Garnett	1/13	1/28
PJ Brown	1/3	1/12
Brian Scalabrine	1/12	1/17
James Posey	1/12	1/12

Table 9.2 shows what a weighted bipartite graph of the 2008 Boston Celtics forwards might look like in matrix form, with each relationship indicating the players skill at the respective position. You may recognize from Table 9.2 that the best players have the smallest weights. This is because for combinatorial optimization, we will most often be pursuing minimization. Most combinatorial optimization research comes from operations research around minimizing travel times or cost in some form of another. We can also visualize the matrix from Table 9.2 as seen in Figure 9.1.

FIGURE 9.1. Visualizing the 2008 Celtics forward graph

You will notice that in Figure 9.1, all the players are connected to both forward positions—indicating that they can play either position. The lines connecting the players to those positions are labeled with a number. This number is the weight representing the player's skill at the position. You can construct a similar looking graph in R using the following code.

```
library('igraph')
forward.mat <- matrix(
  byrow=T,
  nrow=7,
  ncol=7,
  data=c(
    0,0,0,0,0,1/25,1/15,
    0,0,0,0,0,1/13,1/28,
    0,0,0,0,0,1/3,1/12,
    0,0,0,0,0,1/12,1/17,
    0,0,0,0,0,1/22,1/12,
    0,0,0,0,0,0,0,
    0,0,0,0,0,0,0
))

nodes = c("Pierce","Garnett","Brown","Scalabrine","Posey","SF","PF")

forward.graph <- graph_from_adjacency_matrix(
                 forward.mat,
                 mode="upper",
                 weighted=T)

plot(forward.graph,
     vertex.label=edges,
```

```
        vertex.label.font=2,
        edge.label=round(E(forward.graph)$weight,2),
        edge.lty="dotted",
        palette=c("grey","white"),
        layout=layout.circle(forward.graph))
```

LISTING 9.5. Visualizing the Celtics' forward rotations.

The process we go through to create the graph diagram in R is what you might imagine it to be. We construct an upper-triangular matrix representation of Table 9.2 and then process it with igraph's graph_from_adjacency_matrix function. R's igraph comes with nice plotting features that we can take advantage of to make the graph interpretable, including easy labeling.

We will not go into any more depth on the igraph library in this chapter; however, it is recommended that you look into it if you plan to do a lot of work with graphs. The igraph library has a wide range of features and options that provide convenient access to graph visualizations. We can use these visualizations to illustrate the effectiveness of various analytic methods and, in some circumstances, to gain an intuition about the problem at hand.

For our purposes, we can return to the lpSolver library and solve the forward problem. To do this, we will use the lp.assign function. This function takes in a cost matrix—a square matrix of the costs of assigning "sources" to "destinations"—and minimizes the costs. This requires us to construct the cost matrix. To convert Table 9.2 into a cost matrix, we will add three additional columns—to set the number of possible positions equal to the number of players—and give each value in those columns a value of one. These additional columns represent the bench, the place where forwards who are not playing go. Putting a forward on the bench has a cost of one because it is better to have players on the floor than it is on the bench. In your own work, when you are padding a cost matrix, you will want to set these costs to some "worst case" number. This indicates that not being assigned anywhere is worse than being assigned somewhere.

With the cost matrix put together, lp.assign will handle the rest for us. The lp.assign function returns the same lp object that was returned by the lp function, which we used earlier in this chapter. That means to extract the results, we will need to call the solution element. You can see an example of the cost matrix construction and the use of lp.assign below.

```
forward.cost.mat <- matrix(
  byrow=T, nrow=5,
  data = c(
    1/25,  1/15,1,1,1,
    1/13,  1/28,1,1,1,
    1/3,   1/12,1,1,1,
    1/12,  1/17,1,1,1,
    1/22,  1/12,1,1,1))
```

```
lp.assign(forward.cost.mat)$solution

#          [,1] [,2] [,3] [,4] [,5]
#  [1,]     1    0    0    0    0
#  [2,]     0    1    0    0    0
#  [3,]     0    0    0    0    1
#  [4,]     0    0    0    1    0
#  [5,]     0    0    1    0    0
```

LISTING 9.6. Optimal assignments of players to positions in R.

You will notice that the first two columns of our cost matrix are identical to the non-square matrix we represented in Table 9.2. And indeed, we could have arrived at the same result by creating a non-square matrix and combining it with a 1-filled matrix. This technique is useful when we have a large number of placeholder spaces to construct. We will do this in a moment when we tackle the team-sized variant of this problem. For now, let us take a moment to look at the solution matrix. Each column of our solution matrix corresponds to the position that column was assigned to and each row corresponds with the row the player was assigned to. So, the algorithm concludes that Boston should start Paul Pierce at small forward and Kevin Garnett at power forward. The other players, who have 1s in the columns three through five, the bench spots, are backups.

For a more sophisticated example, we will take a look at the 2019-2020 NBA Champion Los Angeles Lakers. The Lakers roster was anchored by their two all-stars: LeBron James and Anthony Davis. The rest of the roster was cobbled together around these two. We have provided a small dataset for this example, describing 11 Lakers, their natural position, their skill at the three position groupings—guard, forward, and center—and their average skill across all positions. That dataset is shown is Table 9.3.

TABLE 9.3. Assorted members of the 2019-2020 Los Angeles Lakers

	Pos	G	F	C	Avg.
LeBron James	F	10	10	8	9.3
Anthony Davis	F	3	10	7	6.7
Kyle Kuzma	F	4	7	3	4.7
Kentavious Caldwell-Pope	G	7	4	1	4.0
Danny Green	G	6	4	2	4.0
Dwight Howard	C	1	3	7	3.7
JR Smith	F	4	4	2	3.3
JaVale McGee	C	1	2	6	3.0
Rajon Rondo	G	5	2	1	2.7
Dion Waiters	G	5	2	1	2.7
Alex Caruso	G	2	1	1	1.3

Table 9.3 provides a good indication of what the Lakers were working with this season. They had one player who could do it all: LeBron James. James has been a perennial all-star since he entered the league at 18 and a viable MVP candidate for the plurality of his career. Davis is an excellent scoring big. The rest of the players would typically be considered role players. The role players come in two shapes: specialists and stretch players. A specialist player, such as Rajon Rondo or Dwight Howard, has a single core strength. Rondo, for instance, is a talented pass-first guard, but struggles shooting and would not make a good forward or center. Howard, a former all-NBA center, is a great defensive center, but at 6'10" and 265lbs, he is not nimble enough to succeed at other positions. In contrast, Danny Green and Kyle Kuzma serve more flexible roles. Green might not be as good as Howard at any one position, but because he is long, can run and shoot, the Lakers can use him in multiple roles.

In this example, we will generate a few different lineups for the Lakers. First, we will generate the Lakers' overall best lineup. This would be the lineup the Lakers would play when they just need their best players on the floor. Then, we will generate a small-ball lineup. This lineup will have three guard spots—instead of two—and no center on the floor. This lineup would be the 3-point shot heavy lineup for when the Lakers needed to score in a hurry or they were looking to run the floor. Lastly, we will put together a breather lineup, for when LeBron James and Anthony Davis are off the floor together. This lineup will be used sparsely, to give the Lakers' two best players a rest.

We will optimize to find the best standard lineup first. To do this, we will need to construct the cost matrix. The cost matrix will consist of the cost of each player playing the available positions. For the standard lineup, the Lakers are going to feature two guards, two forwards, and a center. We will, then, construct a matrix using the corresponding columns from our 2020 Lakers dataset and pad the matrix with bench spots. Lastly, we will pass this matrix into the lp.assign function. The code for this can be seen below.

```
overall.mat <- matrix(ncol=5,
                      data = c(lakers.2020$G,lakers.2020$G,
                               lakers.2020$F,lakers.2020$F,
                               lakers.2020$C))

bench.padding <- matrix(
data=1,
nrow=nrow(lakers.2020),
ncol=nrow(lakers.2020)-5)

overall.cost <- cbind(overall.mat^-1, bench.padding)
lp.overall <- lp.assign(overall.cost)
data.frame(lp.overall$solution[,1:5],
     row.names = lakers.2020$Player)
```

LISTING 9.7. Optimizing the Lakers roations.

You will note in the code that we are constructing our matrix column-wise instead of row-wise. This is because we are pulling columns of data from the data frame we have read the Lakers data into. You will also notice that we are inversing the overall matrix to produce the cost matrix. This is because the raw data, as you can see in Table 9.3, has larger numbers as better than smaller numbers. For combinatorial optimization, we will typically think in terms of minimization—so we need the smaller numbers to be better.

	X1	X2	X3	X4	X5
LeBron James	0	1	0	0	0
Anthony Davis	0	0	0	1	0
Kyle Kuzma	0	0	1	0	0
Kentavious Caldwell-Pope	1	0	0	0	0
Danny Green	0	0	0	0	0
Dwight Howard	0	0	0	0	1

Lastly, looking at the output, we see that the optimal standard lineup includes James, Davis, Kuza, and Caldwell-Pope—the four most talented players on the team—but prefers playing Dwight Howard over Danny Green. An optimization approach prefers Howard over Green because the advantage the team gets by having Howard play center, thus freeing LeBron to play guard and Davis to play forward, is better than having Green on the floor. And indeed, throughout the 2019-2020 season, LeBron started at point guard.

Next, let us modify this scenario for a small ball lineup. For that, we will repeat the process above; however, we will use three columns of the guard skill rating and only two columns of the forward skill rating. Looking at the code below, you can see how that is implemented. You may notice that here we use a different method of turning our positive matrix into a proper cost matrix—we multiply every value by 1. This approach has the benefit of keeping the scale of the original data.

```
small.ball.mat <- matrix(ncol=5,
    data = c(lakers.2020$G,lakers.2020$G,lakers.2020$G,
            lakers.2020$F,lakers.2020$F))

small.ball.cost <- cbind(small.ball.mat*-1, bench.padding)
lp.small.ball <- lp.assign(small.ball.cost)
data.frame(lp.small.ball$solution[,1:5],
            row.names = lakers.2020$Player)
```

Looking at the results of this optimization, we see that the optimal small ball lineup is the same as the optimal standard lineup with Danny Green swapped in for Dwight Howard. LeBron James, all 6"9" and 250 lb of him, still plays guard in this scenario. This was a major advantage for the Lakers over their opponents in their 2019-2020 campaign for the title. Of their top eight players in terms of minutes, none was a center.

And finally, we will find an optimal roster for when James and Davis are on the bench, the so-called breather lineup. To construct this lineup, we will maximize the cost of playing James and Davis at any position on the floor and set the cost of having them on the bench to 0. This will optimize them to the bench. Alternatively, we could omit them from the analysis altogether. For large matrices, the latter is preferable. Besides that change, the code for the breather lineup will be identical to the standard lineup.

```
breather.mat <- matrix(ncol=5,
                    data = c(lakers.2020$G,lakers.2020$G,
                          lakers.2020$F,lakers.2020$F,
                          lakers.2020$C))

breather.cost <- cbind(breather.mat*-1, bench.padding)
breather.cost[1:2,] <- 1
breather.cost[1:2,3:ncol(breather.cost)] <- 0

lp.breather <- lp.assign(breather.cost)
data.frame(lp.breather$solution[,1:5],
          row.names = lakers.2020$Player)
```

LISTING 9.8. Optimizing a basketball lineup without the star players.

You will note the two lines where we adjust James and Davis' cost ratings and how it affects the lineup. Under these constraints, where the cost of playing James and Davis is high, the optimal lineup is to have a Green, Caldwell-Pope backcourt, with JR Smith and Kuzma in the front court, and Dwight Howard playing center.

These are, of course, just three lineups among the countless that an NBA coach would need to weather a season or a playoff run. Though a coach might not need to use all 13 players they are allowed to dress in any given game, they will want to have thought through the many contingencies that can occur in a game: from injury, to illness, to unexpected tactics by the opponent. To the extent that these potential scenarios can be imagined and described mathematically, we can use combinatorial optimization to recommend lineups that respond to them.

Summary

In this chapter, we reviewed applications of optimization to sport analytics. We can use optimization approaches to analyze scenarios in sport where we want to maximize or minimize the value of some parameter, such as points scored or dollars spent. We first looked at how these approaches could be applied to sport business examples such as sport marketing, the planning and management of marketing campaigns, and facilities management and the enhancement of infrastructure. Then we turned our attention to on-field applications of optimization looking at how optimization could be used to maximize the performance of lineups in basketball and hockey. Lastly, we saw how we could modify our linear optimizations to come up with a variety of potential lineups.

Key Terms

Maximum

Minimum

Quadratic function

Concave

Convex

Optimization

Linear functions

Linear programming

Objective matrix

Constraint matrix

Identity matrix

Diagonal matrix

Square matrix

Assignment problem

Graph

Nodes

Vertices

Edges

Exercises

1. In many sports, player performance and player usage take the shape of concave curves. That is to say, players will do better with more activity at the lower end of usage, up to a point, and then their performance will begin to deteriorate. Why might player performance deteriorate when they are asked to do more? Provide two examples from different team sports.

2. In the shoe manufacturing example from earlier in this chapter, basketball shoes took longer to make than football cleats. Imagine there is an improvement to the manufacturing of basketball shoes and now we can make 10 basketball shoes per hour. Does this change how many basketball shoes we should produce each day to maximize our profits?

3. Chess Boxing is a niche sport in which participants alternate rounds of boxing with several minutes of chess. Chess boxing promoters must take care to balance the relative chess and boxing skill of each participant so that both the fights and the chess matches are competitive. Imagine you are a promoter trying to balance a three card fight.

   a. Design cost and constraint matrices under the assumption that discrepancies in boxing and chess skill are equally as bad. Which three matchups would you end up with?

   b. People love watching knockouts. Design cost and constraint matrices that assume that boxing skill discrepancies are half as bad as chess skill discrepancies.

	Chess Skill	Boxing Skill
Andrews	1	10
Berry	10	1
Chang	7	7
Doddson	3	3
Everett	8	5
Fontainebleau	5	8

4. As head of marketing, you have been tasked with allocating your budget across a variety of advertising platforms—to include TV, digital, radio, and sponsorships—to maximize profit. You must invest in at least one unit of each medium and you have $150,000 to spend. A unit of TV costs $15,000 and produces $20,000 in revenue. A unit of digital costs $5 and produces $7.50 in revenue. A unit of radio costs $100 and produces $127 in revenue. And a unit of sponsorship costs $5000 and produces $3500 in revenue. Additionally, you can buy at most 5 units of TV and 50 units of radio. How will you allocate your marketing budget?

5. You're the coach of a little league soccer team tasked with selecting 11 players to your starting lineup. Each player has a skill at attack, midfield, and defense, listed in the table below. Of the

15 players below, which will you start to maximize your team's performance? Assume your team will primarily play the standard 4-4-2 format with 4 defenders, 4 midfielders, and 2 attackers.

- Who will you start if your team was to play a more aggressive 4-3-3?
- Who will you start if your team was to play a defensive 5-4-1?

	Attack	Midfield	Defense
Player 1	6	5	6
Player 2	4	1	3
Player 3	1	2	7
Player 4	3	3	4
Player 5	5	6	1
Player 6	6	3	3
Player 7	2	5	8
Player 8	7	3	7
Player 9	6	4	1
Player 10	5	6	8
Player 11	7	7	4
Player 12	6	6	4
Player 13	5	10	7
Player 14	2	5	8
Player 15	4	4	4

Additional Resources

Cortez, Paulo. 2014. *Modern Optimization with R*. New York, NY: Springer.

Faraway, Julian J. 2014. *Linear Models with R*. Boca Raton, FL: CRC press.

Sallan, Jose M., Oriol Lordan, and Vicenc Fernandez. 2015. *Modeling and Solving Linear Programming with R*. OmniaScience.

CHAPTER 10

Deep Learning in Sport Analytics

J.T. Wolohan

LEARNING OBJECTIVES

After reading this chapter, students should be able to:

- Describe the idea behind neural networks and the influences from classical conditioning and neuroscience
- Identify the popular methods of deep learning, such as convolutional and recurrent deep learning systems
- Identify likely applications for recurrent and convolutional deep learning systems
- Identify major applications of deep learning to sport
- Implement a deep learning system in R

Introduction

Deep learning is one of the most recent analytic techniques, owing its feasibility to a combination of widely available data and compute resources that have come about only in the past decade. Despite its recency, engineers, researchers, and analytics professionals have adopted deep learning approaches for a wide variety of applications, including sport. Throughout this chapter, we will review deep learning theory, approaches, and applications in the world of sport.

Artificial Neural Networks

The first thing most people learn about deep learning is often the technique's misnomer: artificial neural networks. This name has its roots in the 1940s (McCulloch and Pitts 1943), when neither data nor computational power was sufficient to do deep learning. Then, the biology community was beginning to understand how animal brains functioned. In particular, they understood brains to have neurons that "fired" with electrical signals. **Artificial neural networks** were conceived of as a computational parallel to these biological structures. The idea was that a signal—data—would be passed into the neurons—matrices of weights—and that the neurons would fire—calculate interim values—until eventually a signal—a predicted value or class estimate—was output.

This approach is based on the **Hebbian theory** (Hebb 1949) which can, in lay terms, be described as "neurons that fire together, wire together." The idea is that the brain has positive feedback loops for behaviors. When an animal does a thing and then something happens after that, the association between the thing that was done and the thing that happened increases. Consider the historic case of Pavlov's dogs (Bitterman 2006). Pavlov would ring a bell and then feed his dogs. After a while of doing this, Pavlov found that he could ring his bell and—without presenting food to the dogs at all—get the dogs to drool. The dogs' brains had associated hearing the sound of the bell with the food-anticipation behavior of drooling. Because these two sets of neurons—neurons associated with hearing the bell and neurons associated with drooling—fired together so frequently, they had wired together. This is the same premise behind modern clicker training (Fogel, Weil, and Burris 2010). While most well known as an obedience training technique for dogs, clicker training is also popular in sports with highly complex, precise, and multi-planar movements, including tennis, golf, and baseball (Bonner 2010). In these sports, it is common for elite coaches to use clicker training to reinforce positive performance on serves, swings, and pitches. The idea being that the immediate positive feedback can encourage the firing of neurons associated with good serves or swings, while discouraging the firing of neurons associated with poor form.

While these broad strokes are consistent between deep learning—which indeed has neurons that learn from input–output associations—we have since learned that the brain is vastly more complex than even the most sophisticated neural network. For reference, a simulation of the human brain requires roughly three orders of magnitude more computing power than the IBM Watson super-computer. It therefore makes more sense to think about deep learning and cast aside the misleading notion of artificial neural networks.

The moniker "deep learning" comes from the many layers of matrices that are contained in such a system. The large number of layers creates a situation where computers can spontaneously encode many complex patterns to attune themselves to emergent phenomena. However, this also comes with some drawbacks. Because deep learning systems have potentially millions of weights, they are almost impossible to understand. They can learn undesirable behaviors and patterns from data as well as desirable ones. Additionally, deep learning systems require a large amount of data and sub-stantial computing resources to train.

This often makes deep learning approaches only suitable for many of the advanced data sources discussed in the previous chapter. While box score statistics can be fed into deep learning systems, this type of data is often too "small"—containing too few relevant observations to be useful for deep learning. With this data, other techniques should be preferred, such as the linear models discussed in the opening chapters of this book. Advanced data sources, which often receive data generated by a computer, are perfect for deep learning because computers generate high volumes of data with many, many observations relating to any phenomenon of interest.

What Is Deep Learning?

While we talk about deep learning models in terms of neurons, this is a verbal embellishment for what the systems are really made up of: matrices of weights. These weights, when applied with stan-dard matrix algebra, create the firing-like effect discussed earlier—especially when the layers are composed one after another. To examine how this works in practice, let us take a look at a simple deep learning network designed to help golfers pick a club based on distance from the hole.

In this scenario, we will design a deep learning system that has three layers—as the sections of a deep learning system are known:

- An input layer
- A fully connected (dense) interim layer
- A fully connected (dense) prediction layer

In this scenario, the input layer will take the information we have about historical distance-to-hole and club use; the interim layer will offer a chance for the deep learning network to "learn" the appro-priate results; the prediction layer will translate that learning to an outcome. Let us first consider the overall design of the system and then discuss the system layer-by-layer.

Overall, we can think of the system as attempting to learn a function that maps inputs to outputs. The theory underlying neural networks insists that they can stand-in for, or learn to mimic, any continuous function (Kreinovich 1991). In our case, we are imagining a function that takes in club and distance to the hole and estimates the outcome of the round. We can then apply the function across the inputs in question to find the most desirable outcome. For instance, if we are 225 yards from the hole, we can apply our learned network to all the possible clubs and a range of 225. The club with the best outcome should be the club we select for that situation.

This same technique has been used for analysis of soccer. There, Fernández, Bornn, and Cervone (2019) use the position of all 22 players and the ball as inputs and the outcome of the possession as an outcome to learn what the optimal pass-choice is for any given situation. One of the highlights of their research is intuitive finding that ideal pass selection changes based on the location of the ball. When the ball is deep in one's own territory or the midfield, conservative passes are preferred: these passes maintain possession and offer little benefit to the opponent. In contrast, when the ball is in the attacking zone, the team benefits from high-risk passes into the box or to players in space.

You may notice that both of these processes—the hypothetical deep learning system we are exploring here and the actual deep learning system by Fernández *et al.*—are following a pattern we have seen before in these pages. Just like weighted on base average, box plus-minus, and defense value over average, the deep learning approaches attempt to calculate the average success rate of all possible actions. Coaches, then, can adjust their play calling or coaching philosophy toward the actions that are going to have the most positive outcomes.

Putting the overall system description behind us, we can start to think about the input layer. The input layer is a matrix that arranges our data in such a way that is fitting the processing approach of the neural network. There are many ways to arrange data in a matrix and, a priori, it is often difficult to know which arrangement is going to lead to the best results. In our example, we want to include club and distance to the hole in our input matrix. Below, we can see two of the many ways that one might encode this information into a matrix. In option 1, the club is encoded as a number (from 1 to 14, the maximum number of clubs a PGA tour player is allowed to carry) and so is the distance—which represents the number of yards to the hole. In option 2, we encode the club using a technique called **one-hot encoding**. This technique involves taking a categorical variable with several states—14 in our case—and creating a new variable in the matrix for each potential state. We could do something similar with the distance metrics if we wished, encoding short-distance, medium-distance, long-distance, and tee shots. If we want to get more complex, we could encode ball location in our matrix, adding one or more variables for fairway, rough, bunker, etc. Again, this variable could be integer encoded in a single location or one-hot encoded across many.

Option 1	
Club	Distance
...	
9	50
4	200
1	400

Option 2

D	1	2	3	4	5	6	...	P	Distance
...									
0	0	0	0	0	0	0	...	0	50
0	0	0	0	1	0	0	...	0	200
0	1	0	0	0	0	0	...	0	400

FIGURE 10.1. Input matrix options for golf club, distance

As you may have gleaned from the discussion of input matrices above, defining an input matrix is very much an art. The ideal process also depends on the method of the middle layers of the deep learning system as well. Some deep learning systems will respond better to inputs in one format, while others respond better to inputs in another. In general—and making the assumption that we have a large volume of data to train on—we should try to encode as much information in our input matrix as possible. For example, in the soccer case from earlier in the chapter, player position was encoded using detailed X, Y coordinates. With enough information (training data), the deep learning system should be able to learn to disregard unnecessary information just as it learns to pick up on the important information. This process is also known as discriminating "**signal**" from "**noise**."

With our input layer established, we can move on to the dense layer. This is the layer of our deep learning system that does the *learning* aspect of deep learning. In our example system, there is only one of these layers. In a true deep learning system, there will generally be many of these layers. These layers can also take many different shapes and have variable behaviors. Later in this chapter we will review some popular choices of layers, how they work, and some common applications. For now, we can think of this layer as a matrix of weights, each of which is randomly assigned and then adjusted slightly in an iterative fashion until the weights produce sufficient results. Sometimes this layer will never learn to produce sufficient results—in these cases, deep learning models are poorly fit to the task. In other cases, the layer will learn to match the specifics of the data too closely and will generalize poorly to other data. This is called overfitting.

Intermediate layers, like our dense layer, are responsible for finding associations between the input variables we provide and the output value. In our case, the dense layer is responsible for learning associations between club used, distance to the hole, and outcome. Different sections of the layer may pick up on different parts of the problem. For instance, one weight might learn to check if the distance is greater than 500 yards, at which point we would likely want to use a driver of some kind. Another might learn to check to see if we are within 20 yards, in which case a putter is probably most appropriate. Of course, because the learning happens at random, there is no way for us to say a priori what the machine will decide is or is not important. The deep learning model may pick up on human-recognizable patterns, or it may not.

Lastly, our model consists of a dense output layer. This layer is, as one may guess from the name, designed to represent the output of our problem. In our case, the performance of the golfer on the hole. For our problem, we will likely want to use a single-value output layer—one value representing the result of the hole. This, however, is not the only type of output layer we could use. We could, for instance, choose a three-value output layer: one for each under-par, par, and over-par. Our deep learning model, in that case, would learn to project the probability that a given club/distance combination would result in each type of outcome. Choice of output layer is often directly tied to performance on a task. If the output is simplified, the problem is simplified, and often easier for the deep learning approach.

Deep Learning and Sport

While having a sense of how deep learning algorithms work is important, it is also important to understand the history of deep learning algorithms in sport. Deep learning found its first major success in the ancient board game of backgammon. Backgammon, a game where players roll dice and move checkers around a board, outmaneuvering their opponent in order to win, poses a relatively straightforward challenge for a computer. Much like our example above, the computer is presented with a situation—an arrangement of checkers and the numbers displayed on the dice—and must make a decision about how to move its own checkers on its turn. In the mid-1990s, computer programs were able to outplay all but the very best human players and revolutionized the game.

The first deep learning program to earn the respect of top-level human backgammon players was a program called TD-Gammon, named by its creators at the IBM's Watson Research Center for the algorithm the program used. The algorithm was a time-sensitive reinforcement learning algorithm (Tesauro 1995). Reinforcement learning algorithms are algorithms that train by adjusting to the positive or negative feedback they receive. This approach makes a lot of sense in games, where each move can be associated with a game outcome, which is either positive (a victory) or negative (a defeat). These algorithms are often placed next to a system that manages the rules of the game. For instance, a standard computer program that runs the game of backgammon, enforcing its rules, for example, pieces can only move forward.

Though later in the 90s, IBM's Deep Blue chess engine would take a match against Grandmaster Gary Kasparov, it was not until the 2010s that deep learning would be successfully applied to such sophisticated games as chess and go. Training in a similar reinforcement learning fashion, but using the popular contemporaneous convolutional-network approach and much-advanced computing hardware, a group of researchers known as DeepMind, later acquired by Google, would build a single algorithm that could learn to compete at several different piece-position based games, including chess. Indeed, the deep learning approach to chess proved so good, that the AlphaZero algorithm was able to go undefeated against the principal computer chess program at the time: Stockfish (Silver et al. 2018).

And while beyond the world of board games, it is difficult to face algorithms against humans head-to-head, deep learning approaches are widely used throughout sport at present to supplement human performance. For instance, top-level players frequently watch video of their own performances to identify areas for improvement. However, in the past, players would have to watch long sessions of mostly good or satisfactory play to find the few errors that worsened their performance. As players get better, the ratio of errors to uninteresting plays goes up, meaning the athlete would need to watch even more video just to find the incident worth studying. Deep learning approaches, in a task called **action recognition**, can remedy this. Action recognition is a machine learning task where algorithms are applied to identify what sport-specific action is happening in a given frame of video (Mora and Knottenbelt 2017). For instance, in a section of video from a tennis match, we may wonder if that section contains a serve. If so, is it a slice serve? Does it land in play or is it a fault? From which side of the court was the player serving? All of the questions can, to some extent, be answered by computers using deep learning. In baseball, players may wish to see all the sliders the pitcher they will be facing has ever thrown to look for indicators of the impending pitch. Deep learning algorithms can be applied to video of baseball to identify the type of pitch being thrown (Chen et al. 2019).

One of the biggest promises of deep learning is that it will be able to uncover new strategies for professional sports, much in the same way that computer programs have led to leaps in strategy in board games such as chess and backgammon. Quarterback play in the National Football League, for instance, is commonly understood to be of immense value to a team; however, it is notoriously difficult to differentiate a good quarterback on a bad team and a bad quarterback on a good team. Further, the offensive play calling as well as the quarterback's own audibles and decision-making are often indistinguishable, or at least intimately entwined. Deep learning, combined with large volumes of player tracking data, provides an objective and naive way of measuring quarterback decision-making performance (Burke 2019). This approach has the advantage of naivety over traditional expert-informed or box-score-based quarterback assessment systems such as QBR or Quarterback rating. Because the deep learning approach is not (mis)informed by preconceived notions of what good quarterback play looks like, the deep learning models are free to learn this from the data. Ideally, this will lead to coaches and players identifying new strategies of play.

Deep Learning Approaches

In contemporary sport analytics there are two primary types of deep learning systems one will need to use: **recurrent systems** and **convolutional systems**. Recurrent systems are temporal—they have a notion of "time" within the network and are associated with a variety of prediction-based tasks. Convolutional systems are geometric—they have a notion of "space" within the network and associated primarily with tasks that involve imagery, object recognition, or other spatial tasks. In this section, we will explore each of these approaches, before learning how to apply them in the final section of this chapter. We will also touch on reinforcement learning as a special case deep learning system.

RECURRENT DEEP-LEARNING SYSTEMS

Recurrent systems are deep learning systems that have an internal structure that can attune itself to the passage of time in data. These systems are said to have memory of previous data that they have seen. For instance, we might imagine a deep learning system designed to predict the next pitch a pitcher will choose. This system could be fed historical pitch/scenario data and predict the coming pitch. Such a system, if we designed it using a recurrent deep-learning pattern, would remember the pitches the pitcher previously threw and previous situations, and attempt to understand their impact on predicting the next pitch. Intuitively, we can understand why we would want to do that: most pitchers cannot imperviously throw the same pitch again and again. Batters will queue in on the pattern. So pitchers, catchers (who often call the sequence of pitches), and the batters attempt to guess at what their opponent is thinking and change their behavior accordingly. A deep learning system that can remember which pitches were thrown may be able to predict what is coming next in a given sequence, from a given pitcher.

Recurrent deep-learning systems achieve their effect by channeling the information they receive from any inputs along two paths: one dedicated to learning the optimal use of input information and one dedicated to learning the optimal information to remember for future observations. The information from these two paths is combined at each layer of the network and passes outputs along to the next layer. The most common form of a recurrent deep-learning system that you will encounter is the Long Short-Term Memory Network, or LSTM. LSTM layers within neural networks are characterized by three gates: an input gate, which tells the layer what to pay attention to; a forget gate, which tells the layer what to remember and what to forget for the next input; and an output gate, which tells the layer what to pass along to the next layer of the system.

This setup makes LSTM systems excellent for the if-then type of problems common in sport. LSTMs are appropriate for these challenges because, unlike other deep-learning systems which would need to have the historical information codified as an input, the LSTM system can learn from sequences of events. The LSTM system, in this way, can learn its own features by learning what to remember and what to forget about the past. That said, when designing an LSTM system it is still important to ensure that the right data for each event is available. For instance, if we are building the pitch-predictor system described earlier, but we do not include pitch speed, only pitch type, our system will suffer. It will not have a chance to distinguish between high-speed fastball-like sliders and low-speed curveball-like sliders. However, we would not need to indicate previous pitches—that information could be learned by the system.

Sports Analytics

That LSTMs can learn so well from events also makes them especially well suited for sport analytics because we are used to putting out event logs. Many sports already have personnel assigned to producing play-by-play logs. Increasingly, data about who was where doing what is available down to the fraction of a second in sports like basketball, football, and soccer. This raw data, though too voluminous and granular for humans, is perfect fodder for an LSTM to learn from. Likewise, LSTMs will revolutionize esports in the coming decade. LSTM-based deep learning systems are able to beat top gamers in DotA 2 and Starcraft II. The prevalence of these systems, as training partners or coaching tools, will likely have the same impact on esports that Stockfish has had on Chess—helping players discover new techniques and surprising counterintuitive, but effective, plays.

CONVOLUTIONAL DEEP-LEARNING SYSTEMS

Where LSTM systems thrive on sequential data, convolutional deep-learning systems thrive on spatial data. That is, data where the position of things near one another is meaningful. Again, it is intuitive to see how this is applicable to sport. After all, much of sport is about the positioning of objects in space. For instance, positioning a ball into or through a net (shooting), positioning your person around (dodging) or into (tackling) another person, or positioning one object into another object—such as a bat or a racquet onto a ball. Convolutional systems are designed to find patterns in these spatial associations.

The primary application of convolutional neural networks, in sport analytics and beyond, is in image processing. Convolutional systems are used for medical image processing, facial recognition, and sport analytics—and often the same algorithm can be used in all three areas. In professional sport there are many instances where image processing software is useful. For instance, the marketing department may want to find all the three-point shots of the star forward to prepare a promotional video, or a player may want to find all the video clips of their opponent when they dribble left to study for an upcoming matchup. Having an automated system that can tag hours of video by the second for rapid retrieval is invaluable in these cases. Likewise, convolutional systems can be used to get summary data about a team's performance directly from video footage, without the need of human annotators. For instance, we could use a convolutional neural network to enumerate and find the frequency of every offensive formation used by a football team since the first week of the season.

Relative to other sophisticated analytics approaches, obtaining an intuition for how convolutional neural networks work is easy. We can think of convolutional neural networks as scanning an input image—or a series of input images—with a small square, and learning how to encode that information into a desired output format. For instance, if we imagine a convolutional network designed to identify recreational runners in their post-race photos based on their bib number—systems which are prevalent and used by most major road races—we can imagine a computer sweeping over this image with a small square viewport until it finds the runner's bib. It might do this by looking for the distinct colors and rectangular shape of the bib. Then, we can imagine the computer will sweep over that bib area with the intent of identifying the numbers on the bib. That first step may be accomplished by a single convolutional layer, and the latter step accomplished by one or more layers.

At each step of this process, the convolutional deep learning system is learning how to reduce the image input into a more pertinent set of data. One of the primary means convolutional networks have for doing this is an approach called pooling. **Pooling layers** work by taking the strongest or most apparent feature from a given area of the image and reducing the entire image down to just those strong features. We can think of this as very similar to what happens when you shrink an image in Microsoft PowerPoint or Word. The image gets smaller—but we can still make out the most important features. Of course, if you have done this, you will know that at some point, the image becomes unrecognizable and all the information is lost.

There are many varieties of pooling that we may want to use. The most common is called **max pooling.** Max pooling takes the strongest feature from a given area and carries that over. Consider the example of the bib-detection system from earlier. The photos will reflect shadows and light changes on the bibs, but these are not going to be relevant for the detection exercise: we only want to know what the numbers are—not what lighting they are in. A max pooling layer can take the strong dark letters from the bib and remove any fuzziness caused by lighting. Another common method of pooling—average pooling—averages the features from an area of the image. This is often useful when we are dealing with color images. For instance, if we are trying to detect a basketball, picking up on generally orange objects is going to be more important than queuing in on the wide range of oranges that a basketball can take in various lighting situations.

As you are likely noticing, image detection tasks—and the proper design of convolutional deep learning systems—requires us to think about the task of image processing itself. Convolutional deep learning systems are more prone to overfitting than their recurrent counterparts. Remember that LSTM networks have a forget feature built in—this, in part, hinders them from tuning too closely to any specifics of the data ingested. However, any deep learning system can be overfit. Convolutional systems, in contrast, have no such forgetting mechanism. Therefore, convolutional systems are often confused by seeing objects in new locations. For instance, we might imagine training an image detection system for the National Hockey League based on images from their traditional, indoor games. When we go to use the system during the league's New Year's Day Winter Classic, a game which is played outdoors, we might be surprised to find that the system performs rather poorly. Changing backgrounds, colors, or lighting can cause surprisingly large impacts on object detection systems.

A common remedy to this problem has nothing to do with the convolutional systems themselves but rather the data that we train them on. It is common for system developers to modify the input images—sometimes quite dramatically—to increase the randomness of the input data and, by extension, the robustness of the resulting convolutional system. Some trivial examples involve rotating and cropping images in various unusual ways. For instance, if we are training a soccer ball detection system, we may crop some of the images so that only part of the ball is in the image. This helps the system learn to detect the ball when it is partially hidden, say by a player's leg or a goalpost. For the same system, we might also crop out the image of a soccer ball—or more likely: several images—and place those cropped out balls other images far removed from the standard environment we would expect the system to receive data from. We might paste the soccer ball into images of office places, classrooms, living rooms and kitchens, or even outer space and then train on this data in addition to our soccer-game specific data. This is intended to make the system more robust against changing environments.

Reinforcement Learning Systems

Reinforcement learning systems are different than the two major types of deep learning systems we have reviewed in this chapter so far; however, they deserve special attention due to their historical impact on the strategy of games such as backgammon, chess, and poker, as well as their impending impact on esports strategy. Where recurrent deep learning systems and convolutional systems are characterized by the types of layers in those systems—recurrent layers and convolutional layers, respectively—reinforcement learning systems are characterized by how they train. Reinforcement learning systems train from a simple reward feedback mechanism—typically in the form of wins, losses, or points of some kind.

Importantly, these reinforcement learning systems can take raw sensor data as input—requiring the least amount of preprocessing of any deep learning system. Researchers at DeepMind trained a reinforcement learning system to play Atari games simply by creating a situation where the system was shown the pixels that made up the game display and then was ultimately rewarded (or punished) based on the final score it achieved (Mnih et al. 2013). The system had no human oversight during its training process, it simply trained by playing Atari games similar to how a human player might. A prime difference, of course, being that the reinforcement learning system could play and remember many, many situations and moves in a much faster time period than a comparable human player. That said, simple reinforcement learning systems like the one crafted by DeepMind for playing Atari had problems with long-term strategic thinking.

More recently, multi-part deep reinforcement learning systems have been crafted to play specific games requiring long-term strategy, for example, the esports game Starcraft II. A team of researchers out of UC Berkeley designed a deep reinforcement learning system that has components for each of several technical components of Starcraft II play (Lee et al. 2018), including scouting (exploring the field of play to understand what your opponents are doing), worker management (selecting which resources to gather), build order (what units or buildings should be built and when), and tactics (how should units engage in combat with their opponents). These components then feed recommendations to an action recommendation list, from which another algorithm is trained to find and select the best algorithm. You can think of this system as a more complicated version of the LSTMs from earlier in this chapter. Except instead of simply learning to remember and forget, generally, the system is being trained to focus on specific sub-aspects of the game. In contrast to the Atari system, which is fed game pixels and needs very little human input, a system like the Starcraft II playing system is possible only with significant and insightful human input. Similarly, analytic system designers need to understand the nature of sport to design appropriate analytics.

One of the outstanding questions for sport analytics with respect to reinforcement learning systems is whether or not simulation technologies will ever be rich enough to inform on-field decision-making. While we could likely train reinforcement learning systems to play exceptional EA Sports FIFA, Madden NFL, or NBA Live, there is no guarantee that any of the strategies the system learned would carry-over into real world play. For instance, consider the strategies used by premier (human) Madden NFL players. Most elite Madden NFL players use running-inclined quarterbacks because of the premium the game places on speed. In real-life football, even the most gifted running quarterbacks advantage their team less with their legs than their video game counterparts. The Madden NFL simulation is not true enough to reality to benefit real life football. Similar problems exist between professional soccer and FIFA and professional basketball and NBA Live.

In contrast, this may not be the case for team management. Team management simulation video games are a popular alternative to the sport focused video games. Titles such as Football Manager and Out of the Park Baseball provide simulation engines that focus not on playing the games but on running the teams. These games focus on the financial aspects of sport—sport business—including contracts and payroll management, sponsorships, ticket sales, concessions, venue and facilities issues, and more. While incredibly nuanced in their own right, these financial considerations do not require the rigorous physical simulation that on-field play requires, and as such are easier for computers to approximate. It is possible that reinforcement learning systems applied to these games could provide team presidents and general managers insight into the potential ramifications of various decisions. A reinforcement learning system, used in this way. In many respects, an approach along these lines would be similar to the Decision Making Under Deep Uncertainty (DMUDU) paradigm established by the RAND Corporation for public policy, military and intelligence applications (Marchau et al. 2019). In DMUDU, an analyst creates a simulation engine—typically using a Markov Chain Monte Carlo simulation approach—and then runs many, many simulations under a variety of possible assumptions. Game and decision theory is then applied to find the solution that will have the most desirable, or most acceptable, outcomes.

Deep Learning in R

There are lots of software frameworks available for Deep Learning, in R and other programming languages. In this section, we will explore one of the most popular cloud machine learning platforms—H2O.ai—and use the R interface to H2O.ai to perform the task of pitch prediction. Pitch prediction is a task that is familiar to anyone who has seen a baseball game. It involves observing a pitch—or in this case, data about a pitch—and using information to guess what type of pitch a given pitch was. This task can be useful for pitch classification and the automation of analytics and sorting in baseball. Moreover, it serves as a good introductory example to deep learning.

To get started with H2O, you will need to install the H2O library in R and a compatible version of the Java Development Kit. I recommend you download JDK SE 11. Java is the software language that H2O's authors selected for the framework and the R library we will use functions primarily by communicating with that library. This has some advantages, because R is a higher-level language than Java, which gives us easy access to some of the most powerful features of H2O, without needing to worry about any of the minutiae that would prop up if we were to work with the library in its native Java. We can also do our data preprocessing in R, which we are familiar with, and not worry about learning a new programming language.

Once we have H2O and JDK 11 installed, we need to initialize H2O. We will start an H2O instance locally and declare that it can use all the available computing resources on our machine for parallelization. With this step, we are starting our own Java machine learning server on our machine and connecting to it. If we changed a few variables here, such as IP address and port, we could connect to a cloud-based server. This is a powerful feature for analytics organizations, as they can have individual analysts connect to a centralized source of data and computing. That is, the data does not necessarily need to be distributed across all the analysts' machines (especially useful when one is working with big data) and computing can take place at a large, centralized cluster (again, important when one needs large amounts of parallel processing for big data work.) In R, this will be a one line process.

```
library("h2o")
h2o.init(nthreads = -1)
```

Now that we have connected to the H2O server running locally on our machine, let's take a look at some of the data we will be using. In this example, we will be using a small set of pitch data. We can read that data in as we have been reading in CSVs throughout this book and plot it to see how easy or hard it might be to distinguish.

```
data <- read.csv("/path/to/pitch.data.csv")

training.data <- data[,1:3]
training.labels <- data[,4]

plot(training.data$speed,
     training.data$vert.movement,
     col=as.factor(training.labels))
```

Constructing a simple plot, shown in the figure below, we can tell that we have three pitches: fastballs, sliders, and curves. Additionally, it looks as though we will be able to distinguish the fastballs pretty readily: all the fastballs in our sample are above 90 miles per hour, while none of the curves or sliders are. For the curves and sliders, we can rely on speed at either end of the spectrum: the slowest pitches are all curveballs and the fastest are all sliders. However, there is a middle ground area that will be hard to classify. This is the territory where we have fast curveballs that behave like sliders and slow sliders that behave like curveballs. An astute baseball fan might know these types of pitches as a slurve, a curveball-grip pitch thrown at slider speed, which is named as a portmanteau of the two pitches (Figure 10.2).

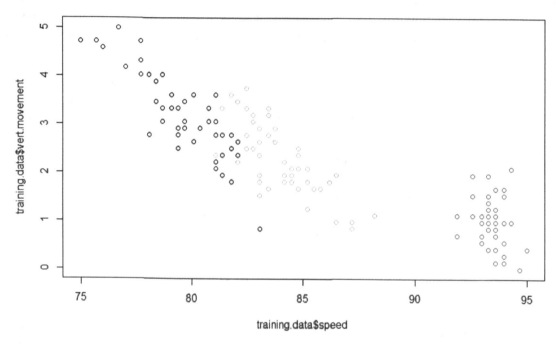

FIGURE 10.2. Fastball, Sliders, and Curves by speed and movement

With that setup, let's run our first deep learning model. Before we run the model, we will need to load our data into the H2O server. Loading data onto the H2O server—in this case the virtual server running on our local machine—makes the data available for the model runners on the server. Once we have done that, we can call one of the model runners—the deep-learning runner—and pass it the parameters we would like for our run. For our first run, we will run a relatively shallow deep learning model that has two hidden layers, each with 3 cells. The logic here is that we have three variables and three pitch types, so maybe there is some magic with the number 3. With most deep learning, there is a little bit of science and engineering and a little bit of art to getting good results. When we have run the model, we will call the summary function on it to view the results.

```
pitch.data <- h2o.importFile("/path/to/pitch.data.csv",
                destination_frame = "pitch.data")

deep.pitch.model <- h2o.deeplearning(training_frame="pitch.data",
                y="pitch",
                hidden=c(3,3),
)

summary(deep.pitch.model)
```

You will note in this code that the y variable of our pitch prediction model is the name of the column in our dataset that contains the label we would like to predict. By default, H2O uses all the other columns as predictors; however, if we were so inclined we could limit the amount of data used by the deep learning system. The hidden parameter is an array that specifies the size of the hidden layers in the system. As we discussed, the more hidden layers, the "deeper" the deep learning network is. In fact, a system as shallow as ours, two three-node layers, may not even qualify as a deep learning system. The summary of the model produces some important output that we will want to understand. Most important are the training metrics.

```
Training Set Metrics:
======================

Extract training frame with `h2o.getFrame("pitch.data")`
MSE: (Extract with `h2o.mse`) 0.1992044
RMSE: (Extract with `h2o.rmse`) 0.4463232
Logloss: (Extract with `h2o.logloss`) 0.5797855
Mean Per-Class Error: 0.2066667
Confusion Matrix: Extract with `h2o.confusionMatrix(<model>,train =
TRUE)`)
===================================================================
Confusion Matrix: Row labels: Actual class; Column labels: Predicted class
          Curve Fastball Slider  Error        Rate
Curve      49       1       0 0.0200 =   1 / 50
Fastball    0      49       1 0.0200 =   1 / 50
Slider     22       7      21 0.5800 =  29 / 50
Totals     71      57      22 0.2067 =  31 / 150
```

In the training metrics we will find a handful of evaluation criteria, namely mean squared error, root mean squared error, and log loss. These are all reasonable ways of comparing model performance; however, for our purposes, it makes the most sense to skip down to the confusion matrix. A confusion matrix is a class x class matrix that shows how our predictions compared to the expected labels. In this instance, it looks like we classified all but one of the curveballs properly, and all but one of our fastballs properly, but did a poor job with the sliders. Indeed, it looks like of the 50 sliders in the dataset, we predicted only 21 correctly as sliders and the rest as curveballs (22) or fastballs (7). This is somewhat surprising given that from the eye test, we know we should be able to distinguish between fastballs and sliders. There is clearly some room for improvement in our model.

For some indication into what is going on, we can look at H2O's variable importance data, also printed by the summary. Here, we can see that the deep learning model is emphasizing vertical and horizontal movement over speed, even though we know that speed is a great differentiator between the pitches. This is one of the drawbacks to machine learning-based approaches: the algorithms determine which variables get weighted in what ways through processes with a large degree of randomness. This can lead to unideal weightings.

```
Variable Importances: (Extract with `h2o.varimp`)
================================================

Variable Importances:
         variable relative_importance scaled_importance percentage
1   vert.movement            1.000000          1.000000   0.424871
2 horiz.movement            0.748141          0.748141   0.317864
3           speed            0.605514          0.605514   0.257265
```

From the variable importances output, we can see that speed only makes up about 25% of the decision-making, even though it should be a prime variable in the discernment process. To see if we can improve our model, let's make our deep learning system deeper. To do this, we will add another hidden layer and increase the size of all of our hidden layers to 10. Instead of a 2-layer model with 3 nodes in each layer, we will now run a 3-layer model with 10 nodes in each. To do this, we must modify the code before and pass in a new array to our hidden parameter.

```
deeper.pitch.model <- h2o.deeplearning(training_frame="pitch.data",
                                       y="pitch",
                                       hidden=c(10, 10, 10),
)

summary(deeper.pitch.model)
```

Examining the confusion matrix this time, we can see that our performance is much improved. As we would have hoped, our error rate on fastballs has dropped to 0. These pitches are so different from the rest that our model can tell them apart 100% of the time. There is still some ambiguity between sliders and curves; however, even here our model is doing much better, guessing only 15 wrong out of the 100 sliders and curves. In particular, our model performed much better on sliders: reducing its error rate to 2 in 50. The curves are now proving the problem child, with an error rate of 26%; however, because these are probably "slurve" type pitches, one wonders if they really fall neatly into either category.

```
Confusion Matrix: Row labels: Actual class; Column labels: Predicted class
           Curve Fastball Slider  Error            Rate
Curve        37         0     13 0.2600 =   13 /  50
Fastball      0        50      0 0.0000 =    0 /  50
Slider        2         0     48 0.0400 =    2 /  50
Totals       39        50     61 0.1000 =   15 / 150
```

Again, we can examine the variable importance table to see what the deep learning model does or does not think is important to predicting whether a pitch is a curve, a slider, or a fastball. In this second model, we see that the pitch speed has become much higher valued. It is still not the most important variable, narrowly trailing horizontal movement; however, it is roughly twice as important as vertical movement in distinguishing between pitches. This maps much better to how we intuited the model should weight the variables, so that should give us some confidence in the robustness of its performance.

```
Variable Importances: (Extract with `h2o.varimp`)
===================================================

Variable Importances:
        variable relative_importance scaled_importance percentage
1  horiz.movement            1.000000          1.000000   0.405903
2           speed            0.946376          0.946376   0.384137
3   vert.movement            0.517264          0.517264   0.209959
```

Of course, once we have a good model, we will want to apply it to new, unclassified data more than we will want to know how it performs on our existing training data. To do this, we will use the predict function. H2O provides this function to make predictions on new data with any H2O model, including their deep learning models. For this example, we will apply it again to our training data and reproduce the confusion matrix from above. Rest assured that you could swap out the data for any data and the process would be the same.

```
predictions <- as.matrix(h2o.predict(
deeper.pitch.model,
as.h2o(data)))[,1]
table(predictions, training.labels)

#              training.labels
# predictions Curve Fastball Slider
#      Curve     37        0      2
#      Fastball   0       50      0
#      Slider    13        0     48
```

Importantly, from this we can see that our confusion matrix remains unchanged. We are getting all the fastballs correct and misclassifying some of our curveballs as sliders. In the code, you can see that we are using the as.h2o function to convert our data frame into an H2O object. This is a convenient way of temporarily converting data in R into a format suitable for H2O.

To try this process out on "new" data, let's quickly bootstrap together some test data by sampling from our existing pitches. To give our deep learning model a run for its money, let's omit any fastballs from our sample as those are easier to predict. In order to do this, we will first take the curve and slide only portions of our data and bring them aside. Then we will create a new dataset by randomly sampling 500 speeds and movements each from our curve and slider observations. This will give us 1,000 new observations—500 curves and 500 sliders—with plausible speeds and movements, though not necessarily in a combination that the model has seen before.

```
curves <- data[which(data$pitch=="Curve"),]
sliders <- data[which(data$pitch=="Slider"),]

harder.predictions <- data.frame(
  speed = c(sample(curves$speed,500,replace=T),
            sample(sliders$speed,500,replace=T)),
  horiz.movement = c(sample(curves$horiz.movement,500,replace=T),
                     sample(sliders$horiz.movement,500,replace=T)),
  vert.movement = c(sample(curves$vert.movement,500,replace=T),
                    sample(sliders$vert.movement,500,replace=T)),
  pitch = c(rep("Curve",500), rep("Slider",500))
)

predictions <- as.matrix(h2o.predict(deeper.pitch.model,
                                     as.h2o(harder.predictions)))[,1]
table(predictions, harder.predictions$pitch)

# predictions Curve Slider
#    Curve       316    128
#    Fastball      0      3
#    Slider      184    369
```

Again, we will also produce a contingency table to see how well our model performed. As we can see, the deep learning model is mostly doing well. It is getting more than 3-in-5 of its predictions right for both curveballs and sliders. There were a few sliders that tricked the algorithm into classifying them as fastballs, perhaps due to the mode still underemphasizing pitch speed. That may be something we would want to look at if we were to try and improve the model further.

Summary

In this chapter, we discussed the history of deep learning, its application to sport and games, and executed an example of a deep learning analysis in R using H2O. We discussed the predominant deep learning approaches of the time, including recurrent networks and convolutional networks. We also discussed the primary applications of these networks, with recurrent networks being excellent for time-based phenomenon and event data and convolutional networks being the de facto standard for image and video processing. In the final practical example, we saw how we could build a deep learning model in R and use it to predict baseball pitches. We also saw how expanding the depth of our deep learning system can influence which variables the system picks up on and how it learns from input data.

Key Terms

deep learning	action recognition
artificial neural network	recurrent system
Hebbian theory	convolutional system
one-hot encoding	pooling layers
signal	max pooling
noise	reinforcement learning

Critical Thinking Exercises

1. In this chapter, we saw how classical conditioning and neuroscience influenced the development of deep learning; however, more recently the paradigm has shifted to emphasize big data over theory. What do you think are the benefits of this turn? What are the drawbacks? In what additional areas can you imagine deep learning being most impactful in sport analytics?

2. What type of deep learning system—a convolutional, recurrent, or reinforcement—would you select if you were going to solve the following problems? Why?
   a. Formation identification from video footage in football
   b. Prediction of the next called play from football play-by-play data
   c. Likelihood of each team scoring next in hockey, from play-by-play data
   d. Optimal path finding in NASCAR or Formula 1
   e. Optimal shot placement in hockey from video data

3. You have a trove of pitch-by-pitch data from a softball league that is interested in developing an algorithm to help them identify which pitch is best to throw in a specific situation. What are some variables that you would want to input into the deep learning model? What type of deep learning system would you use to make these predictions? Why?

4. In the final example in this chapter, we developed a deep learning system that was ultimately perfectly capable of identifying fastballs, but would sometimes confuse sliders as fastballs. Why might this happen? Why were fastballs and curveballs easier to predict than the sliders?

5. One of the hopes with deep learning is that it will provide a way for sport analytics to look at otherwise hard-to-evaluate sport phenomena such as passes in soccer and quarterback play in professional football. What other difficult to measure phenomena across sport would be good candidates for measurement with deep learning? What data would you need to measure those phenomena well? What would be the prediction or task to measure those phenomena?

References

Bitterman, M. E. 2006. Classical conditioning since Pavlov. *Review of General Psychology, 10*(4), 365–376.

Bonner, Julius. 2010. "Improving baseball-pitching through form training: use of video modeling, clicker training, and verbal feedback." MS Thesis. Northeastern University.

Burke, Brian. 2019. *DeepQB: deep learning with player tracking to quantify quarterback decision-making & performance.* Conference paper at the MIT Sloan Sports Analytics Conference (2019). https://www.sloansportsconference.com/research-papers/deepqb-deep-learning-with-player-tracking-to-quantify-quarterback-decision-making-performance

Chen, Reed, Dylan Siegler, Michael Fasko, Shunkun Yang, Xiong Luo, and Wenbing Zhao. (2019). Baseball pitch type recognition based on broadcast videos. In *Cyberspace Data and Intelligence, and Cyber-Living, Syndrome, and Health. CyberDI 2019, CyberLife 2019. Communications in Computer and Information Science*, edited by H. Ning, 328–344, vol. 1138. Springer, Singapore.

Fernández, Javier, Luke Bornn, and Dan Cervone. 2019. *Decomposing the Immeasurable Sport: A deep learning expected possession value framework for soccer.* Conference paper at the MIT Sloan Sports Analytics Conference (March). https://www.sloansportsconference.com/research-papers/decomposing-the-immeasurable-sport-a-deep-learning-expected-possession-value-framework-for-soccer

Fogel, Victoria A., Timothy M. Weil, and Heather Burris. 2010. Evaluating the efficacy of TAGteach as a training strategy for teaching a golf swing. *Journal of Behavioral Health and Medicine* 1(1), 25

Hebb, Donald O. 1949. *The Organization of Behavior: A Neuropsycholocigal Theory*, 62, 78. Hoboken, NJ: Wiley Book.

Lee, Dennis, Haoran Tang, Jeffrey O. Zhang, Huazhe Xu, Trevor Darrell, and Pieter Abbeel. 2018. *Modular Architecture for Starcraft II with Deep Reinforcement Learning.* Association for the Advancement of Artificial Intelligence (www.aaai.org). https://arxiv.org/pdf/1811.03555.pdf

Kreinovich, Vladlik Y. 1991. Arbitrary nonlinearity is sufficient to represent all functions by neural networks: a theorem. *Neural networks* 4(3), 381–383.

Marchau, Vincent A., Warren E. Walker, Pieter Bloemen, and Steven W. Popper. 2019. *Decision Making under Deep Uncertainty: From Theory to Practice*, 405. Switzerland: Springer Nature.

McCulloch, Warren S., and Walter Pitts. 1943. A logical calculus of the ideas immanent in nervous activity. *The Bulletin of Mathematical Biophysics* 5, 115–133.

Mnih, Voldymyr, Koray Kavukcuoglu, David Silver, Alex Graves, Ioannis Antonoglou, Daan Wierstra, and Martin Riedmiller. 2013. *Playing Atari with deep reinforcement learning.* https://arxiv.org/pdf/1312.5602.pdf

Mora, Silvia Vinyes, and William J. Knottenbelt. 2017. *Deep Learning for Domain-Specific Action Recognition in Tennis.* 2017 IEEE Conference on Computer Vision and Pattern Recognition Workshops (CVPRW) (pp. 170–178) (July). IEEE. https://www.doc.ic.ac.uk/~wjk/publications/Mora_Deep_Learning_for_CVPR_2017_paper.pdf

Silver, David, Thomas Hubert, Julian Schrittwieser, et al. 2018. A general reinforcement learning algorithm that masters chess, shogi, and Go through self-play. *Science* 362(6419), 1140–1144.

Sutton, Richard S. 1988. Learning to predict by the methods of temporal differences. *Machine Learning* 3(1), 9–44.

Tesauro, Gerald. 1995. TD-Gammon: A Self-Teaching Backgammon Program. In *Applications of Neural Networks*, edited by A. F. Murray, 267–285. Boston, MA: Springer.

CHAPTER 11

Player Projection Systems in Sport Analytics

J.T. Wolohan

LEARNING OBJECTIVES

After reading this chapter, students should be able to:

- Describe the process of player-performance projection
- Identify situations in which player-performance projection is useful
- Define heuristic-based approaches to player-performance projection
- Compare and contrast simple and complex player-projection systems
- Develop player-projection algorithms in R

Introduction

Sport analytics make the most commotion when they can help us understand what is happening now. When analytics provide a counterpoint to the common narrative about a popular player, or a point in favor of a hated team like the New York Yankees or New England Patriots, commentators are quick to sort into the pro- and anti-analytics camps; with many of the popular former players in the latter camp. Assessing the now, while important, is only part of what analytics can do. One of the key tasks in sport analytics is projecting what will happen in the future: next play, next game, next season. This type of analytics, known as predictive analytics, is critical to the strategy and decision-making of a front office.

One of the most important tasks of a front office is assembling the team: collecting talented players who work well together and win games. It follows naturally, then, that one of the most important forms of analytics is predictive analytics aimed at players. These analytic models, known as player projection models, predict how players will perform in the years to come. These models can be used to find players whose careers' are about to take off and those whose careers are about to drop off.

In this chapter, we will start by reviewing popular methods for performing these player projects. We will review heuristic-based approaches dating back to Bill James (James 1994), as well as more modern machine-learning approaches. We will apply both of these systems in examining Shoeless Joe Jackson's Hall of Fame case. Next, we will review popular contemporary projection systems: Marcel (Tango 2004) and CARMELO (Silver 2015). Lastly, we will build our own projection system for NFL running backs.

Methods for Player Similarity

There are two broad approaches to calculating player similarity: heuristic-based approaches and computational approaches. Both approaches follow the same process: identifying measures and metrics relevant for the projection of interest, weighting those metrics in some way, and identifying similar players based on those weights. Where the approaches differ is in how they get at the weights. Heuristic-based approaches use a predefined set of weights. These weights are often determined by an expert. Computational approaches avoid defining how players are to be compared and arrive at a weighting of metrics through optimization.

Heuristic-based approaches are popular for player similarity calculations for many of the same reasons they are popular in other areas of sport analytics and analytics more broadly: they are simple—often intuitive—to understand. Bill James introduced a points-based approach to comparing players in the 80s that was intended to compare the careers of players. The system, which we will describe below in detail, used a weighting system that we can intuitively understand, for example, home runs are worth roughly seven times as much as a hit—most of us agree that home runs are a more influential indicator of who a player is. Or at least that home run hitters like Barry Bonds and Babe Ruth are more similar to one another than they are to those who hit only the occasional home run, such as Ichiro Suziki or Ty Cobb.

Computational approaches are much harder to understand. Often, we will not even try to understand the interim work that the computer does or the weights that it assigns to different metrics. Instead, we will be satisfied with understanding the process by which the computer arrives at those weights and the error bounds on the outputs of our computational approach. This can be confusing and deeply unsatisfying for those who are skeptical of math or analytics by nature and is often a strike against these approaches.

In this section, we will look at heuristic approaches first—examining James' original player comparison system to predict Hall of Famers in baseball. We will apply the system to a few contemporary players and estimate their Hall of Fame chances. Then, we will look at a technique for player similarity analysis called the K Nearest Neighbors approach. Similarly, we will use this approach to predict whether current players will make the Hall of Fame.

HEURISTIC-BASED APPROACHES

Heuristic-based approaches to player similarity are based on the intuition and choices of the system's author. Bill James' system is based on James' own opinions about how the Baseball Writers of America evaluate players for the Hall of Fame. In some senses, this is no different than any other approach. In every model, the model author has to decide which variables to include and how to include them. What makes heuristic models different is that the authors do not necessarily need to justify these choices with the standard statistical reasoning. Whereas a statistical model will typically assert that they used the fewest variables with the most explanatory power, heuristic models tend to validate with exposition and logical argumentation. For instance, home runs are worth more than singles, so we weigh them higher. That they should be treated differently is not usually questioned; what the weighting scheme should be often is.

James, for his part, devised two heuristic-based approaches to calculating players' career similarities: one model for pitchers and one model for batters. Both models followed the same approach: start with 1,000 and subtract points for the difference between common measurements available for each player multiplied by some weighting factor. For pitchers, James used common pitching statistics such as wins, losses, and ERA; for batters, James used the popular batting statistics such as home runs, batting average, and runs batted in. If you remember back to the chapter where we reviewed player valuation in baseball, you will note that ERA and batting average were not optimal statistics for measuring player value. That is one reason why James' approach is no longer used.

One of the benefits of these heuristic approaches is that they can be represented quite simply in mathematical notation. Where P_a and P_b represent the first player and second players, respectively, C_a and C_b represent their career statistics, and W is a vector of weights for each statistic.

$$f(P_a, P_b) = 1000 - (C_a - C_b) \times W$$

Additionally, we can calculate the similarity between many players at once. If we assume that the career statistics of many players are arranged row-wise in a matrix P, with each column representing a different measurement, we can create a new matrix of similarities S by more or less applying this same formula.

$$S_{i,j} = 1000 - (P_{i,*} - P_{j,*}) \times W$$

For the James' pitcher's model, as we noted, James uses common pitching statistics. In total, James uses appearances, complete games, ERA, games, hits, innings pitched, losses, shutouts, starts, strikeouts, saves, walks, and wins. He also subtracts points for different handedness and varies the ratings

For James' batter model, he used many of the common batting statistics. These include: at bats, hits, games, runs, walks, RBIs, strikeouts, stolen bases, batting average, slugging percentage, home runs, triples, and doubles. Additionally, James classifies each defensive position as having a value. Players who play positions that are more defensively challenging, such as catcher and shortstop, will be rated as more similar than players who play positions which are less defensively challenging, such as first base.

TABLE 11.1. Bill James' similarity weights

Batters		Pitchers	
Metric	Weight	Metric	Weight
Avg.	1,000	W%	500
SLG	500	ERA	50
3B	1/4	L	2
2B	1/5	W	1
H	1/15	G	1/10
R	1/10	S	1/20
HR	1/2	CG	1/20
BB	1/25	IP	1/50
K	1/150	H	1/50
SB	1/20	K	1/30
RBI	1/10	BB	1/10
G	1/20	SO	1/5
AB	1/75	S	1/3

COMPUTATIONAL APPROACHES

On the opposite end of the spectrum from heuristic approaches are computational approaches. These approaches of arriving at similarity measures typically involve identifying a similarity function and applying that function across all the metrics for a player one deems meaningful. Similarity functions are a special type of mathematical function that can be used to find the closeness of two points, vectors, or matrices. They are closely related to distance functions, which seek to find the opposite: how far apart are two points, vectors, or matrices.

You are likely already familiar with some aspects of distance functions. The Pythagorean Theorem, which we noted is the inspiration for Bill James' Pythagorean Win Expectation, is the root of the standard Euclidean Distance formula from geometry. This distance formula takes the square of the sum of the differences between the values of two points in n-dimensional space squared. Because similarity functions are opposite in intent of distance functions, we can take the reciprocal of this function to find a Euclidean similarity or we can use the standard distance function and sort in ascending order.

$$distance(a,b) = \sqrt{\sum_{i=1}^{n}(a_i - b_i)^2}$$
$$similarity(a,b) = -1 \times \sqrt{\sum_{i=1}^{n}(a_i - b_i)^2}$$

A common statistical technique for classification tasks, such as identifying whether or not a player will be a Hall of Famer, based on similarity, is the K Nearest Neighbors algorithm. The K Nearest Neighbors algorithm uses a distance measure to identify the top K similar players and then gives each of those players a number of votes—either one vote per player or a number of votes based on the distance of the voting player to the player they are voting on—and the player would be classified based on those votes. For example, if we are classifying Bryce Harper with a K of 5, we might get a list back that includes Andruw Jones, J.D. Martinez, Kevin Youkilis, Justin Upton, and Frank Robinson. Of these, only Frank Robinson is a Hall of Famer. The four non-Hall of Famers would vote that Harper is not a Hall of Famer, while Robinson casts a vote saying Harper is likely to be a Hall of Famer.

This approach derives its strength from a simple insight: that things which are similar in many ways will likely be similar in other ways. It is an approach that is often overlooked because of its simplicity—it seems almost too simple of an approach—however, it has proven useful for a variety of applications. These applications include predicting the outcomes of soccer matches (Eryarsoy and Delen 2019) and identifying the weaknesses of nations' Olympic preparedness efforts (Shailaja et al. 2020).

Perhaps the best way to understand the nearest neighbors system is to implement it. In the sections that follow, we will implement a nearest neighbors system based on the 2011 season. To do this, we will first create a function that can turn our table of statistics for the 2011 season into a matrix of similarities. Then, we can use that matrix to look up the most similar players for any player of interest. For convenience, we will also create a function that looks up those players and returns their stat lines, so we can validate how similar they are.

We will start with a function to construct the similarity matrix. This function primarily needs to implement the similarity function above: find the distance and multiply it by negative one. We can do that neatly with R's vector arithmetic logic. Before we can do that, however, we will also want to normalize our data.

Normalization is a process by which all the data is placed on a similar scale so that differences in the data are irrespective of the units of the data. That is, if we are taking measurements about height and weight and using them to find similar athletes, and we are measuring the height in feet and the weight in ounces, the weight difference is going to be larger simply because the unit for weight—ounces—is so small compared to the unit for height—feet. No two players are going to be 3 feet apart in height, but many will be 300 ounces or more apart in weight. Normalization resolves this difference so that the differences are treated equally. Once we have done this, we can loop through our data and construct our similarity matrix.

```r
neighbors.matrix <- function(x){
  df <- (x-mean(x)) / sd(x)
  N <- nrow(df)
  df2 <- matrix(0, nrow = N, ncol = N)
  for(i in 1:N){
    for(j in 1:N){
        rmse <- sqrt(sum((df[i,]-df[j,])^2))
        df2[i,j] <- -1*rmse
    }
  }
  return(round(df2,2))
}

neighbors.2011 <- neighbors.matrix(as.matrix(Batting.2011[,mcols]))
row.names(neighbors.2011) <- row.names(Batting.2011)
colnames(neighbors.2011) <- row.names(Batting.2011)
```

LISTING 11.1 Similarity matrix construction in R.

Listing 11.1 shows the code for constructing a similarity matrix on R. You will note that we normalize the data frame first. You may recognize this as standard Z-score normalization. Statisticians favor this normalization process because it takes into account the relative importance of each change in unit. Following normalization, we construct an empty matrix to store our similarity values. We then loop through the rows of our normalized data frame—looping through all the players in our data—and then loop again through all the players. We can then compare each pairing of players by calculating the root mean squared error—the distance measure noted above—and we convert this to similarity by multiplying it by negative one. When this whole process is over, we return the data frame of similarity scores we have constructed.

Lastly, we add some annotations to the similarity data frame. Specifically, we add row and column names. For each, we use the player names listing from the original statistics data frame. We do this for two reasons: one, so we can use lookups by name to retrieve similarities; and two, so we can see the players' names next to the similarity scores when they are returned in R (Listing 11.2).

```
similar.w.stats <- function(player,K=10){
  similar.players <- sort(neighbors.2011[player,],
                          decreasing = T)[2:(K+1)]
  similar.player.names <- row.names(data.frame(similar.players))
  df <- Batting.2011[player,]
  for (name in similar.player.names){
    df <- rbind(df, Batting.2011[name, ])
  }
  return(df)
}
```

LISTING 11.2 Statistics table for most similar players.

Before continuing, we will also put together a handy function that will return the similar players stats, along with their names. This function looks up the most similar players to a given player in the neighbors matrix we just created and then looks up those players stats in the original statistics data frame. With all this information, as well as the statistics of the player we are querying on, the function creates a new data frame containing all of their statistics. We can see this function in action in Listing 11.3.

```
> similar.w.stats("Dustin Pedroia",K=5)
                 Age  Tm   G  PA  AB   R   H X2B X3B HR RBI SB CS BB
Dustin Pedroia    27 BOS 159 731 635 102 195  37   3 21  91 26  8 86
Ian Kinsler       29 TEX 155 723 620 121 158  34   4 32  77 30  4 89
Nick Markakis     27 BAL 160 716 641  72 182  31   1 15  73 12  3 62
Jacoby Ellsbury   27 BOS 158 732 660 119 212  46   5 32 105 39 15 52
Adrian Gonzalez   29 BOS 159 715 630 108 213  45   3 27 117  1  0 74
Melky Cabrera     26 KCR 155 706 658 102 201  44   5 18  87 20 10 35
```

LISTING 11.3 Players similar to Dustin Pedroia.

We can put this function to action looking up the players most similar to Red Sox second baseman Dustin Pedroia. At first glance, the results look pretty convincing. Pedroia is appraised as most similar to Texas second baseman Ian Kinsler, who has a very similar stat line. Both played in 150-something games, had around 725 plate appearances and 625 at bats, and both stole about 30 bases. The two are also both in their late 20s and share a position. That said, we might be able to do better—the hits and home run numbers between the two are pretty far off. And those are relatively meaningful measures—hits being a major contributor to on-base percentage and home runs, of course, being a large contributor to slugging percentage.

```
> similar.w.stats("Joey Votto",K=5)
                Age  Tm   G   PA  AB   R    H X2B X3B HR RBI SB CS  BB
Joey Votto      27   CIN 161 719 599 101 185  40   3 29 103  8  6 110
Prince Fielder  27   MIL 162 692 569  95 170  36   1 38 120  1  1 107
Adrian Gonzalez 29   BOS 159 715 630 108 213  45   3 27 117  1  0  74
Alex Gordon     27   KCR 151 690 611 101 185  45   4 23  87 17  8  67
Miguel Cabrera  28   DET 161 688 572 111 197  48   0 30 105  2  1 108
Ben Zobrist     30   TBR 156 674 588  99 158  46   6 20  91 19  6  77
```

LISTING 11.4 Players similar to Joey Votto.

We can double check our results by doing a second lookup: this time we will use Joey Votto, a power hitting first baseman (Listing 11.4). As desired, Votto appears alongside a bevy of power hitters in their late 20s, including Prince Fielder, another first baseman whom Votto was deemed most similar to. Again, we can clearly see what the algorithm is thinking. Votto and Fielder played a similar number of games, scored a similar number of runs, doubles, and walks. This time, the two are even the same age. Interestingly, Adrian Gonzalez is also a first baseman in his late twenties, and he and Votto are almost identical in terms of games, plate appearances, doubles, and home runs.

While there may be some improvements we could make to our similarity system—for instance, making a principled selection of measurements instead of using all of the available metrics—overall the system works as desired. The nearest neighbors approach identifies players who are similar to our player of interest. When we discuss the CARMELO system below, we will see how this can be used for player projections.

Player Projection Systems

Understanding player similarity is important; however, the task of finding similarity itself is just a start. Once we have found similar players, we want to use that information to make estimations about how a player will perform in the future. If—as a general manager—we can accurately predict how a player will perform in the future, we can make better allocations of our resources than our rivals and hopefully outperform them on the field. For instance, if our rivals have a high estimation of a player on our team and our player projection system suggests that that player's performance will drop off in the next year or two, then we may be able to trade that player for some useful assets at a bargain.

Further, with the onset of fantasy sports, player projection in and of itself has become a money making venture. If we can predict which players will do well in the upcoming season—and if we can do that better than our friends—we should be able to win our fantasy league. For most of us, this will not amount to much money; however, increasingly there are big dollar fantasy leagues where people wager tens of thousands of dollars or more. With the recent advent of daily-fantasy sports, anyone can join in leagues that have prizes of $1 million. And of course, Vegas has long been willing to take wagers on the performance of players before the start of the season. It is common to see prop bets—as these unconventional bets are known—estimating the number of touchdowns a quarterback will throw, the number of home runs a batter will hit, or the number of goals a player will score over the course of a season.

Because of the direct money-making opportunities that arise from these approaches, many of the approaches are kept private by their owners. Which makes sense. If you have information that could be used to make money, and you are giving that information away for free, then you are giving away money. This is especially true for systems design for fantasy and daily-fantasy sports, where the value of the systems is in their ability to capitalize on arbitrage.

There are two related systems which have been described in a reasonable amount of detail. We will cover those systems here. The first system, Marcel (Tango 2004), was designed to be as simple as possible. It is not the best system out there, but it offers good predictions and is competitive with more complex models. Marcel was designed by Tom Tango and has several public implementations. Second, we will look at a system called CARMELO—a backronym for Career-Arc Regression Model Estimator with Local Optimization—which attempts to project the careers of basketball players. The CARMELO system was designed and is maintained by the FiveThirtyEight.com team at ABC, led by Nate Silver, formerly of Baseball Prospectus.

MARCEL

The Marcel model is, in Tom Tango's own words, "the minimum level of competence that you should expect from any forecaster" (2004). Tango did not design the Marcel system to be robust and complete and fully accurate. Rather, he designed the Marcel system to get the job done simply and get out of the way. Tango did not aspire to perfect the art of player forecasting—preferring other, more personally interesting parts of baseball analytics.

Tango's Marcel model is a heuristic-based approach, if we are to classify it using the system above, though Tango—a competent statistician—no doubt derived many of his heuristics from statistical and computational analysis. The system uses the last three seasons of data to make projections about what is going to happen in the next season, by (1) estimating a batter's per plate appearance or a pitcher's per inning rate statistics, (2) estimating how many plate appearances or innings a player will have in the next season, and (3) regressing those values to the mean using age and weighting and league averages. The approach's simplicity is one of its most significant advantages.

Indeed, we can implement the entire Marcel approach in R in just 15 lines of code. When implementing Marcel, we will implement as a higher-order function: a function that returns a function as a result. In our case, the function will take in three seasons worth of data and then return a function that takes a matrix of a player's performance during those 3 years and provide an estimate of their performance the following year. Within our first function we will find the league average, against which we will regress our batter. The function we create within that function—the one we will return—is responsible for merging that information with data from a specific player in order to make the projections.

```
make.Marcel <- function(yr1, yr2, yr3){
  wtd.pa   <- (mean(yr1$PA)*5+mean(yr2$PA)*4+mean(yr3$PA*3))/12
  lg.avgs <- (colMeans(yr1)*5+colMeans(yr2)*4+colMeans(yr3)*3)/12
  wtd.lg.avg <- lg.avgs * (1200/wtd.pa)

  project.Marcel <- function(P){
    player.totals <- (P[1,]*5+P[2,]*4+P[3,]*3)/4
    wtd.totals   <- player.totals + wtd.lg.avg
    wtd.rates    <- wtd.totals/wtd.totals$PA
    age.adj      <- 1+(29-P$age[1])*0.006
    exp.PA       <- (P$PA[1]*.5+P$PA[2]*.1+200)*age.adj
    return(wtd.rates*exp.PA*age.adj)
  }
  return(project.Marcel)
}
```

LISTING 11.5 Marcel projection system in R

The entire system is shown in Listing 11.5—demonstrating how lightweight the Marcel system is in practice—and we will walk through it line by line before taking a look at the approach in practice. The first three lines are to calculate the weighted league average performance. This finds the league average number of player appearances for the last 3 years and the weighted league average for each metric measure over the last three years, and then uses the per-plate-appearance version of each metric to estimate what an average player with 600 at bats would do in two seasons. Recall that the weights are 5 for the current season, 4 for the previous season, and 3 for the two seasons ago. Note that we use the mean function on the plate appearances because those selections are vectors and the colMeans function on the years data frames because they are being treated as matrices.

Next, we begin to create a function inside our function. This second function is the one that is responsible for taking the individual player's performance, mixing it with the league averages, and making a projection. To do this, we calculate the player's totals, as above, and add them to the league average factor we created with the previous function. This gives a sense of how that player should perform; however, the totals we have represent five seasons of plate appearances, not one. To arrive at a single season of plate appearances, we find the player's expected plate appearance adjustment based on their age and the last two seasons performances. We then multiply the per-plate-appearance rates from before by projected number of plate appearances. This provides the estimate. Lastly, we write return

Sports Analytics

statements for both functions. The latter and outermost return statement returns the function we just describe.

With the function in hand, we can turn our attention to making predictions. To do this, we will first—as always—read in some data. For this example, we have four years of MLB batting data from 2008 to 2011. This will allow us to project 2011 based on 2010, 2009, and 2008 numbers. Then, we will apply our Marcel projection function maker to the first 3 years of data to learn how to make projections for 2011.

Having done this, we could build the matrices for each player of interest by hand using rbind; however, because we will want to do this for many players, we will make a function to do it. This function will construct the matrix necessary as an input to the Marcel projection and then make a comparison between the projected data and the actual data. This last part is not necessary if you are just making projects—but it is useful for our purposes because we will want to look up players and the historic projections (Listing 11.6).

```
fn.Marcel <- make.Marcel(Batting.2010[,mcols],
                         Batting.2009[,mcols],
                         Batting.2008[,mcols])

Marcel.predict <- function(player.name){
  player <- rbind(Batting.2010[player.name,][,mcols],
                  Batting.2009[player.name,][,mcols],
                  Batting.2008[player.name,][,mcols])

  projection <- round(fn.Marcel(player),0)
  actual     <- Batting.2011[player.name,][,mcols]
  df <- rbind(projection,actual, actual-projection)
  rownames(df) <- c("Projected", "Actual", "Difference")
  return(df)
}
```

LISTING 11.6 Preparing player data for Marcel projections in R.

With this code ready, we can look up players to see how they compare with our projections. Looking up Albert Pujols and Derek Jeter, we find the following results:

```
> Marcel.predict("Albert Pujols")
            G   PA  AB   R   H X2B X3B HR RBI SB CS  BB  SO HBP IBB
Projected  153 613 520  91 157  34   2 30  95 11  3  80  78   5  24
Actual     147 651 579 105 173  29   0 37  99  9  1  61  58   4  15
Difference  -6  38  59  14  16  -5  -2  7   4 -2 -2 -19 -20  -1  -9

> Marcel.predict("Derek Jeter")
            G   PA  AB  R   H X2B X3B HR RBI SB CS BB SO HBP IBB
Projected  141 588 524 80 150  25   2 12  59 14  4 52 88   6   3
Actual     131 607 546 84 162  24   4  6  61 16  6 46 81   6   0
Difference -10  19  22  4  12  -1   2 -6   2  2  2 -6 -7   0  -3
```

LISTING 11.7 Marcel 2011 projections for Albert Pujols and Derek Jeter.

Comparing the projected statistics against the actual statistics, it looks like the Marcel method performed pretty well (Listing 11.7). Some projections were dead on. For instance, the number of RBIs for each player were within 5 of their actual performance, as was the number of doubles for each player. Other metrics were much farther off. Jeter—never a power hitter—hit only half as many home runs in 2011 as he was projected to, and Pujols ended up with far fewer strikeouts and walks than expected.

Overall, the Marcel system produces reasonable projections with relatively low complexity. In fact, given its performance compared to other approaches, even as measured by the authors of those other approaches (Tango 2012), the Marcel system should be celebrated. If nothing else, the system serves as a baseline upon which player projection systems in baseball must improve, before claiming to be useful.

CARMELO

In Nate Silver's own words:

> *"The basic premise of CARMELO is simple. For each current NBA player, CARMELO identifies similar players throughout modern NBA history and uses their careers to forecast the current player's future."* (2015)

If this sounds a lot like the other systems we have described in this chapter, you are paying attention. The CARMELO system is a basketball adaptation of many of the player-projection systems that were originally developed for baseball.

CARMELO has two categories of metrics it considers: profile metrics and performance metrics. The profile metrics include things like height, weight, age, and draft position. The performance metrics include usage rate, true shooting percentage, 3-point frequency, and free-throw frequency, among others. Metrics from both categories are used to find similar players, using a weighted nearest neighbors approach that considers the year-by-year metrics of players. That is to say, if Chris Paul and Michael Jordan have a True Shooting % of .599 and .603 in the fourth year of their careers, the algorithm will consider them more similar. When Paul goes on to have a TS% of .584 in his fifth year while Jordan records a .614, the algorithm marks them as dissimilar because they are trending in opposite directions.

The similarity scores for all historical players are calculated in this manner. Then the careers of the players that are more similar than not to the player we are making the projection for are averaged together using their similarity scores as weights. That is, the careers of the players most similar to the player whose career we are projecting are given the most weight, and other players are given less to no weight—depending on their similarity.

Additionally, the CARMELO system considers how these historical look-alikes performed relative to their "baseline" expectations—using a method similar to the Marcel system described above. This baselining approach allows the unexpected longevity of players who are expected to decline—perhaps because they rely more on outside shooting that athleticism—to be worked into the projections of similar players. This reflects an assumption on the part of the CARMELO team that players who are similar proportionally will have careers in similar proportion. For example, if Allen Iverson is estimated to be a 10% better version of Tim Hardaway at year 7, then it is estimated that Iverson will follow the same pattern as Hardaway, but 10% better, in year 8.

The precise details of the CARMELO approach change from year to year, and with good reason. The maintainers at FiveThirtyEight.com and ABC continue to work on improving their model. Ultimately, however, there is a lot of similarity between the CARMELO model and models we have discussed in this chapter. The approach's similarity scores follow something in between James' heuristic approach and the computational nearest neighbors approach addressed earlier in this chapter. In addition, the author's cite the Marcel approach as an inspiration for their baselining system (Silver 2015).

Building Our Own Projection System

Lastly, as a conclusion to this chapter, we will build our own player projection system. We will develop a system that projects the future performance of NFL running backs. We will do this using an approach very similar to what we have seen described above by the Marcel system, and even more so by the CARMELO system. We will first use a modification of our KNN system from earlier to identify similar running backs. Then, we will take future seasons from those similar running backs and find a weighted mean based on their similarity to use as a projection.

The first component of our projection system is a modification of our nearest neighbors approach from earlier in this chapter. What we are looking to find is seasons that are similar to the season that was just completed by the player in question. In this sense, we are not looking for players as much as we are looking for player-seasons. For example, we are not interested in finding that Reggie Bush and LeSean McCoy are similar players; however, we would be interested in knowing that Bush in 2011 was similar to McCoy in 2015. We could then use Bush's 2012 and 2013 seasons to project what McCoy might do in 2016 or 2017. In a robust model, we would have a large number of these historical seasons. For our example, we will only use the 4 years from 2013 to 2016 inclusive.

Using our nearest neighbor's code from before, we can then begin to work on our running back season projection function. This function will take in the string naming the player and the season for which we want to make a projection and return the projections for the next two seasons. We will use a weighted-average-based approach for each of the two projected seasons. Our projection function will need to look up the similar player-seasons for a given player and season, find the players above some threshold—in our case it will be the 20 most similar running backs—and then find how those players performed in their next two seasons. Then, those seasons will be averaged together using a weighted average. Those weighted averages will be returned as the projections. The R code for this approach can be seen in Listing 11.4.

In Listing 11.4, you'll note that our function has three sections to it: setup, retrieving the seasons, and then averaging those seasons together. The setup phase involves running our similar.w.stats function from Listing 11.2. Then the output of that function is parsed down to just the names of the similar player-seasons and their similarity weight. Next, in the retrieval phase, we loop through those player names and construct two arrays: one array for the very next player-season and an array for the player-season after that. For example, if we find that Frank Gore in 2013 was similar to Alfred Morris in 2014, we will add Frank Gore's 2015 and 2016 seasons to our lists so that we can look them up and use them for our projections. Lastly, we take those player-season names and weights, lookup the seasons, calculate the averages, and return the projections (Listings 11.8 and 11.9).

```
project.rb <- function(player){
  top.matches <- similar.w.stats(player,k=20)[2:20,]
  match.names <- row.names(top.matches)
  wgts          <- top.matches$similarity
  matched.players <- data.frame(
    player = sapply(match.names, name.to.name),
    year   = sapply(match.names, name.to.year))

  year.one <- c()
  year.two <- c()
  for (i in 1:nrow(matched.players)){
    player <- matched.players[i,]$player
    yr     <- as.integer(matched.players[i,]$year)
    year.one <- append(year.one, paste(player, yr+1))
    year.two <- append(year.two, paste(player, yr+2))
  }

  year.one.avg <- lookup.and.average(year.one, wgts)
  year.two.avg <- lookup.and.average(year.two, wgts)


  results <- rbind(year.one.avg, year.two.avg)
  return(round(results[,2:ncol(results)],1))
}
```

LISTING 11.8 Running back projection model in R

The lookup and averaging is handled by the lookup.and.average function. This function takes an array of strings, each naming a player season, for example, "Frank Gore 2015," and an array of weights associated with each season. The function then looks up those seasons in our data and averages them together based on the weights provided. The code for this can be seen in Listing 11.9.

 The only trick with the lookup function is making sure we only consider player-seasons that actually exist in our data. In some senses, this problem is specific to our data—because we are using such a small sample—however, it is also something that you would have to account for in any player projection system. Players retire, get suspended, get injured, or can otherwise miss seasons for any number of reasons. We do not want to let these missed seasons unravel our projections. In this instance, we simply drop seasons that do not exist. In a more sophisticated system, you may want to consider how to handle player retirements, for instance.

```
lookup.and.average <- function(player.names, weights){
  seasons <- all.players[player.names, ]
  seasons$weight <- weights
  dne <- which(is.na(season[,1]))
  seasons.exist <- season[-dne,]
  season.avg  <- apply(seasons.exist[,2:21], 2,
                       function(x){
                          weighted.mean(x, w=seasons.exist$weight)
                       })
  return(season.avg)
```

LISTING 11.9 Projecting seasons with weighted averages

You will note that R has a built-in weighted.mean function that we can use for calculating our weighted means (Listing 11.9). We use the apply function to calculate the weighted means for each column of our data frame containing the similar player-seasons. The result of this is a new, single-row data frame that holds the weighted average of the similar seasons.

Once this is complete, we can then use our player projection tool to project the next two seasons for any running back from 2013 or 2014. For instance, we can project the 2013 stats of Pittsburgh Steelers' running back Le'Veon Bell into 2014 and 2015. These projections are shown in Listing 11.10.

```
> rbind(project.rb("Le'Veon Bell 2013"),
+        all.players[c("Le'Veon Bell 2013",
+                      "Le'Veon Bell 2014",
+                      "Le'Veon Bell 2015"),3:21])
[,c(1,3,4,12,13,14)]

                    Starts Receiving RecYrds   Att     Yds  TD
year.one.avg          10.9      35.6   294.7 205.8   918.7 5.4
year.two.avg          10.0      27.1   213.0 169.0   667.4 3.8
Le'Veon Bell 2013     13.0      45.0   399.0 244.0   860.0 8.0
Le'Veon Bell 2014     16.0      83.0   854.0 290.0  1361.0 8.0
Le'Veon Bell 2015      6.0      24.0   136.0 113.0   556.0 3.0
```

LISTING 11.10 2014 and 2015 projections for RB Le'Veon Bell

From these projections, we can see how our model fares. In 2014, we projected Bell to start 11 games, and total about 1,200 yards: 300 receiving and 900 rushing. This is roughly the same as his 2013, where Bell had 1,250 yards—400 receiving and 850 rushing. Instead, in 2014, Bell rushes for nearly 1,400 yards and catches twice as many passes as he did in 2013 en route to accumulating 850 receiving yards. The next season, we projected a drop-off for Bell; however, even our bearish project could not predict Bell's unfortunate 2015 season. Bell started out the 2015 season unable to play due to a DUI-related suspension and finished the season injured with an MCL tear. He totaled only 700 yards in 2015; 200 yards fewer than we projected.

Of course, looking at just one player is simply an anecdote. We can feed our projections into a linear regression to get a better sense of how well it's performing. Figure 11.1 shows a regression line fit to our projected rushing yards and the actual rushing yards for all players in our dataset.

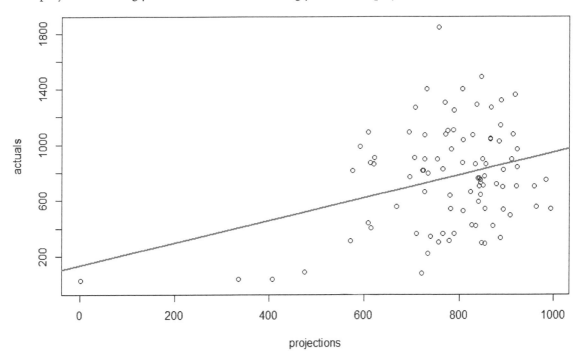

FIGURE 11.1. Regression line and residuals for a running-back projection model.

From this, it is clear that our model is not a great predictor. Indeed, there is one case where we are off by more than 1,000 rushing yards. For most players, however, we are doing okay. We predict 50% of cases within 250 yards of their actual performance. That amounts to about a 16 yards a game difference. If we had just assumed every player would perform at league-average the following season, 50% of players would end up within about 300 yards of their projection. Considered against that baseline, our model is an ever-so slight improvement.

Summary

In this chapter, we have focused on projecting player performances forward in time. This is a valuable endeavor because it can help managers make better decisions about which players to acquire. That is true for both general managers of real teams and the managers of fantasy sports teams—who many not be assembling real teams but are nonetheless gambling with real money. We looked at two techniques for assessing player similarity: a heuristic-based approach and a more statistical approach. We saw that there is some overlap between the heuristic-based approach and the statistical approach in that, in each, the analyst has to make decisions about which statistics to include and exclude from their analysis. One can, of course, include every measurement available, like we did with our running back model; however, there are no guarantees that this is the best approach. Often it will not be and we will want to select metrics that we think are especially important to understanding who a player is. Lastly, we took a look at two projection systems: the Marcel system, a simple system designed by Tom Tango; and CARMELO, a sophisticated system designed by Nate Silver and FiveThirtyEight.com. The Marcel system uses a weighted average of a player's last three seasons and then regresses the player toward league average performance. This turns out to be a surprisingly effective means of predicting player performance in baseball, though, as Tango points out, there is quite large degree of variability when making projections. The CARMELO system is a more robust system, that uses some of the Marcel systems base-lining and then layers on top of it sophisticated player-matching. These two approaches highlight differing beliefs about player projection systems: one believing that year-to-year variance is too wild (and time consuming) to try and predict, and one believing that it can be modeled with a robust enough approach.

Key Terms

Similarity	Z-Score Normalization
Euclidean distance	Marcel
K Nearest Neighbors	CARMELO
Normalization	Weighted average

Critical Thinking Exercises

1. Player projection systems rely heavily on past performance of players to make estimates about how well players will perform in the future. This includes the past performance of both the player in question and others. Can you think of any drawbacks to using a historical approach to projecting performance in this way? In which situations would you imagine historical data not being suitable for making projections? Why or why not?

2. While computational similarity approaches are common now, Bill James' heuristic-based similarity approach can still be useful, especially for sports with a small volume of historical data. Consider the following sports and metrics, which weights would you assign to which metrics and why?
   a. Basketball: PPG, FT%, 2PA/3PA, RBDs, STLs, Assists, Minutes
   b. Football (QB): Attempts, Yards, Interceptions, Touchdowns
   c. Golf: Drive distance, fairway accuracy, strokes gained putting, strokes gained approaching
   d. Tennis: serve speed, first serve accuracy, volley frequency, winners, unforced errors

3. The MARCEL projection system uses only a handful of variables and can, with satisfactory accuracy, project the performance of baseball players in the following season. Why would we prefer a simple system over a system that considered more variables? Are there unique properties about baseball that make this approach successful here? How do you think a simple MARCEL-like system would perform in other sports?

4. One of the keys to creating an effective player projection system is the similarity calculation. As we saw with the baseball examples in this chapter, sometimes these are performance-related metrics and sometimes they are biographical/physical factors like height, weight, or position played. For each of the following sports, select three metrics and three other factors that you might use to calculate player similarity and justify those decisions.
   a. Field hockey
   b. Volleyball
   c. Race-car driving
   d. Football

5. In the final example of this chapter, we developed a player project system for running backs in the NFL. This system uses all the running backs metrics; however, as noted in the earlier questions, we may be better off using fewer metrics as opposed to more. Select a subset of the running back metrics available to be used in the neighbors matrix and re-run the projection. How did the projection of La'Veon Bell change? Does the projection system perform better or worse with the new metrics?

References

Eryarsoy, Enes, and Dursun Delen. 2019. *Predicting the outcome of a football game: A comparative analysis of single and ensemble analytics methods.* In proceedings of the 52nd Hawaii International Conference on Systems Sciences (*HICSS*) (January 2019).

James, Bill. 1994. *The Politics of Glory: How Baseball's Hall of Fame Actually Works.* New York, NY: Macmillan.

Shailaja, Varagiri, Rayala Lohitha, Sreethi Musunuru, K Deepthi Reddy, and J Padma Priya. 2020. Predictive analytics of performance of India in the olympics using machine learning algorithms. *International Journal* 8(5), 1829–1833.

Silver, Nate. 2015. *We're Predicting the Career of Every NBA Player. Here's How.* FiveThirtyEight. com. (October 9, 2015). https://fivethirtyeight.com/features/how-were-predicting-nba-player-career/

Tango, Tom. 2004. *Marcel The Monkey Forecasting System.* Tangotiger .net (March 10, 2004). http://www.tangotiger.net/archives/stud0346.shtml

Tango, Tom. 2012. *Marcel The Monkey Forecasting System.* Tangotiger .net. http://www.tangotiger.net/marcel/

CHAPTER 12

Ranking and Rating Systems in Sport Analytics

J.T. Wolohan

Introduction

One of the most important and hotly debated questions in sport is also the simplest: "who is the best?" That is, which team or athlete is better than which other team or athlete. Across sports, across eras, this is certainly a difficult question. Within a single season or competition, however, we feel like we have a good answer to this question: the best team or competitor is the one who prevails over their competitors and hoists the championship at the end. One of the great aspects of sport is that many of these debates are decided on the field of play.

Of course, just because we believe we have a simple answer does not mean necessarily that the simple answer is correct. And in many cases, analytics shows us that the simple answer is indeed incorrect. Sport analytics has long interested itself in answering the question of which team or which athlete is the best, for a variety of practical and theoretical concerns. Among the practical concerns are seeding competitors in tournaments, balancing or analyzing schedules, awarding of end-of-season trophies, and odds making.

In team sports that have an established "regular season" component, there is often an obvious way to seed an end of season tournament: award teams seeds based on their performance over the course of the season. For many individual sports—notably tennis—the primary mode of competition is through tournament play. This raises the problem of needing to balance the seeding of a tournament. If a tournament is imbalanced, the uneven paths to tournament victory by the competitors may call into question the outcomes of the tournament. In general, most tournaments are organized to maximize expected difference in skill between competitors in the early rounds and minimize the expected difference in skill between competitors in later rounds, such that each subsequent round is more competitive (and more entertaining) than the previous. The process of organizing a tournament—called seeding—is the process of rating the various competitors so that they can be arranged in this order.

Relatedly, one may wish to balance or assess the difficulty of play throughout a season for many of the same reasons. If teams have greatly varying levels of difficulty in their schedules, the fans of the sport will question the results. This is less noticeable in professional sports, where we can often assume a minimally acceptable standard of quality throughout the league; however, in college athletics, this question looms large. How does one compare a Power Five football program—Iowa State—with a Group of Five or Independent school—such as Rice? The two teams play almost incomparable schedules. Iowa State must, as a Big 12 member, play football powers Texas and Oklahoma each year. On the other hand, Rice as a member of Conference USA, plays the less intimidating UT San Antonio and North Texas. To assess the impact of the quality of competition, one needs to have a sense of how the teams all compare to one another.

Alternatively, one may wish to rank teams or players for the purpose of handing out an award. Of all the reasons for wishing to rank teams or competitors, this may be the simplest. If one wishes to provide an award to the best team or competitor, one needs a way of deciding who that best team or competitor is. In order to be fair and transparent, a system of rules or scoring is needed. For the creation of narrative drama over the course of a season, it is also helpful if that scoring system can be updated regularly and intuitively followed by fans.

Finally, we may wish to have a ranking of teams or competitors in order to wager on the match-ups between those competitors. This final reason for ranking teams is very self-encouraging. For instance, consider that you have a reliable ranking system and no one else does: you then have information about the outcomes of games that is better than that of everyone else and can make money off of them by taking their wagers in accordance with your rankings. However, this also encourages those bettors to develop their own ranking systems. If they can construct ranking systems that are better than yours, then they can take money from you by accepting your bets. This is the ratchet effect of Las Vegas on sport analytics. So long as we can glean from sports data information that we can use to make better bets, sport analytics will continue to adopt new approaches and methods.

In this chapter, we review two classes of ranking systems: the Elo rating system and its derivatives and points-based systems and their derivatives. The former, developed for chess, is a general approach that we can use to arrive at probabilistic assessments of the quality of competitors. The later approach, often developed for specific leagues or challenges, is designed to optimize for a different goal: television drama. Additionally, we also cover the use of the PageRank algorithm for ranking teams.

Elo Rating System

Named after its inventor, physics professor Apred Elo, the Elo rating system attempts to take basic statistical ideas and use them to generate a rating system. Elo's system rests on the following idea: we can estimate how skillful a chess player is by observing who they play and the outcomes of those matches (Elo 1978). In order to codify this idea, Elo's approach uses random variables to represent the skill of the chess players and the outcome as one piece of evidence resulting from the meeting of those two players. Based on the result, Elo's method has us adjust the ratings of the two players—increasing the rating of the winner and decreasing the rating of the loser. Importantly, Elo's system adjusts the amounts that each players' rating increases based on the expectation it had about them winning before the match. For instance, if a heavy favorite beats an underdog, the favorite's rating will increase slightly and the underdog's rating will decrease slightly. This is because the rating system largely expected the outcome. If the underdog beats the favorite, however, both ratings move by large amounts. Importantly, Elo's system also accounts for the number of matches played, so that competitor's records stabilize after enough evidence of their true skill has been accumulated.

We can make this more concrete with an example. Two chess players are competing. The first has a rating of 1800 and the second has a rating of 1600. Because the first player's rating is greater than the second player's, we know that the first player is favored. Further, because of Elo's system, we know the percentage chance that the first player is expected to beat the second player. We can calculate that value as follows:

$$\text{WPct}_{\text{player}} = \cfrac{1}{1 + 10^{\left(\cfrac{\left(\text{Rating}_{\text{opponent}} - \text{Rating}_{\text{player}}\right)}{400}\right)}}$$

That is, we expect the first player to win at a rate equal to 1 divided by 1 plus 10 to the difference in the two players ratings divided by 400. This design makes it so a difference in 200 points—as we have in our example—results in a 75% chance of the higher-rated player beating the lower-rated player. This same logic works for both players: if the player ranked 1600 plays in a match against a player ranked 1400 they would be a 3 to 1 favorite; if the 1400 ranked player played in a match against a 1200 ranked player, they would be a 3 to 1 favorite. In this way, the Elo system offers a substantial benefit: it can be used to rank the entire population of potential players from novices to the top professionals.

Turning back to the imaginary match between the 1600 ranked player and the 1400 ranked player, the magic of the Elo rating system comes from updating the players ratings following each match. Because the 1600 ranked player is expected to win, their rating will increase less in a win than it would decrease in a loss. Conversely, the 1400 ranked players rating will increase more in a win than it would decrease in a loss because they are expected to lose. If the higher-rated player wins, their rating will go from 1600 to 1605—a boost of 5 points. If the higher-rated players loses, their rating will go from 1600 to 1585—a drop of 15 points.

If we think about each competitor in a match in the Elo rating system needing to wager points on their victory, it makes sense that the higher-rated player would need to wager more points. After all, they are expected to win. And indeed, the points each competitor needs to wager is proportional to the likelihood of them winning. In our case, we have a 20 point match. The higher-rated player needs to wager 15 points because they have a 75% chance of winning, while the lower-rated player needs to wager only 5 points to match their 25% chance of winning. You'll note that the 15:5 ratio is the same as the 3:1 odds the Elo rating system gives the higher-rated player to win. You will also note that 15 is 75% of 20, 5 is 25% of 20, and that 15 and 5 add up to 20.

In chess, it is possible for players to not only tie, but draw as well. In the case of a draw, each player's rating is updated by a value equal to one half of the sum of their potential outcomes. This value will always point in the direction of the unexpected event; a draw will always benefit the lesser ranked player and reduce the ranking of the higher ranked player. In our case, the higher-ranked player would lose 5 points in a draw and the lower-ranked player would gain 5 points.

More generally, the formula for updating an Elo rating following a match can be described as follows:

$$Rating_{New} = Rating_{Old} + K(Outcome - Expectation)$$

In this formula, K is the number of points the match is for—20 in our case—the Outcome is the result of the match—1 for a win, 0 for a loss, and 0.5 for a draw—and Expectation is the expected probability of winning.

The adjustment of K in Elo rating systems becomes something of an art form. K should be large when matches are particularly reflective of skill changes—such as the first time a competitor is playing in a new league or when a team has recently acquired an important new player. Otherwise, we want K to be small so that individual matches do not cause ratings to over adjust new information. In chess, it is common for youth players to have a K of 40, when they are still learning the game; a K of 20 for matches between players below the Master level; a K of 10 for Master-level players and above. Importantly, this value needs to be adjusted for each sport so that it can properly model the changing skill levels. If we had been using Elo ratings to model NBA basketball teams, we would want to have a relatively high K, while if we wanted to use Elo to model professional tennis, we would use a lower K.

FIFA Rating System

One of the most high-profile applications of the Elo rating system is the rating of national soccer teams. FIFA has used an Elo-like system for rating Men's and Women's national teams since 2018. FIFA uses a formula for updating rankings that directly resembles the general update format above; however, they make unique choices around how to determine K, the weight of a given match, and how to handle the outcomes of games.

In the FIFA rating system, K can vary between 5 points and 60 points for matches of different importance. The least important matches—friendlies—are worth either 5 or 10 points, depending on when they are played. Matches played in competition are worth between 15 and 60 points, with World Cup matches being worth the most. All World Cup matches are worth at least 50 points. World Cup matches in the quarter-finals and beyond are worth 60 points. Varying K in this way makes the most important matches from a competitive standpoint also the most important from a ratings standpoint. It reduces the importance of friendly matches, when many countries' best players may be tied up in league play and emphasizes the events that FIFA cares about. It also significantly boosts the rating of the World Cup winner, who will play several high-value matches and have their rating increased several times on their way to victory. Indeed, when FIFA switched to this rating system in 2018, France became the top rated team having won the World Cup earlier in the year.

FIFA also implements a nuance in their rating system with how they handle the outcome of matches. Intuitively, one could expect FIFA to award the standard 0 for a loss, 0.5 for a draw, 1 for a win; however, FIFA makes exceptions for penalty shootouts. In these cases, FIFA awards 0.75 for the outcome of the winner and 0.5 for the outcome of the loser of the shootout. This has the effect of benefitting all but the heaviest favorites who win by penalty kicks, while always rewarding the underdog.

Lastly, FIFA uses 600 instead of 400 as the divisor for the team ratings in the winning expectation formula.

$$\text{WPct}_{\text{team}} = \frac{1}{1 + 10^{\left(\frac{\left(\text{Rating}_{\text{opponent}} - \text{Rating}_{\text{team}}\right)}{600}\right)}}$$

Increasing this divisor either (1) increases the variance of ratings or (2) captures the greater equity in soccer when compared to chess. From a practical standpoint, the impact is the same: teams need to be farther apart in the FIFA ratings to have the same expected winning chance as they would in standard chess ratings. For example, to have 3:1 odds of winning, a team would need to be 300 points higher rated than their opponent. From the 2020 rankings, one such example could be France (#2 in the world rated 1733) and Jamaica (#48 in the world rated 1438).

Universal Tennis Rating System

Another notable application of the Elo-rating system is in tennis with the Universal Tennis Rating. The Universal Tennis Rating is a system that is designed to rate all players—from complete novices to the top professionals—and form competitive matches. It is designed with competitive local match play in mind. That is, UTR's designers are most interested in solving the problem of "how do we make competitive matches from a diverse pool of amateurs." This is an important problem in tennis because, as a popular recreational activity, the local pool of tennis players may include former college athletes, former high-school athletes, adult-novices of various ages, youth players, and both male and female athletes.

UTR rates all players on a 1 to 16.5. The top players in the world have ratings above 16. The top players on the Women's Tennis Association tour have ratings above 13. Elite college-school aged players will have ratings from 11 to 14. Beginners will have UTR between 1 and 3.

UTR works on the same principles as the Elo rating system, with a few interesting variations: first, UTR uses only the last 30 matches; second, UTR uses an expected score system. Using only the last 30 matches allows players' skill to vary throughout their life, while also allowing the UTR system to vary the K value for things like match veracity or competitiveness. Using an expected score system extracts more information than a single match than using a simple win or loss would.

UTR is calculated by assessing the player's performance and competition over their last 30 matches. This is an extension of a simplified version of the Elo rating system. Using this method, to calculate the rating of a player, we take the sum of the total Elo rating of all a player's opponents, plus 400 times the number of matches won, and divide that by the number of matches played.

$$\text{Rating}_N = \frac{\Sigma \quad \text{Opponent}_n + \text{Wins}(400)}{N}$$

For instance, to calculate the rating of a player over 5 matches, of which they won 2 and lost 3, against players with Elo ratings of 1500, 1300, 1200, 1300, and 1200, we would sum those ratings, add 800, and divide by 5. The resulting Elo estimation would be 1460.

An obvious drawback to this approach is that we do not know which opponents the player beat and which opponents the player lost against. Lacking this information limits the certainty of our estimate. If, however, we know that the player will be playing against a number of players within a relatively small window, we can largely overlook this. For league and tournament play, this is often appropriate. Additionally, because a player will rarely go out of their way to play competition much better than themselves—it is suitable for club play as well.

Glicko-2 System

Since the Elo's system for rating competitors debuted, there have been improvements to the system, most importantly: the Glicko rating system (Glickman 1995). The Glicko rating system, named after its inventor Mark Glickman, adds the additional factor of ratings reliability to the Elo rating puzzle. Glickman's insight here is that not all ratings are equally reliable. The rating of a top chess player may be very reliable, but the rating of a child who is rapidly acquiring new skills and prone to great blunders is much less reliable. Additionally the Glicko-2 system has a notion of rating volatility (Glickman 2003). Volatility is a measure of how much a rating is likely to change. The rating of a basketball team may be stable—up until their star player is injured and the rating becomes highly volatile. We can use the Glickman rating system to model these phenomena while maintaining the probabilistic benefits of the Elo rating system.

Applying the Glicko-2 system, we use a multi-step process that supposes many matches take place simultaneously—similar to the heuristic we saw in the previous subsection. The Glicko-2 algorithm is a five-step process. First, starting ratings and rating deviations are determined or assigned to all competitors. Second, the ratings are converted into the Glicko-2 scale by multiplying by a constant. Third, we calculate rating variance. Fourth, we calculate the estimated rating change. Fifth, we calculate the estimated rating volatility. Sixth, we update the rating, rating volatility, and rating deviation and convert them back to the original scale.

The six step Glicko-2 rating system owes its improvements over the Elo rating system to greater complexity. That trade-off may or may not be acceptable for some applications. Many esports leagues have adopted Glicko-based approaches for their leaderboard systems. Glickman has also adapted the Glicko system for multi-competitor sports such as golf, racing sports, and many of the Olympic sports (Glickman and Hennessy 2015).

Elo Rating System in R

To understand the Elo system better, we will implement it in R. Then we will use our implementation to analyze the 2013 Association of Tennis Professionals season. In doing so, we will compare and contrast three different ways of implementing the Elo system: the standard winner-take all system—where the match winner is the only player to receive points—as well as two systems that weight players victories based on how many (1) sets or (2) games they won.

2013 was a historic year in tennis. Andy Murray won the Wimbledon tournament, breaking a nearly 80-year British drought at the fabled grass court venue. Rafael Nadal won two of the four Grand Slams: the French Open and the U.S. Open, while Novak Djokavic won the ATP Finals and the remaining Grand Slam, the Australian Open, finishing second in the Australian and the French. The yearend ratings had Nadal and Djokavic separated by a razor margin for the number 1 spot, earning Nadal the Player of the Year and Comeback Player of the Year accolades, in light of his distant fourth place finish in 2012.

The Elo rating system can add to the argument about who had a better 2013: Nadal or Djokovic. In order to implement an Elo system, we need only the two algorithms discussed earlier: the Elo win probability algorithm and the Elo rating update algorithm. The Elo win probability algorithm is used to find the likelihood of a player beating another player. The Elo rating update algorithm is used to adjust the ratings of the competitors following a match.

The Elo win probability algorithm takes the two player ratings as inputs and returns a probability. There is an additional scaling factor inherent in the algorithm and, in some cases—as we saw with the FIFA rating system—we may wish to modify this number as well; however, for this example we will use the Elo rating system as originally devised. In the Elo system, the probability of victory is 1 over 1 plus 10 to the power of difference in the ratings of the two players divided by 400.

```
elo.prb    <- function(A, B){
   rd = (B-A)/400
   1 / (1 + 10^rd)
}
```

LISTING 12.1 Elo win probability in R

Listing 12.1 shows the arithmetic for this calculation. We can verify this works by using the example from earlier in this section where we estimated the win probability of a player with a 1600 Elo rating versus a 1400 Elo rating as approximately 0.75.

The next formula we will need to implement an Elo rating system is a rating update formula. This formula uses the probability formula to determine how many points to award the winner and subtract from the loser. This value is equal to K times 1 minus the likelihood of the victory. So, a likely victory receives a smaller update and an unlikely victory receives a large update.

```
elo.match <- function(winner, loser, k=15){
   w.pct <- elo.prb(winner, loser)
   chng  <- k*(1-w.pct)
   winner <- winner + chng
   loser  <- loser  - chng
   return(c(winner, loser))
}
```

LISTING 12.2 Elo rating update algorithm in R

Listing 12.2 shows this algorithm in R code. You'll note that we use the Elo win probability algorithm we designed earlier as the first step, and then multiple 1 minus that value by K to arrive at the value to modify the players scores by. We then add that amount to the winner's score and subtract that amount from the loser's score. You will also note that we define a default K value of 15.

In order to apply this to the 2013 ATP tour, we will need to first prepare the 2013 ATP tour data. This involves reading in the data we need and converting the players' names to factors. We do this so we can construct a data frame that can use the players' names for row-wise look-ups, so we can look up the players' ratings when finding and updating their Elo ratings (Listing 12.3).

```
ATP <- read.csv("ATP.matches.csv")

ATP.players <- factor(c(ATP$winner,vATP$loser))

ATP$winner <- factor(ATP$winner, levels=levels(ATP.players))
ATP$loser  <- factor(ATP$loser,  levels=levels(ATP.players))

ratings <- data.frame(match.elo = array(1500,dim=length(levels(ATP.
players))),
                      set.elo   = array(1500,dim=length(levels(ATP.
players))),
                      game.elo  = array(1500,dim=length(levels(ATP.
players))),
                      row.names=levels(ATP.players))
```

LISTING 12.3 Creating a table of Elo ratings

You will note that create a single large factor first, containing all of the winning players and all of the losing players, before using the levels from that factor to modify the winner and loser columns of the ATP data frame. We do this so that all the players that played in the season can be accounted for in a single table. Had we done the winner and loser columns separately, we would have no way of reconciling the winning players' Elo ratings and the losing players' Elo ratings. Additionally, in the last bit of code here, we construct a new data frame to hold all of these ratings. These are three empty columns with an initial Elo rating of 1500. This data frame also uses the player names as the row names, in the order that they appear in the composite factor we created earlier. Again, this is to allow for lookup of the player's ratings.

Next, it comes to calculating the ratings. To calculate the ratings, we need to loop over all of the matches played during the season in sequential order—remember: Elo rating adjustments are point-in-time estimates, that reflect how good a player or team is right now—and modify the winning and losing player's Elo ratings. We will use three different approaches, one for each of the Elo ratings we'll implement: match-based Elo ratings, set-based Elo ratings, and game-based Elo ratings (Listing 12.4).

```
for (match.num in 1:nrow(ATP)){
winner <- ATP[match.num,5]
loser  <- ATP[match.num,6]

#Matches
winner.m.rtg <- ratings[winner,1]
loser.m.rtg <- ratings[loser,1]

results <- elo.match(winner.m.rtg, loser.m.rtg, k=20)

ratings$match.elo[as.integer(winner)] <- results[1]
ratings$match.elo[as.integer(loser)] <- results[2]

#Sets
for(i in 1:ATP[match.num, 17]){
  winner.s.rtg <- ratings[winner,2]
  loser.s.rtg <- ratings[loser,2]
  results <- elo.match(winner.s.rtg, loser.s.rtg, k=15)
  ratings$set.elo[as.integer(winner)] <- results[1]
  ratings$set.elo[as.integer(loser)] <- results[2]
}
if(ATP[match.num, 18] >0){
  for(i in 1:ATP[match.num, 18]){
      winner.s.rtg <- ratings[winner,2]
      loser.s.rtg <- ratings[loser,2]
      results <- elo.match(loser.s.rtg, winner.s.rtg, k=15)
      ratings$set.elo[as.integer(loser)] <- results[1]
      ratings$set.elo[as.integer(winner)] <- results[2]
  }
}

#Games
for(i in 1:ATP[match.num, 19]){
  winner.g.rtg <- ratings[winner,3]
  loser.g.rtg <- ratings[loser,3]
  results <- elo.match(winner.g.rtg, loser.g.rtg, k=10)
  ratings$game.elo[as.integer(winner)] <- results[1]
  ratings$game.elo[as.integer(loser)] <- results[2]
}
if(ATP[match.num, 20] > 0){
  for(i in 1:ATP[match.num, 20]){
      winner.g.rtg <- ratings[winner,3]
      loser.g.rtg <- ratings[loser,3]
      results <- elo.match(loser.g.rtg, winner.g.rtg, k=10)
      ratings$game.elo[as.integer(loser)] <- results[1]
      ratings$game.elo[as.integer(winner)] <- results[2]
  }
}
}
```

LISTING 12.4 Calculating match, set, and game Elo ratings in R

Sports Analytics

Of the three, the match-based Elo ratings are the simplest. These ratings update the winner's and loser's ratings each once per match, based on their rating at the onset of the match. To do this, we identify the ratings using the lookup, find the resulting ratings, and assign the new ratings back to the winning and losing player. For the match-based ratings, we've chosen to use a K-value of 20. This allows the ratings to vary a reasonable amount, while not being too swingy.

For the set-based Elo ratings, we use a similar process; however, in this case we loop over the number of sets that the winning and losing player won and adjust their scores once for each set. You will note that we update scores with each iteration—we do this to use their in-match rating for subsequent updates, as opposed to their pre-match rating. Another change is that we use a K-value of 15 for the set-based Elo ratings. Because sets are less predictable than matches, we assign a lower K-value so that players ratings do not vary as much from any given unlucky turn of events.

Lastly, we do the same for the game-based Elo ratings. This process is almost identical to the set-based Elo ratings, except instead of iterating through the sets won by the victor and the defeated, we iterate through the games won. This adds even more variation, so again, we decrease the K-value. Dropping the K-value to 10 ensures that Elo ratings will be mostly stable, despite the near guarantee that even the best player will drop a game to the worst player on the tour.

Running this code, we can find the top players by Elo rating for the 2013 ATP season. To do this, we can use the head command on the ratings data frame. Table 12.1 shows the top 10 players ratings across the three different methods.

TABLE 12.1. Top 10 players by Elo ratings on the ATP tour in 2013

Player	Match Elo	Set Elo	Game Elo
Djokovic N.	2005	1868	1544
Nadal R.	2003	1855	1526
Del Potro J.M.	1828	1763	1565
Murray A.	1824	1726	1510
Federer R.	1790	1736	1523
Ferrer D.	1758	1671	1537
Wawrinka S.	1750	1669	1515
Berdych T.	1742	1715	1570
Gasquet R.	1712	1660	1542
Raonic M.	1712	1677	1552

At the top of the table are, as one would have predicted, Djokovic and Nadal, separated by a razor thin margin. Djokovic edges Nadal in all three ratings. Importantly, it was their year-end showdown at the ATP Final that put Djokovic in the lead, as it gave Djokovic a chance to steal points from Nadal and leapfrog him with the victory. In both the match and set calculations, we see that Djokovic and Nadal are well ahead of their elite peers. Djokovic and Nadal's 2000-point ratings would give them just under a 75% chance of beating the Argentine Del Potro or the Wimbledon champion Murray.

While there are some minor differences in ordering between the match ratings and the set ratings, the game ratings vary quite a bit from both of the others. This suggests that games may not be an effective measure of player skill. Considering the game of tennis, this might not be as surprising as it sounds at first. The serving player in tennis has a meaningful advantage over the receiving player, potentially erasing the large differences that would exist. Modeling players' skill at the game level would likely involve giving them two sets of ratings: a service-game rating and a receiving-game rating. We would expect the service-game rating to be much higher than the receiving-game rating for all players.

Point Systems

While probabilistic systems—like the Elo rating system—have an advantage as predictive tools, another goal that rating system designers often have is simplicity. Points-based systems are one of the simplest ways of rating players. In these systems, players or teams accumulate points based on match outcomes over some time period. These points then expire as time passes and players need to compete to earn more points. Typically, more important events will result in more points.

ATP RATING SYSTEM

The Association of Tennis Professional's system is the prototypical points based system. Tennis players accumulate points over a season of play and are rated and ranked according to who has the most points. Players earn points by placing in tournaments, with the most important and competitive tournaments being worth the most points.

Players may use their results from up to 19 tournament placements to calculate their rating. Players must use the four Grand Slam events—the Australian Open, the French Open, Wimbledon, and the U.S. Open—the eight ATP Masters 1000 events, the ATP Finals, and the six best tournaments of their choosing. In order of value, the Grand Slam tournaments are worth the most points, followed by the ATP Finals, followed by the Masters-level events (1000, 500, 250) and the Challenger events.

The ATP rating system can be interpreted simply. The players who are at the top of the rating list in any given year are the players who did the best in the ATP's most prestigious tournaments. Additionally, the system gives the ATP a non-monetary incentive for players to participate in tournaments.

Another points-based rating system is the World Golf Rating system. The World Golf Rating system averages the points a player accumulates playing in tournaments and ranks players according to those averages. Events have points values—with more competitive events being worth more points—and players earn points from those events by finishing higher up the leaderboard.

Events are given ratings based on the number of top-200 golfers playing in that event. Events with more highly ranked players are given higher event ratings. Additionally, some high-profile events have fixed ratings or minimum ratings. For instance, the Major Championships—the Masters Tournament, the PGA Championship, the U.S. Open, and the Open Championship—are each worth a flat 100 points. PGA Tour and European Tour events have a floor of 24 points, regardless of competition; while the tournaments in the Challenge Tour, the European developmental league, are worth at least only 12 points.

Players receive points based on their placement. The winner of the tournament receives the event's full points, while the remaining players each receive a fraction of that value. The top 60 players in a tournament will receive some ratings credit from the tournament, so long as the number of points they receive is at least 1.2. That is, placing 20th is normally worth about 7% of the tournament's points; however, if the tournament is only worth 16 points, this would be only 1.12 points—not enough to be awarded.

Additionally, players rating contribution from tournaments decays over time. The ratings contribution of a tournament decreases in uniform increments weekly beginning 13 weeks after the tournament, and continues for two years. Players may use at least 40 and at most 52 tournaments to calculate their ranking.

The World Golf Rating system has many of the incentive benefits of the ATP Rating system. It encourages golfers to participate in tournaments to hold on to their rating and earn automatic entry into the high-profile tournaments. The system also allows the Golf Tournaments to prioritize their tournaments.

Other Systems

In addition to the aforementioned systems, based on pairwise statistics and points awards, there are additional systems that can be used. In this section, we will look at two additional approaches: the RPI system that is used in College Basketball and the PageRank system.

COLLEGE BASKETBALL'S RATING PERCENTAGE INDEX

NCAA basketball has been using the Rating Percentage Index to help determine its end-of-year tournament seedings since 1981, for men's programs, and 1984 for women's programs. RPI, as the system is known, is a three-factor model that, like the Elo system, considers how much a team wins and how strong their competition has been. The RPI system's three components are winning percentage, opponent's winning percentage, and opponent's winning percentage.

$$RPI_{Team} = \frac{WPct_{Team} + 2 \times WPct_{Opp} + WPct_{OpOp}}{4}$$

Depending on the year, the first factor in RPI was either a raw winning percentage (until 2005) or a weighted winning percentage (since 2005). The weighted winning percentage takes into consideration where games were played. Home wins and away losses count less: 60% of a neutral site game; while away wins and home losses count more: 140% of a neutral venue game.

The second factor, the opponent's winning percentage, is the highest weighted factor in RPI. This factor—commonly called strength of schedule—is the rate at which a team's opponents beat other Division I teams. The winning percentage of opponents updates throughout the season as those opponents win and lose games. So, if Indiana beat Perdue and Ohio State mid-season when Purdue and Ohio State were undefeated, their strength of schedule would be benefit. If late in the season Purdue and Ohio State start to lose, Indiana's strength of schedule will go down.

Third, RPI takes into consideration the winning percentage of teams that a team's opponents plays. Continuing from the previous example, if Indiana plays Purdue and Purdue plays Notre Dame, Notre Dame's winning percentage will be factored into this third component of RPI. The third component of RPI is intended as a way of measuring the opponent's strength of schedule.

Importantly, the RPI of teams in the same conferences are all going to be strongly correlated with one another because they will all share many common opponents. Consider the 15-member ACC. Each of the teams in the ACC will play the other 14 teams at least once, and several twice. This means that any two ACC teams will have at least 13 common opponents. With schedules around 30 games long, these 13 opponents account for nearly half of a team's strength of schedule.

Drawbacks of RPI include its lack of consideration for head-to-head play and for the sequence of wins and losses. In this way, concerns about RPI mirror many of the concerns about the batch Elo-rating heuristic discussed earlier in this chapter. Considering head-to-head play is important because it prevents situations where a team benefits from losing to a good opponent—as they might under the RPI system. Additionally, considering the sequence of wins and losses is important because one of our desires in seeding an end of season tournament is to identify how strong teams are in that moment so that the best teams have the greatest chance of making the most competitive and engaging finale. If we do not consider order, we may unduly favor teams who had strong early season performances but have little shot of winning the title.

Another system that can be used for ranking teams and competitors is PageRank—a ranking algorithm foundational to the internet itself. Google founders Larry Page and Sergey Brin invented PageRank, a formula for assessing the importance of web pages based on the frequency of which other pages linked to them and the importance of the pages that linked to them (Page et al. 1999). When applied to sport, this process can be used to rank teams based on either general measurements, such as wins or points scored, or sport-specific measurements, such as yards gained (in football) or efficiency rating (basketball) (Swanson, Koban, and Brundage 2017; Zack, Lamb, and Ball 2012).

Calculating PageRank is an iterative process. Each team starts with the same baseline rating and then votes for teams they have competed against based on a rule. In its simplest form, teams would vote once for each team that beat them. Each vote would then be worth the team's rating divided by the number of votes, and a team's ratings would be updated to equal the number of votes they receive.

As an example, consider the following scenario. Three teams play one another in round robin style. The first team beats the second and third, and the second team beats the third. If we stipulate that each team starts with a rating of 100, then the first team would end up with a rating of 150, the second team with a rating of 50, and the third team with a rating of 0. The first team's rating would be 100 points from the second team, because it was the only team to beat them, it gets all of their points, and 50 points from the third, which would distribute its 100 points evenly between the first and second teams. Because the third team did not beat anyone, it gets no points.

$$[100\ 100\ 100\ ] \times [000\ 100\ 110\ ] \times [012\ ]^{-1} = [000\ 10000\ 50500\ ]$$

Alternatively, we may choose to evenly distribute across the teams the points that the first team would have given to those who beat it. If we anticipate iterating through this process many times, as we often will, this ensures that those points will stay in circulation. Additionally, this provides a way of giving points to those teams that—like the third team—would otherwise not receive any points. In that scenario, each team's rating would be boosted by 33 points, resulting in 183 points for the first team, 83 points for the second team, and 33 points for the third team.

The PageRank system has several advantages. The PageRank algorithm takes head-to-head match-ups into effect, in contrast to several other systems we have noted. Further, the weighting scheme that PageRank uses often benefits those who play their best against the best over those who would primarily beat lower-level competition. Additionally, PageRank can take into account sport-specific measurements and otherwise be flexible in assigning values. This often feels advantageous compared to the Elo system, which will typically use crude wins and losses. For instance, a PageRank system applied to tennis may have each player vote for their opponent a number of times equal to the number of sets or even games won, so that a 5-7, 7-5, 5-7, 7-5, 5-7 nail biter is treated differently than a 6-0, 6-0, 6-0 straight set victory. In a multi-competitor sport like golf, PageRank could be modified so that a golfer receives votes from every player they finish ahead of equal to the number of strokes by which they beat that player.

PageRank rating and ranking systems, as shown earlier in this section, can be simple. To illustrate this, we will implement a PageRank rating system and evaluate its effectiveness in identifying the top teams of the 2016 English Premier League season. We will use three variations of the PageRank rating system: one that is simple a "winner network," where losers vote for the winners; one that uses goals, where teams vote for the teams that score goals on them; and one that uses the EPL's point system, where teams vote once for teams they draw with and thrice for teams that defeat them.

In order to test this PageRank system, the first step is to implement the PageRank algorithm. As we explored earlier in this section, the PageRank algorithm is a matter of linear algebra. Implementation consists of performing matrix arithmetic. Additionally, we will implement a way to distribute the points of a team that otherwise would not have received any votes as well as a simple loop around the system to allow it to run several times to achieve more robust results.

For a single iteration of our PageRank algorithm, we will take the sums of the columns from the matrix resulting from multiplying the weights, with the current ratings for each team, and the votes for each team. In R, this can be accomplished with the multiplication operator and the colSums function (Listing 12.5).

```r
pageRank <- function(V,
                     ratings=array(1, dim=nrow(V)),
                     iterations=1,
                     boost=T){

  weights <- rowSums(V)^-1

  if (boost==T) {
    I <- nrow(V)
    for(w in 1:length(weights)){
      if (weights[w] == Inf) {
        V[w,] <- array(1, dim=I)
      }}
    weights <- rowSums(V)^-1
  }

  for (i in 1:iterations){
    new_ratings <-  colSums(c(weights*ratings) * V, na.rm=T)
    ratings <- new_ratings
  }

  return(ratings)
}
```

LISTING 12.5 Page rank function in R

In order to implement the ability to iterate, we will wrap the pageRank ratings update in a for loop. After each loop, we will take the results of the update and feed them back into the next update. We do this so that our ratings approach converges. The number of iterations necessary until convergence changes based on the size and composition of the matrix; however, for most examples in sport between 10 and 20 iterations will suffice.

The most code-intensive part of the PageRank algorithm in R involves distributing the votes of a team that would otherwise have voted for no one, e.g., an undefeated team in a winner network. To do this, we will calculate an initial set of weights as usual, take the inverse of this matrix, and fill the row of the votes matrix with 1s for elements in the weights matrix that equal infinity. In this case, the infinities result from inversion of a matrix with cell-values of 0. We then inverse the sums of the rows of the updated votes matrix to find the final weights.

From here, we can validate the PageRank function we created against the example we worked earlier in this section. To do this, we first construct the votes matrix and the PageRank function we have constructed on it. To mirror the example from earlier, we seed the ratings with 100s and specify 1 iteration. Doing this, we can confirm that the output of our function is consistent with our work from earlier in the chapter. The first team has 183 points, the second team has 83 points, and the third team has 33 points (Listing 12.6).

```
> votes.matrix = matrix(c(0,0,0, 1,0,0, 1,1,0),
+                        ncol=3, nrow=3, byrow=T)

> pageRank(V=votes.matrix,
+          ratings=array(100, dim=3),
+          iterations = 1)
[1] 183.33333  83.33333  33.33333
```

LISTING 12.6 Validating the PageRank example

To work a real example, we will dive into the 2016 English Premier League season. Soccer fans around the world were shocked, in 2016, when the unsuspecting Leicester City won the league. Leicester faced 5000-1 odds at the season's onset, but ended up topping the table cleanly: 10-points separated them and runners-up Arsenal. But was Leicester as good as advertised, or did they just benefit from some lucky breaks? To weigh in, we will perform a PageRank analysis of the 2016 EPL season, using a winner-network, a goals network, and a network inspired by the EPL points system (Listing 12.7).

```
EPL.goals      <- read.csv("EPL.goals.csv", row.names=1)
EPL.wins       <- read.csv("EPL.wins.csv", row.names=1)
EPL.pts     <- read.csv("EPL.pts.csv", row.names=1)
rtg.by.goals <- pageRank(EPL.goals, iterations=10)
rtg.by.wins  <- pageRank(EPL.wins, iterations=10)
rtg.by.pts   <- pageRank(EPL.pts, iterations=10)

EPL.df <- data.frame(Wins=round(65*rtg.by.wins,0),
                     Pts=round(65*rtg.by.pts, 0),
                     Goals=round(65*rtg.by.goals,0))

EPL.df[order(-EPL.df$Pts),]
```

LISTING 12.7 Applying PageRank to the 2016 EPL season.

Applying the PageRank algorithm in these three different ways is primarily a task of organizing the votes matrix. For the winner network, we organize the matrix so that each team votes once for each loss they have and issues a half vote for each draw. For example, in this network, if Arsenal beats Aston Villa twice, then Aston Villa would vote for Arsenal twice. If Crystal Palace beats and draws Watford, then Watford would vote for Crystal Palace one and a half times, and Crystal Palace would vote for Watford once.

In the goals network, votes are issued based on who scores goals against whom. If Arsenal scored 5 goals against Aston Villa across their two matches and Aston Villa scored only 1 goal against Arsenal, then Villa would vote for Arsenal 5 times and Arsenal would vote for Villa only once. This approach captures the magnitude of victories, but it has the drawback of favoring offensive teams—which acquire more votes—over defensive teams—which distribute fewer votes, but also accumulate fewer.

Lastly, we implement an EPL-points network. This approach uses the points system of the soccer table to weight the results. Wins are worth 3 votes and draws are worth 1. With this approach, if Arsenal beats Aston Villa twice, then Aston Villa will vote for Arsenal 6 times. If Crystal Palace beats and draws Watford, then Palace will vote for Watford once and Watford for palace 4 times.

In each of these examples, we use 10 iterations as a heuristic. You can verify with 9 and 11 iterations, respectively, that the algorithm has converged by this point. Additionally, you will note here that we take a different approach to weighting the ratings. Instead of providing a ratings matrix a priori, we multiply the final ratings by 65. The effect of this is that all the numbers fall in the range of 0 to 100—a clean spread for most rating systems; 65 was selected for the purpose of viewing this specific example and will not work in all cases (Table 12.2).

TABLE 12.2. Top and bottom 5 teams in the EPL 2016

Team	Wins	Pts	Goals
Arsenal	92	96	87
Leicester City	95	96	86
West Ham United	87	89	88
Manchester United	85	88	63
Southampton	82	87	79
Crystal Palace	49	48	47
Watford	46	45	45
Sunderland	47	44	58
Norwich City	44	43	49
Aston Villa	24	21	36

Running the code and viewing the results, we find the upstart Leicester City at the top of the table in terms of both wins and points, reflecting their surprising Premier League victory. More interestingly, all three PageRank approaches rate West Ham United quite highly, despite West Ham's good but not great performance in 2016. That year, they finished seventh in the official table; however, our PageRank approaches have them in third place. Undoubtedly, this is driven by West Ham saving its best performances for its top opponents, including a 2-0 win and 3-3 draw versus an Arsenal that the PageRank model thought of highly. At the bottom of the table, our PageRank approach agrees with the official rankings except for Newcastle, which the PageRank approach prefers against the standard table. Newcastle was relegated in 2016; however, they would find themselves back in the Premier League two years later, after winning the English Football League Championship.

Summary

In this chapter, we looked at ways of rating and ranking teams and players. At the outset of this chapter, we identified several reasons one might want to rate or rank competitors in sport. Among those are seeding competitors, balancing schedules and seeding tournaments, and odds making. Additionally, when discussing the point-based systems, we saw how the systems could be used to prioritize the competitions more important the league.

Point-based approaches to managing sport leagues make sense for the owners of those leagues who have an interest in funneling those players to their top events. Players can be rewarded for playing in high publicity events with ratings points. Rating systems like RPI, Elo, and PageRank make more sense for more objective systems. International bodies like FIFA for international soccer and FIDE for international chess use Elo-based systems to more credibly determine the world's best.

Much of the innovation in rating systems happens out of the limelight between bettors and esports. Bettors have a financial interest in understanding not only who the best team is, but how much better they are than their rivals. Esports have long had massive, public leaderboards, as well as systems for rating players on those leaderboards. Many of those systems are based on the Elo rating system, with unique variation. The most famous is Microsoft's TrueSkill system for XboxLive matchmaking.

Importantly, as we have seen throughout this chapter, the best and most appropriate means of rating and ranking teams is sport and application specific. Rating a tennis player should have different mechanics than rating a golfer because the sports of tennis and golf can be measured in different ways. Sports that are similar can use similar approaches—one of the reasons the Elo rating system is so popular is that it requires so little information—however, it makes sense to attempt to match the statistical model to the mechanics of play.

Key Terms

Rating

Ranking

Elo rating

K (Elo rating)

UTR

Glick-2 system

Points-based rating

RPI

PageRank

Critical Thinking Exercises

1. What are the benefits of an Elo rating system approach? Why is the rating system able to be applied to sports as different as chess, tennis, soccer, and esports?

2. What are the benefits of a points-based rating system? Why do major sport leagues such as the ATP, PGA, and NASCAR use points-based rating systems? Why might these leagues prefer such rating systems over Elo-based rating systems?

3. Imagine that you are the commissioner of the emerging Professional Lawn Mower Racing League PLMRL. As commissioner, you must decide a way to rank your riders. Are you more likely to pick an Elo-rating based system or a points-based system? Why would you select the rating system you chose?

4. You are an aspiring table tennis player with an Elo rating of 1855. At a national tournament you finish in second place, defeating players with ratings of 1470, 1610, 1590, 1790, and 1833 before losing to the tournament's ultimate winner, who was rated 2081. Following this tournament, what is your rating assuming the following K values?

   a. K = 10

   b. K = 15

   c. K = 25

   d. K = 40

5. You are the coach of a water polo team heading into a round-robin tournament. You estimate that your team is about an 1650 Elo rating, the best team in the pool is rated 1750, and the two other teams are rated 1550 and 1450, respectively.

   a. What are your odds of beating each team?

   b. What are your odds of beating all three other teams?

   c. What are your odds of beating the best-rated team and at least one other team?

References

Elo, Arpad E. 1978. *The Rating of Chessplayers, Past and Present*. New York, NY: Arco Pub.

Glickman, Mark E. 1995. The Glicko system. *Harvard University*. http://www.glicko.net/glicko/glicko.pdf

Glickman, Mark E. 2003. The Glicko-2 system for rating players in head-to-head competition. *Boston University*. http://www.glicko.net/ratings/glicko2desc.pdf

Glickman, Mark E., and Jonathan Hennessy. 2015. A stochastic rank ordered logit model for rating multi-competitor games and sports. *Journal of Quantitative Analysis in Sports* 11(3), 131–144.

Page, Lawrence, Sergey Brin, Rajeev Motwani, and Terry Winograd. 1999. *The PageRank citation ranking: Bringing order to the web*. Stanford InfoLab. http://ilpubs.stanford.edu:8090/422/

Swanson, Nathan, Donald Koban, and Patrick Brundage. 2017. Predicting the NHL playoffs with PageRank. *Journal of Quantitative Analysis in Sports* 13(4), 131–139.

Zack, Laurie, Ron Lamb, and Sarah Ball. 2012. An application of Google's PageRank to NFL rankings. *Involve* 5(4), 463–471.

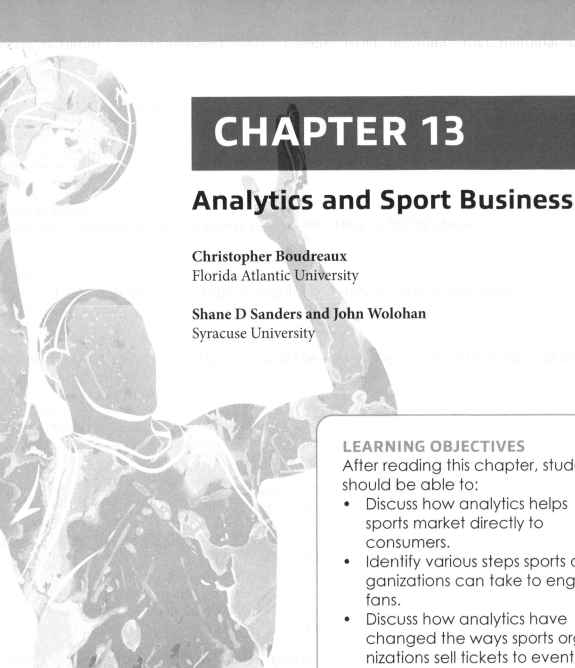

CHAPTER 13

Analytics and Sport Business

Christopher Boudreaux
Florida Atlantic University

Shane D Sanders and John Wolohan
Syracuse University

LEARNING OBJECTIVES

After reading this chapter, students should be able to:

- Discuss how analytics helps sports market directly to consumers.
- Identify various steps sports organizations can take to engage fans.
- Discuss how analytics have changed the ways sports organizations sell tickets to events.
- Discuss the differences between variable ticket pricing and dynamic ticket pricing and how teams use them to maximize revenue.
- Discuss how analytics are used in talent identification.

263

Introduction

In their classic book on marketing "*Positioning: The Battle for Your Mind*," the authors Al Ries and Jack Trout argue that to succeed in selling anything it is essential that you properly position the product in the mind of the consumer. In particular, Ries and Trout argued that you need to position your product, service, or company in people's mind so that it is the first thing people think of when they are looking to buy. According to Ries and Trout, there are two ways to properly position your product in the consumer's mind: (1) be first into the market; (2) advertising and product exposure.

The easiest way to position your product in people's mind is to be first into the market. The first company to occupy that space in the mind of the consumer is going to be awfully hard to dislodge (Ries and Trout 1981). For example, if I mentioned professional hockey in New York, most people would think of the Rangers, not the Islanders. The New York Rangers began play in 1926 and one of the "Original Six" teams that competed in the NHL. The New York Islanders, on the other hand, only started to play in 1972. Since the Rangers had an almost 50-year head start to win the minds and loyalty of the New York hockey fans, even in those years when the Islanders were winning the Stanley Cup, they were never able to dislodge the Rangers as New York's hockey team.

Since there can only be one first in any market, Ries and Trout argue that the other way to properly position your product involves advertising and product exposure. For example, Blue Ribbon Sports, which would change its' name to Nike in 1978, was not the first athletic footwear company. In 1964 when Phil Knight and Bill Bowerman started Blue Ribbon Sports, Adidas and Puma were already well established having provided shoes and athletic outfits to Olympic and professional athletes and teams for decades (Smit 2008). To break into the athletic footwear market, and the minds of the consumers, Nike created a radically new "high-tech" waffle sole running shoes targeted to just to runners. To help promote the shoes to the top American distance runner, Nike signed a sponsorship deal with Steve Prefontaine, the biggest name in US running at the time (Strasser and Becklund 1993). As people watched Prefontaine, and other top American runners such as Mary Decker Slaney, Alberto Salazar, and Carl Lewis competed and won in the new Nike shoes, its brand recognition and position in the mind of consumers improved.

Nike followed that same formula as a late entry into the basketball shoe market. Since the beginning of the NBA, and probably since the beginning of basketball, the basketball shoe market was dominated by Converse and its' All-Star brand. In 1984, however, Nike was on its way to replacing Converse and changing the basketball shoe market forever when Michael Jordan took the court for the Chicago Bulls wearing his red and black "Air Jordans." By sponsoring high profile track and field athletes and taking a shot on an unproven rookie basketball player, Nike was able to reposition itself in the minds of consumers from a niche product into the world's largest supplier and manufacturer of athletic shoes and apparel.

Ries and Trout, however, argue that such positioning is becoming more difficult as society is becoming oversaturated with advertising and media communications and people started tuning out and not hearing a lot of messages. While it is interesting to note that Ries and Trout made their observations pre-internet, and were only talking about advertising on television, radio, and newspapers, their point is equally true today. The only difference is that the internet has exponentially increased the number of advertisements we are bombarded with daily so that most of these messages are just noise. Since Ries & Trout first published their book, technology has advanced in ways they probably could never have envisioned. As a result, "in a world where machine learning now enables the collection and organization of data on a scale that would have been unthinkable just a decade ago – the ability to discern signal from noise is a priceless skill set" (O'Kelley 2016).

As we will see in the rest of the chapter, analytics can be found everywhere in the sports world, not just on the field. Teams and businesses are using analytics to help predict future marketing strategies, help target marketing, to drives sales by to attracting and retaining customers more effectively, improve customer service, and increase sponsorship. In ticketing strategies, analytics are being used to track season and group ticket holders, as well as set variable and dynamic prices. Analytics are revolutionizing the product and retail sales of sporting goods by helping companies with product development and direct to consumer sales that optimize their brand and reduce inventory, and a hundred other ways. In other words, analytics are allowing companies to cut through the all the noise and get their product message into the minds of consumers.

Analytics and Sport Business

> In business, as in baseball, the question isn't whether or not you'll jump into analytics; the question is when. Do you want to ride the analytics horse to profitability... or follow it with a shovel? — Rob Neyer, ESPN. (Davenport and Harris, 2007)

With so much information "data" available to organizations and businesses, it only makes good business sense to use data and statistical models to help guide and inform business decisions (Davenport and Harris 2007). Sports businesses, both on and off the field, have also embraced the use of analytics. As we have already seen, teams, leagues, and companies collect tons of data on players. This information is then used in everything from drafting, signing free agents, contract negotiations, training, and medical care.

Besides players, however, sports fans also generate a lot of data. It is not surprising, therefore, to learn that those same teams, leagues, and companies are also collecting data on fans and potential customers. For example, the Kraft Analytics Group (KAGR), a technology and services company focused on data management, advanced analytics, and strategic consulting in the sports and entertainment industry, is owned by the same group that owns the New England Patriots and the New

England Revolution. KAGR works with clients across the major U.S sports leagues, college athletics, and other key industry players to help them become data-driven and use those analytics to grow the bottom line.

As noted in Chapter 9 "Optimization Methods in Sport Analytics," in today's sports world optimization methods are widely applicable to sports marketing, supply chain, and inventory management. In addition to optimization methods, having a robust ***customer relationship management (CRM)*** system is essential due to the cost of acquiring and retaining new and existing customers, especially in service-based industries. CRM is a process used by companies to help manage their interactions with past, current, and potential future ticket buyers and customers. The CRM process is used across the entire customer lifecycle, spanning marketing, e-commerce, tickets sales, and customer service interactions.

When seeking to engage with avid or casual fans or customers, it is important that organizations begin the CRM process before the fan purchases a ticket or buy a product and continue during, and after the event or sale. By connecting with customers and fans through email and marketing automation technologies, in-venue social and mobile experiences, and personalized automated target marketing campaigns to drive repeat sales and elevate the customer experience, organizations not only make the experience better for the fan but also turn customer interactions into sales. Sutton and Sutton (2015) highlighted how using social media to improve the fan experience is not only respectful of the customer but is also great for return on investment (ROI) and is of the highest priority for many teams and brands seeking to connect with customers.

Marketing

As Ries and Trout argued decades ago, marketing should be about getting your product properly positioned in the minds of consumers. However, in the sports business, it is also important to remember that different fans attend games or purchase products for different reasons, so gaining an understanding of each fans expectations is essential to providing them with the service they may be expecting (Marr 2016). Analytics helps organizations do that. By using data to better understand your current customers, businesses can use that information to keep current customers satisfied and to help find new customers (Miller 2016). For example, as we will see in the ticketing section below, sports organizations use analytics when they develop and maintain CRM systems on potentially new and existing customers, as well as the ticket inventory. Whether the organization is collecting customer data when you purchase tickets, or through in-stadium surveys, teams are constantly collecting and analyzing the demographics and other key variables of their fans.

Using descriptive statistics, organizations typically divide customers into easily defined populations or market segments. Some of the most common groups that marketers segment customers into are demographics, geographic, usage, psychographics, and behavioral. In a typical demographic profile, teams collect data on such variables such as gender, age, education, occupation, and level of income. By collecting this type of demographic information, marketers can get a good snapshot of who their actual customers are. Are they male, female, married, single, old, young, rich, poor, high school or college educated? Only by getting a good picture of the consumers can organizations begin to develop targeted marketing and advertising strategies.

No matter the sport or business, there is a general rule on the market radius in which most of your customers, typically about 80%, will come from within a certain radius. While the radius for professional sports teams is going to be larger than the local health club, the principle applies to everyone. Therefore, collecting geographic or location data, the state, city, or street where people live, allows organizations to better understand the marketing radius and use analytics to help develop E-mail, digital and social media marketing, as well as tracking and measuring a traditional advertising campaigns success.

User data includes product, how much consumers use the product, and the type of benefit they seek from the product. For example, people who use the product (purchase tickets to the game) can be divided in heavy, medium, light, and non-users. Using analytics, organizations track ticket sales and organize CRM systems. These systems can identify heavy users (season ticket holders) and track season ticket renewals and other ticketing data. With this information, teams can understand the needs and wants of heavy users and provide what is needed to help the team keep them buying season tickets. Another example is Nike and athletic shoes. Nike need to understand what various user populations want from athletic shoes. Certain segments of users are going to want high-performance shoes. Others, however, are going to want the shoes to be comfortable or fashionable. When companies can properly segment the consumers and understand what consumers like, they can make informed decisions about future strategy and tactics.

Psychographic data and behavioral data examine attitudes and lifestyle and are more difficult to collect as interval, ordinal, or nominal data than demographics, geographic, or usage data. As a result, the data is usually collected by focus groups or detailed interviews. Because of the complicated nature in collecting the data, and if using a survey, the number of variables and the complexity of the statistical model needed to get a good picture of your customers, most sports marketers do not perform a lot of psychographic or behavioral research.

Understanding who the customers are allows organizations and businesses to make informed decisions on which type of advertising, print, radio, television, email, or electronic method would be most effect in reaching that audience. Once the type of advertising is selected, companies use analytics to weight its effectiveness. For example, using time series regressions companies can track the effectiveness of the advertising and whether it is associated with increased ticket or product sales (Davenport and Harris 2007). Analytics are used to help direct and database marketers build predictive models on who will purchase tickets or products in response to various types of marketing campaigns. By tracking the types of promotions and sales that work, and those that do not, analytics also allows companies to refine their sales and marketing strategies. Teams and businesses can also use a traditional **RFM model**, teams and businesses are able to analyze the recency (date of the last purchase), frequency (number of purchases), and the monetary value (sales revenue) of previous purchases to analyze the effectiveness of the marketing. If teams and organizations want to try and segment the information further, they can either utilize a variety of explanatory variables related to recency, frequency, monetary value, and/or include various customer demographic data (Miller 2016).

It is also important to keep in mind that market analytics do not have to be complicated to be good. The more variables measured, the more complex your statistical model, the greater the chance for confusing or misleading results. In several cases, all you need to do is simply examine demographics, geographic, or usage frequencies to get an accurate picture of fan data.

Sports Apparel and Retail Sales

Nike still uses famous athletes to help position their products and to keep consumers aware of the brand. In soccer, Nike has deals with Cristiano Ronaldo and Neymar; in basketball, it has deals with LeBron James, Kevin Durant, and Carmelo Anthony; in tennis, Naomi Osaka and Rafael Nadal; and in golf, Tiger Woods. While it is doubtful that Nike will abandon this strategy anytime soon, its latest retail and marketing strategy is largely driven by Big Data. Through its initiative "**Nike Direct**," Nike is cutting out intermediaries, like Amazon and some retail stores, and selling directly to consumers. In addition to cutting out the middle-man, Nike's direct-to-consumer initiative also allows Nike to collect lots of customer data. Nike is using this data to improve inventory management with hyper-localized demand predictions, which in turn enhances the consumer experience by ensuring they can find and purchase the products they want (Barseghian 2019).

How is Nike Direct different from traditional retail models? The traditional retail model for companies, Nike, ADIDAS, and Under Armour is that they sell their shoes and apparel to wholesalers, who then sell them to retailers or their own retail stores, who then sell them to you the consumer. This retail-first model has been very successful for these companies, with 87% of Nike's total revenue coming from wholesale customers (Boyd 2019).

Traditional Supply Chain

While not abandoning the traditional retail model, in 2017 Nike announced that it was introducing "a new company alignment that allows Nike to better serve the consumer personally, at scale. Leveraging the power of digital, Nike hopes to drive growth – by accelerating innovation and product creation, moving even closer to the consumer through Key Cities, and deepening one-to-one connection" (Nike News 2017). Nike believes that by interacting directly with consumers, both on- and offline, they can capture better consumer data and hopefully deliver a better customer experience (Barseghian 2019). Nike, of course is not the only sports apparel company doing this, ADIDAS, Under Armour, and others are also seeking to interact directly with consumers too.

Nike Direct Supply Chain

So, what is Nike doing to increase direct interaction and manage customer life cycles? To connect with consumers, Nike announced that it was creating the new Nike Direct organization. By downloading the Nike app, customers have access to the Nike Plus rewards program, which offers exclusives and early access to new products. The app also allows customers to "Ask an Expert" for information on products and advice for whatever sport you play. Training for a marathon and not sure what shoes are best for you, all you need to do is ask the Nike expert, and they will recommend one for you based on your experience and training schedule. Nike also has separate apps for that offer personalized workouts "Nike Training Club," running "Nike Run Club," and where to find and buy the latest sneakers "SNKRS" (Nike News 2017).

By using analytics, Nike wants to optimize their customers lifecycle value. The customers lifecycle value is determined by the cash inflow predicted (amount of future sales) compared to cost of retaining the customer. Predictive analytics on all the data it collects on the apps, and other connected devices like Fitbits, allows Nike to help it better understand the lifecycle of individual customer purchasing habits and predict purchasing decisions (Barseghian 2019). A successful predictive analytics program, however, requires a lot of data. To help Nike collect the data needed, Nike Direct is using the Nike Plus membership to attract and retain customers (Boyd 2019). Therefore, Nike is betting that its ability to model the future, based on the past behavior, will directly influence present sales (Boyd 2019). For example, Nike, by analyzing past purchases and activities, is seeking to predict and identify which customers to target, with which products, and more importantly when to target them. If a customer usually buys a new pair of basketball shoes every fall and it has been 12 months since the last purchase, Nike will know to reach out to that consumer and prompt them with the newest basketball shoes (Barseghian 2019). Nike could also use this consumer data for anticipatory shipping, whereby they ship the items before the customer even orders them because they can predict purchase behavior. If the customer does not need or want the item, they can just ship them back at no cost. Even with the returns, it is estimated that this predictive model would be more profitable for Nike than waiting for the orders to come in (Boyd 2019).

Besides online marketing and sales, Nike can analyze the data collected to enhance the in-store experience. By focusing on very specific geographic locations, the data helps Nike both decide where to build stores and what to put on the shelves. For example, with predictive analytics, Nike can rotate large proportions of the inventory in stores to suit changing tastes (Boyd 2019). This ability to cater to different consumer tastes will be important in the "12 Key Cities" Nike identified in its' "Direct to Consumer" announcement: New York, London, Shanghai, Beijing, Los Angeles, Tokyo, Paris, Berlin, Mexico City, Barcelona, Seoul, and Milan. "Nike projects that these cities and the countries they are in will account for over 80 percent of its growth through 2020" (Nike News 2019).

As illustrated above, companies like Nike and other retailers are using customer data to predict sales, help with inventory management, and even product development. However, these companies also know that predictive analytics of customer behavior are only as good as the data they are based on. As a result, collecting customer data via product and brand apps is vital in making informed decision and future strategies.

Nike Boxes stacked in window of a shoe store.

© mimohe/Shutterstock.com

Ticketing

From the very beginning of sports, gate revenue (tickets sold) has been a major revenue generator for professional and college sports. Whether from single game tickets or season tickets, a team's financial success was measured by how many tickets a team could sell. In setting ticket prices, teams usually considered the three Cs of pricing: costs, consumers, and competition (Miller 2016). The problem for teams, however, was that historically they established the price, or cost of a ticket, before a single game was played. Therefore, there was no way to maximize a team's revenue. For example, if the team outperformed expectations and was making a playoff run, there would be a higher demand for tickets and the extra revenue was lost in the secondary ticket market. Historically, the secondary ticket market was run by ticket spectulators, individuals who resold tickets based on consumer demands for each game. While in most states this activity was illegal, it did not stop these individuals from reselling tickets outside of most stadiums and profiting off the team's success. If, however, the team underperformed, there would be less demand for tickets and teams would be stuck with a lot of unsold tickets because they lacked the ability to lower prices. Setting the appropriate price, therefore, was critical for the long-term management and financial health of the team (Yang, Pursglove, and Manwell 2017).

Today, like in so many other areas in life, data analytics is removing a lot of the guesswork from ticket pricing and enabling teams to make pricing decisions with confidence. With new technological developments and the use of analytics, teams are no longer simply limited to increasing or reducing fixed ticket prices before the season begins. Using data analytics, professional and college teams have moved away from the old fixed-price model of ticking to models based on variable and dynamic pricing that both allow fans more options and flexibility, while increasing revenue for the team. In addition, teams and leagues have moved into the secondary ticket market to recapture revenue lost when demand increases the value on an event.

Variable Pricing

Unlike the traditional fixed price approach, in which teams establish a uniform price per ticket prior to the season, variable ticket pricing is a pricing strategy based on the anticipated demand (Yang, Pursglove, and Manwell 2017). By using a variable ticket pricing strategy, teams can increase game day revenue by setting higher prices for premium games and reducing the prices for games that have little demand to help increase game day attendance. This ticket pricing strategy raises or lowers the ticket price for games based on several variables. For example, if Syracuse University were to use this ticket strategy in basketball, weekend games against Duke, Georgetown, North Carolina, Notre Dame would be priced at the high end, while Monday or Tuesday night non-ACC games would be priced at the low end. Some of the variables teams consider include: the team's own performance, the opponent, day of the week (weekday or weekend), holiday, game time, and scheduled game day promotion. However, since research has shown that game attendance is influenced by a multiple of variables, the list of variables is almost limitless (Paul and Weinbach 2013).

Dynamic Pricing

While teams may use variable pricing to adjust ticket prices based on a set of predetermined set of variables, the prices are still fixed before the season. Therefore, to recoup some of the revenue still being lost with variable pricing, teams are moving to dynamic pricing. **Dynamic pricing**, which has long been common practice in the airline and hotel industries, starts with the variable pricing model. However, instead of just raising or lowering the ticket price for games based on the anticipated demand, dynamic pricing is different in that ticket prices fluctuate based on current demand. While relatively new in the sports industry, the San Francisco Giants were the first team to try it in 2009, dynamic pricing uses advanced computer pricing software linked to the team's ticketing system, to adjust ticket prices higher or lower based on changing factors that affect market demand. Therefore, instead of just setting and fixing prices in the offseason, ticket prices can actually change daily or even hourly based on game demand. Price adjustments are made in real time based on changing variable such as day of week, month, weather forecast, opponent, ticket demand, as well as the prices of tickets on the secondary ticket market. Dynamic pricing therefore allows teams to maximize gate revenues and attendance by raising prices for special games and lowering prices for games with low demand to encourage walkup sales.

Dynamic ticket pricing, therefore, "is more efficient than the traditional fixed priced approach" (Yang, Pursglove, and Manwell 2017). Two other benefits of dynamic pricing are that it allows teams to capture some of the revenue they traditionally lost in the secondary ticket market, while at the same time encouraging fans to purchase their tickets for games early before the price increases.

Secondary Ticket Market

There has always been a secondary ticket market. Because teams historically priced tickets before a single game was played and priced them equally with no price differences to account for the attractiveness (or unattractiveness) of the opponent or date of the game, individuals or syndicates predicting high demand will purchase large numbers of tickets for various events at the fixed price. Although historically illegal in most states, ticket brokers or "scalper" could be found outside most stadiums or arenas selling tickets on the day of the event, where they would haggle with people willing to pay inflated prices for last-minute tickets to the event. With the birth of the internet and the development of online ticket resell platforms like StubHub and Ticketmaster, this old model has been rendered a marginal player in the high-stakes, data-focused secondary ticket market of today (Yang, Pursglove, and Manwell 2017).

With many states having repealed or amended their laws prohibiting the reselling of tickets, secondary ticket markets have developed to allow ticket holders the opportunity to resell their unused or unwanted tickets to buyers for a small commission. In addition, people have started visiting the secondary ticket market prior to the primary market, thinking that the secondary market will yield a better deal on seats (Kirby 2017). Seeing the value of such secondary ticket markets and wishing to recapture some of the lost ticket revenue, which was estimated at a total global value of over $15 billion in 2020, professional and college teams have begun to implement their own secondary ticket market sales strategies (Kirby 2017).

Leagues and teams use the secondary ticket market for several reasons. First, it helps them capture the revenue they would lose when ticket brokers sell their tickets on the open market. Second, research shows that implementing a secondary ticket market strategy can play a significant role in season ticket renewal rates. By reducing the number of unused tickets at each event, season ticket holders are 25% to 30% more likely to renew their season tickets to ensure they can get seats (Yang, Pursglove, and Manwell 2017). If there are empty seats, the need to buy season tickets is lessened. In addition, research shows that people are more likely to purchase season tickets when they know there is a secondary ticket market they can sell their unused tickets in easily. Third, teams use the data they collect on ticket demands to help establish prices in dynamic ticket strategy. Finally, data from the secondary market can demonstrate the true fan interest in the sports product. When a ticket brokers does not invest in a league or team event, it should send warning signals to franchise executives since it is the secondary market where the true indicators of consumer demand exist (Kirby 2017).

Contactless Tickets

Etickets

Another way ticketing has evolved is with the use of contactless mobile ticketing. While teams and leagues have embraced contactless mobile ticketing during the 2020 COVID pandemic, mobile ticketing, however, has been around since the smartphones. As teams move away from physical tickets, digital ticketing allows buyers the ability to manage tickets entirely online. With mobile ticketing, fans will not only be able to purchase tickets electronically but also transfer, resell, or upgrade tickets (Riola, 2017). Mobile ticketing allows teams to better control ticket inventory and prevent counterfeiting.

Employment Analytics

When people think of talent analytics in sports, the first thing that comes to mind is player evaluations. As illustrated from the earlier chapters and the book *Moneyball*, such a conclusion would be highly justified. In professional sports, players are both the most important and expensive resource of teams, with average annual salaries in the millions of dollars, and high-profile athletes running into the tens of millions of dollars annually. With so much money tied up in salaries, it is important that teams use the latest analytics to try to find, hire, and retain the right player. For example, to protect its investments, professional sports teams use biomedical and other performance analytics to help teams gauge players' health and fitness and make draft and contract decisions (see Case Study before).

In addition to employees on the field, ice, or court, sports organizations have also started to move from gut-based judgements to sophisticated analytics to evaluate employees in the front office to make sure that they use data-driven decision-making to put the right employees in the right jobs

(Moyer 2017). While companies have always used some form of analytics to evaluate existing employees, rewarding employees based on sales, new revenue generated, sponsorship revenue, total revenue generated, or some other variable, the use of data analytics in evaluating employee performance is much more sophisticated today. Today, human resource analytics, also known as employment analytics, talent analytics, people analytics, and workforce analytics, play a role in every aspect of the HR function, including recruiting, training and development, succession planning, retention, engagement, compensation, and benefits. In fact, organizations and their human resource departments are using predictive analytics in employment decisions to evaluate candidate's resumes, measure employee performance and engagement, study workforce collaboration patterns, analyze employee churn and turnover, and model employee lifetime value (Mishra, Lama, and Pal 2016).

ANALYTICS AND HIRING

Many companies favor job candidates with stellar academic records from Ivy League or prestigious schools. In fact, with data analytics, organizations are to screen resumes for schools, GPA, major and any other variable it feels appropriate for the job. For example, some companies have realized through quantitative analysis that the ability to take initiative is a far better predictor of high performance on the job than a degree from an Ivy League or prestigious schools (Davenport, Harris, and Shapiro 2010).

In addition to an individual's resume, companies are also data mining a candidate's social media history. Those photos from that wild college party or spring break that you or a friend posted online and tagged, or the social media posts you posted during high school, they are all available to prospective employers. While job candidates might hope that something they did in high school or college will not hurt your future, it is important to understand that most people have a voluminous "digital trail" of data from social networks now available for analysis and that employers are looking at your online history (Davenport, Harris, and Shapiro 2010).

ANALYTICS AND JOB PERFORMANCE

As mentioned above, companies have long used target analytics to reward employees and evaluate performance. In the business of sports, where sales and customer service are two of the main tasks of every job, employees are already focused on the analytics. For example, employees in sponsorships or the ticket office know that they have a set number of tickets or sponsorships they need to sell weekly, monthly, and yearly. If those numbers are not met, the employee not only will fail to earn any bonus money but he or she also risks losing his or her job. While it may not be as easy as counting tickets sold or new revenue raised, companies are using analytics to measure customer satisfaction in the customer service and hospitality areas too. Finally, companies are also measuring the effectiveness of management by surveying employees. According to analysis, operating units with highly satisfied employees have higher revenues, lower costs, greater employee retention, and superior customer loyalty (Davenport, Harris, and Shapiro 2010).

ANALYTICS AND RETENTION

Traditional employment analytics focuses on the present, that is, items such as turnover and cost per hire. While turnover can be a major problem and expense for companies, employee attrition is much less of a problem when you can predict it. To help companies predict future turnover in specific functions or business units, companies are using turnover analytics to look at such factors such as commute time, time since last role change, performance over time or even if someone has signed up for the retirement program. By identifying such employees early, companies can intervene to see if the individuals were hired for the wrong job or simply poorly managed. By spotting potential problems, such as high-risk underperforming employees, companies can take various actions to prevent turnover, reducing empty desk time and phones and panic hiring, which can lead to lower cost, higher quality hiring. In addition to identifying candidates with a higher risk of leaving prematurely or performing below standard, employment analytics can also identify the superstars that companies may wish to move into management programs (Mishra, Lama, and Pal 2016).

Summary

As the above chapter illustrates, sports organizations are collecting and using more data than ever before. Sports businesses have embraced the use of analytics, not just on players but on fans and other customers. Companies hope that by using analytics they will be able to identify future customers, target market directly to them, keep them engaged, as well as predict what types of products or services they may be interested in purchasing based on previous interactions. As illustrated above, teams, leagues, and sporting goods companies are using all the data they collect from fans and customers to help formulate future marketing strategies, ticketing strategies, direct to consumer sales, consumer relations, product development, and the value of sponsorships.

Case Study: NFL Team Payroll Allocation Efficiency

This case study considers the efficiency with which National Football League (NFL) teams allocate their respective player payrolls. The NFL represents the highest revenue sports league globally and interest in the game has increased substantially (Mathewson 2019). From 2001 to 2019, total league revenue increased from $4.28 billion to $15.26 billion, amounting to a 147% increase in inflation adjusted dollars.[1] Team roster and related payroll decisions represent a crucial aspect of team on-field and financial performance in football (Mondello and Maxcy 2009), as well as other professional sports leagues in general.

In the NFL, the offensive "skill positions" (quarterback, running back, fullback, wide receiver, and tight end) are important in terms of average salary and perceived on-field value and in terms of output salience (Draisey 2016). The purpose of this case study is to consider whether teams allocate payroll dollars efficiently across skill positions. To do this, the case study utilizes a path-breaking data set on NFL player Wins Above Replacement (WAR) constructed by Pro Football Focus (PFF). The data is proprietary and was obtained through an academic use agreement with PFF.

If teams are payroll efficient, the case study hypothesizes that the salary premium for a unit of WAR is equal across the observed skill positions (e.g., among players not on a rookie scale contract). If such an equality does not hold, there should be an exploitable inefficiency in the NFL player free agency market. For example, a team could engage in win maximization arbitrage by signing replacement players for skill positions at which units of WAR carry a high salary premium and signing elite players for skill positions at which units of WAR carry a low salary premium. If salaries are indeed inefficiently allocated, this creates opportunities for teams to reallocate their spending toward (highly skilled) quarterbacks (and, to a lesser extent, toward highly skilled wide receivers and tight ends) and away from highly skilled running backs and fullbacks.

Despite the recent growth of football analytics, an ESPN survey of NFL team front offices found that salary-cap and contract analysis is not a substantial element of NFL analytics staff work (Walder

1. https://www.statista.com/statistics/193457/total-league-revenue-of-the-nfl-since-2005/

2020). In fact, according to the ESPN survey no NFL team lists payroll analysis as a primary task of their analytics staff. We might not expect payroll efficiency to yet be obtain in the NFL. To support this claim, Massey and Thaler (2013) demonstrate that teams use decision-making methods that are not guaranteed to be optimal or rational but are only sufficient in reaching the team's short-term goal or exhibit decision-making bias in their valuation of NFL Draft picks. In fact, according to the ESPN survey cited above, teams have not substantially transitioned from traditional decision-making methods toward a more analytic approach when making payroll decisions.

The purpose of this case study, therefore, is to explore whether NFL salaries accurately reflect the positional marginal product of labor, as measured by WAR.

DATA SUMMARY AND VISUALIZATION. The dataset consists of 2,186 NFL skill position player-seasons (n = 2,186). The data represents all fully observed skill position player-seasons between 2006 and 2017. Twelve seasons of data were observed for the 32 NFL teams such that the data set includes an average of 5.69 fully observed player-seasons per team-season. Variables of interest include the player's average annual salary in a season, as well as his position, WAR, and NFL prior seasons of experience. This data was obtained from Pro Football Focus (WAR) and from Pro Football Reference (other variables), and the respective primitive data sets were merged within Stata v16.0. Figure 13.1 below summarizes average player WAR by position.

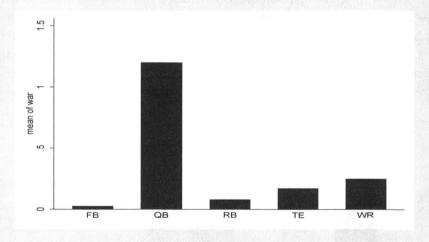

FIGURE 13.1. Quarterbacks have a lot of on-field value

As illustrated by the data in Figure 13.1, quarterbacks generate a great deal of WAR when compared with the other offensive skill positions. Specifically, the average NFL quarterback generated a 1.20 win above the replacement quarterback during the 11-year period. By comparison, the average players at the four other positions combined generate 0.51 wins above replacement (FB = 0.03, RB = 0.08, TE = 0.14, WR = 0.26).

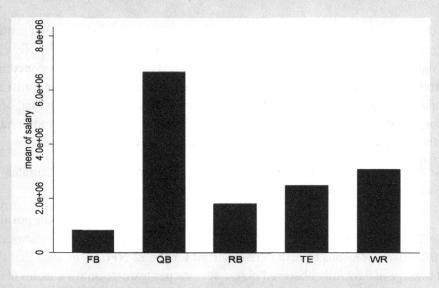

FIGURE 13.2. Quarterbacks earn a higher salary

Figure 13.2 displays average player salary by offensive skill position. Once again quarterbacks lead all the other offensive skill positions and earn a higher average annual salary. However, despite generating more than twice the average WAR of all other offensive skill positions combined, the average annual quarterback salary is only about three-quarters that of the other offensive skill positions combined. As such, it is not clear from Figures 13.1 and 13.2 whether the observed distribution of salaries reflects payroll efficiency. To help examine whether the observed distribution of salaries reflects payroll efficiency, Figure 13.3 shows the average salary per unit of WAR produced for each offensive skill position.

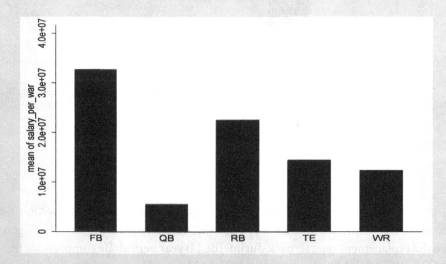

FIGURE 13.3. Average salary per unit of WAR produced by offensive skill position

Sports Analytics

Based on the data in Figure 13.3, quarterbacks are paid substantially less than other offensive skill positions per unit of WAR produced. Figure 13.3 also demonstrates general variation by position in salary per unit of WAR produced. In addition, by comparing Figures 13.1 to 13.3, some interesting ordinal patterns can be observed in the data. For example, a comparison of Figures 13.1 and 13.2 demonstrates that the order of average salaries by position follows the order of average WAR by position. One might think of this as a check of weak form efficiency: Do teams at least pay average salaries to offensive skill positions in the correct rank order (i.e., according to average WAR by position)? Teams pass this weak form payroll efficiency test. Strong form payroll efficiency—rewarding units of WAR equally across offensive skill position—is a much more demanding condition, however. By comparing Figure 13.3 to Figure 13.1, the case study shows that teams unequivocally pay more average annual salary per unit of WAR as the average WAR at a position decreases. In other words, these visualizations suggest that teams may overpay relatively unimportant offensive skill positions and underpay relatively important offensive skill positions. Regression analysis with controls for player experience and season of play will determine whether this is the case.

REGRESSION MODEL. To explore whether NFL salaries do accurately reflect the positional marginal product of labor, as measured by WAR, the case study gathered data from **xx**. This dataset contains **xx** for a total of 1,462 observations. We gathered data on each player's position (QB, RB, FB, TE, WR), WAR, and years of experience.

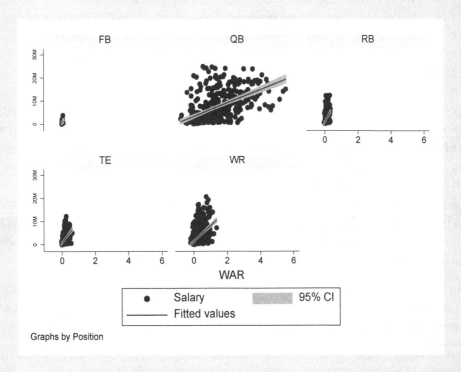

FIGURE 13.4. Scatterplots of Salary and WAR, By Position

The first step in the exploration of the data was to draw a scatterplot between player salary and WAR by each position. Figure 13.4 suggests a positive relationship between WAR and salary for all positions. In addition, Figure 13.4 also supports the claim that teams are overpaying for relatively unimportant offensive skill positions while underpaying relatively important offensive skill positions. Specifically, the slope of the quarterback trend line is least steep among the scatterplots, indicating that the salary response of additional units of WAR is weakest for quarterback. Moreover, the steepest trend lines are observed for the fullback and running back positions.

To control for NFL years of experience, the study performed a position fixed-effect, OLS regression analysis. More specifically, it used the following econometric model:

$$Salary_{it} = \beta_0 + \beta_1 WAR_{it} + \beta_2 Exp_{it} + \beta_3 Exp_{it}^2 + \gamma_k Position_{it} + \delta_k (WAR_{it} * Position_{it}) + \varepsilon_{it} \quad (1)$$

where subscripts i and t denote player i and season t. The dependent variable, salary, is a continuous variable reporting the dollar amount of a player's salary. WAR is a continuous variable ranging from -0.78 to 5.54[2]; Exp and Exp^2 denote the years of experience and its quadratic, respectively. Position is a vector of k = 5 position dummies (QB, FB, RB, TE, WR). In addition to interacting WAR and Position, the study also examines the parameters β_1, γ_k, and δ_k. Further, ε_{it} is our stochastic error term.

RESULTS. The results of the regression analysis are in Table 13.1 of the appending section. In Columns 1 and 2 of Table 13.1 are the regression results of player salary on WAR, experience, experience[2], a set of position dummies, and an intercept. The only difference in the two columns is that column 1 examines a sample of players who are beyond their first contract and column 2 examines the sample of players who are on their first contract. The data is separated in this way because first contract players are subject to the rookie scale, as determined in the NFL Collective Bargaining Agreement and, therefore, unlike veteran players, do not earn their market salary. However, first contract players are of interest in the regression because their salary scale is determined by their draft position. Therefore, first contract players help determine whether certain positions are overvalued or undervalued in terms of NFL Player Draft position. In both cases, there is a similar relationship in the data: WAR and experience are positively associated with player salary, and average annual salary varies significantly by player position. Columns 1 and 2 also provide estimates of the expected salary premium to an additional unit of WAR among the offensive skill positions. This estimate is between $2.3 million and $2.6 million. In other words, the premium for a 4 WAR quarterback over a replacement quarterback is an estimated $9.2 million to $10.4 million according to these point estimates.

Column 3 of Table 13.1 provides the payroll efficiency test that is central to the case study. If NFL teams allocate payroll efficiently among the skill positions, then there will be no significant differences between the salary premium of an additional unit of WAR across positions. However, the

---

2. Quarterback Drew Brees generated 5.54 wins above replacement during the 2011 season. Adding this total to the replacement number of wins for a quarterback, we have that Brees generated about 6 wins during 2011 or almost half of the Saints' 13 regular season wins. In general, the quarterback position generates extreme outcomes, with the 185 highest WAR values in the data and the 11 lowest WAR values.

position dummy WAR interaction terms of the column 3 model shows significant differences relative to the baseline position (Wide Receiver). In particular, the results show that quarterbacks are paid a significantly lower premium for additional units of WAR than are Wide Receivers. However, Running Backs are paid a significantly higher premium for additional units of WAR than are Wide Receivers.

The results from this model suggest WAR has a positive association with player salary, but it is a weaker relationship for quarterbacks than other positions, especially running backs. These differences are economically substantial, as well. Whereas Wide Receivers are paid an estimated $6.77 million premium per additional unit of WAR according to the model, Quarterbacks are paid an estimated $2.41 million premium per additional unit of WAR. On the other hand, Running Backs are paid an estimated $19.1 million per additional unit of WAR. This last estimate appears incredibly large. It should be noted, however, that running backs do not generate substantial WAR in the NFL. As was stated earlier, running backs in the sample generate an average of 0.08 units of WAR in a season, and the maximum WAR value for a running back player-season in the sample was 0.34.

Questions

1. You were recently hired by an NFL team as a salary-cap and contract analyst to develop a draft and free agency strategy. If the team needs to either replace or retain a group of skill position players, what general suggestions do you have for the teams?
2. Are all NFL teams efficiently allocating salary for skill position players?
3. Based on the results of the study, should NFL teams pay for an elite QB and a skilled running back, or a skilled QB and an elite running back?
4. Is it more efficient to draft an elite QB, wide receiver, tight end, or running back?
5. Why are player salaries under their first contract more efficient than players under their second contact?
6. Based on what you know, if you wanted to engage in win maximization arbitrage by skill positions at which units of WAR carry a high salary premium, and which units of WAR carry a low salary premium?

TABLE 13.1. Regression results

	Dependent Variable = Salary		
	(1)	(2)	(3)
WAR	2631543***	2299640***	6770946***
	(194604)	(129321)	(98579)
Experience	659982**	258717***	662911**
	(262896)	(44555)	(258415)
Experience^2	-21621	109492***	-20845
	(13125)	(11116)	(12883)
Position dummies			
FB	-3473418*	-424361	-1722998
	(2103336)	(485300)	(4131865)
QB	31152	425020**	1789747***
	(449567)	(179405)	(590143)
RB	-1048986**	-219398*	-1453172*
	(485170)	(132637)	(784397)
TE	-1424295***	-360650**	-1027193
	(448349)	(157264)	(825153)
Interactions			
WAR * FB			-34900000
			(396000000)
WAR * QB			-4359813***
			(1005958)
WAR * RB			13100000***
			(4929370)
WAR * TE			336634
			(2776091)
Constant	1613116	339412***	98959
	(1215359)	(102289)	(1262129)
Number of observations	724	1,462	724
F-test	59.37***	147.27***	42.56***
Adjusted R^2	0.361	0.412	0.387
> 5 years of experience	X		
< 5 years of experience		X	
> 4 years of experience			X

Note: Model estimated using OLS regression. Standard errors in parentheses. * $p < 0.10$; ** $p < 0.05$; *** $p < 0.01$ (two-tailed test).

```
# Change scientific format
options(scipen = 999)

#Load packages
library(MASS)          #Needed for robust standard error regressions
library(Hmisc)         #Needed for descriptive statistics
library(stargazer)     #Stargzer package for regression exports to tables



#load the libraries
library(lme4)
library(nlme)
library(arm)
library(sjstats)
library(tidyverse)
library(plyr)
library(dplyr)

# Load data from csv
mydata <- read.csv("D:Dropbox/Sports Book Chapter/PFF_WAR_Head_Im-
pact_2006_2017.csv")

#-------------------------------------------------------------------#
#Create position dummies using fastDummies
library(fastDummies)
mydata <- dummy_cols(mydata, select_columns = "Position")

#rename dummies using the plyr package
mydata <- rename(mydata, c("Position_FB"="FB",
                           "Position_QB"="QB",
                           "Position_RB"="RB",
                           "Position_TE"="TE",
                           "Position_WR"="WR"))

#summarize statistics by position
#--------------------------------

#WAR by position
#Proportions
table1 <-table(mydata$Position)
prop.table(table1)

select(mydata, Player_ID, Position, FB, QB, RB, TE, WR, WAR)    #View
selected variables
```

```
#Count by position
mydata %>%
  group_by(Position) %>%
  summarize(n())

#Mean of WAR by position
warplot <- (mydata %>%
  group_by(Position) %>%
  summarize(mean_size = mean(WAR, na.rm = TRUE)))


#Mean of Salary by position - #Save it as salaryplot for the barplot
salaryplot <- (mydata %>%
  group_by(Position) %>%
  summarize(mean_size = mean(Salary, na.rm = TRUE)))



#Bar graphs
#-----------------------------------------------------
#Bar graph of WAR by Position
bp1 <- barplot(salaryplot$mean_size, main="Mean of Salary by Position",
             ylab="Salary",
             names.arg=c("FB", "QB", "RB", "TE", "WR"))

#Bar graph of Salary by Position
bp2 <- barplot(warplot$mean_size, main="Mean of WAR by Position",
        ylab="Wins Against Replacement (WAR)",
        names.arg=c("FB", "QB", "RB", "TE", "WR"))


#Create new variables
#-----------------------------------
mydata %>%
  group_by(Position) %>%
  mutate(position.mean.values = mean(Salary))
```

Key Terms

Positioning

Variable ticket pricing

Dynamic ticket pricing

contactless mobile ticketing

RFM model

Predictive Analytics

Demographics

Secondary ticket market

Fan Engagement

Direct Marketing

customer relationship management (CRM)

Critical Thinking Exercises

1. Develop a list of variables that you think might impact game attendance?
2. What are some of the benefits companies like NIKE hope to achieve when they compete with analytics?
3. In developing a ticketing strategy, what are some of the most common variables teams should consider?
4. In talent analytics, compile a list of some of the key variables an NFL team might find important. What about a sales associate?
5. In developing your marketing strategy for the upcoming season, suppose you have the following fan data: 80% of season ticket buyers live within one-hour drive of the stadium; 75% of season ticket buyers are male; 70% of new season ticket buyers renew; 90% of season ticket buyers who are entering their fourth season or greater renew. Using the above data, think about all the marketing decisions that can be made more effectively and efficiently.

References

Barseghian, Alex. 2019. *How Nike is using analytics to personalize their customer experience.* Forbes (October 7). https://www.forbes.com/sites/forbestechcouncil/2019/10/07/how-nike-is-using-analytics-to-personalize-their-customer-experience/#ad9f2171611c

Boyd, Clark. 2019. *How Nike uses predictive analytics: A data with destiny.* Medium (September 9). https://medium.com/swlh/how-nike-uses-predictive-analytics-821907a90187

Breedlove, John. 2017. Developing and measuring the effectiveness of data-driven direct marketing initiatives. In *Sport Business Analytics*, edited by C. Keith Harrison and Scott Bukstein. New York: Auerbach Publications.

Thomas Davenport, T. 2014. What businesses can learn from sports analytics. *MIT Sloan Management Review* (June 3), 10–13. https://sloanreview.mit.edu/article/what-businesses-can-learn-from-sports-analytics/?gclid=EAIaIQobChMI9KTln4vW7QIVBb_ICh1ZxQbrEAAYASAAEgLKt_D_BwE

Davenport, Thomas H., and Jeanne G. Harris. 2007. *Competing on Analytics: The New Science of Winning.* Boston: Harvard Business School Press.

Davenport, Thomas, Jeanne Harris, and Jeremy Shapiro. 2010. Competing on talent analytics. *Harvard Business Review* (October). https://hbr.org/2010/10/competing-on-talent-analytics

Draisey, Trevor. 2016. *The determinants of NFL player salaries.* https://scholarworks.uni.edu/cgi/viewcontent.cgi?article=1218&context=hpt

Kirby, Troy. 2017. Ticket markets in sport: Is the secondary market becoming the primary market. In *Sport Business Analytics*, edited by C. Keith Harrison and Scott Bukstei. New York: Auerbach Publications.

Marr, Bernard. 2016. *Big Data in Practice: How 45 Successful Companies Used Big Data Analytics to Deliver Extraordinary Results.* Chichester, West Sussex: John Wiley & Sons.

Massey, Cade, and Richard Thaler. 2013. The loser's curse: Decision making and market efficiency in the National Football League draft. *Management Science* 59(7), 1479–1495.

Mathewson, T. J. 2019. *TV is biggest driver in global sport league revenue.* Global Sports Matters (March 7). https://globalsportmatters.com/business/2019/03/07/tv-is-biggest-driver-in-global-sport-league-revenue/

Miller, Thomas W. 2016. *Sport Analytics and Data Science: Winning the Game with Methods and Models.* Old Tappan, NJ: Pearson Education.

Mishra, Sujeet N., Dev Raghvendra Lama, Yogesh Pal. 2016. Human Resource Predictive Analytics (HRPA) for HR management in organizations. *International Journal of Scientific & Technology Research* 5 (5), 33–35.

Mondello, Michael, and Joel Maxcy. 2009. The impact of salary dispersion and performance bonuses in NFL organizations. *Management Decision* 47 (1), 110–123.

Moyer, Brandon. 2017. Talent analytics: Utilizing analytics to evaluate employee performance. In *Sport Business Analytics*, edited by C. Keith Harrison and Scott Bukstein. New York: Auerbach Publications.

Nike News. 2017. *Nike, Inc. Announces New Consumer Directs Offense: A Faster Pipeline to Serve Consumers Personally, at Scale* (June 15). https://news.nike.com/news/nike-consumer-direct-offense

Paul, Rodney J., and Andrew P. Weinbach. 2013. Firework saturation and attendance in minor league baseball. *International Journal of Sport Finance* 8, 123–138.

Paul, Rodney J., and Andrew P. Weinbach. 2017. An exploration of dynamic pricing in the national hockey league. In *Breaking the Ice: The Economics of Hockey*, edited by Bernd Frick. Chem, Switzerland: Springer International Publishing.

Ries, A., and Jack Trout. 1981. *Positioning: The Battle for Your Mind.* New York: McGraw-Hill.

Riola, Jay. 2017. Analytics and ticketing innovations at the Orlando magic. In *Sport Business Analytics*, edited by C. Keith Harrison and Scott Bukstein. New York: Auerbach Publications.

Smit, Barbara. 2008. *Sneaker Wars.* New York: Harper Collins.

Strasser, J. B., and Laurie Becklund. 1993. *Swoosh: The Unauthorized Story of Nike and the Men Who Played There.* New York: Harper Business.

Sutton, Bill, and Dan Sutton. 2015. Where to find answers about management, brand strategy. *Sport Business Journal*, 23.

Veeck, Bill, and Edward Linn. 1962. *Veeck - As in Wreck.* Toronto: G.P. Putnam's Sons.

Walder, Seth. 2020. *2020 NFL analytics survey: Which teams are most, least analytically inclined?* ESPN.com (September 24). https://www.espn.com/nfl/story/_/id/29939438/2020-nfl-analytics-survey-which-teams-most-least-analytically-inclined

Yang, C-W, Lindsay Krol Pursglove, and Allison Manwell. 2017. The sport product and pricing strategies. In *Marketing for Sport Business Success* (2nd ed.), edited by Brian Turner and Kimberly Miloch. Dubuque, IA: Kendall Hunt.

CHAPTER 14

Analytics and Esports*

John Wolohan

> ### LEARNING OBJECTIVES
> After reading this chapter, students should be able to:
> - Distinguish the differences between esports and egaming.
> - Explain some of the methods used by digital game developers to collect player and game data to adjust and improve esports.
> - Display knowledge of the current state of the esports industry and of the industry's growth.
> - Explain why esports will never be an alternative to live sports, but a complimentary product in its own space.
> - Explain how sport marketing organizations are attempting to convert esports fans to their core product.

*Special thanks to Chad DeLuca, Director, Twitch Properties at Twitch and Chris Henderson, Associate Manager, Marketing Partnerships at 2K League National Basketball Association (NBA) for allowing me to interview them and for educating me about the business of esports.

Introduction

When looking for the beginning of esports, most people point to 1972 and the release of the video game *Pong* by Atari. Having personally spent many hours playing the game at a friend's house, I can say that Pong was a very simple **Player vs. Player (PvP)** game based on a table tennis game in which players controlled a paddle and moved it up or down the screen to hit a moving dot (ball). Moving from the arcade to the home, in 1975 Atari began to sell the game with the Atari Home Video Computer System (VCS), which included a console, two joysticks, a pair of paddles, and a game cartridge. For the first time, individuals no longer had to go to an arcade to play arcade games but could simply hook them up to their televisions and compete at home against their friends. In the early 1980s, Atari would also develop or license such popular games as *Space Invaders, Asteroids, Donkey Kong, Pac-Man,* and *Missile Command* to help grow the home video gaming industry (Chikhani 2015).

While Atari and *Pong* may have been the first successful home VCS, it was not the first game system sold for commercial home use. Although not as successful at Atari, earlier in 1972, Magnavox released the Magnavox Odyssey VCS that could be programmed to play a variety of games, including ping pong, checkers, and four sports games (Chikhani 2015).

However, if we go back another decade, we can really see where video games got their start: college computer science and engineering labs across the country. College students with access to bigger and more powerful computers began to create games in their labs to play with their friends. One such game was *Spacewar* which was invented at MIT by Steve Russell in 1962. Spacewar, which was a two person PvP game, allowed players to control individual spaceships that could thrust, turn, and fire torpedoes at each other (Brand 1972). As described by Rolling Stone in 1972, the game had such a following in the computer science labs at universities that most nights you could find students "locked in life-or-death space combat computer-projected onto cathode ray tube display screens, for hours at a time, ruining their eyes, numbing their fingers in frenzied mashing of control buttons, joyously slaying their friend and wasting their employer's valuable computer time" (Brand 1972). In fact, the game was so popular in the computer science community that despite the lack of the official term "esports," the first esports tournament involved Spacewar when the Stanford University Artificial Intelligence Laboratory hosted the "first Intergalactic Spacewar Olympics" in 1972. Contestants, mainly computer science students, battled on the lab's only PDP-10 computer with the winner receiving a year-long subscription to Rolling Stone magazine and all participants receiving free beer (Brand 1972).

While arcade and home videos games increased in popularity as technology and video graphics improved, it was not until the late 1970s that two major changes in the industry set the stage for today's esports competitions. The first major change was the ability of video games to save individual high score from game to game. Now, players were not only playing against the game, but also competing against the high scores of other players (Taylor 2012). Being ranked among the top 10 high scores on the game became a badge of honor and bragging rights for arcade game players, with some spending hours and lots of quarters seeking the chance to put their three initials on the leaderboard. The second change was the introduction of esports tournaments. In 1980, the game maker Arai hosted a "Space Invaders" national championship with regional tournament winners from Chicago, Dallas, Los Angeles, New York, and San Jose. The tournament attracted more than 10,000 people and received a large amount of media attention.

In the early 1990s "as the arcade scene went bust … the sofa became the primary sport where gamers played against their friends and family, and the multiplayer experience began to move into the game world" (Taylor, 2012, 5). In the 1990s, the next big step in the gaming evolution came when gamers began connecting their consoles and personal computers through local area networks (LAN), and later the Internet, to multiplayer gaming. LANs allowed players to interconnect their computers within a limited area such as a residence, school, laboratory, university campus, or office building (Hood 2018).

By connecting their computer networks, multiple players could compete against each other and interact with each other from different computers, which improved the social aspect of gaming. With gamers connecting via their computers, the world moved one step closer to today's esports with the release of the first-person shooter game *Doom* in 1993 (Chikhani 2015). Finally, in 1997, and official esports league was born. This league was referred to as Cyberathlete Professional League and was considered the pioneer of what esports has become today (Hood 2018).

Due to the normalization of egaming and the internet, along with advances mobile technology and smartphone, the last step (for now anyway) in the evolution of esports came in the 2000s. With games now available on smartphones, game developers began creating games for the mainstream pop culture in a way never before seen. For example, the mobile game *Angry Birds* made developers Rovio $200 million in 2012 and broke two billion downloads in 2014 (Chikhani 2015).

With changes in technology happening all the time, it is clear that the next evolutionary change in the industry is only a year or so away. However, until that happens, it is interesting to note how the billion dollar a year modern-day esports industry has taken on several similarities to traditional sports leagues. For example, Riot Games, which is owned by the Chinese Internet Company Tencent, began selling franchises for $10 million for its game *League of Legends* (LoL) in 2017. At the same time, Activision Blizzard began selling franchises for $20 million for its *Overwatch* league. In addition, professional sports leagues have started running their own esports leagues. The best example of this is the *NBA2K* League, which is 5 versus 5 game play using the players custom avatars, not NBA players, and played over a 14 Weeks of regular season. At the end of the regular season there is a 10 team Playoff, with $420,000 Prize money for the Champions.

What Are Esports?

First, a quick refresher on how is it spelled? This text and various organizations like Twitch use the spelling: Esports or esports; not eSports or e-sports. While other academics and organizations may use a different spelling, to be consistent, this text will use the spelling: Esports or esports. With the spelling out of the way, the next question

Gamers at their computers at an online esports event.

is: what are esports? And is there a difference between esports and egaming? When you see the word *egaming*, it is usually used to refer to the entire electronic gaming industry from video consoles to PC and mobile games, online streaming services, as well as the esports industry. Therefore, when you sit down with friends to play *NBA2K21* or *Madden NFL21* you are egaming. Esports (or electronic sports) describes the professional world of competitive, organized video gaming. Professional esports consists of individual competitors and teams in organized leagues competing against each other. The most watched esports genres are multiplayer online battle arena, first-person shooter, real-time strategy, and player vs player games.

MULTIPLAYER ONLINE BATTLE ARENA (MOBA)

Multiplayer online battle arena (MOBA) are strategic games that involve multiple players working as a team competing against other teams. Game play usually takes place on an interactive map that is, apart from the players, often populated with computer-controlled entities. These entities can be enemies, allies or unaffiliated with either team. and serve a variety of roles. Teams are often built so that players' talents compliment other team members in terms of attacking, defending, and healing. As players experience, their avatar levels up to upgrade weapons/armor (example: *League of Legends* and *Heroes of the Storm*).

FIRST-PERSON SHOOTER (FPS)

First-person shooter (FPS) games allow you to play or experience the game through the eyes of your avatar. As the name would indicate, the game involves the player shooting his or her weapon at various targets or enemies in the game. FPS games are different from third-person shooter games, in that with third-person shooter, the player can see the character they are controlling (usually from behind, or above), while with FPS games their weapon is usually floating around in front of you along with a map, your health and ammo count. As a result, you can only really see what is in front of your avatar (examples: *Call of Duty*, *Counter-Strike: Global Offensive*, and *Battlefield*).

REAL-TIME STRATEGY (RTS)

Real-time Strategy (RTS) games allow multiple players to simultaneously play the game in real time. With all the players beginning on the same map, RTS games require individual players to strategize on the best way to grow their army and position defenses and other structures to help defend their position on the map. In addition, players must decide when to expend resources to construct buildings, gather materials, research improvements, train soldiers, or create additional units for gathering resources, while at the same time attacking their opponents and destroying their structures and armies.

The term "real-time" is specific in that once the game starts and players must react to events in the game as the game progresses (examples: *StarCraft*, *Age of Empires* and *Warcraft*).

PLAYER VS. PLAYER (PvP)

Player vs. Player (PvP) can be broadly defined as any game that involves two or more players competing against each other. While these games are called PvP, it should be noted that individual players can also compete against the computer. As we will explore later in this chapter when we discuss rankings, PVP games can present several competitive issues due the differences in player ability and skill. By ranking players, game developers seek to prevent experienced players from competing against new and inexperienced players. Traditional PvP games include fighting and sports game (examples: *Mortal Kombat*, *Madden*, and *NBA2K*).

Esports Competitions

Esports competitions can attract viewing crowds that rival most traditional professional sports events and are watched and followed by millions of fans all over the world, either by attending live events or tuning in on TV or online. In 2020, over 380 million people attended live esports events for *Fortnight*, *Dota 2*, and *League of Legion*. The 2020 *League of Legends* **World Championship achieved a peak viewership of 3.8 million,** averaging more than 1.1 million viewers, and saw over 139 million hours of viewership (Dixon 2020). Streaming services like Twitch, which was launched in 2011, and YouTube have greatly contributed to the growth of the esports industry by broadcasting live tournaments all over the world. In addition to broadcasting the world's biggest tournaments, Twitch also produces its own competition series and gives esports athletes a platform that allows fans to watch their favorite gamers play in real time (Willingham 2018).

Below are the top 10 games on Twitch by total hours watched. The ranking can be filtered on both esports hours and total overall hours. Esports hours consists of content from professionally organized esports competitions and does not include individual (pro-player) streams. This content combined with consumer content makes up the total hours watched.

Rank	Game Title	Publisher	Total Hours	Esports Hours
1	Dota 2	Valve Corporation	42.8 million	14.5 million
2	Counter-Strike: Global Offensive	Valve Corporation	60.7 million	12.7 million
3	Rocket league	Psyonix	23.3 million	5.5 million
4	Valorant	Riot Games	42.3 million	3.2 million
5	League of Legends	Riot Games	96.3 million	2.8 million
6	FIFA 21	Electronic Arts	43.1 million	2.1 million
7	Hearthstone	Blizzard Entertainment	25.7 million	1.0 million
8	StarCraft II	Blizzard Entertainment	4.1 million	0.8 million
9	Age of Empire II	Ensemble Studios	2.7 million	0.6 million
10	PLAYERUNKNOWN'S Battlegrounds	PUBG Corporation	11.2 million	0.6 million

Newzoo December 2020
https://newzoo.com/insights/rankings/top-games-twitch/

According to the Newzoo, a market analytics company, in its' 2020 Global Esport Market Report, the esports industry was worth an estimated $1.1 billion in 2020, a year-on-year growth of +15.7%. Of that amount, $822.4 million in revenue will come from media rights and sponsorship. In addition, according to Newzoo, the total global esports audience was estimated to expand to 495.0 million people in 2020, a year-on-year growth of +11.7%, with the majority from North America, China, and South Korea (Newzoo 2020). China, with a total audience three times as big as the United States, is currently is the biggest esports market. The gaming industry worldwide took in $180 billion for 2020, a 20% increase in revenue, and that the NFL, NBA, MLB and NHL combined (Monahan 2021).

The top 10 esports markets ranked by revenue estimates[1] for 2020 are:

---

1. The revenues are based on consumer spending in each country and exclude hardware sales, tax, business-to-business services, and online gambling and betting revenues.

Rank	Country	Revenues
1	China	$40,85 million
2	United States	$36,92 million
3	Japan	$18,68 million
4	South Korea	$6,56 million
5	Germany	$5,96 million
6	United Kingdom	$5,51 million
7	France	$3,98 million
8	Canada	$3,05 million
9	Italy	$2,66 million
10	Spain	$2,65 million

Newzoo's 2020 Global Games Market Report.
https://newzoo.com/insights/rankings/top-10-countries-by-game-revenues/

Colleges and universities have even gotten in on the action and started to sponsor teams and offer scholarships. While the National Collegiate Athletic Association (NCAA) in April 2019 declined to move esports under its governance umbrella, citing the facts that esports are predominantly played by males (which creates possible Title IX complications) and the violent nature of some of the games (Zavian 2020), another problem cited with esports and the NCAA is the organization's amateur model. As mentioned above, esports competitors can earn money via sponsorships and streaming, both of which would conflict with the NCAA's stance on amateurism. As the NCAA moves in 2021 to loosen its stance prohibiting its athletes from capitalizing on their names, images, and likeness (NIL), it will be interesting to see if the NCAA reevaluates its position on esports.

In the meantime, with the NCAA unwilling to sanction esports, the void was filled by many smaller organizations, like the National Association of Collegiate Esports (NACE), American Collegiate Esports League (ACEL), and the Electronic Gaming Federation (EGF). Under those banners, esports programs are popping up all over the country, with NACE alone having over 170 member schools that have provided more than $16 million in esports scholarships. Understanding the value of sponsorships to esports competitors, NACE allows students to license their NIL rights to sponsors and develop their own broadcast channel and licenses (Zavian 2020).

Analytics and Esports

Like any sport or business, the world of gaming is extremely competitive. The top players in esports compete for larger and larger cash prizes and sponsorships, while game developers and publishers constantly seek to develop the next cutting-edge game. Developing games and bringing them to market, however, is not cheap. "Large scale, blockbuster "AAA" games typically take at least two years of full-time work by teams of hundreds of people to create and bring to market" (Marr, 2016, 274). For example, in 2020, game developer CD Projekt Red released the *Cyberpunk 2077*. The sci-fi roleplaying game, which featured Keanu Reeves and an avant-garde soundtrack cost $317 million to develop. Despite not living up to the pre-marketing hype, the game performed poorly on older consoles and gamers complained about the graphics, the game still sold 13 million copies (Monahan 2021). While the cost may be significant, the risk–reward payoff is also significant. For example, the top-grossing mobile game worldwide in November 2020 was Tencent's *Honor of Kings* with over $230 million in user spending (Chapple 2020).

MOST POPULAR CORE PC GAMES

Below are the Top 20 Most Popular Core PC Games worldwide, ranked in order of the number of unique players who played them during December 2020.

Rank	Game Title	Publisher
1	League of Legends	Riot Games
2	World of Warcraft	Blizzard Entertainment
3	Minecraft	Mojang
4	Tom Clancy's Rainbow Six: Siege	Ubisoft
5	Apex Legends	Electronic Arts
6	Among Us	InnerSloth
7	Valorant	Riot Games
8	Grand Theft Auto V	Rockstar Games
9	World of Warcraft Classic	Blizzard Entertainment
10	Roblox	Roblox Corporation

Newzoo December 2020
https://newzoo.com/insights/rankings/top-20-core-pc-games/

All this competition has forced gamers and developers to look for any edge they can find. As a result, much like it has in traditional sports, data analytics has become an important part of esports. This is especially true since, due to the nature of the games being played on computers and game consoles, every decision or strategy a player makes during the game can be recorded and analyzed (Marr 2016). "Gone are the days when playing a video game was a solitary experience where the gamer was disconnected from the rest of the world and interacted only with the machine in front of them" (Marr, 2016, 275). While individuals can still play by themselves and compete against the game, the majority of today's egamers are playing online. This function not only allows individuals to compete against other players down the street or around the world but also allows game developers and hosts to track exactly what players are doing and how they are interacting with the game. Every keystroke, bullet fired, upgrade, or special equipment or weapon purchased through the publisher's digital store, to chatting with their friends using social features, is analyzed, and studied to improve the game experience and increase profits (Marr 2016).

Besides game developers, just as in traditional sports, analytics are being used by esports teams to help develop strategies for the team to improve performance, develop game strategies, and defend against an opponent tendency. However, instead of traditional analytics such as VORP, Corsi, or RUG, with the development of esports comes new analytics.

Esports analytics has been defined as: "the process of using esports related data, primarily behavioral telemetry but also other sources, to find meaningful patterns and trends in said data, and the communication of these patterns using visualization techniques to assist with decision-making processes" (Schubert, Drachen and Mahlmann, 2016, 1). As discussed in previous chapters, this definition is similar to the analytics used by traditional sports analytics.

ENCOUNTER METRICS

Encounter Metrics are often used in first-person shooter and Multi-Player Online Battle-Arena games (MOBAs) games and are compact and descriptive metrics used to understand initial settings and possible outcomes of each encounter. Since some games can last hours, and it is possible that two relevant actions take place on two separated parts of the map in parallel, data analysts need to develop techniques for breaking down matches into analyzable sections of decisive game play before player and team performance can be evaluated in detail. The ability of being able to segment matches is highlighted by the game developer Valve's decision to introduce "fight recaps" for someone watching a live *DOTA* match or a replay (Schubert, Drachen, and Mahlmann 2016).

One of the segments, esports analytics, breaks games down into components referred to as encounters. An encounter is established when players from opposing teams are in range to affect each other (Schubert, Drachen, and Mahlmann 2016). The encounter information collects all sorts of information on game play, tracking every kill, every death, equipment choices, tactical moves, bullet fired, and other statistics unit values so that game developers and players all benefit from a finely polished game. Players and game companies can process and analyze the information to finely tune and adjust characteristics of weapons and equipment as well as adjust due to player skill levels. For example, because of machine learning, in some games a particular weapon will be adjusted or "nerfed," meaning that the damage the weapon does was drastically reduced, based on the players skill.

One of the best examples of the usage of these metrics is when Bungie, the video game developer of *Halo*, faced an issue within the development of the third installment of their flagship game franchise. On the map titled "Valhalla" in the *Halo 3* beta test, if a player spawned at the red team's "Lake Base" they were almost immediately killed. With players unable to fight back or even get a shot off, most players logged off almost as immediately if they found themselves on the Red Team when the map came up in rotation during matches (DataScienceGraduatePrograms.com 2018).

Faced with the problem of an unbalanced game, Bungie and Microsoft, the maker of the Xbox game console for which *Halo* was a major title, monitored and analyzed every player action, every bullet fired, every character death. Based on the collected information from thousands of players in millions of matches, on player death locations, the problem with players spawning at the Lake Base became obvious. With this information, Bungie was able to make a few minor adjustments to the geometry of the map and tweaks to equipment characteristics to make the game more balanced. *Halo 3* went on to become that year's best-selling video game in the United States.

Another benefit of the encounter metrics is that they reflect changes in player skill and adaptation to the game itself. For example, Valve Software, a game developer, and digital distribution company, and at one time the most profitable company per employee in the United States, as well developers of such games as *Half-Life, Counter-Strike, Left for Dead*, and *DOTA* uses encounter metrics to reduce meta gaming. Meta gaming is the use of a player's real-life knowledge concerning the state of the game to determine their actions, which is considered unsporting or cheating in the competitive gaming and is one reason why Valve's games are some of the most popular in professional gaming competitions is because their games tests a player's skill, not knowledge of the game (DataScience-GraduatePrograms.com 2018).

ENHANCING GAME DESIGN

In addition to tracking encounter metrics, esports game developers have another important reason for monitoring the behavior of players and collecting player data, enhancing game design. Every decision or strategy which is played out during the game gives game developers insight into what players enjoy, how they adapt to challenges, and what is just too difficult to be fun (Marr 2016). The information collected helps boost game design, so that game developers can quickly adjust and improve the games.

In fact, game programmers have been using a form of machine learning to assess how hard users were finding the game and adjust difficulty levels in some situations to avoid frustrating players as far back as 1983 (Data Science Graduate Programs.com 2018). This type of data is important because building interactive and complex scenarios for games not only requires creativity, but also a proper understanding of what works well for users. Here is where data analytics can lend a helping hand. For instance, analytics helps companies detect problematic gameplay moments for users by tracking play time, users' interactions, quitting points, and gaming style. Indeed, data can show that some levels might be too dull, some might be too challenging, and some might simply contain bugs that do not let users move forward. In addition, game programmers can use advanced machine learning to generate encounters for players at a pace and in places that it judges most effective to ratchet up tension and improve multiplayer group dynamics (Data Science Graduate Programs.com 2018). Machine learning also allows the games to optimize the narrative and engagement levels to individual players. As a result, the games can detect which aspects of certain games are most appealing to the player. For example, if a player who shows an affinity for a certain aspect, he or she might be presented with more scenarios that offer opportunities to use those skills or might have their loot drops subtly boosted with certain items to keep players engaged over time (Data Science Graduate Programs.com 2018).

Data analytics, therefore, allows game developers to scrutinize these variables and help gaming companies position their product better, designing more immersive games, bringing more personalization, and, just as important, generating more profits. For example, King Digital Entertainment, the developer of *Candy Crush Saga* saw that users were massively abandoning the game at level 65. Once King Digital was able to discover that a particular gaming element did not let users make it past level 65, it was able to quickly redesign the game and the element was deleted, and user retention improved (Yurevich 2019). Another example was Valve Software, the gaming company behind such hits as *Half-Life, DOTA, and Counter-Strike*. With *Counter-Strike*, Valve collected and analyzed certain user data, including which guns the teams chose, how their behavior changed during the game, how they killed, and how they died. Based on this information Valve was able to fine-tune the game balance and to make sure that the game is fair and that there are no sticking points in the game design (Yurevich 2019).

Case Study: Encounter-Based Metrics

Before moving on with the chapter, let us stop and imagine that you are an analyst at a video game development company. Your company released a Beta 2 weeks ago for a new online multiplayer First-Person Shooter. At first, participation was very high, and responses were great, but participation dropped dramatically over the last 5 days. You arc asked to investigate the matter by your supervisor by analyzing the in-game data your company has collected over the length of the Beta. You are asked to report on why participation dropped and submit recommendations on what should be adjusted.

The information is as follows:

Kill Information by Weapon				
	Kill: Death Ratio	Accuracy of shots	Headshots (By % Fired)	% of Usage per 20 minute round
MP5	1.06	21.3	15.5	16.8
M4-A1	1.47	26.4	19.6	25.8
AK-47	1.11	20.2	15.8	15.7
AUG	1.04	21.4	15.7	14.9
P-90	.82	15.2	13.2	8.6
FN Scar	1.07	22.1	16.2	18.2

Average length of life by Spawn Point (by Second)																	
Team A									Team B								
Map A			Map B			Map C			Map A			Map B			Map C		
Spawn 1	Spawn 2	Spawn 3	Spawn 1	Spawn 2	Spawn 3	Spawn 1	Spawn 2	Spawn 3	Spawn 1	Spawn 2	Spawn 3	Spawn 1	Spawn 2	Spawn 3	Spawn 1	Spawn 2	Spawn 3
62	50	37	65	58	47	61	58	52	67	48	62	70	33	36	65	55	54

Win Rate by Team/Map					
Team A			Team B		
Map A	Map B	Map C	Map A	Map B	Map C
33%	61%	53%	67%	39%	47%

Based on the above information

- Can you identify some of the possible reasons for the decline in Beta participation?
- If so, what can you suggest to resolve these issues and improve the gaming experience, and in turn the final game?

REAL-LIFE STATISTICS

Sport games not only use encounter metrics to track every move a gamer makes on the court or field but they also use real-life statistics to adjust player abilities within the game. For example, in games like Electronic Arts' (EA) *FIFA*, which has sold over 260 million games, *Madden*, which has sold over 130 million games, or 2K Sports' *NBA 2K*, which has sold over 100 million games, if a real player competing in the actual sports has a breakout or disappointing year on the field or court, his player ratings in the game will change based on their in-season performance (Cox 2020). The use of actually player game data, and in some cases the Athletes Biometric Data (ABD), raises some interesting legal and ethical issues and will be covered more in Chapter 16 Legal and Ethical Issues.

Disregarding the legal and ethical issues involved in using such player data, EA Sports has been able to grow *FIFA* into one of the six best-selling video game franchises by using such real-time analytics. The only games ahead of *FIFA* are: *Grand Theft Auto*, *Call of Duty*, *Super Mario*, *Pokemon*, and *Mario* (Cox 2020).

KEY PERFORMANCE INDICATORS (KPIs)

Like the NBA or the English Premier League (EPL), the world of gaming is extremely competitive. There are winners and losers. The competition, however, is not only just between the players, but also between game developers who are constantly trying to come up with innovative way to outdo their competitors. As technology improves, this has driven up the costs of game development as gamers are demanding better graphics and more real life-like games. For example, in 2020 by the time CD Projekt Red released *Cyberpunk 2077* the company had already spent over $330 million between development and marketing costs (Monahan 2021).

In their attempt to accurately measure a game's overall success, developers seek to measure several Key Performance Indicators (KPIs). The KPI seek to measure data on the number of daily active users (DAU) in a game; the number of monthly active players (MAU); the number of new or unique users (Unique Users); and most importantly average revenue per user (ARPU). Calculating these KPIs with analytics and optimization methods (See Chapter 9) helps game developers better understand the reasons who is playing the game and why people are playing the game or abandoning it (Yurevich 2019). Game developers can use these KPIs to track certain trends, positive and negative. For example, if there are certain upgrades, equipment, or resources within the game that can be purchased to help players advance, and the game is attracting new DAU and MAU users, game developers can use this information to reconsider their pricing policy. If, however, the game is not attracting DAUs, reducing the cost of the game and upgrades may stave off defections (Yurevich 2019).

BOOSTING MONETIZATION

Another way data analytics are used by game developers and gaming companies is to determine pricing strategies. It has become common practice for game developers to sell game add-ons, such as different "skins" weapons, resources, and other game components to users for an additional small fee, known as a micro transaction. For example, *Fortnite* sold "NFL skins" via the Fortnite Item Shop for $15 or 1,500 V-bucks. This allowed players to dress their game avatars in their favorite NFL team's uniform. The use of microtransactions also allows players, who are not willing to spend the time to manually level up, or who prefer to customize their armor or weapon, to purchase the resources, armor or weapons they need to advance to higher levels quicker.

By using player data, game developers can maximize revenue by identifying what the users want and need in the game and offering it to them. The ability to sell these game add-ons, is especially important for free-to-play game developers since players do not pay for the game up front, but through the use of microtransactions are charged small amounts of real money when the players buy game extras or enhancements. The free-to-play business model is also known as "Freemium" (Marr 2016)

For example, Zynga, which calls itself a social game developer because of its focus on running games on mobile and social networking platforms, not only offered users of its' free-to-play game *Farmville* the opportunity to purchase additional animals, but it also created rare species to stimulate users *(Yurevich* 2019). *Farmville*, which was "sunsetted" in 2020, was an agriculture-simulation game created by Zynga and launched on Facebook in 2009. From 2009 to 2011, *Farmville* was the most popular game on the social network, with over 34.5 million daily active users in 2010 (Naughton 2021).

Since *Farmville* required players to check on their farm every day, otherwise your crops would die, Zynga and Facebook were able to collect an endless amount of player data. Game developers use all this data collected online to make real-time adjustments to determine exactly what players want from a game and to keep them engaged. Using real data, the business can make decisions on what to tweak or change to increase customer satisfaction by providing gamers a personalized product, while at the same time balancing the financial demands of the company and employees. Finally, although *Farmville*, was sunsetted in 2020, it should be credited with moving the gaming industry away from exclusively using expensive, gaming consoles, like PlayStation and Xbox, and DVDs game disks to free-to-play and online gaming (Naughton 2021).

SUNSETTING

Sunsetting, or discontinuing a game, is one of the interesting problems gamer developers face with "forever franchises," those games that can top $100 million in a year and sustain a business for five years or more. Because of the cost of maintaining these games, they eventually need to be discontinued by the developers because they are not worth the cost of updates. However, because of the game's longevity, they usually have millions of global users, discontinuing or sunsetting a game can cause some difficult public relations problems. In some cases, players have spent hundreds of hours accumulating resources and advancing through the various levels over a period of years. For example, *Age of Empires: Castle Siege* was a massive online multiplayer game developed by Smoking Gun Interactive and Microsoft Studios. Released in 2014, the goal of *Castle Siege*, was to maintain and develop a castle that produced resources, which could be used to train troops and upgrade buildings, as well as research new technologies. The armies, or troops, of the player were then used to attack other players' castles to loot their resources and to earn crowns or defend your castle from attacks. While players could slowly gather resources, train troops, and advance through the levels, the game also allowed microtransactions to aid in rapid development of a castle and to improve defensive and attacking capabilities. By purchasing more resources, like gold or stone, players could defend the castle against enemy attacks more efficiently and unlock new technologies. In addition, while players played the game individually against other players, you attacked someone or they attacked you, it was also possible to join an alliance with other players. Once in an alliance, players could share resources or troops, thereby helping other players in the alliance advance faster, or share tips and other strategies. After 5 years, however, Microsoft Studios announced that it was sunsetting *Age of Empires: Castle Siege*. A decision, which Microsoft claims was because of the cost of updating the game and adding levels to keep users engaged, frustrated players (the author included) who had contributed a lot of hours and money building up their castles and resources.

Esports Ranking Systems

As previously addressed in Chapter 12 "Ranking and Ranking Systems in Sport Analytics" esports, like golf, tennis, or other individual and some team sport, use a ranking system. While it has already been noted that many of the innovations in rating systems occurred because sports bettors and casinos had

Esports fighting game tournament EVO 2019 Evolution Championship Series.

© Leonel Calara/Shutterstock.com

a financial interest in understanding not only who the best team is but how much better they are than their rivals, esports tournaments and game developers also have an interest in rating players. By ranking players based on their skill and experience, games allow players to compete against other players of equal skill and experience. The ranking system, therefore, seeks to ensure that new or less experienced players are not matched up against more skilled and experienced players.

How do esports ranking systems work? While there are different rankings for all different games, a majority of esports utilize the "Elo" rating system to match up opponents by individually rating them. The Elo rating system, developed by physics professor Arpad Elo for chess, is designed to calculate the skill levels of players in zero-sum games. In particular, the Elo rating system takes into consideration the player's current rank to predict whether a player will win or lose. If the two players were of equal rank, they would be expected to win and lose an equal number of games against each other. If, however, one player's rating is higher than the other player, she would be expected to win a greater percentage of the games played.

The player's rating moves up or down depending on whether they win or lose against other rated players. As a result, the Elo ranting system is self-correcting. If a player is ranked too low, she will move up the ratings after they win a few games. If a player is ranked too high, she will lose rating points until the ratings reflect the true playing strength (Moncav 2020). A slightly modified version of the Elo system has been used by professional esports leagues and various online games to rank players and balance competitions.

Another ranking system based on the Elo rating system, with unique variations, is Microsoft's TrueSkill system for XboxLive matchmaking. Initially developed to match players and teams in *Halo*, TrueSkill, like the Elo system, moves player and team rankings up or down based on wins and losses and can be updated after every match. Another benefit of TrueSkill is that even though teams are composed of several players, it allows tracking of players as they move from team to team. TrueSkill, however, is not widely used because the algorithm is patented and trademarked by Microsoft, so it is not available without a fee.

Esports and Traditional Stick and Ball Sports

One of the biggest complaints about the growth of esports and egaming is that fewer children are outside playing actual stick and ball games. Critics of esports complain that millions of teenagers are glued to their coach or computer screens. While it may be true that millions of young boys and girls around the world spend hours egaming, it is also true according to the National Federation of State High School Associations (NFHS) 2018-19 Annual High School Athletics Participation Survey that 7,937,491 high school students in the United States participated in high school sports. Of the almost 8 million participants, the third-highest total ever recorded by NFHS, 4,534,758 were boys and 3,402,733 were girls (NFHS 2019).

With esports posing no real threat to the next generation of professional stick and ball athletes, sports marketers of the various professional sports leagues and even the International Olympic Committee (IOC) have begun to embrace esports as a complementary product. For example, sports leagues are examining how they can use esports to both broaden their brand while reaching a traditionally younger demographic of users. By getting younger fans of the egames interested in the NBA, NFL, MLB, NHL or FIFA, sports marketers hope that they can transition them into becoming fans of their core product, whether through attending games in person or consuming the games on television.

A good example of this desire to convert esports fans into fans of the core product is the Olympics. Worried about the median age of viewers for Olympic television broadcasts, which was 53 during the Rio Olympics in 2016, the IOC has decided to add esports (Lombardo and Broughton 2017). In 2018, the IOC took the first step toward including esports when, prior to the PyeongChang Winter Olympic Games it allowed Intel and ESL to host a *Starcraft II* tournament using the Olympic rings. Although not an official Olympic event, the fact that the IOC allowed the tournament to use the Olympic rings was significant (Bloom 2018). The next step was announced for the 2022 Asian Games, in Hangzhou, China, when esports will be a medal event. The final step was the announcement that esports would be a demonstration sport at the 2024 Paris Games. The IOC is hoping to run simultaneous virtual and live events of certain individual and team sports.

However, there are still several hurdles to clear, such as establishing a single International Federation (IF) to oversee esports and help integrate it into the Olympic governance model. This is an especially difficult issue because, unlike basketball or track and field, esports games are built around the intellectual property of private, for-profit game developers (Bloom 2018). Without their approval, the IOC cannot use the games, and without the most popular games, will people watch?

While both sides are trying to resolve the various issues, the relationship seems like a win for both sides. First, the IOC will be able to connect to a younger and different demographic, which is good for the Olympic brand in the long run and good for sponsors and television networks in the immediate time. Unlike the Olympics, with its aging viewer population, median age 53, the median age for esports viewers in the United States is 29, with 39% of the total audience in the 25- to 34-year-old range (Sims 2020).

As for esports, being a part of the Olympic games would bring in additional money to the development of esports athletes. For example, each Olympic sport receives funding from the IOC, the IFs, the National Federations (NFs), and the National Olympic Committees (NOCs) to help train and develop athletes for future Olympics. In addition, the Olympic Games would provide esports some legitimacy and allow its athletes to attract additional sponsorship dollars (Bloom 2018).

Summary

From their humble beginnings to the advanced technology of today's video games, one thing has remained constant, players are still "locked in life-or-death" battles "for hours at a time, ruining their eyes, numbing their fingers in frenzied mashing of control buttons, joyously slaying their friend and wasting their employer's valuable computer time" (Brand 1972). What has changed, however, is the increased use of analytics to record and track players. As esports has become big business, it is not surprising to see teams and individuals using analytics to improve their playing skills by tracking tendencies and potential areas that they may need to improve or exploit.

However, where data analytics really pay off in esports is game development. Gaming companies are continuously collecting, visualizing, and analyzing data on how players use their games. Game developers can earn millions of dollars with the right game. However, there is a fine line between making a game interesting and something that players will continue to play and something that is either to easy, which players will quickly abandon because it is boring, and too difficult, which players will abandon in frustration. As noted above, data analytics allows game developers to discover problems early and hopefully maximize profits while minimizing problems.

As has happened throughout the 50-year history of esports and egaming, the industry is evolving. Esports and egaming have evolved from college computer labs to arcades to home consoles to home PCs and social networks to mobile gaming, a segment of the industry that generated over $15 billion in 2020. In the 2020s, gaming is replacing social media as the "place" friends meet up.

Due to the pace of technology changes, it is impossible to forecast what the gaming industry will look like 5 years after this book is published. For example, with the Oculus Quest Virtual Reality (VR) home headset, VR is bringing gamers "into" the game. VR, however, even with the ever-evolving technology is still not there yet. What is certain, however, is that esports and egaming are two of the fastest growing segments of the entire sport and entertainment industry.

Key Terms

Data Mining

Egaming

Esports

Esports Analytics

Encounter Metrics

Multiplayer Online Battle Arena (MOBA)

Player vs. Player (PvP)

First Person Shooter (FPS)

Real-time Strategy (RTS)

Critical Thinking Exercises

1. What are reasons behind the exponential growth of esports throughout the world?
2. Why are team analysts and coaches becoming so necessary in the industry?
3. How are sport marketers and traditional sports leagues attempting to convert esports fans to their core product? (for example, FIFA fans to soccer fans)
4. What are some of the esports developers are using analytics to track users to improve the product and increase profits?
5. How are analytics used differently or the same in Esports and traditional sports like baseball or basketball?

References

Bloom, David. 2018. *What Olympic Recognition Could Mean for Esports, and Vice Versa*. Forbes. (October 18). https://www.forbes.com/sites/dbloom/2018/10/18/esports-olympics-recognition-ioc-esl-advertising-sponsors/?sh=1ee46f3f3b05

Brand, Stewart. 1972. *SPACEWAR: Fanatic Life a Symbolic Death Among Computer Bums*. Rolling Stone (December 7). https://www.wheels.org/spacewar/stone/rolling_stone.html

Chapple, Craig. 2020. *Top Grossing Mobile Games Worldwide for November 2020*. Sensor Tower (December 8). https://sensortower.com/blog/top-mobile-games-by-worldwide-revenue-november-2020

Chikhani, Riad. 2015. *The History of Gaming: An Evolving Community*. The Crunch (October 31). https://techcrunch.com/2015/10/31/the-history-of-gaming-an-evolving-community/#:~:text=Atari%20not%20only%20developed%20their,shopping%20malls%20around%20the%20world

Cox, Sam. 2020. *Best Selling Games of All Time—Top 10 Sports Video Games*. 888 Sports (October 14). https://www.888sport.com/blog/all-sports/top-10-best-selling-sports-video-games-of-all-time

Data Science Graduate Programs.com. (April 9, 2018). *Big Data is the Biggest Game Changer to Hit the Gaming Industry in Decades*. https://www.datasciencegraduateprograms.com/2018/04/big-data-is-the-biggest-game-changer-to-hit-the-gaming-industry-in-decades/

Dixon, Ed. 2020. *2020 LoL World Championship draws 3.8m peak viewers*. Sports Pro. (November 5). https://www.sportspromedia.com/news/league-of-legends-world-championship-2020-final-audience-viewing-figures#:~:text=Esports%20tournament%20racks%20up%20139m,up%20from%20last%20year's%20137m.&text=The%202020%20League%20of%20Legends,year's%20high%20of%203.9%20million

Hood, Vic. (2018, October 16). *Esports: Everything you need to know*. Techradar (October 16). https://www.techradar.com/news/esports-everything-you-need-to-know

Lombardo, John, and David Broughton. 2017. Going gray: Sports TV viewers skew older. *Sports Business Journal*. https://www.sportsbusinessdaily.com/Journal/Issues/2017/06/05/Research-and-Ratings/Viewership-trends.aspx

Marr, Bernard. 2016. *Big Data in Practice: How 45 Successful Companies Used Big Data Analytics to Deliver Extraordinary Results*. Chichester, UK: John Wiley & Sons.

Monahan, Sean. 2021. Video games have replaced music as the most important aspect of youth culture. *The Guardian*. (January 11). https://www.theguardian.com/commentisfree/2021/jan/11/video-games-music-youth-culture

Moncav, Melany. 2020. *What is Elo? An explanation for competitive gaming's hidden rating system*. DOT Esports (March 6). https://dotesports.com/general/news/elo-ratings-explained-20565

Naughton, John. 2021. *How FarmVille and Facebook helped to cultivate a new audience for gaming*. The Guardian. (January 9). https://www.theguardian.com/commentisfree/2021/jan/09/how-farmville-and-facebook-helped-to-cultivate-a-new-audience-for-gaming

Newzoo. 2020. *Global Esports Market Report 2020*. https://newzoo.com/insights/trend-reports/newzoo-global-esports-market-report-2020-light-version/

NFHS. 2019. *Participation in High School Sports Registers First Decline in 30 Years*. NFHS News (September 5). https://www.nfhs.org/articles/participation-in-high-school-sports-registers-first-decline-in-30-years/

Schubert, Matthias, Anders Drachen, and Tobias Mahlmann. 2016. Esports Analytics through Encounter Detection. MIT Sloan Sports Analytics Conference. (March). https://www.researchgate.net/publication/295861293_Esports_Analytics_Through_Encounter_Detection

Sims, Alexander. 2020. "Understanding The Esports Viewing Demographic." *The Next Level: The Business of Esports.* April 27. https://tnl.media/esportsnews/2020/4/22/understanding-the-esports-viewing-demographic

Taylor, T. L. 2012. *Raising the Stakes: E-Sports and the Professionalization of Computer Gaming*. Cambridge, MA: MIT Press.

Taylor, T. L. 2018. *Watch Me Play: Twitch and the Rise of the Game Live Streaming*. Princeton, NJ: Princeton University Press.

Willingham, A. J. 2018. *What is eSports? A look at an explosive billion-dollar industry*. CNN. (August 27). https://www.cnn.com/2018/08/27/us/esports-what-is-video-game-professional-league-madden-trnd/index.html

Yurevich, Kseniya. 2019. Data Analytics Streamlines Gaming Industry. Here's How. Datanami. August 29. https://www.datanami.com/2019/08/29/data-analytics-streamlines-gaming-industry-heres-how/

Zavian, Ellen. 2020. *The NCAA whiffed on esports. It's paying a price but can still learn a lesson*. Washington Post (August 6). https://www.washingtonpost.com/video-games/esports/2020/08/06/ncaa-whiffed-esports-its-paying-price-can-still-learn-lesson/

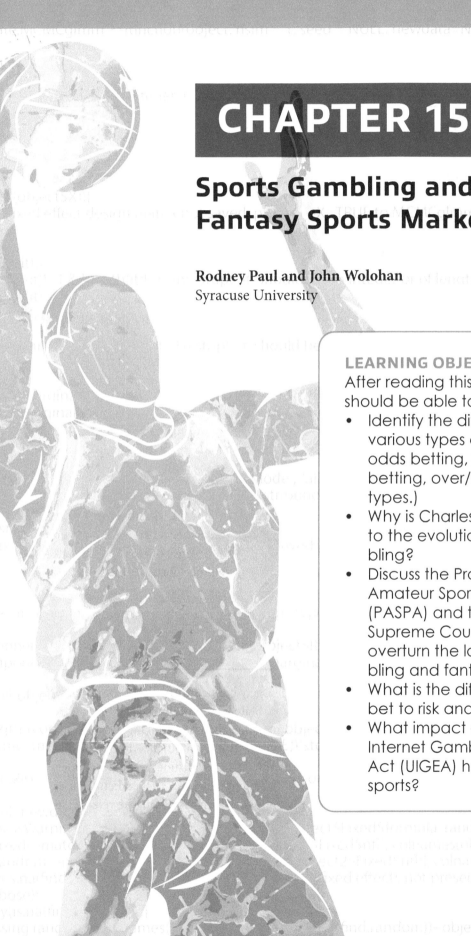

CHAPTER 15

Sports Gambling and Fantasy Sports Markets

Rodney Paul and John Wolohan
Syracuse University

LEARNING OBJECTIVES
After reading this chapter, students should be able to:
- Identify the difference between various types of sports bets (e.g., odds betting, line or spread betting, over/under, and other types.)
- Why is Charles McNeil important to the evolution of sports gambling?
- Discuss the Professional and Amateur Sports Protection Act (PASPA) and the impact of the Supreme Court's decision to overturn the law on sports gambling and fantasy sports.
- What is the difference between bet to risk and bet to win?
- What impact did the Unlawful Internet Gambling Enforcement Act (UIGEA) have on fantasy sports?

Introduction

"There are three things a gambler needs: money, guts and brains. If you don't have one, you're dead" (Boyle 1986).

On Sunday 3 February 2019, the New England Patriots defeated the Los Angeles Rams 13 – 3 in the NFL Super Bowl. While the game was generally unremarkable, something happened that day that is going to have a long-term impact on American sports. The game marked the first Super Bowl in which bettors in states outside of Nevada could legally place bets on the game (Wolohan 2020). As a result, on what is usually the single biggest day of the year for the sportsbooks in Nevada, they handled about $12.65 million or about 8%, less than the Super Bowl record of $158 million, bet in 2018 (Wolohan 2020).

However, while bettors in Nevada may have only wagered $145.94 million on the game, bettors wagered $34.9 million in New Jersey's sportsbooks, $2.2 million in Delaware, and another $4.6 million in Mississippi. In all, a record $187 million was legally bet on the 2019 Super Bowl, almost $30 million more that in 2018 (Wolohan 2020). By the end of 2020, according to figures published by the New Jersey Division of Gaming Enforcement (NJDGE), the state's total sports wagering **handle** (the total amount wagered in bets; revenue is how much the casino keeps) was over $5 billion for the calendar year (Mulligan 2020). In addition, the $930 million bet during November 2020, of which gross revenue for the state was $50.6 million, was up 16.0% compared to October 2020 and 65.7% higher than November 2019 (Mulligan 2020). More importantly, the number dwarfs Nevada's $659.9 million record handle generated in October 2020.

Of the $930 million, $872.1 million came from online betting, and the other $60 million came from retail (casinos and other sports books). With 20 – 25% of New Jersey sports bets coming from people from New York, and the state facing a $60 billion budget deficit because of the COVID pandemic, it is not surprising that New York is also hoping to introduce online sports betting in 2021.

A Short History of Sports Gambling in the United States

At the end of the 19th century, all forms of gambling were largely banned throughout the country. Beginning in the 1920s and 1930s, because of the Depression, State laws prohibiting gambling were gradually loosened. The first state to legalize sports gambling, other than horse racing, was Nevada when it passed the Wide-Open Gambling Bill of 1931 (Davies and Abram 2012). Although it did not include sports gambling at first, the Bill was expanded by 1949 to include betting on sports (Wolohan 2020). Sports betting however did not really become popular until 1940, when Charles McNeil, a securities analyst in Chicago, introduced a revolutionary form of betting he referred as "wholesaling odds" (Boyle 1986). Prior to McNeil's new method, bettors were limited to betting on games using the standard system of odds. Under that system, if the odds were 4 to 1 that Syracuse would beat the University of Massachusetts in football, to win $100 betting on Syracuse you would have to be willing to bet (and lose) $400. Although, all Syracuse had to do was win the game for you to win the $100, the higher the odds the more financially risky the bet.

McNeil's new form of betting, which is currently called **point spread betting**, **line betting** or **straight betting**, allowed gamblers to bet that a team would either win or lose by a certain number of points. The point spread, which McNeil determined using data on team performance, weather, common opponents, and other variables was designed to make the teams more equal and less financially risky for bettors. Under McNeil's system, if the line in the Syracuse v. Massachusetts games was Syracuse (-10), Syracuse would have to defeat Massachusetts by more than 10 points for you to win your bet on Syracuse. If Syracuse lost or won the game by fewer than 10 points, you lose the bet on Syracuse. If Syracuse won by exactly 10 points, it is considered a "push," and no one would have won, and your bet would be refunded. What makes this form of gambling more appealing to gamblers is that on a $100 bet on Syracuse, bettors would generally have to only risk $110. If you bet $2,000, you would generally need to pay $2,200 if you lost. The extra 10% fee is called the "vigorish," "vig" or "juice" on spread or line bets and is essentially a fee the house collects from bettors for allowing them to bet. The fee may be different at different sports books, so it is always smart to know what the vig is before placing your bet.

Even with line betting appealing to more sports bettors, other states were still slow to adopt sport betting. One of the reasons for the delay was taxes. While not specifically banned by the Federal government, due to the NCAA basketball scandals, Congress in 1951 passed a law imposing a 10% tax on all sports bets and required all sports books to purchase a license. As a result, legal sports betting could only be found in an increasing smaller number of "turf clubs" in Nevada, while the other 49 states seemed content to raise tax revenue via legalized horse racing (Davies and Abram 2012). In 1974, when Congress reduced the federal tax on sports bets from 10% down to 2%, sports betting once again became an option for states to increase their tax revenue (Davies and Abram 2012). The first state was Montana, when it passed the Card Game, Bingo, Raffles, and Sports Pool Act. In 1976, Delaware legalized a form of sports gambling when it introduced a Scoreboard lottery. However, unlike Nevada, Delaware did not allow gamblers to bet on individual games. Instead, the Delaware game required bettors to pick seven winners in seven selected NFL games. Although Delaware discontinued its football lottery after only one year, it reinstituted the game in 2009.

In 1983, the Federal tax on sport betting was reduced again, from 2% to 0.25%. The reduction in tax rates now made betting on sports more profitable for gamblers and states. For example, the Nevada handle rose to $894 million after the second tax cut in 1983 (Chen 2019). This led to more states looking to add sports betting, which Oregon did in 1989, when it initiated a game like Delaware's Scoreboard lottery. Oregon allowed betting on NFL football games through a game called Sports Action, which is a part of the Oregon Lottery. Oregon, however, discontinued the game after the

2006 NFL season as part of an agreement with the NCAA. By the early 1990s, at least thirteen other states, including Illinois, California, and Florida, were exploring the possibility of allowing legalized sports betting in their states (Wolohan 2020).

Worried the sudden proliferation of sports-based lotteries could pose a threat to the integrity of their sports, the NCAA and major professional sports leagues petitioned Congress for help. In 1992, Congress passed the ***Professional and Amateur Sports Protection Act (PASPA)***. In addition to protecting the integrity of the sports, the goal of PASPA was to stop the spread of State-sponsored sports gambling by limiting it to those states that had already enacted legislation. The law therefore exempted Nevada, Oregon, Montana, and Delaware since they had previously allowed sports betting (Wolohan 2018).

SPORTS GAMBLING POST 2018. As a result of the financial crisis in 2008, New Jersey was facing a significant shortfall in state tax revenues enacted the Sports Wagering Act in 2012, legalizing sports betting in New Jersey's casinos and racetracks. However, before the state could take a single bet, the NCAA and professional sports leagues filed suit in federal court. In a legal odyssey that lasted over six years, the United States Supreme Court in 2018 shocked the sports world by ruling that the Federal Government had overstepped its powers when it passed the PASPA and that the law was unconstitutional. By 2020, a mere two years after the Supreme Court's decision in *Murphy v. National Collegiate Athletic Association (NCAA)*, the number of states to have passed legislation legalizing sports gambling as of November 2020 had reached 25 states: Arkansas; Colorado; Delaware; District of Columbia; Illinois; Indiana; Iowa; Louisiana; Maryland; Michigan; Mississippi; Montana; New Hampshire; New Jersey; New Mexico; New York; Nevada; Oregon; Pennsylvania; Rhode Island; South Dakota; Tennessee; Virginia; Washington; and West Virginia. There are another three states that have introduced active legislation: Massachusetts; Ohio; and Vermont. In addition to the 28 states that have passed or have active legislation legalizing sports gambling, there were another 15 states where sports gambling legislation failed to make it out of the state legislature (American Gaming Association 2020).

The reason so many states are rushing into the sports betting market is the belief that legalized gambling can provide additional tax revenue. Once again, we look at the $930 million New Jersey sportsbooks reported in November 2020, a monthly record for any state with legalized sports betting, including Nevada. The amount was especially impressive since the state's casinos were operating with limited capacity in that the NBA and NHL were not playing games. Of the $930 million handle, New Jersey's reported gross revenue was $50.6 million. The betting market in the United States is only expected to grow bigger. In September of 2020, VIXIO Gambling Compliance forecast the U.S. sports betting market to be worth $8.4 billion in total annual revenue by 2024. The vast majority of the $8.4 billion is expected to come from online sports betting, as opposed to sportsbooks at casinos (VIXIO, 2020).

Professional sports teams are also cashing in on sports gambling. Besides sponsorship deals, which teams had in place before PASPA was repealed, teams are beginning to allow sportsbooks inside their stadiums and arenas. For example, in 2021, the Washington Nationals announced that Bet-MGM would open a sportsbook inside the Nationals stadium as part of a long-term deal to become the exclusive sports betting sponsor of the Nationals. The Nationals will share in revenue from the sportsbook, calculated based on handle. Along with the retail outlet, which MLB mandates cannot be accessed from within the ballpark on game days, BetMGM gets access to operate its mobile app within two blocks of the ballpark. While the deal was the first for an MLB ballpark, NBA, NHL, and Major League Soccer teams have already opened their facilities to sportsbooks. The NFL still prohibits teams from opening retail sportsbooks in their stadiums. However, stadiums in states with legal sports gambling, like the New Jersey Meadowlands Stadium, may offer betting lounges allowing mobile betting options.

Sports Betting Markets

While there are endless ways you can bet on an event or game, below are some of the most popular ways gamblers can bet on sports these days.

TOTAL OR OVER/UNDER BETTING

Total or over/under betting allows gamblers to bet that the total number of points, runs, or goals that will be scored by both teams in the game, half, quarter, or period will be either over or under the total estab-

Sport betting at Caesar's Palace in Las Vegas

lished by the sportsbook. For example, if the over/under line for the total predicted points for a game in a basketball game between Syracuse and North Carolina is 140.5 and Syracuse won 75 – 64, you would win your bet if you bet under since the combined final score was 139 points, which is under the 140.5 line. If, however, North Carolina score in the last shot of the game and the final score was Syracuse 75 – 66 North Carolina, you would lose the bet because the point total is now 141, over the 140.5 line.

MONEY LINE BETTING

Money line betting is simply betting on which team you expect to win, regardless of the score. While this form of betting is less common then point spread or line betting, it is still common in baseball and hockey. The minus sign (-130) always indicates the favorite and the amount you must bet to win $100. The plus sign (+120) always indicates the underdog and the amount you win for every $100 bet. The higher the number, such as +300, +500, +5000, the greater the underdog and the more likely the team is to lose.

The following illustrates how money line betting work:

> Boston Bruins -130
> New York Rangers +120

If you wanted to bet on the Boston Bruins to win, you would need to bet $130 for a chance to win $100. **If the Bruins won, y**our return would be $230 – the original $130 stake (bet) and the $100 bet profit. If the Rangers win, you lose the original $130 bet. However, if you bet on the New York Rangers to win, your return would be $220 – the original $100 bet and the $120 profit. Once again, if the Bruins win, and you bet on the Rangers to win, you lose the original $100 bet.

PARLAY BETTING

In sports betting, a parlay bet is when you make two or more bets and tie them together into one bet. You can combine point spread with over/under bets. For example, suppose that in one game the Buffalo Bills were a 3-point favorite over the Baltimore Ravens, with an over/under of 45 points and in another the Kansas City Chiefs were a 10-point favorite over the Cleveland Browns, with an over/under of 50 points. If I bet on Buffalo -3, Cleveland +10 and the over in the Kansas City game. For me to win, Buffalo would need win by more than 3 points, Cleveland would need to win outright or to lose by less than 10 points, and the point total of the Kansas City / Cleveland game would need to be over 50 points. If any of the bets in the parlay loses, the entire parlay loses. However, if all the bets wins, the bettor receives a bigger payout than if they bet on each game individually (Winston 2009).

Parlay size	Actual Odds	Standard Payout Odds	House Percentage Edge
Two bets	3-1	2.6-1	10
Three bets	7-1	6-1	12.50
Four bets	15-1	12-1	18.75
Five bets	31-1	25-1	18.75

The size of the parlay will depend on the sportsbook, but it is possible to parlay the entire NFL weekend schedule. While the payouts can be significant, it is important to remember that the more bets included in the parlay the more likely you are to lose. In fact, a UNLV Center for Gaming study showed that from 1992 to 2015 Nevada sports books had nearly a 30% hold on parlays. The hold is the amount the sports keep after all the bets are paid out. The hold for straight line bets was less than 5% (Appelbaum 2019).

TEASER BETTING

In sports betting, a teaser bet is a variation of a parlay bet that allows the bettor to move the point spread or the over / under line up or down a designated number of points. For example, suppose that in one game the Buffalo Bills were a 3-point favorite (-3) and in another the Cleveland Browns were a 10-point underdog (+10). A two team 6-point teaser involving these teams moves the point spread 6 points on each game. Therefore, if you took the Bills and the Browns, to win the teaser Buffalo would now just have to win outright or to lose by less than 3 points and Cleveland to win outright or to lose by less than 16 points. The catch, however, is that it requires that multiple bets be tied together and that to win your bet both teams would have to cover the new point spread. If one of the bets in your teaser ties or pushes with the spread or total, it is removed from the teaser (Winston 2009). For example, a three-team teaser that finishes with one push would be graded as a two-team teaser and see its payout drop from +160 to -110.

The most common teaser is a 6-point teaser; however, you can also find 6.5-point and 7-point teasers. Teasers must include two or more bets (although some books require three or more), and the more the bets added, the higher the potential payout but also the higher the risk. The table below shows the payouts for 6-, 6.5-, and 7-point teasers. Note that payouts can vary sportsbook to sportsbook.

Teaser size	6 Points Odds	6.5 Points Odds	7 Points Odds
Two-Team Teaser	-110	-120	-135
Three-Team Teaser	+160	+140	+150
Four-Team Teaser	+265	+240	+215
Five-Team Teaser	+450	+400	+350
Six-Team Teaser	+700	+600	+500

PLEASER OR REVERSE TEASERS

Pleaser or reverse teasers allow you to add or subtract a designated number of points and then bet with that move, such as dropping a total from 46 to 40 points and betting the Under rather than gaining an advantage with the Over. For example, a two-team 6-point reverse teaser would move the Buffalo Bills from a 3-point favorite to a 9-point favorite and the Cleveland Browns were a 10-point underdog to a 4-point underdog. The pleaser therefore increases the number of points the Bills would need to win by, while at the same time reducing the number of points the Browns could lose by. Because pleasers modify the spreads and Over/Under totals in a disadvantageous direction, the risk of losing those bets is higher but the potential payout reflects that and offers a greater return.

PROP BETTING

Prop betting is a bet on anything outside the traditional betting line. Most prop bets are similar to money line bets in that you are simply betting on whether an event will occur. For example, in the Super Bowl between Tampa Bay and Kansas City, the prop of which team will score first would look something like this:

> Kansas City (-150)
> Tampa Bay (+130).

Here are a few other examples of popular prop during the 2020 Super Bowl included:

- How long will it take for Demi Lovato to sing the national anthem?
- Will either team score in first 5 1/2 minutes of the game?
- Which team will score first?
- Which player will score the first touchdown of game?
- Total interceptions in game?

FUTURE BETTING

Future betting is like prop betting in that it allows gamblers to bet on future events. For example, bettors must correctly select a team to win an event that takes place in a later time than the current day. The money wagered will be tied up until there is an outcome and bettors will receive fixed odds when they place the wager. For example, in January 2021, three months before the start of the 2021 MLB season and nine months before the 2021 World Series, if I wanted to bet on the 2021 World Series, I would find the following odds (odds are listed at 10/1, so that if you bet $100 you win $1,000):

Team	Odds	Fractional
Los Angeles Dodgers	+450	9/2
New York Yankees	+550	11/2
San Diego Padres	+900	9/1
Atlanta Braves	+1000	10/1
Chicago White Sox	+1000	10/1
New York Mets	+1400	14/1
Minnesota Twins	+1500	15/1
Tampa Bay Rays	+1500	15/1
Houston Astros	+1800	18/1
Oakland Athletics	+1800	18/1
Boston Red Sox	+5000	50/1
Pittsburgh Pirates	+10000	100/1

In the above example, the future odds of the New York Yankees are listed as a 11/2. Therefore, if you were to bet $100 on New York to win the World Series and the Yankees won, then you would win $550 (5.5 ÷ 1 × 100). You would collect $650, which includes your win and stake ($100). The stake is the initial dollar amount that you wager on the MLB future, either at a sportsbook or through an online sportsbook. If you wanted to bet $100 on the Red Sox, you would collect $50,100 if they won the 2021 World Series.

The Role of Analytics in Setting the Betting Line

Sports gambling and fantasy sports are both numbers games. Therefore, it is not surprising that analytics is used by both oddsmakers and many bettors. Since the goal of any casino or sportsbook is to make money, sportsbooks use analytics to determine the lines (point spreads, totals, odds, etc.) for every game or event. To do this, sportsbooks use proprietary statistical models using a "zillion different factors" that could affect a spread, such as home field advantage, the competitive strengths of each team, points scored, points against, strength of schedule, margin of victory, and even weather (Silverman 2020). For example, scoring overall should go down as the weather worsens, which is important for over/under betting, but not so much for point spread, while home-field advantage might increase if the visiting team is coming from the West Coast to the East Coast for an early game.

Since bookmakers are more skilled at predicting the outcomes of games than most bettors, economics researchers generally modeled sportsbook behavior under the balanced book hypothesis (Winston 2009). In particular, the belief was that since each bettor must pay a vig or commission and sportsbooks were guaranteed to make a profit if the price or line was even, based on the bet 11 to win 10 rules, it was assumed that sportsbooks would seek to set the line so that half the money went on one team, while the other half went on the other (Winston 2009). If we think back to Chapter 9 and Optimization Methods, any betting imbalances should lead the sportsbook to change the price in the direction of the more popular side of the wager to again try to even the betting action. The original studies of market efficiency in sports wagering markets by Zuber et al. (1985) and Sauer (1988) utilized this assumption in their studies. To illustrate how this might work in practice, Jason Scott, vice president of trading at BetMGM says that instead of employing people to dive deep into football analytics, his digital team focuses on the betting side of the business by developing computer algorithms to identify how a group of bettors using BetMGM's digital platform are betting on the point spread. Based on this data, BetMGM will change the price trying to find what he calls the "true price," that point "where the sharps aren't picking on either side because they don't think they've got an advantage" (Silverman 2020).

Nick Bogdanovich, director of trading at William Hill US (Caesars), however, called equal action a "pipe dream," while Johnny Avello, director of bookmaking at DraftKings, considers it to be "very rare" when a bookmaker can balance out a game (Silverman 2020). This position is supported by research that has rejected the true price or balanced book hypothesis.

Instead, bookmakers try to systematically exploit bettor biases by choosing prices that deviate from the market clearing price and allow betting imbalances to accrue as a profit-maximizing strategy Levitt (2002). While this strategy can potentially expose the bookmaker to risk on any game, over the course of a season, the risk borne is minimal. Paul and Weinbach (2008, 2009, 2011) and Humphreys et al. (2014) found that bookmaker profit maximization provides a simple explanation for sportsbooks, allowing significant imbalances to occur as data from actual sportsbooks revealed that bettors consistently and predictably prefer big favorites in the sides market and betting the over in the totals market, but that sportsbooks still offer closing lines that do not reject market efficiency, offing an unbiased forecast of game outcomes. Therefore, sportsbooks are actually using both game data (performance statistics related to both teams in a game) and historical betting trends of their clientele (i.e. where the money is likely to be bet) to determine their prices and making the decision as to when to change the prices. The models used are highly analytical and updated in real time to effectively price the marketplace.

INDIVIDUAL BETTOR. For the individual bettor, it is said that the safest bet in all of sports gambling is to bet on the horse that is the favorite win to show, basically come in third place or better. However, if you do not want to bet on the horses, another safe way to bet on sports is to bet to risk instead of bet to win. When you bet to risk, you are betting a specific amount regardless of the odds. For example, if the New England Patriots are a -150 favorite on the money line and you want to bet $100 on the Patriots. If you bet to risk, this means you are risking $100. Based on the - 150 favorite price, this means if the Patriots win the game you win roughly $66.67, plus you get the $100 you risked back. If the Patriots lose the game, you lose the $100 that you risked.

If you bet to win $100 on the Patriots, this means you would need to risk $150 up front based on the - 150 money line price. If the Patriots win, you win $100 plus you get the $150 that you risked back. If the Patriots lose, you lose the $150 that you risked. While on the surface, it might seem as though betting to win is the smarter bet when it comes to betting underdogs, you need to consider that betting to win on underdogs cuts into your potential profits and forfeits the advantages of plus money payouts (Appelbaum 2020).

ANALYTICS AND POINT SHAVING

One of the reasons the NCAA and the professional sports leagues fought so hard to keep sports gambling restricted to Nevada was the potential it could have on undermining the integrity of their games. **Point-shaving**, which is viewed as a soft form of corruption, is designed to manipulate the margin of a game without manipulating the game's overall outcome. Point shaving, however, is an illegal form of insider trading upon which those in the know can profit at the expense of those on the outside (Chang and Sanders 2009).

While there are opportunities for athletes in every sport to shave points or throw games, in many respects, the sport with the greatest potential for point shaving is basketball. With only five players on the court at a time, and players playing both offense and defense, any given player can potentially exert a great deal of influence upon the game by committing turnovers and missing defensive assignments.

With the average yearly NBA salary at 7.7 million in 2020, the greatest threat of point-shaving is within NCAA Men's Basketball. In fact, one of the most famous instances of match fixing in sports happened between 1947 and 1951, when at least 86 college basketball games were fixed by at least thirty-five college players from several colleges in the New York City area and the University of Kentucky. Twenty of the players, and fourteen gamblers, were eventually arrested and served time in prison (Wolohan 2020). Despite all the efforts by the NCAA and the criminal penalties handed down to the players, statistical evidence shows that point shaving in college basketball may still be commonplace today. For example, based upon distortion in the distribution of NCAA Men's Basketball game outcomes (from 1989–1990 through 2004–2005), Wolfers (2006) estimates that 6 percent of strong favorites "have been willing to manipulate their performance" such that an estimated 1 percent of games or 500 games in the sixteen-season sample "involve gambling-related corruption" (Wolfers 2006, 283).

Fantasy Sports Markets

The most common myth on the birth of fantasy sports traces its origin to 1980, when Daniel Okrent, a writer for *Sports Illustrated,* and a few other sportswriters would gather weekly at the La Rotisserie Française restaurant for a fantasy baseball league (Vinton 2009). The **Rotisserie league**, as it was called, required individual players, or team owners, to draft or select baseball players at the beginning of the season to create a team. These teams would then compete over the entire season and team owner would be awarded points based on how well the baseball players performed statistically during the day, week, or season. Rotisserie league team owners were awarded points for the traditional baseball statistics, such as runs, hits, and stolen bases. The winner at the end of the season was the team owner with the most points.

While the Rotisserie league may have been the first fantasy baseball league, fantasy sports can be traced game back almost 20 years earlier to 1962 when Wilfred "Bill" Winkenbach, a limited partner in the Oakland Raiders, and a few other Raiders personnel and local sports writers developed the basic rules for fantasy football (Newman 2020).

Daily Fantasy Sports (DFS)

While fantasy sports were gaining in popularity, from one million in 1992 to an estimated 45.9 million in 2019 (Fantasy Sports & Gaming Association 2020), it was not until 2006 when Congress passed the **Unlawful Internet Gambling Enforcement Act (UIGEA)** that DFS took off as a business. The law, which was meant to prohibit online

DraftKings app on a smartphone

poker and other forms of gambling, specifically exempted online fantasy sports. About a year after the passage of the law, instant fantasy sports or Daily Fantasy Sports (DFS) was created, and Draft-Kings and FanDuel, the two largest DFS companies, grew into a multi-billion-dollar business (Meddy 2016). Unlike traditional fantasy-sports where team owners drafted players at the beginning of the season and competed over the entire in the same league, DFS allows team owners to create a new team daily or weekly and compete and cash in on one-day events (Chen 2019).

While prior to 2018 and the Supreme Court's decision in *Murphy v. NCAA*, professional sports leagues treated traditional sports gambling like the plague. At the same time, however, the leagues and television openly entered partnerships with DFS. The first league to enter a partnership agreement with a DFS (DraftKings) was Major League Baseball in 2013. Although a ghost deal, in that there was no press release announcing the deal, the deal allowed DraftKings to have signage in MLB stadium and a DraftKings banner ad on MLB.com (Chen 2019). In exchange, MLB received an equity stake in DraftKings. By 2015, FanDuel would have an exclusive deal with the NBA and over 12 professional sports teams would have partnerships or equity in one of the two major DFS. As for television, the networks began accepting DFS advertising in 2014 and by 2015 ESPN had entered a $250 million deal with DraftKings (Chen 2019).

Analytics and Fantasy Sports

Like traditional fantasy sports, it takes a lot of skill to win at DFS. Players need to watch games, follow the trade and injury reports, while analyzing all the player information that is generated each night (Caspian Kang 2016). However, even with advanced statistical modeling, to win at DFS a person would need to win roughly 53 percent of their bets to beat the "rake," the roughly 10 percent service fee DFS companies take out of each wager (Caspian Kang 2016).

The average player would probably have been happy to take those odds. In 2015, in the first half of the MLB season, 91 percent of DFS player profits were won by just 1.3 percent of players (McKinsey & Company 2015). The reason why the top DFS players were winning all the money is because DFS offered no protections for novices. In DFS, the top players with the help of advanced analytics and computers programs could enter every contest each day. In addition, unlike the novice player who enters one or two lineups per contest, since DFS did not limit the number of rosters a player could enter a tournament or event, the top players enter dozens or hundreds of rosters for each tournament (Barbarisi 2017). For example, one player on DraftKings entered nearly every MLB contest on the site, from the $10,600 buy-in contests to the $1 buy-in tournaments (McKinsey & Company 2015).

Due to the bad press DFS companies received over the practice, they have tried to modify some of their rules to even out the odds between the novice and "sharks." In addition, both FanDuel and DraftKings began to limit the number of entries a player could submit for certain contests by hosting single-entry contests. This prevents sharks, who traditionally enter hundreds of different lineups per contest, from entering more than a single entry. Of course, these rules do not apply in the big money contest, since DFS companies need the sharks to enter multiple times to build up the prize pool.

As discussed in Chapter 11 "Player Projection Systems in Sport Analytics" with the money involved in fantasy sports, player projection in and of itself has become a prime concern for bettors. If you can predict which players will do well in the upcoming season—and if you can do that better than your friends or people you are competing against—you should be able to win your fantasy league or in the money in DFS. And of course, Vegas has long been willing to take wagers on the performance of players before the start of the season. It is common to see prop bets on the over/under on the number of touchdowns a quarterback will throw, the over/under on the number of games a will win, or who will win MVP or Cy Young awards during the upcoming season.

Because of the direct money-making opportunities that arise from these approaches, many of the approaches are kept private by their owners. Which makes sense. If you have information that could be used to make money, and you are giving that information away for free, then you are giving away money. This is especially true for systems design for fantasy and daily-fantasy sports, where the value of the systems is in their ability to capitalize on arbitrage.

As described in a reasonable amount in Chapter 11, there are two well-known player projection systems. The first system, Marcel (Tango 2004), was designed by Tom Tango to be as simple as possible. As noted previously, it is not the best system out there, but it offers good predictions and is competitive with more complex models. The second system we examined was called CARMELO—a backronym for Career-Arc Regression Model Estimator with Local Optimization—which attempts to project the careers of basketball players. The CARMELO system was designed and is maintained by the FiveThirtyEight.com team at ABC, led by Nate Silver, formerly of Baseball Prospectus.

Regardless of the system, however, the analytics used in fantasy sports are like those used in the sports betting market. The key difference is that with fantasy sports, the analysis is incorporated on an individual player level rather than at the team level. Another key difference is how prices (salaries) are set in daily fantasy compared to those in the sports betting market (point spreads, money lines, totals). In the sports betting market, sportsbooks can adjust prices based upon real-time information such as injuries or suspensions. In daily fantasy sports, prices are fixed once they are released to the public for the duration of the daily contest. This creates advantages for participants who pay attention to recent news and find players who are likely to see an increased playing time or suddenly face more favorable matchups.

While many of the empirical models built for fantasy sports are like those used directly by team analytical staffs, it should be noted that fantasy sports are aimed at the offensive side of the game. Players are awarded points based upon their scoring prowess or other similar offensive stats. Even fantasy games where defenses are drafted, such as in NFL daily fantasy games, the main bulk of defensive scoring is when the defense scores a touchdown. Therefore, analytics at the team level spends many more resources analyzing and modeling defensive play than traditional fantasy operators or players.

Case Study: Daily Fantasy

The daily fantasy marketplace can be examined using data available online. The data that will be used here are from DraftKings and incorporate the daily salary data for each player and their performance data in terms of points earned. The daily salaries can be exported each gameday directly on any contest viewed on the website. At the bottom right of the list of players available to draft there is a link allowing you to export to CSV. Clicking on this will download the file, and it can directly be used in R (or it can be opened in Excel to view in a spreadsheet). After any contest, overall scoring of all players can similarly be downloaded from the website by going to Contests. Under My Contests – History, clicking on any contest will show the results. Below the results is an Export Lineups to CSV link that will provide the scoring for each player. A merge of the files will combine salary and result in addition to other useful information. While the data shown here uses data from 2016–2017 through 2018–2019, visualizations and basic models will be possible after only a short time of gathering data on the website. For historical data, there are a variety of outlets that sell data on daily fantasy games for a nominal fee.

To examine if the daily fantasy market on DraftKings is efficient, we will use a simple linear regression model approach. In a regression model, there is a dependent variable (left-hand side of the equation), which is the variable to be explained, and one or more independent variables, the explanatory variables. The dependent variable is the Y variable, and the independent variables are the X variables. Linear regression determines a model of best fit based upon the data given in relating the explanatory variables to the dependent variable. A linear regression model output in

R provides the coefficients for the independent variables, their standard errors, their t value (coefficient divided by its standard error), and the associated probability value of the t value in terms of statistical significance.

The coefficient can be interpreted as, all else equal, how the independent variable influences the dependent variable. The first key element of the coefficient is the sign. A positive sign means that the independent and dependent variable have a positive relationship (move together), while a negative sign means they have a negative relationship (move apart). A simple rule of thumb for statistical significance is to look for t values of 2 or more in absolute value. Although this rule of thumb is handy, the output in R provides the exact level of statistical significance in its last column of numerical output, which is also accompanied by *-notation, which shows statistical significance. A single * represents statistical significance at the 5% level (or less), while ** is at the 1% level and *** at the 0.1% level.

The simple model presented here provides a testing of the concept of market efficiency in the daily fantasy marketplace. The efficient markets hypothesis assumes that all available information is incorporated into the current price of an asset. The asset in the case of the daily fantasy marketplace for the NBA is the player. The price of the asset is the salary for the daily fantasy game posted on the website. Under the weak form of market efficiency, all past information should be included in the current price of an asset. Semi-strong form market efficiency expands upon this and includes current news as a factor that should be included in the current price of an asset.

Under the null hypothesis of market efficiency, the daily fantasy salary of a player should incorporate all factors relevant to his performance for that day. Simple and recognizable factors that are well known to influence performance should be fully reflected in the daily fantasy salaries of the players. Therefore, the player salary is included in the regression model as an independent variable. Other factors included as independent variables in this example include home court advantage and opponent. These variables are dummy variables. A dummy variable is binary in nature. It takes a value of one if yes, zero if no. The way R classifies a series of dummy variables is to use the first alphabetically as the reference category. When including dummy variables in a regression model with an intercept, one category must be dropped or there will be the so-called "dummy variable trap" where the regression is perfectly specified and cannot be run. The reference category could be any of the series of complete dummy variable categories and all other results are compared to the reference category. The null hypotheses under market efficiency is that the coefficient on the home dummy should be zero and the coefficients on the opponent dummies should jointly be zero.

Below is the code used in R to run a simple regression model based upon daily fantasy salaries and points scored for DraftKings. Each line of code is preceded by comments noting the purpose and function of each.

```
> # Read file
> NBA_DK <- read.csv("Draftkings_NBA.csv")
> # change scientific notation output
> options(scipen = 999)
> # model - Dependent: Points on Draft Kings; Independent: Salary on
Draft Kings, Home/Away Dummy, Opponent Dummies
> NBA_DK_Model <- lm(formula = DKP ~ DK.Sal + H.A + Opp, data=NBA_DK)
> # printout of regression model results
> summary(NBA_DK_Model)

Call:
lm(formula = DKP ~ DK.Sal + H.A + Opp, data = NBA_DK)

Residuals:
    Min      1Q  Median      3Q     Max
-74.132  -8.057  -0.876   6.645  64.875

Coefficients:
               Estimate  Std. Error  t value           Pr(>|t|)
(Intercept) -9.23566046  0.18403124  -50.185 < 0.0000000000000002 ***
DK.Sal       0.00604230  0.00001641  368.250 < 0.0000000000000002 ***
H.AH         0.56881613  0.06006545    9.470 < 0.0000000000000002 ***
Oppbkn      -0.23040425  0.23492120   -0.981             0.326707
Oppbos      -0.83101549  0.23036300   -3.607             0.000309 ***
Oppcha      -0.45895889  0.23535809   -1.950             0.051173 .
Oppchi      -0.28301407  0.23544892   -1.202             0.229359
Oppcle      -0.49048540  0.23178537   -2.116             0.034337 *
Oppdal      -1.07133395  0.23469772   -4.565        0.0000050060338 ***
Oppden      -0.54803850  0.23334512   -2.349             0.018845 *
Oppdet      -1.08442199  0.23583144   -4.598        0.0000042639537 ***
Oppgsw      -0.52581528  0.22887800   -2.297             0.021600 *
Opphou      -0.45365766  0.23049307   -1.968             0.049047 *
Oppind      -0.89515928  0.23223784   -3.854             0.000116 ***
Opplac      -0.72472189  0.23351617   -3.104             0.001913 **
Opplal      -0.18429107  0.23549425   -0.783             0.433880
Oppmem      -0.99851075  0.23458176   -4.257        0.0000207753842 ***
Oppmia      -1.15755571  0.23360453   -4.955        0.0000007235502 ***
Oppmil      -0.42063940  0.23338824   -1.802             0.071498 .
Oppmin      -0.62087281  0.23492132   -2.643             0.008221 **
Oppnor       0.05217275  0.23474301    0.222             0.824116
Oppnyk      -0.64001241  0.23698647   -2.701             0.006922 **
Oppokc      -0.60424085  0.23170451   -2.608             0.009114 **
Opporl      -0.56454766  0.23480329   -2.404             0.016203 *
Oppphi      -0.34544578  0.23303275   -1.482             0.138239
Opppho      -0.07249102  0.23480185   -0.309             0.757525
Opppor      -0.66038925  0.23207284   -2.846             0.004433 **
```

```
Oppsac     -0.52805585   0.23525165   -2.245              0.024793  *
Oppsas     -1.17161012   0.23155756   -5.060     0.0000004205418  ***
Opptor     -0.94462427   0.23033792   -4.101     0.0000411570364  ***
Opputa     -1.54847417   0.23229526   -6.666     0.0000000000264  ***
Oppwas     -0.33544193   0.23363170   -1.436              0.151070
---
Signif. codes:  0 '***' 0.001 '**' 0.01 '*' 0.05 '.' 0.1 ' ' 1

Residual standard error: 10.48 on 121640 degrees of freedom
Multiple R-squared:  0.5278, Adjusted R-squared:  0.5276
F-statistic:  4385 on 31 and 121640 DF,  p-value: <
0.00000000000000022
```

The regression model results reveal that the market for setting salaries on DraftKings is not efficient in that it does not incorporate all information about player performance into the prices in the marketplace. While the posted salary for a player on DraftKings has a positive and statistically significant effect on points earned by the player, it does not fully account for other factors known in advance to influence player performance. For instance, the dummy variable for the player playing at home (H.AH) has a coefficient of approximately 0.569 and is statistically significant at the 0.1% level. This reveals that the simple situation of playing at home will yield an additional half-point-plus in points earned by that player on the average. Therefore, the home court advantage is not fully priced into daily salaries on the website. In addition, the inclusion of dummy variables for the opponent, with the first team alphabetically, the Atlanta Hawks, as the reference category, reveals various opponents where a player will score more or fewer points, that is again not fully factored into the daily salaries. Atlanta just happened to have opposed players score the most fantasy points against them in this sample as all the individual team dummy variable coefficients were negative compared to Atlanta. All else equal, relative to the Hawks, some teams prevented fantasy scoring against them at rather sizable magnitudes. Utah (uta), San Antonio (sas), Miami (mia), Detroit (det), and Dallas (dal) all allowed more than a point fewer per game, on the average, for fantasy opposing players (each was found to be statistically significant at the 0.1% level). Other teams were also found to generate statistically significant results at the 5% level or less, resulting in players scoring fewer points against these teams. This again suggests a simple strategy for daily fantasy players to pay attention to the defensive prowess of a player's opponent as it is not fully priced into the daily salaries in the game.

Beyond this simple model, it is easy to envision testing other factors which also may influence player scoring that may not be fully integrated into daily salaries. Factors such as rest (pretty straightforward to calculate by observing the difference in dates between games), travel distance (creating a matrix of travel distances from NBA city to city), streakiness (previous game performance or some measure of exceeding or not meeting expectations), and any other factor that can be estimated can be included in the model and tested. Any inefficiencies can then be built into optimizing lineups given the value built into various circumstances surrounding individual games.

Although some factors, such as the dummy variables for opponent, can be somewhat unappealing and noisy to visualize, the results surrounding the home court advantage for players in daily fantasy games can be shown rather simply in a chart. The following code in R uses ggplot2 to make a simple plot of salary vs performance for all players in the sample. The plot is assigned to p1. DK.Sal (player salary) is assigned to the X-axis and DKP (points) is assigned to the vertical axis. Colors of the points on the chart are separated into red and teal (default colors), with red representing a player who is playing in a game on the road, while the teal points show players playing at home. The chart includes a linear trend for each group (away and home) and is included in the chart through the stat_smooth function. In this case, a linear trend is chosen (method=lm) and the standard error bands are suppressed (se=FALSE). The R code and visualization of the data is shown below.

```
> # Use ggplot2 for visualization
> library(ggplot2)
> # assign plot with DK Salary on X-axis, DK Points on Y-axis, and
H/A as color
> p1 <- ggplot(NBA_DK, aes(x=DK.Sal, y=DKP, color=H.A))
> # show plot with linear trend lines for Home and Away
> p1 + geom_point() + stat_smooth(method=lm, se=FALSE)
```

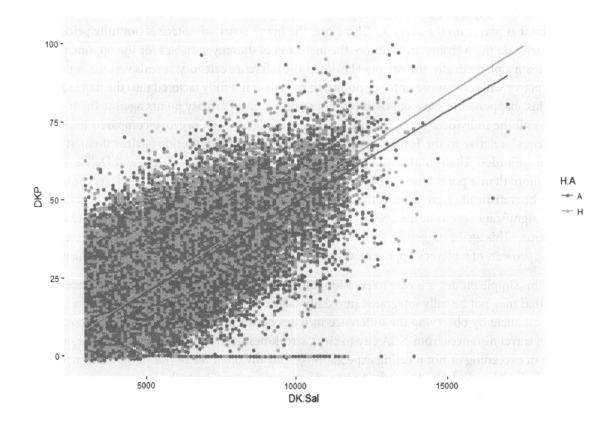

The plot shows the relationship between posted salaries on DraftKings and Points Earned by each NBA player. Red represents players who were away from home, while teal represents players that played at home. The teal trend line lies above the red trend line. This shows that players generally score more daily fantasy points at home, rather than on the road, and that the salaries of players do not fully reflect this. If daily fantasy salaries were priced efficiently, this should not be the case. In an efficient market, the salary of the player who is playing at home would be higher than if the player were playing on the road, by the exact amount to reflect the higher scoring that is expected to occur when that player plays on their home court. In other words, if the salaries were efficient in this marketplace, the trend lines shown should be the same as the home court advantage would be fully reflected in the daily salaries posted on the website. Since they are not, selecting players at home, rather than on the road, offers a slight advantage in roster construction as playing at home results in over a half-point more on average per player than when playing on the road.

A major question arises as to why daily fantasy markets can reject market efficiency with easily identifiable factors such as home court advantage leading to higher scores than players' salaries would imply. One potential rationale is that price setters for daily fantasy games do not realize the importance of these factors. This argument is highly suspect as knowledge of home court advantage has been known and discussed for a long time and home court advantages are consistently built into betting point spreads and odds on games. A second potential reason could be the economic argument of menu costs, meaning that it is costly to change the price on an item once set, but given the electronic nature of posting prices on the website and that the prices are generated by an algorithm, this also seems highly unlikely.

A more plausible story as to why inefficiencies exist in the daily fantasy marketplace is that the price setters purposefully do not adjust all prices for these easily recognizable factors. They may do this for two reasons, one from a legal perspective and the other from a consumption perspective. On the legal side, if daily fantasy were to be treated as gambling it could be deemed illegal in certain jurisdictions. Whether this sort of activity is classified legally as gambling may depend upon this being deemed a game of chance or a game of skill (like poker). If the market were efficient and prices perfectly reflected all available information, winners would essentially be random, and this would purely be a game of luck. On the other hand, if certain simple strategies can be illustrated to outperform others, then the contest becomes one of skill rather than pure luck (although luck is obviously still important as player performance is highly volatile). The other reason the market may not be efficient is that participants enjoy searching for winning strategies and spending time contemplating and building their lineups. Without returns to skill of selecting players, the contests may eventually become less interesting and participation, and profits for the companies offering the games, may fall. In any case, the market for daily fantasy does not appear to be perfectly efficient; therefore, using statistical analysis to analyze and forecast player performance may not only be enjoyable, but it could lead to better performance in daily fantasy contests.

Summary

If anything, the COVID-19 pandemic in 2020 showed that the future of sports gambling and fantasy sports markets is mobile. As mentioned in the introduction, New Jersey in November 2020 generated $872.1 million that came from online betting, and only $60 million from retail (Mulligan 2020). While people will eventually return to casinos and sportsbooks again, the ease with which mobile sites now allows individuals to bet on sports is not going to be replaced by a trip to the casino.

Besides going mobile, bookmakers also continue looking for more ways to generate bets from the public by offering interesting proposition "prop" bets that relate to individual games and players. The diversity of offerings of prop bets, which was once primarily the domain of Super Bowl betting, will extend to more games and sports. In addition, the duration of prop bets will likely continue to fall as bets will be made for shorter time periods including quarter-by-quarter, period-by-period, inning-by-inning, and even getting down to individual possessions or plays. Mobile technology is going to allow betters to keep continuously involved and betting multiple times during a single game.

In daily fantasy sports, companies already offer shorter-term offerings (i.e., first and second half individual contests in football) and more styles of play. What will be interesting to follow, however, is whether DFS will continue to grow as options to bet on games become legal in more states and its' ease rivals that of DFS. Whether seeing a less profitable future for DFS, are just wanting to expand into the sports betting market the two biggest DFS companies FanDuel and DraftKings are now major players in the sports betting market.

Key Terms

Daily Fantasy Sports (DFS)	Point Shaving
DraftKings	Betting Odds
Match Fixing	Prop Betting
Point Spread	Teaser Bets
Money Line betting	Unlawful Internet Gambling Enforcement Act
Parlay Bets	(UIGEA)
Rotisserie League	Professional and Amateur Sports Protection Act
Sportsbooks	(PASPA)

Critical Thinking Exercises

1. Why would gamblers prefer line or spread betting over straight odds betting?
2. Before the Supreme Court overturned PASPA, there was a debate within many states over whether fantasy sports, and in particular daily fantasy sports, was a game of skill (not illegal gambling) or a game of chance (illegal gambling), what is your opinion?

3. When betting, if you want to limit your risk is it better to bet to win or bet to risk? Please explain why?
4. What is meant by the bet 11 to win 10 rule?
5. What are some of the variables that would help in fielding a winning DraftKings team?

References

American Gaming Association. 2020. *Interactive Map: Sports Betting in the U.S.* (2020). https://www.americangaming.org/research/state-gaming-map/

Appelbaum, J. 2019. *How Does a Parlay Work in Sports Betting.* Action Network. https://www.actionnetwork.com/how-to-bet-on-sports/general/why-sports-bettors-should-avoid-parlays

Appelbaum, J. 2020. "Why Sports Bettors Should Bet to Risk, Not to Win." *The New York Post.* August 31.

Barbarisi, Daniel. 2017. *Dueling with Kings: High Stakes, Killer Sharks, and the get Rick Promise of Daily Fantasy Sports.* New York: Touchstone.

Boyle, R. H. 1986. "The Brain that gave use the Point Spread." *Sports Illustrated.* March 10.

Chang, Y-M., and Sanders, S. 2009. "Corruption on the court: The causes and social consequences of point-shaving in NCAA basketball." *Review of Law and Economics* 5, 269–291.

Chen, Albert. 2019. *Billion Dollar Fantasy: The High Stakes Game Between FanDual & DraftKings that Upended Sports in America.* Boston: Houghton Mifflin Harcourt.

Davies, Richard, and Richard Abram. 2012. *Betting the Line: Sports Wagering in American Life.* Columbus: Ohio State University Press.

Fantasy Sports & Gaming Association. 2020. Industry Demographics. https://thefsga.org/industry-demographics/

Humphreys, Brad, Rodney J. Paul, and Andrew P. Weinbach. 2013. Consumption benefits and gambling: Evidence from the NCAA basketball betting market. *Journal of Economic Psychology* 39, 376–386.

Caspian Kang, Jay. 2016. How the Daily Fantasy Sports Industry Turns Fans into Suckers. *The New York Times.* January 6.

Levitt, Steven D. (December 2002). How do Markets Function? An Empirical Analysis of Gambling on the National Football League. *National Bureau of Economic Research.* Working Paper 9422. http://www.nber.org/papers/w9422

Levitt, Steven D. 2004 Why are gambling markets organized so differently from financial markets? *The Economic Journal* 114(495), 223–246.

McKinsey & Company. 2015. *For daily fantasy-sports operators, the curse of too much skill.* September 1. https://www.mckinsey.com/industries/technology-media-and-telecommunications/our-insights/for-daily-fantasy-sports-operators-the-curse-of-too-much-skill

Mulligan, Richard. 2020. *New Jersey sports betting handle passes $900m in November.* IGB (December 15). https://igamingbusiness.com/new-jersey-sports-betting-handle-passes-900m-in-november/

Newman, Nico. 2020. *History of fantasy sports.* Fantasy-Sports.net. (April 14). https://fantasy-sport.net/history-of-fantasy-sports/

Paul, Rodney J., and Andrew P. Weinbach. 2008. Price setting in the NBA gambling market: Tests of the levitt model of sportsbook behavior. *International Journal of Sport Finance*, 3 (3), 2–18.

Paul, Rodney J., and Andrew P. Weinbach. 2009. Sportsbook behavior in the NCAA football betting market: Tests of the traditional and levitt models of sportsbook behavior. *Journal of Prediction Markets* 3(2), 21–37.

Paul, Rodney J., and Andrew P. Weinbach. 2011. Bettor biases and price setting by sportsbooks in the NFL: Further tests of the Levitt hypothesis of sportsbook behavior. *Applied Economics Letters 18(2), 193–197.*

Sauer, Raymond D., Vic Brajer, Stephen P. Ferris, and M. Wayne Marr. 1988. Hold your bets: Another look at the efficiency of the gambling market for national football league games." *Journal of Political Economy* 96(1), 206–213.

Silverman, Michael. 2020. *How do NFL oddsmakers set point spreads in a COVID-riddled season?* Boston Globe. (October15). https://www.bostonglobe.com/2020/10/15/sports/how-do-nfl-oddsmakers-set-point-spreads-covid-riddled-season/

Tango, Tom. 2004. *Marcel The Monkey Forecasting System.* Tangotiger .net (2004). http://www.tangotiger.net/archives/stud0346.shtml

Vinton, Nathaniel. 2009. *How fantasy became reality: Rotisserie's rise from Yoo-Hoo showers to Yahoo! Dollars.* Daily News. (March 29). https://www.nydailynews.com/sports/baseball/fantasy-reality-rotisserie-rise-yoo-hoo-showers-yahoo-dollars-article-1.371889

Winston, Wayne L. 2009. *Mathletics: How Gamblers, Managers, and Sport Enthusiasts Use Mathematics in Baseball, Basketball, and Football.* Princeton, NJ: Princeton University Press.

Wolfers, Justin. 2006. "Point shaving: Corruption in NCAA basketball." *The American economic review* 96(2), 279–283.

Wolohan, John. 2018. *How legal sports betting could benefit the pro leagues.* Fortune. http://fortune.com/2018/05/21/supreme-court-sports-betting-legal-leagues/

Wolohan, John. 2020. *Sports Gambling.* Chapter in Doyice Cotten & John Wolohan. *Law for Recreation and Sport Managers* (8th ed.). Dubuque, IA: Kendall Hunt.

VIXIO Gambling Compliance. 2020. *Get Ahead of the Game: U.S. Sports Betting Tracker.* VIXIO Gambling Compliance. (September).

Zuber, Richard A., John M. Gandar, and. Benny D. Bowers. 1985. Beating the spread: Testing the efficiency of the gambling market for national football league games. *Journal of Political Economy* 96(1), 206–213.

CASES

C.B.C. Distribution v. Major League Baseball Advanced Media, 505 F.3d 818 (8th. Cir, 2007).
Murphy v. National Collegiate Athletic Association (NCAA), 138 U.S. 1461 (2018).

LEGISLATION

Professional and Amateur Sports Protection Act, 28 U.S.C. §3701, et. seq.
Unlawful Internet Gambling Enforcement Act, 31 U.S.C. §5362

CHAPTER 16

Legal and Ethical Considerations

John Wolohan

LEARNING OBJECTIVES

After reading this chapter, students should be able to:

- Provide a working definition of the term Athlete Biometric Data (ABD).
- Identify some of the legal issues involved with player data.
- Identify some of the ethical issues involved with player data, especially medical data.
- Identify some of the considerations when collecting professional athletes' biometric data compared to college athletes.
- What role should the players' unions play in the collection of Athlete Biometric Data?

Introduction

As illustrated in this book, over the last 20 years analytics have increasingly controlled larger parts of our lives. As analytics become more ingrained in every type of business, it was not surprising that their use has moved into the areas of sports. If there is one thing more ingrained in our daily lives than analytics; however, it is the law. Therefore, while this book has so far addressed how analytics are being used in individual sports and sports business, this chapter focuses on how analytics intersects with the law. In particular, the chapter explores the legal and ethical issues of using Athlete Biometric Data (ABD) and what rights the players, teams, leagues, and product suppliers have to the data.

Before moving on, however, a brief word on what is not covered in this chapter. Since the text is designed for students interested in sports analytics, not the practice of law, the chapter does not cover the growing use of analytics in the practice law. Lex Machina, the practice of using big data, predictive analytics, and machine learning to help lawyers with legal decisions and strategies, is overhauling the legal profession. Lawyers are increasingly using analytics to track patterns and *take a* more data-based approach to their decision-making. Analytics are being used to help lawyers build legal strategies that predicts the success rate of a specific motion in specific courts and judges, the potential monetary award value of certain claims, and whether to settle a case or go to trial. However, while this area is interesting, the authors have agreed that Lex Machina is probably a topic for a book on analytics and the law.

Collection and Use of Athletes' Biometric Data (ABD)

The first wearable technology device used to collect biometric data was developed in 2006 when Nike and Apple partnered to launch the Nike + iPod, an activity tracking device that allowed consumers to measure and record their running or walking distance, time, and pace through a sensor embedded in your shoe (Jessop and Baker 2019). Today, it is common for recreational, college, and professional athletes to have their every move recorded with some form of wearable technology or video analysis to quantify the many factors that influence performance, such as training load, recovery, and establishing early-warning signals that stop athletes from overtraining, which often results in injury (Marr 2016).

Once collected, the athlete's data can be analyzed at an individual level to create an individual profile, or it can be aggregated across the population (team) to develop another insight into injuries and treatment patterns (Marr 2016). A good example of how analytics can improve athlete performance is the USA Women's Olympic cycling team at the 2012 London Olympics (Taylor 2015). Before the 2012 Olympics, the women's cycling team had not won a medal in 20 years. With no real expectations for the 2012 Olympics, in preparation for the games the team started collecting and recording athletes' blood glucose levels and blood oxygen saturation with medical devices. In addition, the athletes filmed, tracked, and analyzed brain waves during sleep, and even sequenced their DNA (Taylor 2015). Using the data collected to improve their training, the women's cycling team went on to win the silver medal at the 2012 Olympics.

Athlete Biometric Data (ABD) has been defined as "a measurable and distinguishable physical characteristic or personal behavioral trait used to recognize one's identity, including but not limited to name, nicknames, likeness, signatures, pictures, activities, voice, statistics, playing and performance records, achievements, indicia, data, and other information identifying a particular athlete" (Gale 2016). The use of biometric data and medical information in the sports industry is not new. Teams have historically collected a wide variety of data, including cardiac and respiratory related data like heart rate, breathing rate, and blood pressure and blood sample analysis for various health reasons and for drug testing (Osborne 2017). Today's athletes are being monitored more than ever.

The collection of all this information, beside improving athletic performance, can also have a darker side. One of the most public examples of the misuse of athletes' data is the Texas Tech Women's Basketball program under coach Marlene Stollings. Stollings used the results of the wearable heart rate monitors that she required all players to wear during every practice, game, and workout to punish players whose heart rate dropped below 90% capacity for more than two minutes of game time (Epstein and Libit 2020). Players who did not meet the 90% requirement had their playing time reduced and were required to do extra conditioning drills. As a result of the emphasis on maintaining an elevated heart rate, at least two players began using over-the-counter drugs to keep their heart rates up. Stollings abuse of the players was so bad that 12 players transferred out of Texas Tech in the two years she was coach there. While Stollings was fired in 2020 after a USA Today story in which her players likened her methods and use of analytics as "basically a torture mechanism," it is difficult to believe that she is the only coach misusing player data (Epstein and Libit 2020).

As illustrated by the Texas Tech and USA Women's Cycling Team cases above, using wearable technologies and video, teams and organizations can monitor and collect ABD during every practice, game, and sleep, ranging from a player's physical fitness, stamina, and heart rate to body temperature and whether he/she is suffering from any nagging and/or reoccurring injuries (Garlewicz 2020). It is hoped that by creating individual profiles and grouping them together to discover similar profiles, teams can increase player performance, create a competitive advantage, improve the fan experience, or generate new revenue streams (Brown and Brison 2020). Teams also collect biometric data to establish biometric baseline for the athletes to design appropriate training programs, prevent and monitor injuries, and improve injury rehabilitation (Osborne 2017).

The collection of all this biometric data, however, raises some serious legal and ethical questions. For example, while athletes have always surrendered some degree of personal privacy, such as medical information, the use wearables allows teams to collect biometric data that is beyond what is collected from an athlete's physical (Brown and Brison 2020). This is especially true when teams mandate that athletes to wear devices 24 hours a day that can track their activities and GPS. Since this type of data goes well beyond the athlete's health and moves into the athlete's private life, it is critical for there to be a clear understanding of the intended purpose of the data collection.

Current Federal and State Laws

With these legal and ethical questions in mind, teams and organizations need to be aware of current federal and state laws concerning the collection and sharing of health information. The general rule in the United States is that businesses are permitted to collect personal information, including health information (Determann 2020). There are, however, exceptions to the general rule. As of 2021, four states, Illinois, Texas, Washington, and California, have laws regulating the collection of biometric data. None of the four states regulate data collected by wearable technology.

The Illinois Biometric Information Privacy Act, passed in 2008, defines a "biometric identifier as a retina or iris scan, fingerprint, voiceprint, or scan of hand or face geometry" (Illinois Biometric Information Privacy Act, 740 ILCS 14/10). The law, however, does not cover "information captured from a patient in a health care setting, ... information collected, used, or stored for health care treatment, or X-ray or film of the human anatomy used to diagnose, prognose, or treat an illness or other medical condition or to further validate scientific testing or screening" (Illinois Biometric Information Privacy Act, 740 ILCS 14/10).

The Texas law, the "Capture or Use of Biometric Identifier," which went into effect in 2009, defines "biometric identifier" as a retina or iris scan, fingerprint, voiceprint, or record of hand or face geometry and prohibits the collection of such identifiers for a commercial purpose without informed consent (Texas Business and Commerce Code § 503.001). The Washington biometric law, which was signed into effect in 2017, regulates the way individuals and non-government entities collect, store, and use biometric identifiers. Washington's prohibits the "automatic measurements of an individual's biological characteristics, such as a fingerprint, voiceprint, eye retinas, irises, or other unique biological patterns or characteristics that is used to identify a specific individual" without prior consent. Biometric identifier, however, do not include "information collected, used, or stored for health care treatment" (Washington, RCW 19.375.010). The primary difference between Washington and Illinois is that it does not provide a private right of action in its law.

While broader in scope than the other three, the California Consumer Privacy Act (CCPA), which went into effect in 2018, requires employers to comply with requirements about the collection, storage, and use of employee information, which includes biometric information (California Consumer Privacy Act 1798.1000 (v) (1) (e)). In particular, the California law requires any "business that controls the collection of a consumer's personal information shall, at or before the point of collection, inform consumers ... of personal information to be collected and the purposes for which the categories of personal information are collected or used and whether that information is sold or shared" (California Consumer Privacy Act 1798.1000 (a) (1)).

At the federal level, personal health information (PHI) is protected under the Health Insurance Portability and Accountability Act (HIPAA), which governs the collection, use, dissemination, and protection of individually identifiable health information created, received, maintained, or transmitted for covered entities and their business associates for the purpose of providing health care (Gale 2016). However, HIPPA, like the state laws, only regulates biometric data when it is collected by health care providers as part of an individual's health care. Otherwise, HIPPA does not regulate its collection. Therefore, for a professional athlete's biometric data to be protected under HIPPA it must be collected and deemed as part of the athlete's PHI (Gale 2016).

Another problem with trying to apply HIPAA to professional athletes' biometric data is that the official guidance provided by the Department of Health and Human Services (HHS) notes that professional sports teams were unlikely to be covered entities that would need to abide by HIPAA privacy rules (Osborne 2017). Further, HHS noted that even if teams were to be covered, it is fully within the right of the employer to "make an employee's agreement to disclose health records a condition of employment" (Osborne 2017). As a result, the leagues can simply compel players to disclose PHI (waive HIPAA privacy) and subsume the information into the employment record of each player. The NFL CBA, for example, says that players must agree to disclosure of their relevant HIPAA information. Once part of the employment record, the contents of the record are no longer protected under HIPPA (Osborne 2017).

The protection of biometric data is also important to recreational athletes. With the increased use of personal health devices and mobile tracking applications like Fitbit that collect, track, and disseminate biometric data, the security and privacy of the data collected should be of importance to everyone using such a device (Gale 2016). For example, in 2020 Amazon introduce the "Halo" activity tracker. In addition to just tracking the user's health and activity data, Halo also tracks sleep patterns and comes with a built-in microphone that records user's conversations 24 hours a day (Romano 2020). The user's data, including voice, sleep, and health, is then stored on Amazon's internal servers. Although Amazon has promised to never sell the data, the fact that a trillion-dollar business wants to record your conversations 24/7, as well as track your health and activity data, has drawn comparisons to dystopian science fiction classics like "Terminator" and "The Metrix" where computers run the world (Romano 2020).

Even if Amazon does nothing with the data, health insurance companies are now offering policy holders free devices, Halo, Fitbits, and other trackers, in exchange for sharing their sleep, heart rate, and activity data. If this data sharing were to become widespread within the insurance industry, an individual's data may become a key factor in how much the individual pays for insurance or whether they can even get insurance at all.

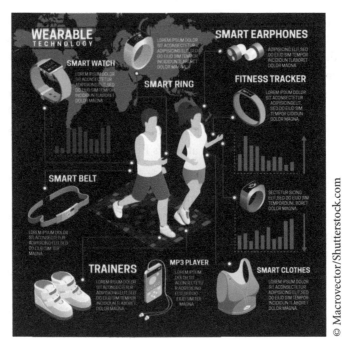

Wearable technology

Who Has the Rights to Use Player Medical Data?

Analytics and the use of algorithms are already developing and spreading rapidly into the world of medicine as doctors use greater amounts of personal information to tailor treatments to individual patients. This use of large datasets with sophisticated predictive algorithms to identify complex connections between multiple patient characteristics to make decisions related to health care is called "Blackbox medicine" (Price 2015). The use of Blackbox medicine has been hailed as the next step in health care because it is believed that this type of individual or personalized medicine can save and extend lives by suggesting more effective treatments, while at the same time reducing the cost and risk of unnecessary medical interventions (Price 2015).

With all this patient information being collected and analyzed, it is important to identify who has the right to access the player's medical data and what type of medical information is protected? For example, the way athletes' injuries are discussed on sports talk radio, online, and on television, you would think that an athletes' personal medical data is public information and readily shareable. However, while it may be reasonable for a sports radio host to comment in the abstract about an athlete's injury, those treating the injured athlete are required under HIPAA and various state laws to protect the athlete's private medical data. However, as noted above, the laws do not provide a lot of protection for ABD. Therefore, professional sports leagues and athletes have begun negotiating the protection of player data under the collective bargaining agreement.

Collective Bargaining Agreements (CBA)

With no clear protection of biometric data at the federal level, professional athletes and teams have started to take steps to impose protections for ABD through the collective bargaining process. A collective bargaining agreement (CBA) is a contract between the league and the players over the terms and conditions of employment within the league. Generally, in professional sports the CBA addresses issues ranging from drug testing, minimum salaries, and free agency to and anything else that can affect the athlete's employment. In the latest set of CBAs, one of the major bargaining issue between the players' associations and owners has been the collection, security, and ownership of biometric data, as well as privacy and commercialization of data. The following section looks at how the various professional leagues and the players' associations have addressed the ABD issue.

National Basketball Association (NBA)

The NBA's current CBA, which runs from 2017 until 2024, outlines a set of rules governing the use of wearables. According to the CBA, "Wearables" shall mean a device worn by an individual that measures movement information (such as distance, velocity, acceleration, deceleration, jumps, changes of direction, and player load calculated from such information and/or height/weight), biometric information (such as heart rate, heart rate variability, skin temperature, blood oxygen, hydration, lactate, and/or glucose), or other health, fitness, and performance information" (NBA CBA Section 13. (a), 2017). Under the agreement teams are only allowed to request players wear ABD devices in practice, not in games, and players have the right to decline. In addition, before a team can even request that a player use a wearable, it must "provide the player a written, confidential explanation of: (i) what the device will measure; (ii) what each such measurement means; and (iii) the benefits to the player in obtaining such data" (NBA CBA Section 13. (g), 2017).

While the CBA grants players "full access to all data collected on him … the data collected may be used for player health and performance purposes and Team on-court tactical and strategic purposes only" (NBA CBA, Article XXII, Section 13. (h), 2017). According to the CBA, however, the data cannot "be considered, used, discussed, or referenced for any other purpose such as in negotiations regarding a future Player Contract or other Player Contract transaction (e.g., a trade or waiver) involving the player" (NBA CBA, Article XXII, Section 13. (h), 2017). Finally, the CBA states that "no player data collected from a Wearable worn at the request of a Team may be made available to the public in any way or used for any commercial purpose" (NBA CBA, Article XXII, Section 13 (i), 2017).

Since data collection and use of ABD can sometimes cross an ethical line, it is important that teams and athletes have strategies and structures in place to prevent that from happening. One of the best ways to do that is to establish some sort of data ethics committee. Although not unique, the NBA's CBA mandates that "the NBA and the Players Association form a joint advisory committee (the "Wearables Committee") to review and approve wearable devices for use by players" (NBA CBA

Section 13. (a), 2017). These ethics committees are going to be increasingly important as leagues and teams continue to expand the type of biometric data they collect and sell. In addition, with the speed in which wearable technology is evolving, these committees can help the league and the players keep up to date with technological changes and privacy protocols.

Major League Baseball (MLB)

MLB's CBA, which runs to 2021, also covers wearable technology. As part of the CBA there is a letter between the union and the Commissioner's office which states that:

> "any use of a wearable technology by a Player (including use on-field, off-field and/or away from the ballpark) shall be wholly voluntary and that before a Player can voluntarily agree to use a wearable technology, the Club must first provide the Player a written explanation of the technology being proposed, along with a list of the Club representatives who will have access to the information and data collected, generated, stored and/or analyzed the Wearable Data" (MLB CBA, Attachment 56, 2017).

According to the CBA, all the player's "Wearable Data shall be treated as highly confidential at all times" … "shall not become a part of the Player's medical record," and shall not be disclosed without the express written consent of the Players' Association (MLB CBA, Attachment 56, 2017). In addition, if requested by the player, all the player's data must be destroyed by the club.

Like the NBA, MLB's CBA requires that the league and the Players' Association establish a Joint Committee on Wearable Technology ("JCWT") that will meet twice a year to review the potential use of any new wearable technology in games or pre-game activities and make recommendation regarding whether to approve such technology. In addition, the JCWT examines player safety, data management, privacy and confidentiality, and any other topics that are deemed relevant by two or more members of the Committee (MLB CBA, Attachment 56, 2017).

National Football League (NFL)

The NFL's CBA, which runs until 2030, requires that the NFL and NFLPA establish a "Joint Sensors Committee" made of three members from the league and three members from the union, none of whom may not have an ownership or other financial interest in any company that produces or sells any Sensor, to review and approve Sensors for NFL and Club use (NFL CBA 2020). Since 2013, as part of its Next Gen Stats sports statistics program, the NFL has been working with Zebra Technologies to insert nickel-sized radio-frequency identification (RFID) sensors in the footballs and the players' shoulder pads to measure and track their location, speed, and distance traveled.

The NFL CBA requires that all NFL players wear sensors during all practices and games. Sensors are defined as "any device worn by an individual player used to collect, monitor, measure or track any metric from a player, biometric information, or other health, fitness and performance information" (NFL CBA 2020). If the league wants to collect any data from players outside of NFL games or practices (e.g., Sleep Studies) if must get advance approval from the NFLPA (NFL CBA 2020).

Unlike the other leagues, the NFL's CBA allows the league to "use data concerning players' performance and movements collected from Zebra Sensors during NFL games commercially, including but not limited to, with broadcast partners, as long as the league provides advance notice to the NFLPA of such use" (NFL CBA 2020). The NFL hopes that this new data will not only improve the broadcast experience, but also enhance fan engagement as well as provide an additional resource for coaches and trainers and create additional revenue streams for the owners and athletes.

Even though the CBA allows the NFL to use the data, the CBA also clearly states that "each individual player owns his personal data collected by Sensors and wearing Sensors shall not require or cause an individual player to transfer ownership of his data to the Club or any other third-party" (NFL CBA 2020). Players may not, however, use data collected from approved Sensors for any commercial purpose. Nor may any data collected from Sensors be referenced or cited by any Club, player, or player's representative in contract negotiations (NFL CBA 2020).

National Hockey League (NHL)

Not all professional sports leagues have specifically addressed the question of biometric data, however. For example, the NHL's CBA or the detailed Memorandum of Understanding (MOU), which extended the CBA until 2026, does not mention the use of wearable technology or any athlete tracking device (NHL CBA, 2013). However, while the CBA may be silent on wearables, the NHL CBA does provide guidance on the player's electronic medical records. In particular, the CBA states that "Clubs shall be required to input and cause the input of the types of medical and/or health records agreed upon, and reviewed annually by, the Joint Health & Safety Committee into the Athlete Health Management System or its equivalent ("AHMS")." The NHL and teams are also required to maintain any electronic medical and/or health records in a secure, centralized system such as the AHMS (NHL CBA 34.3 (b) Medical Information (i) 2013). The NHL CBA also provides a detailed list of when clubs, the League, and the NHLPA may use and disclose a player's medical information "without the express, prior, written consent of the Player or as required by law" (NHL CBA 34.3 (c) Disclosure of Medical Information (I - X) 2013).

While not addressed in the CBA, the NHL introduced the Puck and Player Tracking system for the 2019–2020 season. Besides the equipment needed in the arenas, the tracking system also requires one sensor placed on the shoulder pads of every player on each team and in each puck. This will allow the league and teams to track every movement of the puck and each team's players during a game. The system will have the ability to track the players at 200 times per second. Like the other leagues, the NHL hopes that the data collected will enhance the fan experience inside the arena and for those watching on television, via mobile devices or, in some cases, both with a digital stream broadcast dedicated to showcasing puck and player data (Gulitti 2020).

Women's National Basketball Association (WNBA)

Beginning with the 2020 CBA, which runs until 2027, the WNBA and the WNBA Players Association agreed "that use of wearables and other in-game technology provides a unique opportunity to the WNBA with respect to enhanced broadcasts, differentiated fan experiences, player health and revenue generation and will work together to develop a comprehensive policy regarding wearables and other in-game technologies" (WNBA CBA, Section 13. Wearables, 2020). For the 2020 season, WNBA players could opt-in to a voluntary program between the WNBA and Oura in which the players would wear an Oura Ring and track daily biometric such as increased body temperature, heart rate variability, resting heart rate, respiratory rate, and sleep and activity patterns. Oura Rings can measure body temperature directly from the skin.

Major League Soccer (MLS)

At the time this chapter went to press, the new MLS CBA running from 2020 to 2025 was unavailable to the public. However, the old CBA which ran from 2015 to 2020 stated that the league or team medical staff may require a player to wear "any physiological monitoring device" in connection with training throughout the pre-season and season, if the device does not to impede the player's performance (MLS CBA, Section 9.10, 2015). The metrics collected include GPS tracking such things as distance covered, speed, as well as biometric data such as heart rate, body fat, VO2 max, omega wave, and urine hydration levels (Booton 2019). While the league and teams are not allowed to share the results of such testing with coaching staffs, technical directors, and other personnel, the CBA requires that the League and Team share the results of such testing with the Player. In addition, the results cannot be publicly disseminated unless consented to by the Union (MLS CBA Section 9.10, 2015).

Like other leagues, however, the MLS has expressed an interest in collecting more biometric data during games via wearables with the intent of improving broadcasts and the fan and viewing experience. As Don Garber Commissioner of MLS said. "What could be more exciting than Landon Donovan stepping over a penalty kick and seeing his heart rate?" (Booton 2019).

Data Security and Privacy

Along with the collection of data, another big challenge facing leagues and player unions is data security. It is essential that leagues and teams address the risks to player data by developing protocols for protecting and storing the data. A good example of how most leagues address this issue is the NFL's CBA which requires all clubs "comply with all federal and state laws regarding the storage, use and privacy of such data" (NFL CBA 2020). The NBA also addressed the issue in their CBA when it directed the joint committee to set cybersecurity standards "for the storage of data collected from

Wearables," and to vet any device requested by teams and ensure team compliance with those standards (NBA CBA Section 13. (c), 2017).

Once again, however, the problem is who owns and controls the data. Data collected from wearable devices can either be stored in the database owned by the technology companies or by the team. Ownership of data varies, depending on when the information was collected. For example, depending on the type of data, if it was collected during regular season games, the data may be under the ownership of the league. If it was collected during practice or other event, it is under the ownership of the team (Sikka et al. 2019).

Not every league has rules dealing with the storage and security of biometric data, however. For example, MLB only states that: "any and all Wearable Data shall be treated as highly confidential at all times, including after the expiration, suspension or termination of this Agreement, shall not become a part of the Player's medical record" (MLB CBA, Attachment 56, 2017). While there is no evidence that MLB's lack of specific safeguards played a role, one of the most infamous security breaches in sports involved St. Louis Cardinals scouting director Chris Correa hacking into the Houston Astros scouting database. Correa was able to gain access to the Astros database simply by reportedly using someone else's password. Once he gained access, Correa was able to look at the Astros' medical evaluations of possible draft picks, internal scouting reports, and trade discussions with other teams. When discovered, MLB penalized the Cardinals by taking away their top two 2017 draft picks and fining them $2 million. Correa, who claimed to have acted alone, was sentenced to a forty-six month sentence in federal prison and ordered to pay the Astros $279,038.65 (ESPN 2017).

The Cardinals case is not the only high-profile breach of athlete's data. In 2016, the World Anti-Doping Agency (WADA) confirms that a Russian cyberespionage group operator by the name of Tsar Team (APT28), also known as Fancy Bear, illegally gained access to WADA's Anti-Doping Administration and Management System (ADAMS) database via an International Olympic Committee (IOC)-created account for the Rio 2016 Games. The group accessed athlete data, including confidential medical data such as Therapeutic Use Exemptions (TUEs) related to the Rio Games. The data concerning 41 athletes from 13 countries, including American athletes: Simone Biles, Elena Delle Donne, Serena Williams, and Venus Williams, was eventually released to public, accompanied by the threat that they will release more (Axon 2016).

It was believed that the hackers gained access to WADA's ADAMS through spear phishing of email accounts. In spear phishing attacks, emails that look real but contain malicious links are sent to known targets by attackers. The links go to websites that prompt users to enter credentials that are then stolen and used to access the data. As the above breaches illustrate, it is critical for all parties to understand the risks associated with the collection of biometric data and to ensure all necessary protections are taken.

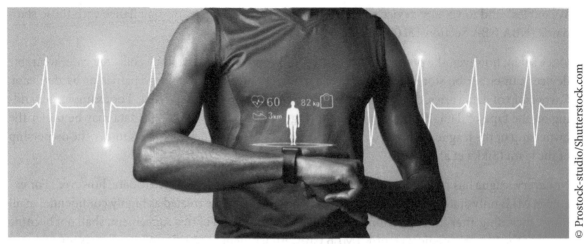

Athlete checking fitness tracker

Athletes' Biometric Data in College Sport

While professional athletes are well compensated and have labor unions representing their privacy interest, the same is not true for college athletes. Unlike professional athletes, college athletes have little bargaining power over the collection of their biometric data. In addition, without a comprehensive federal regulation of biometric data, college athletes have very little control over the use of their personal data or the power to prevent schools from requiring them to wear data collection devices. As a result of their scholarship with the schools, even though the risk associated with the misuse of their biometric data is substantial, college athletes must consent to the collection and use of their data.

What makes this imbalance of power even more troubling is that colleges and universities are beginning to sell their athlete's data as part of sponsorship deals. A perfect example of this is the 15-year, $ 173.8 million contract negotiated between Nike and the University of Michigan that contained a clause granting Nike the right to utilize "activity based information ... including, but not limited to, speed, distance, vertical leap height, maximum time aloft, shot attempts, ball possession, heart rate, running route, etc." collected in "... any and all media ... in connection with the manufacture, advertising, marketing, promotion and sale of Nike products and digital features and programming" (Tracy 2016). The Michigan agreement with Nike, and the deals other sport apparel brands like Adidas and Under Armour have with other universities, make it clear that these brands are no longer interested in only negotiating for the right to outfit the college and university athletic program with uniforms and cash but are also seeking the exclusive right to access and utilize their athletes' biometric data (Jessop and Baker 2019). As a result of these deals, apparel and technology companies are collecting the athletes' data without compensation and using it to develop new products or improve their algorithms (Sikka et al. 2019).

While college coaches like to claim that the biometric data collected on their students give them a competitive advantage, the absence of college athletes from the bargaining table during these negotiations over their data between colleges and the sport apparel brands and other data collection device corporations is not the only legal and ethical concern for college athletes. College athletes who hope to play professionally also need to be fearful that potential professional teams will gain access to an athlete's data, thereby costing the athlete a potentially lucrative professional career. By analyzing player's practice and game data, and discovering who has what condition or injury, what treatments are working, and what are the player's projected performance levels after recovery, teams can learn a lot about players and impact decisions on who to draft, or provide leverage in contract negotiations.

Another major concern for athletes' centers around whether the constant monitoring of biometric data and GPS data is an unreasonable invasion of their privacy. With modern data collection devices, coaches can tell where players are 24 hours a day, 7 days a week and when their heart rate or other biometric data fluctuates. Since the NCAA has no policy defining or limiting the scope of how NCAA schools collect data from college athletes, by leaving the issue to individual schools, the NCAA has exposed college athletes to a major privacy risk.

Non-Medical Legal Considerations

In the United States, individuals have a certain right of privacy in their own personal information. Of course, the legal protection available to individuals relies on several factors, such as the type of information being disclosed, whether the individual has waived their privacy right or consented, and whether the information is publicly available. The following section examines the legal protections available for an athlete's non-medical data.

RIGHT OF PUBLICITY

In *Haelan Laboratories v. Topps Chewing Gum, (1953)* the courts extended an individual's right of privacy to include a "Right of Publicity" to protect athletes and other celebrities against commercial misappropriation and prevent the unauthorized use of an individual's name, image and likeness, or other recognizable aspects of one's persona.

While the issue of professional athletes' image rights and right of publicity have generally been addressed in the leagues' CBAs and individual player contracts, athletes and leagues should still be aware that because of the unique characteristics of biometric and other personal performance data, the use of such data in broadcasts, team promotions, video games, fantasy sports, gambling, and other commercial purposes without consent of the athletes could be a violation of the athlete's right of publicity (Garlewicz 2020). At the college level, the issue of an athletes' image rights and right of publicity are going to be even more important to sort out. With college athletes scheduled to gain control over their Name, Image and Likeness (NIL) rights, it is doubtful that colleges will be able to continue selling the players' data without their consent. Therefore, colleges and companies like Nike are going to need to reconsider how they use athlete data in the future.

While there are no cases examining the use of biometric data as a publicity right, a good example of how the courts look at player personal data is *Palmer v. Schonhorn Enterprises*, (1967). Arnold Palmer and three other professional golfers sued Schonhorn Enterprises for invasion of privacy after the company without their permissions used their names and career data in a game. In defense, Schonhorn Enterprises argued that the player information contained in the game was readily obtainable public data and available in newspapers, magazine articles, and other periodicals. Therefore, it should not be denied the privilege of reproducing it (Wolohan 2020).

In finding for Palmer and the other golfers, the court held that while it is true that the publication of biographical data does not per se constitute an invasion of privacy, the use of the data for the purpose of capitalizing upon the players name in a commercial project other than the dissemination of news or articles or biographies does (Palmer v. Schonhorn Enterprises 1967). In support of this conclusion, the court held "it is unfair that one should be permitted to commercialize or exploit or capitalize upon another's name, reputation, or accomplishments merely because the owner's accomplishments have been highly publicized" (Palmer v. Schonhorn Enterprises 1967, 79).

GAME DATA & STATISTICS. As future cases were to illustrate, the key to the Palmer decision was the facts the players' names were used in a commercial venture (Wolohan 2020). For example, the court in *National Basketball Association v. Motorola* (1997) held that game data was not protected. Motorola manufactured and promoted the SportsTrax paging device, a hand-held device that provided owners with real-time information about professional basketball games. In particular, the SportsTrax's pager displayed the following data on NBA games in progress: (i) the teams playing; (ii) score changes; (iii) the team in possession of the ball; (iv) whether the team is in the free-throw bonus; (v) the quarter of the game; and (vi) time remaining in the quarter. SportsTrax updated the information every two to three minutes, with more frequent updates near the end of the first half and the end of the game (*National Basketball Association v. Motorola* 1997). In finding that data was not protected, the court held that NBA games were not protected under copyright law because they do not fall within the subject matter of federal copyright protection because they do not constitute "original works of authorship" under 17 U.S.C. § 102(a) (*National Basketball Association v. Motorola* 1997).

In rejecting the NBA's misappropriation claim, the court held that to establish a claim for common law misappropriation an individual must demonstrate four elements: 1) the defendant used the plaintiff's property, 2) the appropriation of plaintiff's property provided the defendant some advantage, commercially or otherwise, 3) lack of consent, and 4) resulting injury. The court found that the NBA failed to produce any evidence that anyone regards SportsTrax as a substitute for attending live NBA games or even watching them on television. In fact, the SportsTrax is marketed as being designed "for those times when you cannot be at the arena, watch the game on TV, or listen to the radio" (National Basketball Association v. Motorola 1997, 854). Therefore, the court held there was no misappropriation.

PLAYER DATA & STATISTICS. While seemingly decided in *Palmer v. Schonhorn Enterprises* (1967), the question of who owns player statistics and data was once again examined by the court in *C.B.C. Distribution v. Major League Baseball Advanced Media*, (2007). With an estimated 45.5 million people in the United States playing fantasy sports (Wolohan 2020), the issue of who owns the players' data and statistics was a financially important one for the professional leagues and players' associations. The party that owned the data would be able to control the right of others to use the players' profiles and statistics and sell the data.

C.B.C. Distribution sought a declaratory judgment against Major League Baseball Advanced Media to establish its right to use, without license, the names of and information about major league baseball players in connection with its fantasy baseball products. Advanced Media counter-claimed, maintaining that CBC's fantasy baseball products violated the players' rights of publicity and that the players, through their association, had licensed those rights to Advanced Media, the interactive media and Internet company of Major League Baseball.

In ruling against MLB Advanced Media, the Eighth Circuit found that the information used in CBC's fantasy baseball games is all readily available in the public domain and that it would be a strange law that a person would not have a First Amendment right to use information that is available to everyone (*C.B.C. Distribution v. Major League Baseball Advanced Media* 2007). Therefore, when balanced against CBC's First Amendment rights in offering its fantasy baseball products, the Eighth Circuit ruled the players' rights of publicity was not enforceable.

The decision in *C.B.C. Distribution v. Major League Baseball Advanced Media* (2007) was followed by the Supreme Court of Indiana in *Daniels v. FanDuel* (2018) when the court found that online fantasy sports operators do not violate the Indiana right of publicity statute when the organizations use the names, pictures, and statistics of players without their consent because the use falls within the meaning of "material that has newsworthy value," an exception under the statute (Daniels v. FanDuel 2018).

This issue is also being litigated outside the United States. As this chapter was going to print, in the United Kingdom a group of over 400 English Premier League (EPL), English Football League, National League, and Scottish Premier League soccer players were considering lawsuit against gaming, betting, and data-processing companies who utilize their personal statistics without consent or compensation. In particular, the players argue that while teams legally collect the players' personal data to help improve their performance and the performance of the team, the gaming and betting companies are using the players data without their consent or compensation.

Case Study: Is he Worth the Money?

When used correctly, professional athletes hope that analytics can vastly extend their careers by providing them with the proper balance of diet and exercise and help them avoid injury through over-exertion. The flip side of that argument, however, is that while most CBAs specifically exclude using a player's biometric data in contract negotiations, it is difficult to believe that teams are not making decisions on individual players based on their data compared to other players. This is especially true when an athlete is trying to recover from an injury.

The following case study, as general manager of an NBA team, you need to determine the contract value of free agent Kevin Durant. Durant, one of the top players in the NBA, tore his Achilles tendon while playing for the Golden State Worriers, in the 2019 NBA finals. In the case of Kevin Durant, since whether because of his age, skill level, or the degree of injury, it was impossible to generalize any potential outcome based on past data. As one of the best players in the NBA, is Durant an outlier, who is substantially different from all the other players who have suffered such injuries (the measured population) or is he simply another data point in the equation? As a result, each team considering whether to offer Durant a max contract worth over a hundred million dollars had to base their decision on data patterns across different datasets and combine that data to reach an informed decision.

Suppose you are the owner of an NBA team during the summer of 2019. You have cleared a lot of salary cap space in the hope of acquiring some of the big-name free agents on the market that summer. The biggest of which is Kevin Durant, an eight-time NBA All-Star who many believed to be one of the top three players, if not the best player, in the NBA. While you are interested in offering Durant a contract, you are concerned about the potential price tag. Durant is reported to be asking for a contract in the $40 million a year range.

To gather as much information as possible, the team asks Durant to supply some of his pre-injury ABD from prior years. Kevin Durant, however, claims that the Golden State Warriors refuse to release the data to any other teams. Golden State, which is also seeking to resign Durant, claims that since they collected the data with Durant's permission, they are the rightful owners of the data, not Durant, and therefore do not have to release it.

Based on the following information, found on Spotrac.com, the largest online resource for team and player contract, prior to his injury, Durant had a career average of 27.0 points, 7.1 rebounds, and 4.1 assists per game. In addition to his statistical production, Durant also had a career average of 39.9 minutes a game. Also, based on player contracts already signed for the 2019–2020 season, you know that the values of the top six player contracts for next season are:

1. $40.2 million – Stephen Curry, Golden State Warriors
2. $38.5 million – Russell Westbrook, Houston Rockets
3. $38.5 million – Chris Paul, Oklahoma City Thunder

4. $38.2 million – James Harden, Houston Rockets
5. $38.2 million – John Wall, Washington Wizards
6. $37.4 million – LeBron James, Los Angeles Lakers

You also know that in the last 10 years, six other NBA players suffered Achilles injuries like Durant's. On average, Achilles injuries affect players over 30 the worst, often shortening their careers to just another season or two. Durant will turn 31 just before the start of 2019 – 2020 season. Only one of the six players who suffered an Achilles injury reached his pre-injury peak, but only for additional couple of years. While you know that every player is different and that an Achilles injury for one player does not affect everyone the same way, these are the facts you have:

Player	Age	PPG Pre-Injury	PPG Post-Injury	RPG Pre-Injury	RPG Post-Injury	MPG Pre-Injury	MPG Post-Injury
Player 1	27	25	16	13	8	32.6	25.7
Player 2	30	19	11.7	6.5	5.7	33.8	23.3
Player 3	28	15	12.5	3.7	2.3	33.9	30.0
Player 4	34	27.3	18	6.3	2.8	38.6	28.2
Player 5	28	20	7.2	10	8.3	38.5	28.9
Player 6	30	14	7.3	2.8	1.8	30.6	17.6

Based on this and other information you found on Spotrac.com, the owner wants you to answer the following questions:

1. Even though Durant consented to the collection of his ABD in his Warriors contract, doesn't he own his own ABD?
2. What are the chances of Durant maintaining his high level of performance?
3. How many years and at what value are you willing to offer a new contract?
4. How can you quantify his future value?

Chapter 16: Legal and Ethical Considerations   345

Summary

"Media coverage tends to portray ABD collection as a potentially Orwellian tactic in which professional and college teams are able to maintain twenty-four-hour tabs on players by mandating wearable or injectable data collection instruments" (Osborne 2017, 57). Having all this information, it is argued, provides teams with an unfair advantage over the players in contract negotiations and personnel decisions. While it is impossible claim with certainty that simply collecting biometric and player data will lead teams and organizations down such an Orwellian path, as the above sections illustrate, athletes are justified in some of these concerns. The issues surrounding the collection, security, and ownership of biometric data, as well as privacy and commercialization of the data are far from settled by the courts or leagues. With little in the way of federal protection, and only four states as of 2020 having enacted any laws protecting ABD, athletes and their unions are on their own in trying to police the collection and use of their data. While college athletes may not have the same bargaining power as their professional counterparts, that does not mean that the colleges and manufacturers of data collection devices are free to collect and use the athlete's data. This is especially true as college athletes gain greater control of the NIL rights and the right to control their personal data.

The key take away from the chapter, therefore is that to profit off the data, whether for use in broadcast, video games, sports betting, or improved player performance, it is crucial that teams get their athletes' consent to the specific use of the data collection. While professional athletes can gain this consent through the use of player contracts and the collective bargaining process, the current unfair bargaining power between colleges and their athletes raises concerns over the voluntary nature and enforceability of their consent.

Key Terms

Athlete Biometric Data (ABD)

Blackbox medicine

Collective Bargaining Agreement

Health Insurance Portability and
  Accountability Act (HIPAA)

Lex Mechina

Machine Learning

Personal Health Information

Predictive Analytics

Right of Privacy

Right of Publicity

Wearable Committees

Wearable Technology

Critical Thinking Exercises

1. Who owns an athlete's biometric data?
   a. Does it matter if the athlete is professional athlete?
   b. College athlete?
   c. Recreational athlete?
2. Should professional athlete be able to contract away ownership of their own data to their team? What about third-party businesses?
3. Should Colleges and Universities ethically and legally be allowed to collect their athletes' biometric data and sell it?
   a. What about as part of a sport apparel sponsorship deal?
   b. What about as a separate contract?
4. Should college athletes be able to opt out of any agreement where their ABD is sold and used by third parties?
5. Are companies that use analytics more likely to commit ethical violations when collecting and using data without legal restraints?
6. Does the ability to gather and use data because it can, lead organizations to collect data even when they should not?

References

Axon, Rachel. 2016. WADA confirms U.S. athletes' data was hacked, blames Russians. *USA Today.* September 13. https://www.usatoday.com/story/sports/olympics/rio-2016/2016/09/13/wada-confirms-us-athletes-data-hacked-blames-russians/90306006/

Booton, Jen. 2019. *MLS Seeks Player Tracking in Upcoming CBA Negotiation* (June 5). https://www.sporttechie.com/mls-soccer-player-tracking-wearables-data-cba-negotiation/

Brown, Sarah M., and Natasha T. Brison. 2020. "Big data, big problems: Analysis of professional sports leagues' CBAs and their handling of athlete biometric data. *Journal of Legal Aspects of Sport* 42, 63–81.

Epstein, Jori, and Daniel Libit. 2020. Texas Tech women's basketball players describe toxic culture: 'Fear, anxiety and depression.' *USA Today* (August 5). https://www.usatoday.com/in-depth/sports/ncaaw/big12/2020/08/05/marlene-stollings-texas-tech-program-culture-abuse-players-say/5553370002/

ESPN.com. 2017. *Chris Correa Maintains Allegations Houston Astros First Stole Information from St. Louis Cardinals,* ESPN. http://www.espn.com/mlb/story/_/id/18592311/chris-correa-maintains-allegations-houston-astros-first-stole-information-st-louis-cardinals

Gale, Kristy. 2016. Evolving sports technology makes its mark on the internet of things: Legal implications and solutions for collecting, utilizing and disseminating athlete biometric data collected via wearable technology. *Arizona State University* (5) 337–380.

Gale, Kristy. 2016. The sports industry's new power play: Athlete biometric data domination. Who owns it and what may be done with it? *Arizona State University* (6), 7–84.

Garlewicz. Adam. 2020. Athlete biometric data in soccer: Athlete protection or athlete exploitation? *DePaul Journal of Sports Law* (16), 1–33 (Spring, 2020).

Gulitti, Tom. 2019. *NHL plans to deploy Puck and Player Tracking technology next season* (January 25). https://www.nhl.com/news/nhl-plans-to-deploy-puck-and-player-tracking-technology-in-2019-2020/c-304218820

Marr, Bernard. 2016. *Big data in practice: How 45 successful companies used big data analytics to deliver extraordinary results.* Chichester, UK: John Wiley & Sons

Jessop, Alicia, and Thomas A. Baker III. 2019. Big data bust: evaluating the risks of tracking NCAA athletes' biometric data. *Texas Review of Entertainment & Sports Law* (20), 81–112.

Osborne, Barbara. 2017. Legal and ethical implications of athletes' biometric data collection in professional sport. *Marquette Sports Law Review* (28) 37–84.

Price II, W. Nicholson. 2015. Black box medicine. *Harvard Journal of Law and Technology* (28), 420–454.

Romano, Benjamin. 2020. Amazon's Halo: Next level fitness watch, or dystopian tracker? *The Syracuse Post-Standard* (September 20).

Sikka, Robby S., Michael Baer, Avais Raja, Michael Stuart, and Marc Tompkins. 2019. Analytics in sports medicine: Implications and responsibilities that accompany the era of big data. *The Journal of Bone and Joint Surgery* (101), 276–283.

Taylor, Tom. 2015. How the U.S. women's cycling team transformed itself with technology. *Sports Illustrated*, May 14. HTTPS://WWW.SI.COM/EDGE/2015/05/14/PERSONAL-GOLD-DOCUMENTARY-US-WOMENS-CYCLING-TEAM

Tracy, Marc. 2016. With Wearable Tech Deals, New Player Data Is Up for Grabs. *New York Times* (September 9). https://www.nytimes.com/2016/09/11/sports/ncaafootball/wearable-technology-nike-privacy-college-football.html

Wolohan, John T. 2020. Image Rights. In *Law for Recreation and Sport Managers* (8th ed.), edited by Doyice Cotton and John Wolohan. Dubuque, IA: Kendall Hunt.

CASES

C.B.C. Distribution v. Major League Baseball Advanced Media, 505 F.3d 818 (8th Cir. 2007).

Haelan Laboratories, Inc. v. Topps Chewing Gum, Inc., 202 F.2d 866 (2nd. Cir. 1953).

National Basketball Association v. Motorola, 105 F.3d 841 (2nd Cir. 1997)

Palmer v. Schonhorn Enterprises, 96 N.J. Super. 72; 232 A.2d 458 (N.J. Super. 1967)

Legislation

California Consumer Privacy Act of 2018 §§1798.100 - 1798.199.100

Health Insurance Portability and Accountability Act of 1996 (HIPAA), Pub.L. 104–191

Illinois Biometric Information Privacy Act, 740 ILCS 14

Major League Baseball Collective Bargaining Agreement, Attachment 56 - Wearable Technology, p. 334 - 336 (2017–2021)

Major League Soccer Collective Bargaining Agreement Section 9.10, p.26 - 27 (2020–2025).

National Basketball Association Collective Bargaining Agreement, Article XXII Player Health and Wellness, Section 13 Wearables, p.357 – 361 (2017–2024).

National Football League Collective Bargaining Agreement, Article 51, Section 14, p.291 - 294 (2020–2031).

(National Hockey League Collective Bargaining Agreement (2013–2022).

National Hockey League/National Hockey League Players' Association Memorandum of Understanding Extending the CBA until 2026.

Texas Business and Commerce Code § 503.001. Capture or Use of Biometric Identifier

Washington State RCW Title 19, Chapter 19.375 Biometric Identifiers

Women's National Basketball Association Collective Bargaining Agreement, Article XX Physical Condition, Medical Examinations and Injuries, Section 13 Wearables, p.169 – 170 (2020–2027).

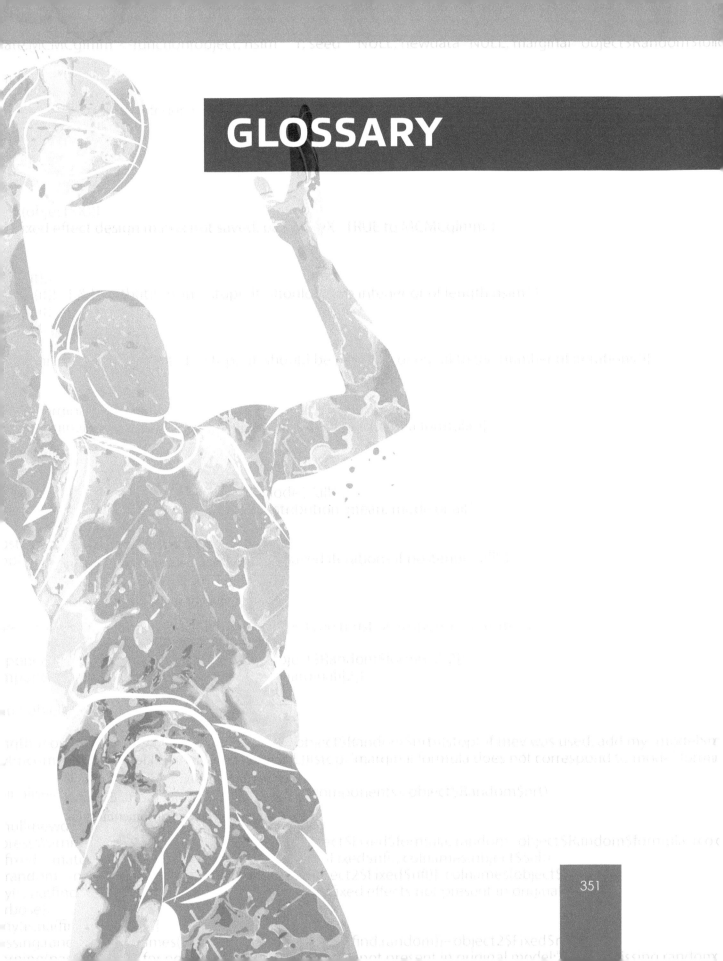

Adjusted Yards per Attempt (AYPA)—A quarterback's Yards per Attempt (YPA) minus sack yards, adjusted by a 45-yard penalty for each interception thrown; 45 yards is chosen because it is approximately equivalent to the Expected Point (EP) value of an interception.

Air yards—is measured by the number of yards the ball travels in the air during a receiving play.

$$air\ yards = total\ yards - yards\ after\ catch.$$

Air yards per attempt—is measured by the total number of air yards divided by the number of attempted throws by a quarterback.

Batting Average (BA)—is measured by the number of hits divided by at bats. Modern sabermetrics considers batting average a weak measure of performance because it does not correlate as well as on base percentage.

$$BA = \frac{Hits}{At\ Bats}$$

Corsi—a metric that is popular in hockey is the Corsi used to measure shot attempt differential while at even strength play. This includes shots on goal, missed shots on goal, and blocked shot attempts toward the opposition's net minus the same shot attempts directed at your own team's net.

$$Corsi = \frac{Shots_{For} + Blocks_{For} + MissedShots_{For}}{Shots_{Against} + Blocks_{Against} + MissedShots_{Against}}$$

There are numerous variations of the simple Corsi, below are two of the most common:

The **Corsi Rate** or Corsi Percent are the two components of Corsi expressed as a percentage. This metric is useful because it can help differentiate between a player who has a low Corsi score because their team both took a few shots and their opponent took few shots and a player whose Corsi score is low because their team and their opponents take about an equal number of shots.

$$Corsi = \frac{Corsi_{For}}{Corsi_{Against}}$$

$$Corsi_{Rate} = \frac{Corsi_{For}}{\left(Corsi_{For} + Corsi_{Against}\right)}$$

Defense-adjusted Value Over Average (DVOA)—used in football takes the core ideas from Win Probability Added—that each player should get credit for their performance on a play based on how much it contributes to their team's likelihood of winning—and combines it with the fundamental observation from WAR—that a baseline player would have done *something* and sometimes that something will even be a good thing. The more positive the DVOA rating, the better the player's performance. Negative DVOA represents below-average offense. DVOA (and its cousin, VOA, which is not adjusted based on opponent).

Defense-adjusted Yards Above Replacement (DYAR) is a way to evaluate running backs by assigning a value of the performance on plays where a running back carried/caught the ball compared to replacement level, adjusted for situation and opponent, and then translated into yardage. The simple version of DYAR means a running back with more total value.

Effective Field Goal Percentage—is the number of total field goals made (two pointers and three pointers), plus one half the number of 3-point field goals made, divided by the total number of field goal attempts. So, a player who made 3 of 8 shots, including 2 of 3 three point shots, would have an Effective Field goal percentage of 50%. Since three-point shots are worth an extra point than 2-point-shots, they are 50% more valuable. This leads directly to the following formula for Effective Field Goal Percentage:

$$eFG\% = \frac{FG + (.5 \times 3P)}{FGA}$$

Effective Field Goal percentage is a useful means of comparing similar types of players; however, shot volume is still going to factor heavily into the utility of Effective Field Goal percentage. Low-volume shooters who take high-percentage shots—think centers and power forwards—will still have a higher rating in this metric when compared to shooters who are taking higher volume or lower-likelihood shots.

Expected Points Added—attempts to measure the offensive contribution of individual players by taking the difference of the amount of points an offensive player contributed to their team, by comparing observed points accumulated in situations in which that player was involved against the expected points a generic team would have accumulated. EPA is the measure of a play's impact on the score of the game. An individual player's EPA is the sum of the EPA of the plays in which that player was directly involved. Being directly involved is defined as an offensive player who ran, threw, or kicked the ball, was targeted by a pass, or flagged for a penalty.

Full-strength plus-minus—only counts goals that are scored while both teams are at full strength are counted toward a player's plus-minus. This eliminates power play, penalty shot, empty net goals, and shootout goals. When an even strength goal is scored, the plus–minus statistic is increased by one ("plus") for those players on the ice for the team scoring the goal; the plus–minus statistic is decreased by one ("minus") for those players on the ice for the team allowing the goal. The full-strength plus minus is often used as the "standard" plus minus.

Hat Trick—Occurs anytime a player scores three goals in a game. Commonly associated with hocky, soccer, and lacrosse, the term was first used in cricket for a bowler who retired three batsmen with three consecutive balls. If a bowler could accomplish such an almost impossible feat, the club would reward the bowler a new hat.

Ice-time adjusted Corsi—attempts to normalize Corsi over the length of the game, or over the length for which a player is typically on ice, in order to facilitate comparisons between players who play different numbers of minutes. A good number of minutes to use to normalize the Corsi statistic by is 20—a number of minutes that most starters for a given game will surpass, but few second stringers will. This would seem to make Corsi an indicator of a player's impact on a game should they be in a starter role.

$$Corsi_{20} = \frac{(Corsi_{For} - Corsi_{Against})}{Minutes} \times 20$$

On-Base Percentage (OBP)—is a metric that measures the number of hits, walks, times a player is hit by a pitch, over the number of at bats, walks, times hit by a pitch, and sacrifice hits. Sabermetrics like this statistic more often than batting average since in considers the number of times a batter gets on base via a walk, or being hit by a pitch, in addition to hits.

$$OBP = \frac{H + BB + HBP}{AB + BB + HBP + SF}$$

On-base plus slugging (OPS)—a player's on-base percentage and slugging percentage.

Passer Efficiency System (College Football)—is a simple linear weighting of four measures—passing yards, passing touchdowns, passing completions, and interceptions—divided by the number of pass attempts.

$$Passer\ Efficiency = \frac{(8.4\ x\ YDS)+(330\ x\ TD)+(100\ x\ COMP)-(200\ x\ INT)}{Attempts}$$

Passer Rating (National Football League)—is calculated using five variables: pass attempts, completions, passing yards, touchdowns passes, and interceptions. Each of those variables is scaled to a value between 0 and 2.375, with 1.0 being statistically average. Passer rating in the NFL is on a scale from 0 to 158.3, with an 88.6. rating indicated an average performance, and a 100+ rating indicated an excellent performance.

The four separate calculations can be expressed in the following equations:

$$a = \left(\frac{COMP}{Attempts} - .3\right) x\ 5$$

$$b= \left(\frac{Yards}{Attempts} - .3\right) \text{ x } 0.25$$

$$c= \left(\frac{TD}{Attempts}\right) \text{ x } 20$$

$$d= 2.375 - \left(\frac{INT}{Attempts} \text{ x } 25\right)$$

If the result of any calculation is greater than 2.375, it is set to 2.375. If the result is a negative number, it is set to zero. Then, the above calculations are used to complete the passer rating:

$$Passer\ Rating = \left(\frac{a+b+c+d}{6}\right) \text{ x } 100$$

Player Efficiency Rating (PER)—The Player Efficiency Rating metric, originally devised by early basketball analytics pioneer John Hollinger, has largely fallen out of favor now. However, the basic theory behind PER is to calculate how much a player contributes to their team's performance by assigning point values to all of the things they do and then weighting those actions by how frequently they occur based on minutes played and pace of play. For example, in the part of Hollinger's PER formula that deals with blocks and steals, he assigns a full average value of a possession to a steal and a fractional average value of a possession to a block. This is because, as we noted above, not all blocks are recovered by the defensive team.

Plus–minus—also written as +/- or ±, is metric that attempts to measure a players joint offensive and defensive contributions to his team. It has a simple implementation: one takes the number of points the team scored while a given skater was on the ice and subtracts the points scored by the opponent while that skater was on the ice.

$$\pm= Goals - GoalsAgainst$$

There are two additional implementations of plus-minus worth knowing: full-strength plus-minus and situational or weighted plus-minus.

Pythagorean Wins developed by Bill James, the formula takes a team's runs scored and raises it to some exponent and then divides this value by the team's runs scored and runs conceded to some exponent. The original exponent was two (2), but more precise exponents are now used to estimate a team's expected wins.

$$Wins = \frac{RunsFor^2}{RunsFor^2 + RunsAgainst^2}$$

Runs Batted In (RBI)—The number of runners who score due to any hit, fielder's choice, out, walk, or hit by pitch by the batter.

Runs Created (RC) is used to measure the number of runs a hitter contributes to his team over a season. While this metric has many forms, each increasing in complexity, the simplest of them is:

$$RC = OBP \times SLG \times AB$$

It should be noted that this simple metric falls apart for truly exceptional players because their OBP and SLG numbers will be much, much higher than that of a normal player.

Situational plus-minus—considers the numbers of players on ice at the time of a given goal and credits the player with a value equal to the number of players on the player's team over the number of players on the opposing team. Teams that are short-handed when they score, then, will be credited with values greater than one, while teams that score while on the powerplay will receive credit equal to less than a regular goal.

Slugging percentage (SLG) is calculated as the total number of bases a player earns on hits divided by the number of at bats. This is a good statistic for measuring a batter's power since it gives more weight to extra-base hits with doubles, triples, and home runs, relative to singles. Slugging percentage, like batting average, is a simple ratio of two other statistics: total bases and at-bats.

$$SLG = \frac{TB}{AB}$$

Targets (Tgts)—The number of pass attempts directed at a particular receiver.

Total bases (TB) is the number of bases a player reached on any hit.

$$TB = 1 \times 1B + 2 \times 2B + 3 \times 3B + 4 \times HR$$

Total Quarterback Rating (QBR)—is an ESPN proprietary statistic that is designed to measure the total effectiveness and performance of a quarterback. The metric takes into account all of a quarterback's contribution to a game. Moreover, each play is weighted based on the game and the strength of the opposing defense. This means that statistics in garbage time of a blowout game hold less merit than statistics in a close game. QBR functions on a 0–100 scale and represents a percentile of overall quarterback performances since 2006. Meaning that if a quarterback has a QBR of 90, then their performance in that game is, on average, better than 90% of other quarterback performances.

True Shooting Percentage is a metric that attempts to measure a player's shooting skill, to include their performance on free throws, which Effective Field Goal percentage omits. To do this, True Shooting Percentage normalizes the number of points a player scores by the number of field goal attempts they take, plus an average rate of foul-shots awarded. The formula for this is as follows:

$$TS\% = \frac{PTS}{2\,(FGA + .44 \times FTA)}$$

This metric has the effect of both crediting players who make more three-point shots as well as players who can get to and score from the line. Conversely, players who are unable to get to and score from the foul line at an average rate will be punished by this metric.

Usage Rate—Usage Rate is a metric that attempts to measure how integral a player is to their team's offense. Players with high Usage Rates are expected to do a lot of work to make the offense function; players with low Usage Rates are more of a cog in the system and come by their metrics a little more serendipitously. To calculate Usage Rate in basketball we take the number of field goals, free throws, and turnovers a player accumulates, multiplied by one-fifth the team's minutes played, and divide that by the player's minutes played times the same quantity for the team. The formula for this is shown below.

$$Usg\% = \frac{(FGA + .44 \times FTA + TOV) \times \frac{MP_{TM}}{5}}{MP \times (FGA_{TM} + .44 \times FTA_{TM} + TOV_{TM})}$$

Value Over Replacement Player (**VORP**)—The metric VORP attempts to calculate the marginal value of a player based on the difference between the runs they have created, the outs they have made, and the expected performance of a replacement-level player who is an average fielder at that position and a below-average hitter player over that same period.

For batters, the formula for VORP is below:

$$VORP = OutsMade \times \left(\frac{RunsCreated}{OutsMade} - \frac{ReplacementRunsCreated}{ReplacementOutsMade} \right)$$

For pitchers, VORP is the number of innings a pitcher has pitched, times the replacement rate of giving up runs—their Run Average (RA)—minus the pitcher's specific RA over 9. In this case, 9 is used because Run Average is a metric that attempts to look at how many runs a pitcher would give up in a standard 9 inning game. The is below:

$$VORP = IP \times \frac{ReplacementRA - RA}{9}$$

IP = Innings pitched

RA = Run average

As was the case with hitters, run average should be normalized for park effects before VORP is calculated. Pitcher VORP is on the same scale as that of hitters.

Walks plus Hits allowed per Inning Pitched (WHIP) is a statistic that looks at a pitcher's efficiency by counting the number of batters a pitcher allows to reach base per inning by walks or hits.

Weighted on-Base Average (wOBA) is a version of on-base percentage that attempts to assign linear weights to the positive outcomes that a batter can create while at bat: walking, getting hit by pitch, single, double, triple, or home run, and divide these by the number of opportunities a batter has to create these positive outcomes. The value for each method of reaching base is determined by how much that event is worth in relation to projected runs scored (example: a home run is worth more than a single). Importantly, weighted on-base average cannot be calculated using a player's stat line alone. It is typically calculated specific to a given season and the value of walks, singles, doubles, triples, and home runs for a given season.

$$\text{wOBA} = \frac{.72 \times NIBB + .75 \times HBP + .90 \times 1B + .92 \times RBOE + 1.24 \times 2B + 1.56 \times 3B + 1.95 \times HR}{Plate\ Appearance\ (PA)}$$

HBP = Hit by Pitch

NIBB = Non-intentional walk

Plate Appearance = AB + NIBB + SF + HBP

RBOE = Reached Base on Error

Win Probability Added (WPA)—is similar to Expected Points Added except instead of points, we use win probability—the likelihood of the team winning the game—and instead of only awarding players who touched the ball as we do in Expected Points Added, we reward every player on the field. An individual player's WPA is the sum of the WPA of the plays in which that player was directly involved. Being directly involved is defined as an offensive player who ran, threw, or kicked the ball, was targeted by a pass, or flagged for a penalty. Defensive players are credited for WPA when they tackle or sack the ball carrier, are credited with an assisted tackle or sack, cause a fumble, defend a pass, or are flagged for a penalty.

Wins Above Replacement (WAR)—a statistical formula calculating a player's total contributions to his team wins and losses. However, unlike most of the metrics used in this book, WAR does not have a standard implementation. Rather, various baseball analytics groups publish their own versions of WAR, often with proprietary and undisclosed logic behind them.

The logic, however, is much the same as VORP: Calculate the difference between the player in question and a replacement-level player, and then convert this value into wins. A simple version of WAR can be estimated using VORP and a rule of thumb that says 10 runs contributed is equivalent to 1 win. That is, a VORP of 10 is a WAR of 1, a VORP of 30 is a WAR of 3, a VORP of 60 is a WAR of 6, and so on.

Yards After Catch (YAC)—The yards gained by a receiver after catching a pass.

Yards per Attempt (YPA)—Yards gained per pass attempt.

Yards per Reception (YPR)—The average yards a receiver gains per reception, including Air Yards (AY) and Yards After Catch (YAC).

Yards per Target (YPT)—A receiver's average yards gained per pass attempt directed at him.

INDEX

Demographics, 266–268
Dense layer, of deep learning system, 203–204
Descriptive statistics, 6–7
Design matrix, 96–97
    for APM, 96
Diagonal matrix, 185
Direct marketing, 268–270
Discrete random variables, 41
Domain, 43
Domination, 157
Draft Kings, 318
Drive, 116, 120–121
Dynamic ticket pricing, 271–272

E

Edges, 189
Effective Field Goal Percentage (eFG%), 99–102
Efficiency, 99. *See also* Player Efficiency Rating
Egaming, 289, 290
Electronic Gaming Federation (EGF), 293
Elo rating system, 243–245, 301–302
    in R, 247–252
Employment analytics, 273–274
    and hiring, 274
    and job performance, 274–275
    and retention, 275
Encounter metrics, 295–300
Enhancing game design, 296–297
Esports, 288–289
    analytics and, 293–294
        encounter metrics, 295–296
        enhancing game design, 296–297
        popular core PC games, 294–295
    case study, 297–300
    competitions, 291–293
    defined, 290
    encounter-based metrics, 297–300
    first-person shooter, 290–291
    multiplayer online battle arena, 290
    Player vs. Player, 291
    ranking systems, 300–302

real-time strategy, 291
    and traditional stick and ball sports, 302–303
Esports analytics, defined, 295
Ethical considerations, legal and. *See* Legal and
    ethical considerations
Euclidean Distance, 225
Expected points, 117
Expected Points Added (EPA), 117–118
Expected utility, 158
Experimental design, 9

F

FanDuel, 318
Fan engagement, 266
Fantasy sports markets, 317
    analytics and, 318–320
    case study, 320–325
    daily fantasy marketplace, 320–325
    Daily Fantasy Sports, 318
Federal and state laws, 332–333
Fielder's choice, 64
FIFA rating system, 245–246
Finite games, 161
First-person shooter (FPS), 290–291
Football
    advanced metrics for, 115–117
        Defense-Adjusted Value Over Average,
            119–126
        Expected Points Added, 117–118
        Win Probability Added, 118–119
    box score metrics for, 110–115
For loop, 28
40/60/first-down rule, 122, 125
Full-strength plus minus, 87
Future betting, 314–315

G

Game-based Elo ratings, 249–251
Game data & statistics, 342–343

federal and state laws, 332–333
non-medical legal considerations, 341–343
player medical data, rights to use, 334–338
Lex Machina, 330
Likelihoods, 38
Linear function optimization, 181–183
maximizing lineups for ice hockey, 184–187
stadium improvement decision-making with, 183–184
linear programming, 181
Line betting, 309
Logistic regression, 95
Long Short-Term Memory Network (LSTM), 206–207
Loop, 28–29

M

Machine learning, 330
platforms, 210–216
Major League Baseball (MLB), 318, 336
Major League Soccer (MLS), 338
Marcel model, 229–232
Marginal value, 74–75, 78
Marketing, 266–268
Markov Chain, 146
Markov Chain Monte Carlo simulations, 145–148
Match Fixing, 317
Match-based Elo ratings, 249–251
MATLAB, 20
Matrices of weights, 201
Maximin strategy, 167
Maximization, 177
Maximums, 177–180
Max pooling, 208
McNeil, Charles, 308–309
Mean, 48–49, 137
Mean of distribution, 45–47
Measure of centrality, 7, 47–50
Measures of frequency, 7
Measures of position, 7
Measures of variation, 7

Median of distribution, 49–50
Medical data, player, rights to use, 334–338
Microsoft Excel, 20
Minimax decision rule, 154
Minimax regret, 168
Minimax strategy, 167–169
Minimization, 177
Minimums, 177–180
Mixed strategy, 161
Mobile betting, 311
Mode, 47–48
Monetization, boosting, 299–300
Moneyball approach, 74
Money line betting, 311–312
Monte Carlo analysis, 130, 135–136
applied introduction to, 130–135
Monte Carlo experimentation, 130
Monte Carlo methods
binomial distribution, 137–138
bootstrap Monte Carlo, 144–145
bootstrapping and jackknifing, 140–144
Markov Chain Monte Carlo simulations, 145–148
Monte Carlo analysis, 135–136
applied introduction to, 130–135
normal distribution, 137
uniform distribution, 138–139
Monte Carlo simulation, 130–145
Markov Chain, 145–148
Multiplayer online battle arena (MOBA), 290
Murphy v. National Collegiate Athletic Association (NCAA), 310, 318
Mutually exclusive, 39

N

Nash Equilibrium, 161
National Association of Collegiate Esports (NACE), 293
National Basketball Association (NBA), 335–336
National Basketball Association v. Motorola, 342, 343

National Collegiate Athletic Association (NCAA), 293
    Men's Basketball, 317
National Football League (NFL), 336–337
    team payroll allocation efficiency, 276–284
National Hockey League (NHL), 337
Neuroscience in deep learning. *See* Artificial neural networks
New Jersey Division of Gaming Enforcement (NJDGE), 308
Nike Direct, 268–269
Nodes, 189
Noise, 203
Non-medical legal considerations, 341–343
Normal distribution, 42, 45–47, 137
Normalization, 226
Number of trials, 137–138

O

Obedience training technique, 200
Objective matrix, 183
Observations as random variables, 40–42
Offensive VORP in R, 76–78
Okrent, Daniel, 317
Olympics, 302–303
On-base metrics, 63
    in R, 70–74
On-base percentage (OBP), 63–64
    contrasting batting average and, 64–66
    in R, 70–74
On-base plus slugging (OPS), 67–68
    in R, 70–74
One-hot encoding, 202
Optimal assignments of players to positions, 192
Optimization, 176
    combinatorial optimization, 187–188
    linear functions, 181–187
    minimums and maximums, 177–180
    rotation selection in basketball, 188–195
Ordinary Least Square (OLS) regression model, 8
Output layer, of deep learning system, 204

Overfitting, 203
Oversimplification, 160
"Over-valuing the big" problem, 103

P

PageRank, 255
    implementing in R, 256–259
Palmer v. Schonhorn Enterprises, 342, 343
Parlay betting, 312
Passer efficiency, 111–113
Passer rating, 111–113
Passing metrics, 111–113
Payoff, 156
Payoff matrix, 156
Payout matrix, 160–162
Payroll allocation efficiency, 276–284
PC games, 294–295
Perfect information, 163
Personal health information (PHI), 333
Pitch prediction, 210–211
Pitching VORP in R, 79–82
Placeholder variable, 28
Plate appearances, 64
Player
    contributions to wins, estimating, 82
    data & statistics, 343
    efficiency rating, 102–103
    -evaluation analytics, 62
    evaluation in basketball, 98–102
    measuring, 62–63
    medical data, rights to use, 334–338
    value in hockey, 86–91
Player Efficiency Rating (PER), 99, 102–103
Player projection systems, 222, 228–229
    building own, 233–237
    CARMELO, 232–233
    Marcel model, 229–232
    methods for player similarity, 222–223
        computational approaches, 224–228
        heuristic-based approaches, 223–224
Player similarity, methods for, 222–223